Platforms, Power, and Politics

Platforms, Power, and Politics

An Introduction to Political Communication in the Digital Age

Ulrike Klinger
Daniel Kreiss
Bruce Mutsvairo

polity

First published in 2024 by Polity Press

Polity Press
65 Bridge Street
Cambridge CB2 1UR, UK

Polity Press
111 River Street
Hoboken, NJ 07030, USA

ISBN-13: 978-1-5095-5357-0
ISBN-13: 978-1-5095-5358-7 (pb)

A catalogue record for this book is available from the British Library.

Library of Congress Control Number: 2023933008

Typeset in 10.5 on 13 pt Quadraat Regular
by Cheshire Typesetting Ltd, Cuddington, Cheshire
Printed and bound in Great Britain by TJ Books Ltd, Padstow, Cornwall

For further information on Polity, visit our website:
politybooks.com

Contents

Acknowledgments

We have a lot of people to thank for their help in making this book possible.

Uta Rußmann, Anders O. Larsson, and Johannes B. Gruber read previous versions of the book, and their feedback was immensely helpful as we revised and restructured the manuscript. We're also indebted to the anonymous reviewers for their very constructive and detailed suggestions for revisions.

Frederik Körber was an invaluable help in managing citations and references over the course of writing this book, as we kept adding and deleting paragraphs and pages. Walter Pepperle designed a previous version of the cover art, helping us to develop an idea into an actual cover.

At Polity, we would like to thank Stephanie Homer – who lent key support for this book's production and marketing – and especially Mary Savigar. Mary believed in this book and its authors very early on and throughout the process, and provided valuable insights every step along the way as it moved from an idea to a reality. We thank her for believing in our ambition and vision for this volume.

Ulrike Klinger would like to thank the Center for Information Technology and Society (CITS) at the University of California, Santa Barbara, for hosting her as a visiting scholar from September 2021 to March 2022 – especially Joe Walther and Bruce Bimber. The amazing creative and intellectual atmosphere of UCSB provided the perfect environment while writing large parts of this book.

Daniel Kreiss would like to thank colleagues at the University of North Carolina Center for Information, Technology, and Public Life (CITAP) for enduring numerous discussions of this project during its conception and writing. It has been an honor to work alongside such a trailblazing and brilliant group of researchers, and he hopes that our shared intellectual agenda is reflected here as an animating spirit in this book. Daniel would also like to thank the John S. and James L. Knight Foundation, and especially John Sands, for all the support over the years and for funding essential research in the fields of misinformation, disinformation, and journalism during the platform era, much of which is cited throughout this book and without which it would not be possible. Finally, Daniel would like to thank colleagues across the Knight Research Network; he hopes this book captures the vibrant research and debates about platforms in the field.

Bruce Mutsvairo would like to thank Ingrid Volkmer, Benedetta Breveni, Hayes Mabweazara, Ahmed al Rawi, and Saba Bebawi for sharing thoughts on recent developments in journalism across Australia, Africa, and the Arab World.

1 Introduction: Political Communication in the Platform Era

The opening chapter provides an overview of this book. It introduces the relationship between technology and political communication and provides an overview of media and politics during the platform era. The chapter also defines a number of core terms used throughout the book, including media, digital media, the Internet, social media, platforms, and technologies. Finally, the chapter provides chapter descriptions and an overview of the pedagogical features of the book.

OBJECTIVES

By the end of this chapter, you should be able to:

- detail the relationship between media, technology, and political communication
- provide working definitions of key terms used in this book
- understand how to use this book
- know the content that will be covered in this book.

1.1 Introduction

After serving as German chancellor for four consecutive terms, from 2005 to 2021, Angela Merkel gave a long farewell interview just before leaving office. In addition to discussing many other things, she reflected on how digital platforms have changed politics and political discourse during her 16-year chancellorship:

> Interviewer: When you think about Germany, what worries you?
>
> Merkel: That the political climate in the country has become harsher. When I became chancellor, there was no smartphone. Facebook was a year old, Twitter wasn't invented until a year later. We live in a completely changed media world, and that has something to do with it, too.
>
> Interviewer: What does that mean for politics?
>
> Merkel: It changes political communication. We have to ask ourselves: How do we reach people? How do we ensure that there are discourses in

> which different opinions are respected and not everyone hides in the opinion corner where they feel confirmed? Today, you can have your personal opinion confirmed by many more people than you even know. I'm afraid that we're increasingly running into problems when it comes to compromise-building, which is essential in a democracy.
>
> (Gammelin et al. 2021)

Merkel's observations are a great starting point for the journey we will embark on in this book. The long-serving German chancellor is not alone in worrying about the "harshness" of political discourse, the distorting effects of social media on public opinion, and media bubbles as a barrier to compromise. While politics has never been a place of harmony and joy, and hate and so-called "fake news" are as old as humankind, the former chancellor is certainly right that digital platforms have impacted what political information people see and how they receive it, how citizens discuss politics and with whom, and how political leaders interact among themselves and with the public. At the same time, many popular perceptions and much common wisdom about social media and their impact on politics and social life are more mythical than reality. For example, people have long bemoaned "filter bubbles" and "echo chambers" – broadly, the idea that the Internet and social media lock people into impenetrable clusters of like-mindedness. However, social science research shows that these ideas do not capture how people actually engage in politics and encounter political information online. Indeed, to the contrary – and perhaps counter-intuitively – social media, and the Internet more generally, provide environments where citizens encounter, sometimes by accident, more diverse opinions and sources of information, as well as political contestation, than in their lives "offline."

This book is about the fears, and hopes we have about platforms and social media and their effects on politics and democracy. It provides a survey of the things we know, the issues we have to reconsider, the things that are less of a problem than we thought, the problems we are just beginning to think about, and the many, many things we do not know (yet!). We draw our discussion primarily from the vast, complex field of political communication research, and especially the research on platforms and their relationship with politics that has been going strong for the past 15 or so years. This research will help us map the threats to and opportunities for democracy that platforms give shape to, and help us think in more nuanced and critical ways about the intersection of platforms, power, and politics.

1.2 Technology and Political Communication

Technologies are central to political communication, as they are to all social life. The forms of debate, storytelling, evidence, conversation, and public address that are central to human societies have long grown up alongside, and been shaped by, technologies. While we tend to think of "technology" narrowly in terms of things such as cars, virtual reality sets, or social media, in its broadest definition technology means knowledge, skills, processes, methods, and tools. Take political communication, for instance. Before writing, oral cultures developed extensive technologies to extend human memory. These included things such as songs and poetry that helped codify and accumulate knowledge and pass it between people and across generations. With the development of forms of writing – for example, on parchment – the rules and eventually laws of societies became more durable, specified, and the basis for institutions.

The codex (bound volumes that preceded the modern book) and the printing press helped make knowledge and information more portable, widespread, and, ultimately, accessible beyond religious and political authorities (Blair et al. 2021; Eisenstein 1980). The development of post offices, mail, and telegraph networks played key roles in knitting regions and nascent states together during the nineteenth century, including through the circulation of the newspapers and pamphlets that helped give rise to the imagined political communities of nation states (Anderson 2006; John 2009). The middle of the nineteenth through the dawn of the twenty-first century witnessed the refinement of point-to-point communication, including the telegraph and early radio, and the explosion of truly mass media-facilitated communication over increasingly greater, and even global, scales (Crowley & Heyer 2015). In many countries around the world, political communication during the second half of the twentieth century was structured around a set of mass media technologies – especially television – and routinized ways in which political and media elites could communicate with, create, mobilize, and shape local, national, and global publics.

Enter the Internet. The Internet grew to increasing prominence in social, cultural, economic, and, indeed, political life by the turn of the twenty-first century. The origins of the global Internet lay in the US and Europe in the 1970s and 1980s, but it reached widespread popular adoption in many Western democracies only in the mid to late 1990s (Benjamin 2019; Mailland & Driscoll 2017; Turner 2010). The Internet was primarily accessible through computer labs, desktop computers, and then laptops, during this time. With the boom in mobile phones and smartphones globally in the early and mid-2000s, especially in many regions of the world outside of the Global North, the Internet became central to social life and political communication around the globe. In political contexts, during this time elected leaders, parties, and candidates, as well as many other political actors, began a slow, unsteady, and often halting process of increasingly using the Internet through multiple different devices to do things such as address the public and campaign for office. Journalism outlets were also experimenting with ways to engage audiences in new ways, from dedicated internet sites to the adoption of new multimedia styles of storytelling.

The rise and explosive growth of social media, and technology platforms more generally, in the mid-2000s through the start of the second decade of the twenty-first century in turn brought much debate – and sweeping social, political, and economic changes. By 2010, "platforms" had grown to truly global proportions. Many of those most familiar to audiences around the world – American companies such as Meta (Facebook) and Google, and their subsidiaries such as WhatsApp and YouTube – have extended far beyond their national origins to become fundamental infrastructure for much in the way of commercial, political, and social life in countries around the world. The commonly referred to "Arab Spring" of the 2010s appeared to reveal the Internet's new, democratizing power, when anti-government protests and uprisings organized in significant part online swept through countries such as Libya, Tunisia, Egypt,

Yemen, Syria, and Bahrain and deposed a number of political leaders. It seemed to many researchers (Boulianne 2015; Diamond & Plattner 2012; Howard & Hussain 2013) that social media were fueling a new wave of political participation, helping citizens exercise accountability over political leaders in countries around the world, and facilitating democratization efforts in authoritarian countries.

And yet the "Arab Spring" ended with generally failed democratic revolutions. Meanwhile, the 2016 UK European Union Membership Referendum (commonly known as "Brexit") and the election of former US President Donald Trump, amid concerns over Russian state-sponsored propaganda and abuse of personal data by firms such as Cambridge Analytica, turned the narrative about social media, platforms, and politics much darker and less optimistic. Concerns over the spread of misinformation, disinformation, and propaganda on social media platforms have only proliferated since then – with some people even asking whether democracies can survive the Internet.

This narrative, however, sits uneasily alongside the continued global spread, fueled by social media, of unprecedented movements for gender, racial, social, and economic justice, such as the global Black Lives Matter and Rhodes Must Fall movements (Bosch 2017; Kilgo & Mourão 2019; Richardson 2019), whose activists tore down monuments to white supremacy in countries around the world and worked to hold police and states accountable for abuses of power against racial and ethnic minorities.

The platforms discussed throughout this book include those mentioned above, as well as the non-profit Wikipedia and private, global US companies such as Instagram (owned by Meta), Amazon, Twitter, Reddit, and Snapchat. In much of the world, US companies dominate the platform landscape, even though there are numerous smaller platforms, nationally and regionally, that matter for political communication. Indeed, some commentators have even suggested that we are moving to an era of a "splintered Internet," where countries create their own firms and infrastructures according to specific state-granted political freedoms and content rules, instead of having one global Internet generally aligned with the expressive and commercial aims of US-based companies (Walker et al. 2020).

SPOTLIGHTED CASES

In countries such as China and Russia, for example, domestic companies provide similar products and services to US-based firms, but with strict content guidelines determined by the state. These platforms include Russia's VKontakte and China's Alibaba, WeChat, Weibo, Baidu, and Tencent. That said, new platforms such as the Chinese company-owned TikTok (known as Douyin in China) have also burst upon the scene to capture the time and attention of global users, including taking them away from comparatively more established platforms. These companies, like their American counterparts, tailor their content rules for the countries they operate in – which is often the price of doing business, provoking fierce debates about the harm, or benefits, they cause to democracy or democratization efforts.

Not only do new platforms continually emerge, their user bases evolve over time, as does their design and what scholars call "affordances" – broadly the activities that users perceive they can do on platforms, and what platforms technically make it possible to do (Bucher & Helmond 2018; Nagy & Neff 2015). Some platforms – such as Facebook – have become sites that many, many people use for diverse purposes, crossing generations in countries around the world. Others – such as WhatsApp – have broad user bases that utilize them as basic communications infrastructure for much of everyday life. Still others, such as Twitter, have more niche uses for well-defined communities such as journalists and political and entertainment elites. Others, such as TikTok, have found particular appeal in well-defined user bases, including among creatives and young people (Literat & Kligler-Vilenchik 2023). Platforms are both different (supporting different types of communication) and continually add new functionalities in their attempts to grow, and keep, audiences – especially adopting features they see others successfully rolling out. And users also innovate on platforms! Most famously, the Twitter hashtag (#) and @ symbol before usernames were both user innovations to group and direct tweets before being formally adopted by the company.

1.3 Platforms and Global Political Communication

This book provides an overview of the various actors, institutions, and processes involved in political communication during the platform era. The information environments that we inhabit are in part created, and increasingly dominated, by global platform companies. At the same time, the political systems these companies and their technologies operate in matter too. We cannot understand contemporary political communication without simultaneously accounting for the diversity of political communicators, the technological underpinnings of global public spheres, *and* the workings of governments and political institutions and systems in countries and regions around the world. In other words, while platforms are central actors in countries across the globe in the twenty-first century, they exist alongside and are shaped by many different forms of media and media institutions more generally, as well as states, institutions, norms, laws, social groups, social structures, economic systems, and cultures.

Let's unpack this a little bit. First, as the political scientist Andrew Chadwick (2017) has pointed out, media are *hybrid* and exist in *systems*. To take an example, even in our screen-saturated world, we still communicate face to face. We still watch television and listen to the radio (forms of mass media) even as we share videos on YouTube. In our daily lives, we seamlessly talk to our friends and families, listen to podcasts, and share updates on social media (and sometimes all at the same time!).

This is the very definition of hybrid! Thinking about any one of these things in isolation abstracts away from the fact that we use many different forms of media and communication contextually (depending on considerations such as what we want to accomplish, the settings we are in, the ways we want to pass the time, etc.) and continually in the course of our daily lives. And many different forms of media and communication are arranged into *systems* where they interact with one another.

SPOTLIGHTED CASE

Let's think about another example to illustrate *hybrid* media systems. Imagine that a political leader tweets a controversial opinion. Their followers might agree and retweet it, amplifying it. And so might the political opposition, quote-tweeting it to criticize or ridicule the political leader. Journalists might then take note, and interview party members to get a response. Pundits on opinion television might start breathlessly stating their positions on the brewing controversy (while promoting themselves on Twitter!). Non-governmental organizations (NGOs) might rally in the streets in protest against the political leader, all the while producing visually arresting images for journalists and social media that in turn get a lot of engagement and drive more coverage, tweets, and, of course, controversy. Other party members might then feel pressured to take action, such as sanctioning the party leader.

As in the box above, media systems are hybrid and many different forms of media and communication interact with one another. This happens *sequentially* – during a controversy, different political and media actors interact in dynamic, responsive ways. In the example above, journalists, party members, and civil society groups all responded to one another as the controversy unfolded. At the same time, what is also clear is that we have to think about not just media systems, but also *political* systems. Established political actors and institutions, such as political party members, journalists, and NGOs, used platforms – and many other media – in ways that aligned with their strategic goals, professional understandings, and economic incentives. Media equally matter, though. Platforms provide new contexts for political elites to share their opinions – including instantaneously to their thousands (or millions) of followers on platforms such as Twitter – and they provide members of the public with unprecedented ways to engage around those opinions and to share their own. In this sense, politics shapes how media are used, but media also shape political communication strategies, processes, and contexts.

On a broader level, nations provide the context and orientation for platforms and media institutions to emerge, function, thrive, or die. Nations provide the economic and regulatory contexts that platforms and media institutions develop and work within. This includes defining the communicative rules that platforms and media outlets must follow (for example, laws regulating activities including hate speech, defamation, libel, pornography, etc.). Nations also provide frameworks for political systems, including through legal rules (such as constitutions), organizational and political-cultural contexts (such as parties and norms of public life), and political-economic contexts (Hallin & Mancini 2011).

But nations are not the only things that matter! Media have long been transnational, including operating at regional and even global scales, as have political institutions and systems – and so are platforms. We can think of journalism outlets such as the British Broadcasting Corporation (BBC) and Al Jazeera English as truly "global" media, even if they might not operate in every country. Outlets such as the

SPOTLIGHTED CASE

Political systems indelibly shape media systems and political communication. At the same time, media and political communication shape the workings, and potentially even the structure, of political systems. To take a US example, political reforms furthering open party primaries (where anyone can run for office, not simply people chosen by the party elite) during the 1970s led to the greater role of media in electoral processes and the increased independence of candidates. These changes helped open the doors to office for celebrity candidates, such as Donald Trump, who have in turn shaped the parties they are a part of – as well as the nations they lead.

French-language Africa 24 have a presence in French-speaking countries in western and northern Africa, France, and the Middle East. From a political perspective, look no further than the United Nations (global) and the European Union (regional) as examples of transnational institutions. The Internet itself is governed not only by national rules, but also by formal and informal international bodies and networks that create protocols and standards (DeNardis 2009), such as the global Internet Corporation for Assigned Names and Numbers (ICANN) that is responsible for things such as domain names.

Meanwhile, national economies have long been embedded in global systems, including globalized forms of racial and social differentiation. As the sociologist Tressie McMillan Cottom (2020) has argued, platforms operate in a global economy premised on international and national rules, patterns of low-paid labor – especially in the Global South – and the monetization of global forms of culture. Indeed, to understand the effects of platforms in societies, one should look beyond digital practices in the "west" (Arora 2019). Historically, media have been central to international, diasporic communities and cultures, which use them for identity and information.

In our own era, platforms serve as essential infrastructure for immigrants, refugees, and other global communities knit together through shared culture and identity (e.g. Retis & Tsagarousianou 2019). Ideas travel globally through platforms and media, produced by international scientific and social scientific institutions, writers, artists, and religious groups, which give shape to our understandings of morality, gender, class, sexuality, and race and ethnicity (Adams & Kreiss 2021). Ideas developed locally or within specific countries can spread far beyond them and help to structure politics and political conceptions around the world (Hooker 2017). Look no further than the global #MeToo movement that shone a light onto women's experiences in workplaces across the world (Mendes et al., 2019). Meanwhile, international human rights frameworks and legal and cultural understandings shape things such as the content moderation engaged in by platforms (Douek 2020), as do the national contexts companies originate or operate in. International advocacy organizations such as Human Rights Watch and Amnesty International make media, document abuses, and strive for accountability on a truly global scale (Powers 2018).

SPOTLIGHTED CONTENT

We want to pause a moment and consider the terms that we are using. One important aim of this book is to provide examples of political communication as it looks in countries around the world. To do that, we deliberately use terms such as "Global South" and "Global North." We do so despite the criticism such terms have received in some academic disciplines. These criticisms include claims that such terms homogenize diverse populations. In contrast, we see the concept of the "Global South" defined not by geography, but by the collective determination of historically and currently dominated nations and groups to achieve social and political agency. This struggle comes in the context of a well-documented history of sociopolitical marginalization and economic subjugation through European and US empire-building, colonialism, and Cold War geopolitical occupation, war, and interventions (including US-sponsored coups). We recognize these groups' and nations' determination to shape their destiny through struggle, knowledge production, and independence. In doing so, we follow scholars such as Gayatri Spivak (2008), Marlea Clarke (2018), and Anne Garland Mahler (2018), just to name a few, who have made a case for the analytical value of such concepts.

Political and media systems are also dynamic entities that are constantly changing. For far too long, much public and policymaking discourse and academic scholarship in the democratic West presumed that democracies are stable and political systems are generally enduring. Many have had faith in progress-oriented narratives that the world is trending in democratic directions – where suffrage is inevitably expanded, systems of exclusion such as racism are relics in the process of being dismantled, and polities will eventually achieve equality and justice. This is especially a feature of research on media development begun during World War II and continuing through the global Cold War and its aftermath. Researchers assumed both that greater media freedoms and commercialization would mean progress toward multi-ethnic, multi-racial, pluralist democracy, and that, once achieved, there was no going back.

However, history has taught us that these assumptions are generally wrong. They are flawed in presuming both that (1) political and media systems are fundamentally stable, and that (2) their underlying dynamics push toward greater democratic liberalism. It is easier to see this now than it was at the end of the last century. The decade from 2010 to 2020 revealed *both* democratic gains and democratic backsliding (or crises) in countries around the world. As such, this book argues that democracy – like any political system – must be continually performed, legitimated, and protected by many institutions and political actors, including citizens themselves. Like any other political system, democracy is always an achievement that needs to be cared for in order to be sustained.

Sometimes, over many decades, political systems democratize and are able to maintain these hard-won gains (Voltmer 2013) – but it is always a contingent achievement and never permanent. The global rising tide of illiberalism, racism, and authoritarian leaders, movements, and parties in many countries around the world reveals this. To take the US case, it was only with the passage of bills such as the Civil Rights

Act in 1964 that the country became a truly multi-ethnic, pluralist democracy, whose stability is still fraught today given the growing extremism of the white political right (Mills 2017). Despite many idealistic sentiments and active misremembering, the US was at best a hybrid regime for much of its history, with colonially subjugated populations within its borders living on reservations (which still persist to this day) and white authoritarian one-party rule in its southern regions and circumscribed citizenship on the basis of race and ethnicity existing across the nation through the 1960s. And deep inequalities in policing, wealth, political representation, and health persist across racial lines.

Similarly, despite claims of being democratic, European colonial empires set up elaborate systems of racial, ethnic, and religious differentiation to extract resources from their colonies (Chakravartty & Da Silva 2012). While many of these colonial regimes have manifestly ended, their consequences are still deeply with us in patterns of global inequality – all of which shapes political communication and media systems around the globe (Aouragh & Chakravartty 2016).

Throughout this book, we use a number of key terms – including *media*, *digital media*, *the Internet*, *social media*, *platforms*, and *technologies*. These are all closely related terms – but they are different! While we go into greater depth in some individual chapters, we wanted to briefly define them there.

First, by "media," we simultaneously mean devices that carry messages and information (such as television sets, radios, computers, mobile phones, etc.), entities that produce those messages and information (multi-media outlets such as CNN and the BBC, newspapers, etc.), and, broadly, the complex environments that we navigate every day when we encounter things and others in the world.

Second, by *digital media*, we mean media that consist of information in digital bits of 1s and 0s – which is at the heart of much modern communication (i.e., computers, Apple Watches, video games, digital photographs, etc.). The *Internet* is a global network of computers and other devices linked together through a number of different means (from cables that run under the ocean to satellites in the sky). Not all digital media are on the Internet, of course – but the Internet is premised on the connections between and information shared by digital devices.

Social media refers to sites that have as their basis, at least in some part, user-generated content shared with other users. These users can be individual people or institutions (such as a media outlet). Communication on social media can take various forms. These include communication directly between users, communication that flows across users' social networks (or their set of social ties), or communication that is presented in some algorithmically determined way based on interests or behavior. (An *algorithm* is a set of defined rules for doing something, such as displaying content on a social media platform.) At their heart, social media feature some form of user-generated content (the 'social' in 'social media').

We spend an extensive amount of time defining *platforms* in Chapter 3. Briefly, for now, *platforms* refers to data-intensive technologies that rely on algorithms to deliver content, goods, services, relationships, etc., to users. To provide a few examples, the Nintendo Switch is a platform for video games, Facebook is a platform for social relationships and market transactions, Amazon is a platform for goods and services (such as cloud computing), and Google is a platform for information services, search, and collaborative work.

Finally, by *technologies*, we broadly mean artifacts (whether they are material or virtual), knowledge, processes, and organization. Think about all of these things together! Technologies are not always, and not just, physical and virtual things you hold in your hand, such as iPhones; they are also the organized knowledge required to build and use them. To understand technology, you have to understand how it is produced and consumed, social narratives about what it is and who should use it, how it is designed, what it does, and what people perceive that it does. You also have to understand how institutions – routine ways of doing things – are built around technologies.

1.4 Structure of the Book

With this book, we introduce readers to political communication in the age of platforms. We focus on the ways in which platforms have become central to how political communication works across many contexts, from public spheres to journalism to politics and entertainment.

Chapter 2 introduces the definitions of our key concepts and provides an overview of varieties of political communication across the globe. We also outline our approach and provide a model for understanding the role of platforms in political communication.

Chapter 3 focuses on platforms, detailing their political power and impact on political life as distribution channels, infrastructures, technologies, policymakers, and profit-making firms. This chapter is especially focused on the intersection between platforms and political actors such as campaigns, journalists, governmental bodies, and citizens, and addresses platform products, design, and affordances.

Chapter 4 discusses the relationship between platforms, public spheres, and public opinion. This chapter shows what has changed with respect to public spheres, how, and with what consequences for political communication. The chapter also provides an extended discussion of how platforms shape public spheres and public opinion in countries around the world.

Chapter 5 offers our analysis of journalism during the era of platforms. This chapter discusses how we should think about journalism in an era of democratized publishing, the increasing debates over journalistic professionalism and objectivity amid growing international movements for political and social equality, changing business models for journalism, trends toward data journalism, and the legitimacy of and trust in journalism as an institution.

Chapter 6 introduces readers to strategic communication, shifting our attention to things such as political advertising, political marketing, public relations, and public diplomacy. We discuss the history of political strategic communication, what practitioners do and the ethical considerations involved, and how platforms have changed nearly all aspects of mobilizing publics and shaping public discourse.

Chapter 7 focuses on campaigns, elections, and referendums in democratic states. The chapter details the history of campaigning and elections, and discusses what transitions during the platform era mean for voters, political information, and discussion, as well as the people and organizations who practice politics.

Chapter 8 provides an account of social movements, protest cultures, and revolutions within democratic and non-democratic states during the age of platforms. We begin by discussing the history of ways of making claims on the state or powerful elites and institutions, before detailing the relationship between media, platforms, and movements and the various outcomes of movements, in different regions around the world.

Chapter 9 provides an analysis of the relationship between media, platforms, and governance. It provides us with an opportunity to explore the relationship between political communication and policymaking processes, legal systems, executive agencies, and bureaucratic functioning, with a focus on goals and strategies for policymaking and regulation over platforms. The chapter ends with a case study of an innovation in platform governance: the Facebook Oversight Board.

Chapter 10 focuses on a set of current and pressing issues of central concern to contemporary democracies, namely the relationship between how we come to know and accept things as true or propaganda, misinformation, disinformation, and polarization. The chapter takes up questions about how informed the public should be and the role knowledge-producing institutions play in democracy.

Chapter 11 takes up questions about social and political identity, populism, and extremism in the platform era, detailing case studies from different social and political contexts. We pay particular attention here to the role of media in what scholars call "democratic backsliding" (Haggard & Kaufman 2021), or the erosion of democratic institutions and governance.

Chapter 12 details the relationship between entertainment media and politics. Indeed, political communication does not only happen around expressly political things! We aim here at showing how ostensibly non-political things have political meaning, such as lifestyle selfies on Instagram, reality shows, and video games, and how this affects us politically and socially in a world where many genres of political communication are being reinvented.

Chapter 13 summarizes the book, offering conclusions and points for further exploration and discussion.

1.5 Pedagogical Features

This book has a number of key features that we hope will make for an engaging read. First, the chapters are designed to be read *either* in the sequence of this book, or as standalone introductions to the concepts they cover. We deliberately set out to write a book that could be applicable across many different courses and contexts, and that covered content ranging from journalism and strategic communication to campaigning and disinformation. As such, while no doubt reading the book straight through will provide deeper context for understanding the content covered by specific chapters, the individual chapters can also stand on their own and be readily accessible to those encountering their ideas for the first time.

Second, as you have no doubt noticed, the text features a number of elements that are designed to help students understand the core ideas in this book. At the start of every chapter, we outline a number of objectives – things we hope you will take away from the text. Each chapter covers a lot more! However, we hope to capture the main ideas of the chapters in these objectives so you can be sensitive to them while reading. Each chapter also has what we call "Spotlighted Content" or "Spotlighted Case(s)." These are extended discussions of core concepts or detailed examples that we offer to illustrate key themes in the text. We conclude chapters with a set of discussion questions – these are useful for instructors and readers for thinking through the key themes of the chapter (and hopefully talking through in classes or among peers!). Finally, each chapter has a brief list of suggested readings to accompany this text, for readers who would like to go further into the subjects addressed in the chapter.

2 Definitions and Variations of Political Communication

Chapter 2 provides an overview of a number of key concepts in political communication, as well as details how political communication looks different in various media and political systems in countries and regions around the world. This chapter provides a guiding definition of political communication, details shifts in media and political systems with technological change, and discusses the relationship between platforms, political communication, and political processes. It concludes by providing a model of platforms and political communication as they are embedded in media and political systems and shaped by historical, cultural, social, and economic forces, which they in turn shape.

OBJECTIVES

By the end of this chapter, you should be able to:

- define political communication
- contextualize political communication from a global perspective
- understand the transition from the mass media era to the platform age
- explain the relationship between political systems, platforms, and political communication
- reflect on how political communication is mediated.

2.1 Introduction

This book is about political communication. And, broadly speaking, political communication is communication about politics. Even more, communication *creates* what people understand to be political. By *communication*, this book means any form of symbolic expression, whether it entails spoken words, texts, visual symbols, digital videos, or, most likely, some combination of all the above.

Some of these forms of communication have long lineages of being important politically, while newer ones are central to the ways we communicate about politics today. For example, oration has long been a preferred form of authoritative address for political elites, whereas digital video has exploded in popularity globally in the last decade. Digital video has become a means for everything from campaigns introducing candidates to everyday people documenting war and police abuses. Indeed, we are awash in new forms of storytelling through multimedia on global video-hosting platforms such as YouTube (which has more than 460 million users in India alone) and Youku (more than 500 million users in China). Whether printed or digital, texts provide vehicles for political ideas and debate, and they can range from newspapers, books, and the white papers of think tanks to tweets, Facebook posts, and pamphlets circulated by social movements. Visual symbols include everything from flags and images on Instagram to campaign and party logos and emojis.

As such, *communication* is an expansive concept and takes many different forms through different media, including the human voice. Communication is something people do verbally and non-verbally all the time, beginning the moment they enter the world. Communication becomes *symbolic* when people develop the capacity to create, convey, and understand meaning. What makes it *political* is when communication concerns the distribution of power or resources in a society; who the members of that society are and should be; the problems that collectively need to be identified and solved; the ways we should live and what values and goals we should have; the very nature of the community itself and its relations with other communities; or who legitimately holds power and what the nature of that power is. In short, politics deals with relations, power, identity, and decision-making.

This book takes as its starting point that *political communication* concerns public life – the things we share with others and our relations with others. This is an expansive definition, and deliberately so. It includes not just the things we take for granted as political – such as elections and policymaking. But also those things that people *want* us to have a collective response to, whether they concern manners, morals, or issues – anything that relates to our ways of living together.

Even ostensibly private things can suddenly become matters of public concern, depending on what people talk about when they talk about politics – or disappear from public concern when they stop talking about politics (Wells et al. 2017). What is considered private versus public is often the result of communicative struggles that are inherently political.

SPOTLIGHTED CASES

Here are a few examples of how what was formerly private became political. Women in countries around the world successfully redefined what had once been commonly seen as violent "private" spousal relations as "domestic violence," transforming it into a public issue. Even further, naming what occurred between husbands and wives as *violence* was also a broader political argument about *equality* that defines how we should treat one another in private and public life and what the role of the state should be with respect to protecting its citizens. The same goes for Black activists pointing to discrimination in private real estate markets, religious advocates arguing for public standards of dress or prayer in public schools, and lesbian, gay, bisexual, transgender, queer/questioning, intersex, or asexual plus (LGBTQIA+) activists fighting for equality in labor markets and public accommodations.

In addition, things that we do not ordinarily think about as being political are full of political meaning. Politics is all around us. Think about entertainment programs that convey ideas about how to live and who has money and power, even if these things are tangential to the main plot. Think about TikTok videos that celebrate self-expressive joy and free expression. Think about all the athletes around the world who knelt during their national anthems or wore black armbands during "end racism" campaigns and global Black Lives Matter protests. And think of all the advocates around the world who argue that representation – in sports, entertainment, media, corporate board rooms, and education – matters for the types of future that children believe they can achieve.

2.2 Types of Political Communication

Accordingly, the *types* of actors that produce and engage in political communication are many and diverse – whether they are people, organizations, institutions, media, or even technologies. Indeed, *everyone* or *everything* is a potential political communicator if their expression relates to matters of public concern – or argues that something should be a matter of public concern. When a member of the public gives an interview to a journalist to express her concerns about a polluting business nearby, it is political communication. When a woman comes forward publicly about a harassing famous boss, she is engaging in political communication. When a person comes out publicly as LGBTQIA+, they are engaging in political communication in affirming who they are in ways that have political implications (Garretson 2018). When a religious person declares a set of tenets that they believe a moral or just society as a whole should adhere to – that is political communication. When people produce entertainment media that represent immigrant lives and communities, this is inherently political communication as well.

And when a global platform company such as Meta (formerly Facebook) designs an algorithm to remove what it defines as "racist" content, someone builds a bot on Twitter to try to shape public opinion around an election, or TikTok's algorithms shape the "for you pages" of its users in ways that influence how they think about their social identities, these are also forms of political communication. Indeed, not only are the corporate employees and engineers behind the policies and algorithms engaging in political communication, these technologies, such as bots and algorithms, are engaging in political communication by restricting, promoting, or shaping the incentives for certain types of content (Brevini & Swiatek 2020; Noble 2018; Tripodi 2022).

While political communication is all around us all the time, there are *institutionalized* political communicators who play more defined, specialized, and routine roles in journalistic, political, and public communication processes. These types of communicators are at the heart of this book. By "institutionalized," we mean that certain political actors play defined roles in political processes and communicate in generally patterned and routinized ways that persist over time (Cook 1998; Schudson 2002). These political communicators include journalists, political pundits, political parties and elected representatives, social media managers, political candidates, political advertising agencies, think tanks, political marketers, political public relations practitioners, press secretaries, advocacy and social movement organizations, government agencies, transnational bodies such as the European Union – and many, many more besides. These are the individuals and organizations that address publics routinely and play established and often well-defined roles in public debate, electoral politics, and governance processes across the world, as well as the creation, circulation, and diffusion of ideas and arguments that shape what people see as matters of public concern. This includes the issues that need to be addressed and their causes, ideas how polities should be structured, and arguments about who has legitimate power and status.

The addressing of publics and debates within public spheres take shape through *media* and *genres* that are institutionalized according to particular settings and contexts for political communication. One way to think about media is in terms of *technologies* and the *organizations*, *institutions*, and *cultures* that surround them. To take an example, television sets are forms of media, but to truly understand television we also need to consider the *content* that they display, the *organizations* that manufacture and produce content for them, the *cultures* (Brock 2020) that shape that content and norms for their use, and the regulatory and economic landscapes that govern how television sets are produced and what content can be shown, how, and when. *Genres* are patterned ways of communicating that exist across media, which are in turn also shaped by the organizations that produce media, the economic and other reasons they have for doing so (such as audience demand), and the regulations that shape discourse in the public sphere. Think about how news broadcasts usually follow a particular, patterned format, with an anchor who narrates headlines according to shared standards of newsworthiness. There are many different genres in political communication. What appears on the news pages of a newspaper differs, for instance, from what appears in the opinion section and on cable news. Taken together, genres constitute the patterned ways in which political and media elites and everyday people alike express, discuss, and debate public issues.

Finally, there are often defined settings and contexts that shape political communication. How elected officials address parliaments or other governing bodies is different from how they speak at a campaign rally or to their colleagues behind the scenes in legislative offices. Declarations of war, funerals, and public health crises are all contexts that call for staid, somber, and authoritative addresses, respectively, by political and state leaders, whereas other settings (such as national holidays) might be causes for celebration or uplift. Citizens speak differently in legislative hearings than in public meetings. Citizen discourse also differs substantially across platforms, with their different social norms and rules around things such as anonymity. For example, on platforms such as Facebook that require real names, people can be more cautious about expressing controversial opinions, given the ways "contexts collapse" (Marwick & boyd 2011), drawing work, social, and familial ties together. Different political and media actors, meanwhile, have different norms and expectations for political expression, especially when communicating across fields. Think about the often deferential way journalists communicate when asking questions of political leaders, versus their approach to citizens such as victims of a crime or eyewitnesses to a natural disaster.

2.3 Overview: Varieties of Political Communication across the Globe

Political communication is not the same everywhere and for everyone, of course. Historical, social, economic, and cultural contexts matter profoundly for political communication, including shaping who has power in societies. Political communication is textured by different state and regime types, political systems, party systems, electoral systems, media systems, and journalism cultures (e.g. Esser & Pfetsch 2020). One way to illustrate this is the paradox of the "Americanization" of election campaigns. On the one hand, elements of US presidential campaigns spill over and influence campaigns in other Western democracies, such as in the use of professional public relations experts or social media to obtain microdonations and for microtargeting. On the other, campaign managers from outside the US will tell you that, no, unfortunately they cannot just copy-and-paste the playbooks from the Obama 2012, Trump 2016, or Biden 2020 campaigns, as they would not work in the specific political setting or media system in their country (e.g. Lilleker et al. 2020).

In fact, US elections are unique among Western democracies. The presidential system gives extraordinary power to the White House, and a polarized two-party system means that parties do not share power in governing coalitions, but that the winner (however slim the victory) takes it all (the presidency or House and Senate majorities). The presidential prize that can be won (or lost) is so big that both sides spend enormous amounts of resources in the race, focused on only a handful of states due to an election system based not on the popular vote, but a complicated and anachronistic institution: the Electoral College. Because of this specific setting, innovations often arise in US presidential election campaigns – there are abundant financial resources, strong incentives to implement new technologies and to move beyond the known strategies, comparatively few regulations (especially compared to Europe), and no reason to be soft on your opponent (Kreiss 2016).

Compare this to the situation in Switzerland, for instance. Here we find a multiparty system in a parliamentary democracy premised on power sharing. After each election, the parties in parliament elect a government, the Federal Council, a collegial body of seven members with equal rights. The presidency rotates among them each year, but it is the council as whole that collectively serves as head of state. Since 1891, the idea behind this government formation has been to include all major political movements in the government. This, of course, means that there is no opposition – all major parties are part of the government, and they govern by the consensus principle. It is also a political tradition to not vote out a sitting member of the Federal Council. Thus, elections hardly ever change anything – parties can hardly win or lose anything, and politicians meet again in roughly the same coalitions after the election. It is also impossible to vote out the government. Against this backdrop, there are few incentives to spend many resources on campaigning or pursuing innovations, or to be tough on your competitors. This is an entirely different story when it comes to referendum campaigns, which is the Swiss playground for political conflicts and ideological battles.

These two cases illustrate how very differently the stage can be set for political communication – *even* given the fact that the US and Switzerland are both wealthy Western democracies with highly media-literate and technology-savvy citizens. There is much more variation in the world beyond these two countries, of course. For example, the role of platforms in political life can look very different across countries. Even as social media and platforms influence democratic political change in some countries (Howard & Hussain 2013), some leaders have proven remarkably adept at holding on to power, and even at dying in office, at whatever cost. These leaders often use informational tactics on platforms to stifle the political opposition and democratic movements.

SPOTLIGHTED CASES

Despite early optimism that the Internet would bring democracy to countries around the world, authoritarian and anti-democratic leaders have adapted to changing media environments. Some African countries, such as the Democratic Republic of Congo, Chad, Cameroon, and Zimbabwe, have blocked internet access in the wake of anti-government protests – despite government denials. Meanwhile, even amid sweeping changes in media and technology, authoritarian leaders have died in office (Chad's Idriss Déby), have had to be forced out via a military coup (Robert Mugabe of Zimbabwe), or, as in the case of Cameroon's Paul Biya, who has held power since 1975, have established de facto one-party systems and simply refuse to give up power.

Indeed, some political leaders have proven markedly adept at bending information environments to suit their will. Critics and researchers have documented Russian President Vladimir Putin's ability to control informational dynamics within his own country through propaganda and other manipulative tactics that have enabled him to maintain and expand power domestically, even while exporting these tactics abroad to strategically weaken his adversaries (Cooper 2020; Miazhevich 2018). In other countries, such as Venezuela, state-run media outlets sit alongside commercial media and social media that represent various groups and ideological perspectives vying for political power, dynamics which undemocratic leaders work to manipulate to shore up power (Lupien 2013).

Most political communication research originates from and focuses on democracies – those countries or transnational entities, such as the European Union, that hold elections and protect the basic political rights of individuals and associations (what scholars call "liberal democracy"). However, scholars have increasingly come to realize that democracy is a matter of degree, and states are always in a process of becoming or unbecoming, just as authoritarian states face constant pressure to change as well. Between consolidated and comparatively stable democracies on one side and totalitarian states on the other, we find many forms of "defective democracies" (Merkel 2004) (such as in new states where institutions are imperfectly realized), "hybrid regimes" (Bogaards 2009) or "anocracies" (Pate 2020) (hybrid or mixed regimes featuring democratic and authoritarian elements, such as Nigeria), "democracies with adjectives" (Collier & Levitsky 1997) (such as military-backed democratic regimes), or democratic "backsliding" (Haggard & Kaufman 2021) (the erosion of democratic or civic institutions in countries around the world, such as the United States). Democracies emerge and they can die (Keane 2009; Levitsky & Ziblatt 2018). Across history, democracies are the exception, not the rule, and therefore they should not be taken for granted. For their part, authoritarian systems can be overthrown or gradually shift toward democracy, or break down into war and ethnic cleansing.

There is also political communication in all of these mixed and non-democratic states, of course. Consider the extreme cases of authoritarian, totalitarian, or one-party states. Political communication can include everything from state propaganda, leader proclamations, state-friendly journalism, and military parades to the subtle, coded communication of opposition groups, independent press organizations, and discontented citizens who cannot dissent openly. In these countries, explicit censorship means that journalists and political activists cannot write and publish as they see fit. It also means that criticism in politics, journalism, literature, poetry, and theatre plays is expressed "between the lines," and that citizens and activists use coded language in everyday life and on social media (Tilly et al. 2020).

As noted above, digital platforms were initially praised for democratizing closed regimes, or at least creating the conditions for democracy to thrive. Researchers and journalists held up paradigmatic examples such as the democratic movements that swept the Middle East and North Africa in the early 2010s (the "Arab Spring") as examples of this democratizing relationship between information and communication technologies and authoritarian regimes (e.g. Howard 2010; Mutsvairo & Bebawi 2022). Since that time, however, there has been considerable rethinking. It might be less dangerous to hold up a cardboard sign in public (and run away once the police show up) than to voice discontent or mobilize protest online, traceable by IP addresses or digital forensics.

States such as China have exercised control over what their populations can access in terms of information, including on American-run platforms that desire to do business in them, and regularly engage in tactics to manipulate digital information and social processes (Field et al. 2018; Lu & Pan 2021; Pan 2019). Indeed, what content standards US-based companies should have across vastly different regimes is an important debate in contemporary political communication research and Western policymaking discourse (e.g. Helberger et al. 2018). At the same time, contests between platforms for market share often reflect larger geopolitical struggles between states over values and economics. While Meta's WhatsApp has long been widely used across Africa, in recent years WeChat, owned by a Chinese company, has been making inroads, aided in part by the growing influence of China's political and economic supremacy across the continent. In the United States, there are fierce debates over the Chinese company-owned TikTok potentially being a tool for influence over the American public, in addition to widespread fears about the safety and security of data about Americans on the platform.

Meanwhile, processes of democratization can be interrupted or reversed. Scholars have established various definitions and measurements of democratic consolidation (Coppedge et al. 2020; Schedler 2001). The progress of democratization and the quality of democracy depend on factors such as the guarantee of civil liberties, the rule of law, the resilience of the electoral system, the checks and balances within the political system, political participation, and the role of the military and potential anti-system actors in the state. Researchers have ways of assessing and comparing all of these things through democracy indices, such as Freedom House, the Bertelsmann Transformation Index, the Sustainable Governance Indicators, or the Varieties of Democracies index.

In the past two decades, there has also been an explosion of work on democratic decay, backsliding, and crisis (Bennett & Livingston 2021; Levitsky & Ziblatt 2018), amid growing evidence and widespread concern that even apparently consolidated democracies are under threat from the pressures of inequality, polarization, would-be autocratic leaders, anti-democratic parties, or, most dramatically, coups that take power through force (Haggard & Kaufman 2021). At the same time, many of these things are taking shape amid unprecedented movements for racial and social justice that threaten dominant interests and privileged social groups, which can provoke intense backlash (Hajnal 2021) – precisely the story of the attempted coup in the US on January 6, 2021 (Cline Center 2021).

As such, it is best to see political systems as always in flux. The past two centuries, after all, have witnessed the gradual expansion of suffrage in countries around the world, to include men without property, people from non-dominant racial and religious groups, and women. In countries such as Argentina, democratic governments were overthrown (some with the help of the United States) and then reinstated through elections. And yet, even these things are far from settled, with the resurgence of right-wing, exclusionary movements in countries across the globe that seek to restrict citizenship and reinforce rigid hierarchies across social groups. For example, since 2019, India, considered the world's most populous democracy, has experienced considerable backsliding on the heels of a Hindu nationalist leader and political party consolidating power.

Democracy must be upheld through laws and institutions as much as norms – including those that shape political communication. History has made it clear that democracies prove fragile when political communicators cease to respect the legitimacy of the opposition; undermine electoral accountability; stoke racial and ethnic divisions in the service of protecting or pursuing unequal power; deny people equality; circumscribe citizenship or rights to favor certain racial, ethnic, or religious groups; or refuse ever to compromise. The relationship between these things and platforms, social media, and technology more generally is complicated and actively debated. There are clearly challenges to forms of authoritarian rule when people communicate shared grievances and organize, mobilize, and make themselves visible to one another. Technology offers social movements important new opportunities for mobilization (Bennett & Segerberg 2013). At the same time, digitally enabled mobilization does not necessarily translate into the institutions and organizations necessary for durable democratic change (Tufekci 2017).

Over the past decade, there has also been an explosion of work on platforms and threats to democracy. A conclusion of this research is that platforms are tools for those contesting power, especially elites who seek to stoke and inflame division in pursuit of political advantage. But platforms are not neutral tools – through their design, policies, monetization strategies, and power over attention they amplify certain forms of political speech (such as the emotional and extreme) and dramatically lower the costs of some types of communication (such as video). These things in turn provide opportunities for non-institutional media and political interests, which has meant more rapidly mobilizing social movements and threats to institutional parties, including their loss of control over, for example, nominating contests. It has also meant increased opportunities for coordination across shared political interests (such as ruling parties and elites and organized digital movements that work in tandem with them). Even all this is complicated. The same platforms that facilitate movements for democracy and justice also create conditions for disinformation and propaganda in the service of power – undermining the tolerance, accountability, and faith in institutions at the center of democracy. Non-institutional media and parties are democratizing in some contexts, and levers of power for authoritarians in others.

In sum, changes in media and technology do not necessarily bring democracy. There are many varieties of political communication – in democracies and authoritarian countries, in political systems with 2 or 17 political parties in the legislative branch, and in nations with public service broadcasters, private media duopolies, or some pluralistic mix. Political communication is constantly evolving in response to changes in media and political systems – even as political communication changes media and political systems in turn. Let's now look in greater detail at the relationship between political systems and political communication.

2.4 Political Systems and Political Communication

The "political" can be thought of generally along three dimensions: the *polity* – which includes things such as constitutions and institutional designs that are structural (i.e., they provide the rules of the game); *politics* – the arena of conflicts between political actors; and *policy* – often the aim of political conflicts, such as the passage (or revocation) of laws and regulations.

All three are interconnected. The design of a political system impacts the goals of political actors, how they behave and communicate, and what they are incentivized to do. Political practices and norms, such as around conflict negotiation, that are part of the arena of politics impact how, and even whether, new policies can enter the political agenda. Political actors create the details of policies in line with their goals, constituencies, values, and understanding of the political climate, which shapes how they communicate about and fight for them. Actors who pursue unpopular policy goals, for instance, often opt for non-public mobilization strategies such as lobbying, instead of trying to pressure policymakers through public appeals. Most importantly, politics and policy are highly dependent on the structural setting of a specific polity – and therefore so is political communication.

SPOTLIGHTED CONTENT

Political systems can be parliamentarian (most European countries) or presidential (e.g. the US, France, and Turkey). Heads of state can be elected directly (France) or indirectly (US and Germany), and there are also constitutional monarchies with royalty that, by birthright, can have real power (e.g. Liechtenstein and Thailand), or be confined to symbolic functions (e.g. the UK, Japan, and Sweden). In the United Arab Emirates, Brunei, Oman, Saudi Arabia, Vatican City, and Eswatini (formerly Swaziland), an absolute monarchy still rules. Political systems can be built around one party (e.g. China), two main parties (US, UK), or multiple parties that may or may not form government coalitions (e.g. Netherlands, Germany, Italy, and Australia), depending on the ideological distance within the party system.

To understand the role of political communication and platforms in polities, and their effects, therefore requires accounting for their embeddedness in political systems. Parliamentary systems tend to be rather stable because parties are a result not only of the electoral system, but also of the social structure and social conflict lines within a society, such as urban and rural, labor and capital, church and state, center and periphery, and the various racial, ethnic, and social identity groups in polities. Political systems can be competitive (mostly in two-party systems) or consociational (aiming to include most groups and interests in society and seeking consensus). These ideal types only rarely exist in the real world, however. For example, in most European countries we find mixed versions (e.g. Belgium, Germany, and Austria).

Party systems can be polarized (mostly in two-party systems) or fragmented, especially where the threshold to enter parliaments is rather low. In the Netherlands, for instance, there is no threshold, and as little as 0.67 percent of votes can be sufficient to gain 1 seat in parliament. In the 2021 election, this resulted in 17 parties being represented in parliament. In most multi-party democracies, there is a threshold around 5 percent, and all parties below this vote share remain outside of parliamentary representation. This influences how small or new parties campaign, because often this threshold is connected to receiving public financial resources for campaigning.

Political parties are key actors in political communication, and they come in an array of different types. We can differentiate parties along the ideological spectrum (left versus right), their position (in the government versus in the opposition), their size (members or vote share), or group them into party families (such as conservative, progressive, or nationalist). All this impacts how they will engage in political communication or run a campaign. For example, a major incumbent party with a large member base will follow different strategies than a new, small party in a challenger position without a broad member base and with fewer resources. Moreover, parties pursue a variety of objectives that may cause internal conflicts. They might have policy goals (such as a new climate policy) that may be particularly important for the party member base. At the same time, they might also aim at maximizing votes and gaining or keeping office, which may be particularly important for the party elite. Coalition negotiations may lead to conflicts, such as when parties need to decide what is more important to them, their policy agenda or gaining office in a prospective government, or when there are differences in the values, priorities, or goals of the coalition members.

All of these dynamics have significant implications for understanding the strategies behind political communication. A communications campaign may be strategically directed at presenting the party as a viable minor coalition partner, rather than winning, and themes may be chosen accordingly. Party resources have a major impact on campaign strategies. In some countries, parties are based on a membership model (e.g. most European countries), while in other countries parties survive primarily from their supporters' donations and therefore spend more time soliciting wealthy donors and fundraising off of political controversies (e.g. the US). Parties also receive varying degrees of public resources across countries, based on many different regulations and transparency rules.

SPOTLIGHTED CASE

In Switzerland, political parties are treated just like any other private association, with no obligation at all to make their financial assets and revenue transparent, while in many other democracies parties are obliged to publicly report how much they spent on campaigns and where the money came from.

Political communication is indelibly shaped by these features of the polity, such as the institutional dynamics around parties. Election systems are another important variable in political communication. Elections may aim at majority representation (i.e., the party with the highest vote share wins a majority in parliament or the government as a whole). This is mostly the case in two-party systems. It is a system that generally yields clear majorities, creates conditions for stable governments, favors government change with the transfer of power, and enables clear political accountability. On the downside, all votes that were not cast for the winner are generally excluded from power. In contrast, electoral systems aiming at proportional representation favor a fair representation of all voters and are found mostly in multi-party systems, where they yield government coalitions and provide good chances for new and small political parties. On the downside, government coalitions can more easily break and there are many potential vetoes among minor parties – making wielding power more difficult. This can lead to political instability. Italy is an excellent case to illustrate this, with 67 governments since 1945 at the time of this writing. Finally, campaigning is different in first-order elections (national elections) and second-order elections (regional, local, or transnational elections such as the EU), the latter of which are characterized by lower turnouts, worse prospects for governmental parties, a tendency toward protest voting, and the perception that less is at stake.

Political communication is also shaped by the policies and rules countries create governing things such as elections and campaigning. In many democracies, access to TV and radio airtime is regulated and allocated to parties, for instance, often in ways that reflect their vote share in the last election. Whether and how parties and candidates can buy airtime for political ads influences their campaign strategies. When airtime for ads is equally distributed among parties through regulations, there is no point raising money to buy prime time slots on TV. On the other hand, if a small, new party with limited resources is forced to buy TV airtime and cannot afford it, platforms such as social media might become more central to their campaign strategies.

One reason we see all the varying (and confusing!) implications and effects of platforms in different countries are these differing political systems, democratic institutions and cultures, social structures (such as inequality), and social groups in the polities they are embedded in. The communication of political elites, campaigns, movements, activists, citizens, and government officials does not take place in a vacuum and rarely happens out of thin air. The structure of polities, rules and norms of politics, and existing policies all shape how political communicators use platforms, to what ends, and with what effects.

SPOTLIGHTED CONTENT

To understand the origins, intent, dynamics, and outcomes of political communication, we have to consider the context. Consider a few much focused on examples relevant to democracies around the world today. Small groups who organize and radicalize new members in Facebook or Telegram groups based on deeply rooted ideologies and social identities forged over generations, and then take their messages to the streets or storm political institutions, may not overthrow a stable, consolidated democracy (at least not immediately). They may, however, shake the foundations of a young, barely institutionalized democracy or a sclerotic, dysfunctional regime that has lost the support of its citizens. Elite attempts to polarize citizens for electoral gain using social media might not pose any significant democratic consequences in a parliamentary democracy with strong parties that have to make common cause through coalitional politics to wield power. Those same polarization attempts might look very different, however, in countries with long-standing racial and ethnic animosities, inequalities, histories of violence, and growing economic precarity, or when two parties stand in for very large social divides – such as in the US.

The attempts by an authoritarian leader to gain power might not be a cause for concern in a country with strong parties that reject them, but in moments of crisis or weakness this might open the door to the undoing of democracy.

To summarize, political actors behave and communicate in ways that are structured and incentivized by the political systems they operate in. The structure of the polity, arena of politics, and policy conflicts at stake shape political communication and how political actors use media – even as these things affect the workings of politics in turn (what is known as the "politics–media–politics" model: Wolfsfeld et al. 2022). Because of this, technological and strategic innovations do not always travel well from one nation to another, nor are the effects of platforms the same in every setting (Lorenz-Spreen et al. 2023). All of which is another way of saying that political communication is highly dependent upon the political context in which it takes place, even as media systems also provide the context within which political actors vie for power through communication. We turn now to consider media systems.

2.5 Media Systems and Political Communication: from Mass Media to Platforms

The sociologist Niklas Luhmann (2000) famously argued that whatever we know about society or the world, we know through media. In fact, in their most recent book, *Political Communication in Contemporary India*, Yatindra Singh Sisodia and Pratip Chattopadhyay (2022) spotlight the influential role the media play in shaping political decision-making in the South Asian nation. Hardly anyone has ever met their president, prime minister, or monarch in person, and comparatively few have personally witnessed major historical events first-hand, such as the fall of the Berlin Wall in 1989, the terrorist attacks of September 11, 2001, or the nuclear disaster at Fukushima in 2011. In large, as geographically dispersed societies, we simply cannot eyewitness or experience much of politics first-hand, despite its tremendous impact on our public and personal lives.

As such, political communication is almost *always* mediated. This means that it has to travel from sender(s) to recipient(s) through media of some sort – most commonly in our time mass media and/or digital platforms. Even in-person political events such as candidate speeches are often mediated – by microphones, teleprompters, and staging. Local political events that live audiences can witness directly are often produced for mass mediated audiences (see Lang & Lang 2009). Much of politics is about strategic political actors trying to convey messages through media (such as journalism), ideally without any distortion of the original message. If citizens try to gain the attention of political elites or a broader public, their objective is often to gain as much visibility as possible in the media. Often, these citizen, activist, or movement groups are far more reliant on journalists (what powerful elites say is often *inherently* newsworthy after all!) and have to meet their definitions of what is newsworthy – for example, by creating spectacles that both appear authentic and will play well on television or digital video (Sobieraj 2011). Social media and platforms more generally, however, have provided movements with unprecedented opportunities to gain public visibility, and that has also indelibly shaped journalism and created new forms of public accountability for elites (Richardson 2020).

All of which means that media – understood expansively – are at the core of political communication. Concepts such as the "marketplace of ideas" underline media's importance to democracy. The media of a particular era significantly impact, shape, and structure political communication. Historically, mass media stood as *the* gateway to the public sphere, the core arena for politics. Today, however, there is what the US legal scholar Yochai Benkler (2006) has called a networked "public sphere" (or space for public discourse, covered extensively in Chapter 4), facilitated by platforms that host and gather together many different types of media and political actors. These actors not only use media and platforms to find audiences, they increasingly prioritize media logics (such as performing for television and social media) over political logics (such as engaging in good faith debate with members of the opposing party). Indeed, one of the key sets of documents made publicly available by the US-based Facebook whistleblower Frances Haugen were internal reports at the company that European Union political parties often took more extreme positions on policy issues on social media because they performed better – received more widespread attention, distribution, and engagement.

This shift means significant changes in political communication. We have nearly a century of research on how media select for the information and commentary that journalists and other media actors believe is important, often through professional standards, ideological and identity orientations, and commercial concerns. In the case of legacy media, it is journalists and their news values – "all the news that's fit to print" is the tagline of the *New York Times* – which shape what information is presented to the public and how. At the same time, these news values also look different across print/text and broadcast, and are also shaped by the audiences represented and appealed to by outlets – for example, partisan media that seek to advance a political agenda, or media rooted in a particular community for which they are an advocate.

In the case of digital platforms, algorithmic systems provide the recommendations that make implicit judgments as to what is important to people and what they will engage with, such as whether it is content shared by close social ties or is similar to content a user has interacted with before. Often, these algorithms are designed to keep users on platforms – ultimately so they can be monetized for the sale of digital ads. Yet some platforms take a more editorial role, such as selecting content to feature (e.g., governmental information during Covid-19), flagging and correcting misinformation (such as when elections are disputed), or designing to promote quality content or "healthy" conversations (such as when Twitter asks you if you want to read something before sharing it). This includes information from government agencies or trusted news sources during elections and public health crises. As we discuss in the next chapter, these are forms of content moderation – broadly, the decisions that platforms make about what content to take down and leave up in accordance with their rules – and take shape according to platforms' standards, values, and perceived user needs and desires, as well as external pressures from governments, journalists, and civil society organizations.

With media at the core of contemporary political communication, the varieties of media systems matter. Media systems have evolved over time, and the advent of new technologies has transformed them continually, although older technologies rarely become obsolete – instead, newer and older technologies sit side by side. And there is a close relationship between media systems and political systems.

Take news media, for example. While "news" is a centuries-old genre for making society visible to itself (Pettegree 2014), it is not simply a representational media. Newspapers are a global phenomenon, and have been tools for projects of empire and proselytizing. Portuguese missionaries established India's first printing press (Priolkar 1958). British missionaries are credited with launching newspapers in sub-Saharan Africa. Newspapers have also been vehicles for political projects and diasporic political communities. English-speaking West Africa is often considered the first region on the African continent to embrace newspapers. *The Royal Gazette* and *Sierra Leone Advertiser*, first published in 1801, are touted as the region's oldest newspapers (Mano 2010) (the first printing press brought to Africa in 1792 was destroyed upon arrival [Hunter 2018]). These newspapers were founded by a Black American settler, part of a larger community of many former slaves who escaped from their slave masters and fought for the British during the revolutionary war, and later founded Freetown, Sierra Leone. And Charles L. Force, a former American slave, established the *Royal Gold Coast Gazette*, first published in Ghana in 1794, and later launched the *Liberia Herald* in 1820.

Meanwhile, newspapers and political parties often evolved in tandem in Europe and the United States. In the 1700s and 1800s, many newspapers served as vehicles for political factions and political parties. During this time, politics in many European countries was largely newspaper-based. During the French Revolution, for instance, many politicians started their own newspapers. Between February and March 1789 alone, over 200 newspapers were founded in Paris (Habermas 2013: 277–8). Similarly, in the lead-up to the American Revolution, newspapers helped galvanize widespread frustration about taxes into a union of colonies fighting together for independence. During the 1800s, political parties in the United States and Europe often used newspapers as their organizational basis.

Only during the late 1800s and 1900s did many newspapers in countries such as the US separate from political interests given shifts in economics, printing technology, consumer demand, and reformer desires to have information be free from partisanship so citizens could make up their own minds. With the advancement of printing presses and new commercial models for the press appealing to mass, non-partisan audiences in "democratic market societies" (Schudson 1978) during the late nineteenth century, newspapers became more accessible to and affordable for almost everyone. This continued throughout the first decades of the twentieth century in the United States and Europe, as mass, general-interest newspapers appealed across partisan lines amid a professionalizing journalism project that was codifying its ethics, values, and standards. Unevenly, to be sure, as "yellow" (or sensational) journalism, the racist southern white press in the US that aided and abetted the overthrow of Reconstruction and implementation of Jim Crow segregation, and concerns over tabloids continued to be a feature of journalism throughout the twentieth century in the US (Lippmann 2022; McQueen 2018; Roberts Forde & Bedingfield 2021). And scholars, policymakers, and the public alike worried about the functioning of the mass press given its central importance to US and European political systems, which only grew over the course of the twentieth century. During the peak of the newspaper boom in Europe, in 1929, there were 147 newspapers in Berlin alone, many of them with morning, afternoon, evening, and sometimes even nightly, issues (Patalong 2021).

These concerns about the power of media only grew as the twentieth century witnessed an explosion of new, especially "mass," media technologies, and the increasingly large-scale adoption of older ones (such as radio). "Mass" is an imprecise concept, but generally refers to the capacity of a medium to reach large audiences (one-to-*many*, as opposed to one-to-one). With the growth of mass radio and television media, in particular, came concerns about the power of these technologies over the public, with the twentieth century featuring prominent debates over whether these media were strengthening or weakening democracy, or how they were otherwise affecting public life. In reality, media innovations rarely give birth to democracy *or* lead to its destruction. Instead, media get enrolled in what we are already organized to do politically, and they can be directed toward many different ends. While radio enabled citizens to hear the voice of their monarch or president for the first time, it was also an important propaganda tool for the Nazi regime in the 1930s. While TV brought the US Civil Rights Movement's struggle and presidential debates into living rooms (such as the famous John F. Kennedy versus Richard Nixon American presidential debate) and allowed the entire world to witness mankind's first steps on the Moon, media scholars also feared that we were "amusing ourselves to death" (Postman 2006).

Then along came the Internet and, later, social media, raising initial, overly enthusiastic hopes for the creation of a more inclusive, participatory, deliberative, and indeed global democracy, the end of censorship and big institutions, and, along with the end of the Cold War, "the end of history" (Fukuyama 1989) and the final victory of democracy. By 2016, however, in the wake of that year's United Kingdom European Union membership referendum (i.e., "Brexit") and the election of Donald Trump in the United States, researchers across the world were analyzing a new disinformation disorder, worrying about an epistemic crisis, and arguing that coordinated inauthentic behavior (including by states) and large-scale manipulation of public opinion were undermining democracies around the world. Meanwhile, by 2020 there were growing fears in the United States and Europe that an Internet built largely on American frameworks of "free expression" and "free markets" was becoming "splintered" as countries such as China and Russia developed their own platforms with stricter, state control over expression and information.

Over time, overly utopian and dystopian "techno-deterministic" (the simplistic idea that technologies cause large-scale social and psychological changes) views generally give way to more nuanced and differentiated perspectives on media and communication systems as they actually work within political systems. This resembles the history of research on the effects of media on individuals. Over the past century, analyses of media effects ranged from initial beliefs in strong, linear media effects on citizen's opinions (c.1930s–1950s) to increasingly more sophisticated research traditions that documented how media effects are psychologically, situationally, socially, and contextually dependent (Neuman 2016; Dunaway & Soroka 2021; Neuman & Guggenheim 2011). Most scholars today adopt a model of "contingent effects," detailing things such as the way in which social relationships and social identities shape what people believe, including with regard to the content of news. Researchers have also generally tracked changes in how communication flows, such as a move from direct mass communication from political elites to the public to, increasingly, through networks of social contacts. The latter was always important, but has taken on new prominence now with social media.

All of this tells us that people are rarely dupes of media; they tend to seek out, be exposed to, consume, and believe media in line with their pre-existing identities, social ties, preferences, attitudes, and beliefs. Despite this body of research, fears persist over the power of the media to distort the public sphere, manipulate the masses, and otherwise undermine democracy. In fact, media are often a convenient scapegoat (and an apolitical one) for what are often more fundamental, and irreducibly political, conflicts among social groups over power.

2.6 A Model of Platforms and Political Communication

To sum up, *any* understanding of platforms and political communication requires accounting for the larger media and political systems they are embedded in. Media systems, such as commercial markets for news, the existence of public service broadcasting, and the level of media concentration and media pluralism, have an impact on the ways that elites, journalists, and others engage in political communication, including on platforms. Media systems and journalism cultures are also a result of political systems and regime types – after all, non-democratic systems may feature higher censorship, lower levels of journalistic professionalization, and less autonomy for journalists than do democratic systems. Even in democratic systems, rising harassment, threats, and violence amid extremism can result in people hiding their political views and organizing in secret (Van Duyn 2021). All of which affect how journalists and citizens use platforms. And, broadly, features of political systems shape the role of platforms within them, such as the ends that political actors pursue, even as the communicative work that gets done on platforms in turn shapes the form and durability of political systems.

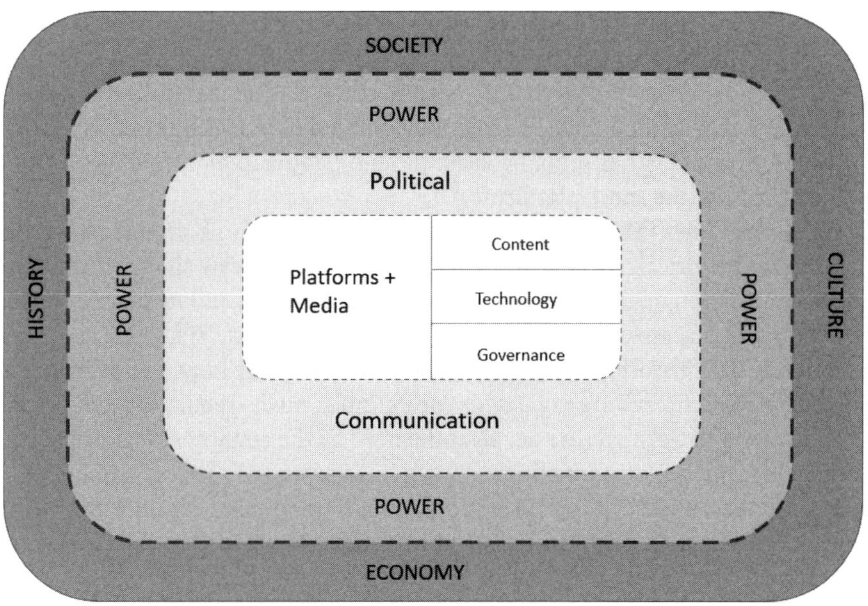

Figure 1 A model of political communication in the digital age. Source: Created by the authors.

We propose the model in figure 1 for the relationship between platforms, political communication, and the embeddedness of both in broader political and media systems.

Let's break down some of these elements.

(1) We see platforms at the core of contemporary political communication, alongside other forms of media and arranged into systems. Platforms are increasingly the primary way in which citizens encounter political information and engage with it, as well as communicate with others around things that concern their shared lives. Political *content* on platforms is created by political and media actors of all stripes, including journalists, activists, political strategists, elected officials, and citizens themselves. Platforms are not neutral distribution channels, however. Platform *technologies*, such as their affordances and algorithms, as well as their *governance* – through policies, regulations, business models, and the organizations behind them – shape the ways political content is distributed and flows on and across platforms. In other words, platforms are not just code. To understand how political communication works on platforms, we need to look beyond the content found on them and reflect also on the technologies and governance that shape how they work, in addition to the dynamics of the political and media systems they are embedded in.

(2) Political communication depends highly on context – which is why, even if platforms were the same everywhere (and they are not!), political communication would still be different. If we want to understand the impact of platforms on polities, including their role in political communication phenomena such as disinformation or populism, we must take into account the specific historical, social, cultural, and economic contexts they operate in,

as well as the relations of power shaped by these structural forces that play out upon them (Kuo & Marwick 2021). This is why we aim throughout this book to provide examples that go beyond the Western, generally democratic, context of the United States and Europe, and take into account how political communication varies globally, even though people in many nations around the world use the same platforms.

(3) The dashed lines in our model capture how power runs in both directions. Power rooted in historical, social, cultural, and economic contexts shapes how political communication operates and the workings of platforms and media. For instance, most platforms are commercial, and therefore operate in capitalistic economic contexts. The historical experiences of nations influence how, and even whether, media and platforms are regulated. For example, media regulation and platform governance in Germany are deeply influenced by the country's Nazi past and the remembrance of genocide (as shown by the country's strong prohibitions against "hate speech" directed at racial, ethnic, and religious minorities, and bans on Holocaust denialism and Nazi propaganda).

Platforms and media, however, have power, too. They do not command armies or shape class structures in society, but the content they differentially host, promote, and disseminate, the technologies they unleash upon society, and their internal governance decisions impact what citizens know (or do not know); what they share, how, and with whom; and how they form opinions, mobilize, or radicalize. Platforms (and media) shape which political actors, wielding which communication styles, gain visibility and attention in ways that affect the workings of political institutions, such as parties. Thus, platforms and media are not just shaped by forms of social, political, cultural, or economic power – they themselves wield power over the societies and political and media systems they operate in.

2.7 Summary

The remainder of this book is about the intersection of these forces. We move through chapters on platforms that detail the ways they are shaped by political and media systems, as well as historical, economic, social, and cultural phenomena, even as they affect these things in turn by providing people and organizations with new capacities to act and communicate. In the end, we embrace the idea that platforms and media and political systems mutually shape one another. Social, political, economic, and historical forces and contexts shape platforms, including how they work, what they are designed to do, their uses in practice, and their applications. But the design and functioning of platforms in turn shape social, political, and economic contexts, and do so throughout time in ways that shape the future contexts that political actors must navigate. We turn now to focus on platforms.

Discussion Questions

- Political communication varies considerably depending on local context – including political structures, media systems, political cultures, and the historical experiences of countries. What is the most influential institutional feature in your country that shapes political communication?
- This book is based on a very expansive definition of political communication. Think about how to turn this perspective around. What would be the narrowest definition of political communication, and what area(s) would it cover (or not cover)?

Suggestions for Further Reading

Dunaway, J., & Graber, D. A. (2022) *Mass Media and American Politics*. Washington, DC: Congressional Quarterly Press.

Jungherr, A., Rivero, G., & Gayo-Avello, D. (2020) *Retooling Politics: How Digital Media Are Shaping Democracy*. Cambridge University Press.

Kaid, L. L. & Holtz-Bacha, C. (eds.) (2007) *Encyclopedia of Political Communication*. Los Angeles, CA: SAGE Publications.

Mazzoleni, G., Barnhurst, K. G., Ikeda, K. I., Maia, R. C., & Wessler, H. (eds.) (2015) *The International Encyclopedia of Political Communication*, 3 vols. Chichester: John Wiley & Sons.

McNair, B. (2017) *An Introduction to Political Communication*. London: Routledge.

3 Platforms and Their Power

Chapter 3 focuses on platforms, analyzing their political power and impact as intermediaries, distribution channels, infrastructure, technologies, and profit-making firms. The chapter is especially interested in the intersections between platforms, political institutions, journalism, and governmental bodies, as well as how platforms create new, technologically mediated social spaces. This chapter addresses platform products, design, affordances, and economics as they affect politics, and their self-governance through things such as content moderation policies (the book analyzes various state attempts at external, governmental regulation in Chapter 9 on governance).

OBJECTIVES

By the end of this chapter, you should be able to:

- understand platforms and their roles in society
- analyze the dimensions of platform power
- understand technological power, including affordances and algorithms.

3.1 Introduction

Elon Musk, one of the richest people on Earth and an eccentric, libertarian entrepreneur, bought Twitter in autumn 2022. He promptly took the company private. In his chaotic first few weeks as the self-described "Chief Twit" of the company, people around the world were reminded of the volatile character of platforms. Platforms come, and platforms go. Platforms change their designs, affordances, and appearances as they evolve over time – or rapidly change. The rules governing them from the inside and outside change.

However, the sheer speed with Musk seemed to undo Twitter as the world knew it was breathtaking. In only a few days he laid off thousands of employees, seemingly capriciously, not only potentially breaking labor laws and regulations in various countries, but also losing some of the senior managers responsible for key issues such as data protection. There was no communication department anymore, and many remaining employees were called back from remote working to Twitter's headquarters. Musk, it seemed, liked to break things and run an established company and platform previously publicly traded in start-up mode.

There were consequences of this change in ownership. Firing the company's content moderators led to increased levels of hate and harassment (Center for Countering Digital Hate 2022). Re-activating far-right activist accounts brought a surge of racist and extremist content. At the same time, alternative platforms to Twitter gained much attention. Mastodon, a non-profit, open-source, de-centralized network of servers (called "instances") received a large share of the "Twitter migration" and had an explosion in new and active accounts. It remains to be seen whether moving to Mastodon was just short-term hype, or if a non-profit, ad-free platform run by its own administrators making their own rules will become a significant alternative to Twitter. What is important, however, is that Musk's Twitter takeover was a powerful reminder that we should not trust platforms with all our data, rely on them as spaces for public discourse, or otherwise believe they will serve as digital services for eternity.

Many people also experienced first-hand how what researchers call "network effects" work. "Network effects" refers generally to how value lies in the number of people who use a service or a platform. Twitter users cannot simply transfer the followers they took years to gain to any other platform, let alone a new platform that is just getting started. Even with alternatives to the Musk-led platform, for many leaving Twitter means losing voice, reach, and community. And, given the role of collectives such as Black Twitter in holding police accountable and #MeToo in holding men accountable, it means losing potentially much more than that too.

3.2 So, What Are Platforms?

This seems like a simple question, but it is actually really complex! We refer to "platforms" casually every day when we search for information on Google, post on Facebook and TikTok, or purchase something on Amazon. But what makes each of these things the same thing? Search on Google is different from video on YouTube, after all. We take our lead from scholars José van Dijck, Thomas Poell, and Martijn de Waal (2018: 9) who define a "platform" as a "programmable architecture designed to organize interactions between users." As these researchers go on to write:

> A platform is fueled by *data*, automated and organized through *algorithms* and *interfaces*, formalized through *ownership* relations driven by *business models*, and governed through *user agreements*.

This is complicated – so let's break it down a bit. This is a very helpful definition that gets us to what is so unique about our era – and that is a central part of this book. Namely, the fact that behind most contemporary political communication are commercial platforms that organize much of political (as well as social and entertainment!) life and interactions across a stunningly diverse array of *users*. In the realm of politics alone, *users* include campaigns, voters, elected representatives, political parties, social movements, think tanks, citizens, and advocacy organizations, among many others.

SPOTLIGHTED CASES

What does it mean that platforms "organize interactions among users" in the context of politics? Let's think about a few concrete examples. Facebook does not produce journalism directly. Nor does it directly determine what news people consume. Instead, Facebook provides a way for news media to reach audiences. Facebook also assesses journalistic credibility through Facebook News and elevates some outlets to serve as fact-checkers. Facebook also provides users with the ability to personalize the media they see through their own choices and engagement. The platform shapes public attention through the algorithmic design of its "newsfeed," which displays content to users with the goal of increasing the time they spend on the platform (which is the way Facebook monetizes users). Similarly, Google does not maintain the vast majority of webpages the search engine links to. The platform indexes billions of pages of content, makes them searchable, and ranks them based on what it determines are the collective preferences of billions of users and structures of links. In the process, Google shapes the very ways billions of users navigate the web and content providers find audiences – with significant political implications (Noble 2018; Tripodi 2022).

While platforms vary, the definition provided above captures the common elements that underlie how many different platforms work to organize billions of daily interactions (Gillespie 2010). Platforms are centrally reliant upon data – the trillions of pieces of information they collect on who users are and what they like, how they behave, what they reveal, how they communicate and interact, and what they create. While they are very different, Facebook relies on data to prioritize the content to display to users, just as Google relies on user and link data to structure its search results. Especially important here is that *data* exist in systems, such as the algorithms that rely on data to deliver content, the interfaces that respond to data from and about users, the business models that help platforms generate revenue, and the data that enable platforms to determine threats to security and compliance with policies. Platforms rely on data about their users to design their features and ensure they are meeting their desires and needs. And, indeed, platforms produce those very desires through data-driven, targeted advertising – which most platforms rely on for monetization.

Indeed, data about users is valuable currency – so much so that some researchers have seen data as the cornerstone of contemporary capitalism and the basis for markets for advertising and goods and services (Van Dijck et al. 2018; Zuboff 2019). Data not only feeds the algorithms that shape what users see and do, in part by prioritizing particular types of content and interactions to monetize them – data is also a commodity that platforms sell to advertisers and data brokers. Data is the basis upon which platform companies directly sell their users to advertisers. They often do not provide data on users to advertisers directly; instead, they distill billions of points of data into categories of users that they auction off to advertisers (McGuigan 2019). These categories are often premised on probabilistic assessments of who is likely to purchase a particular good or service on the basis of prior behavior, attitudes, or preferences, as well as demographic characteristics.

Just as data are central to their operations, all platforms are programmable, in the sense that they are designed architectures. Design organizes those interactions between users, and between users and information. Platforms can be *digital* architectures, *hardware* architectures, or both. In the former category, think about web-based applications such as Facebook and Amazon (which also rely on immense physical architectures, such as servers). The latter includes the Apple iPhone, Nintendo Switch, and the increasing array of hardware products that companies such as Meta and Google are investing in to deliver various services (and generate data). Look no further than virtual reality and the so-called "metaverse."

So, for example, on a platform such as Facebook, programming determines the framework for what users disclose about themselves to other users and to the company itself, how users can interact with one another (such as becoming friends), how they make themselves visible to each other (such as by sharing content and liking or commenting on posts), and how content is displayed. Users can be individuals like me and you, but also political campaigns, political parties, major brands, and local businesses. Programming also determines how users interact with information. Think of a Google search – the results that are returned are the complex outcome of how the company weights webpages based on the authority of their connections to other sites Google sees as credible (what it calls "PageRank"). These are programming choices, and as such are *social* choices – not neutral features of the technology (Noble 2018; Svensson 2021).

The functioning of platform algorithms and interfaces is a primary way that platforms keep users engaged and coming back to spend time on them, thus generating more interactions with advertising and therefore even more revenue for the companies that maintain them. Indeed, this is central to their business models. Many of the American and other global platforms are offered as (mostly) free services, paid for primarily through digital advertising that commoditizes the data, time, attention, content, and relations of users. While users certainly derive value from these mostly free services, the economic returns of the time and attention spent on platforms and data generated by them flow back to their owners, shareholders, and employees (in the form of salaries, or sometimes stock options). In order to derive (ostensibly) free value from platforms (while also helping to collectively produce their profits through user-generated content), users have to adhere to platforms' terms of service (or "user agreements"), which govern what they can do, including what they can say on them.

As our model shows, platforms are now at the center of media systems, and therefore political systems. This does not mean that platforms are the *only* forms of media in contemporary media and political systems. It means that platforms are the most important forms of media in politics because they are central to what every actor does. Journalists are centrally reliant on platforms to communicate with audiences, as are politicians for their communication with constituents. Citizens get the bulk of their political information from platforms (including the products of professional news media). Consider the role of Apple and Spotify in political podcasting as well. And, in a world where streaming through sites such as Netflix and Hulu has eclipsed broadcast and cable in the United States, platforms are now central to other forms of media (such as entertainment).

This means that commercial platform companies (in much of the West) and state-backed companies (such as those owned or directed by Russia and China) play an increasingly central role in shaping, structuring, and even governing public spheres and political processes in countries around the world. Through their design, functioning, and content policies, platforms shape public attention, the distribution of political information, and the forms, types, and content of political expression that people engage in. In countries around the world, platforms shape the distribution of news, the audiences for media outlets, the format and types of stories, newsgathering, the user-generated political expression that is allowed (often in accord with international human rights frameworks), flows of political information, and possibilities to affiliate with others in groups. It's for these reasons that authorities in conflict-hit Ethiopia in August 2021 announced state-sanctioned measures to build the Horn of Africa nation's own social media platform to rival the dominant Facebook, Twitter, and WhatsApp (Oluwole 2021).

SPOTLIGHTED CONTENT

To take one example of how platforms shape politics, they make distribution less of a capital-intensive effort for publishers. This means that newer, often resource-leaner, outlets that publish digital-only have newfound ability to grow, monetize content, and gain sizable reach and attention – a big part of the problem around monetized "fake news" websites! At the same time, individual citizens with smartphones, social movements pursuing their causes, and authoritarians with an intent to subvert their accountability also have new opportunities in the era of platforms. Indeed, it is the contests between many different actors like these in platform-mediated environments that define a lot of political communication today.

3.3 What Platforms Mean for Political Communication

Like everything else, what platforms mean for political communication, public opinion, the stability of governments, distribution of power in societies, and political processes is complicated. Platforms have given rise to an unprecedented richness and diversity in political information, and have enabled citizens to access a stunning array of sources. They have also facilitated the ability of commercial entities to monetize entirely "fake news" content and have made the sharing of mis- and disinformation – especially by political elites – to wide audiences much easier and faster than during the era of mass media. Given that they optimize for engagement, the most extreme or emotional content on platforms often finds greater reach and spread online than in offline contexts, where social norms can make people hesitant to say controversial things.

Is all this bad? Maybe. While some have pointed to the polarization that platforms create (Bail 2022), others demonstrate that communication on platforms promotes political participation (Boulianne 2020) and has been central to *global* movements for democracy and racial and social justice (Jackson et al. 2020). Platforms create the conditions for new forms of documentation and witnessing that help

Table 1 The most important platforms for political communication

Country	People who use social media for news (2021)(%)	Most popular platform for news (2021)
EUROPE		
United Kingdom	41	Facebook
Germany	31	Facebook
France	38	Facebook
Italy	47	Facebook
Spain	55	Facebook
Portugal	55	Facebook
Ireland	51	Facebook
Norway	44	Facebook
Sweden	47	Facebook
Finnland	45	Facebook
Denmark	46	Facebook
Belgium	38	Facebook
Netherlands	37	Facebook
Switzerland	47	WhatsApp
Austria	48	Facebook
Hungary	63	Facebook
Slovakia	56	Facebook
Czech Republic	50	Facebook
Poland	59	Facebook
Romania	58	Facebook
Bulgaria	67	Facebook
Croatia	54	Facebook
Greece	69	Facebook
ASIA		
Turkey	61	YouTube
Japan	24	YouTube
South Korea	42	YouTube
Taiwan	54	Line
Hong Kong	61	Facebook
Malaysia	72	Facebook
Singapore	57	Facebook and Whatapp
Philipines	72	Facebook
India	63	YouTube and WhatsApp
Indonesia	64	WhatsApp
Thailand	78	Facebook
AMERICAS		
United States	42	Facebook
Canada	55	Facebook

Table 1 (cont.)

Country	People who use social media for news (2021)(%)	Most popular platform for news (2021)
Brazil	63	Facebook
Argentina	66	Facebook
Chile	69	Facebook
Mexico	67	Facebook
Colombia	70	Facebook
Peru	70	Facebook
AFRICA		
South Africa	75	Facebook
Kenya	76	WhatsApp
Nigeria	78	WhatsApp
Australia	47	Facebook

Source: Table based on Reuters Institute for the Study of Journalism's *Digital News Report* 2021 (https://reutersinstitute.politics.ox.ac.uk/digital-news-report/2021/interactive). Created by the authors.

hold powerful actors, such as the police, accountable (Richardson 2020). In other words, platforms are celebrated for promoting political engagement and allowing a greater diversity of voices into global public spheres, even as they raise fears of disinformation, polarization, populism, and extremism.

All of these things raise significant questions, and concerns, about how political communication works in our era. In a world of platforms, who has the power to shape public attention and matters of public concern – and to what ends? Who has the power to shape policymaking agendas? Who has the power to determine what can, and cannot, be said? How do platforms affect the balance of power between various actors, from movements to elected officials? And, who should have power in the public sphere?

3.4 Platforms Are Not Neutral Technologies

Imagine a football or soccer pitch. The rectangular green bordered by crisp white sidelines that clearly demarcate boundaries. The midfield line and center circle. The marked-off penalty and goal areas. At first thought, it is hard to imagine a more neutral technology – it's just a pitch, it treats everyone equally, allowing nothing but skill, endurance, strategy, and team organization to shine.

After further consideration, however, it becomes clear that even this simple technology is not neutral. Whether the turf is artificial or real grass favors certain athletes who perform better on one than the other. Not every soccer pitch is the same size, so players will find relative advantages and disadvantages differentially across games. The dimensions might reward some types of skills and forms of training, for instance – such as endurance running – and not others – such as sprinting. Left-footed and right-footed players clearly have different strengths on different sides of the field, and different angles to be played to their strengths. If a football pitch is not neutral, think of a global platform such as Facebook. It too has an ostensibly neutral set of features, available to everyone. In most countries, anyone 13 and up can create a Facebook profile after answering questions about a predetermined set of categories. Anyone can post a range of images, videos, and text; comment and follow friends, neighbors, and causes; and share what others have posted. And anyone can see and respond to advertisements, the monetary lifeblood of the platform.

Again though, on further consideration, we would be hard pressed to imagine a more complicated, and less neutral, technology. The Facebook algorithms – which help determine what content gets reach and attention – reward emotion and are designed for engagement, not *necessarily* reason and deliberation (Bucher 2021). The content that gets the most attention – whether it is something your uncle, the *New York Times*, the United Nations, or a president shared – is conditioned by a mix of timing (favoring recency), follower (or 'friend') structure, the features of the message (such as emotional content, and cat videos!), the context it is released in (what else is vying for attention, what do people want to pay attention to at a particular point in time?), and engagement (content that performs well – such as getting likes and shares – gets even more visibility). Even more, this complex mix of ingredients changes depending on what the platform continually determines encourages people to spend more time on it, and new people to sign up.

All of this has vast consequences for political communication. We will provide three examples. First, in its enormous reach and power over attention, Facebook structures the marketplace for digital journalism, making or breaking many publishers reliant on web traffic (Bailo et al. 2021a; Meese & Hurcombe 2021) and digital ads. Second, Facebook's policies on political ads, including its definition of allowable targeting and its real-time auctions of audiences, shapes how candidates run for office (Barrett 2021). Finally, Facebook groups provide millions of people around the world with an easy way to organize at scale, including around harmful conspiracy theories that undermine democratic deliberation (Krafft & Donovan 2020; Malinen 2021).

Technological infrastructures underpin much of contemporary political communication – and they are globally coordinated and dependent upon thousands of decisions that are in themselves political, such as the creation of standards (DeNardis 2014). Like media, technologies are not inherently good or bad. Nuclear technology can be used both to generate electricity and to build weapons of mass destruction. But technology is not neutral either. Thinkers have long argued that technologies carry with them the intentions of those societies, groups, people, organizations, and institutions who created them and whom they serve – their norms and values, worldviews, interests, and business models. And technologies are often the *outcomes* of conflicts between many stakeholders. For example, with regard to algorithms, the technology that mediates much of political and social life in countries around the world, Tarleton Gillespie (2014: 167) argues that we "must not conceive of algorithms as abstract, technical achievements, but must unpack the warm human and institutional choices that lie behind these cold mechanisms." This makes algorithmic ethics necessary (Ananny 2016).

In other words, platforms are not purely mathematical and electrical entities. As detailed above, platforms are designed and curated communication systems, and they come in many varieties. Platforms have been deliberately designed to function and perform in specific ways. In many cases, as we noted above, they are commercial, for-profit entities and have data at the core of their business models (which they use to monetize their users). Communication on digital platforms does not take place in a vacuum or in a neutral space, but in a space which neither political actors nor citizens have complete ownership or control over – although they can and do assert a lot of pressure, whether it is regulatory or in the court of public opinion, both of which can have significant impact on the policies and functioning of platforms (Barrett & Kreiss 2019).

The particular *ways* in which platforms make certain things easier to do, incentivize certain forms of speech and action, and structure reach and attention means they have taken on central roles in shaping political communication around the world. And they do so in ways we are only beginning to grapple with today. Facebook (and Instagram and WhatsApp), Google and YouTube, TikTok/Douyin, Twitter, Snapchat, VKontakte, Alibaba, Wechat, and Weibo are increasingly, unmistakably, and powerfully setting the rules and providing the structures for much of public (and private!) communication in political and social life.

SPOTLIGHTED CASES

To take an example, in the US and Europe, YouTube has received a lot of attention for its potential role in politics, especially in the context of radicalization (Munger & Phillips 2022). YouTube uses data about users – such as their preferences for particular kinds of content and their responsiveness to particular types of advertising – to recommend content to those users. Recommendations are fundamentally the platform's guesses about what users will be most likely to enjoy or respond to, given the company's desire to keep them engaged and therefore spending more time on the platform. YouTube, like nearly all platforms, wants to keep its users engaged for commercial reasons. More engagement means more market share for the streaming platform and, ultimately, more revenue from digital advertising.

As many have pointed out, the complicated thing about platforms is that what is often good for *business* might not be good for *democracy*, or *society* more broadly. If the content that is most likely to keep users engaged is the most extreme, outrageous, polarizing, or emotionally charged, or otherwise leads people down a path of becoming more extreme in their political views, it might lead people to lose their tolerance of those with opposing views, see the political opposition as illegitimate, or embrace extremism and violence. The research jury is still out on these things, however. There is ample debate and mixed evidence, for instance, about whether social media leads people to more extreme views, or whether it reinforces existing preferences. Or, most likely, some combination of both, with political beliefs leading to media choices that further reinforce political beliefs (Young & Bleakley 2020). But it is also worth noting that many extreme views across history are ones majorities in many countries see as morally good today – such as an embrace of equality for LGBTQIA+ people, and civil rights for people of color.

Indeed, the very same algorithms and their incentivizing of content assisted the massive growth and political power of the international Black Lives Matter movement (Jackson et al. 2020) *and* the Stop the Steal rally that led to the assault on the US Congress. All of which means that, when evaluating the relationship between platforms and democracy, we always have to consider the *ends* toward which they are used, and by whom. That said, a starting point of concern is more than justified because platforms such as YouTube are primarily commercial enterprises, without the same commitment to public welfare or, in democratic countries, rights and equality that institutions of the state or professions such as journalism often have.

Let's consider now the sources of platform power over the political and media systems of which they are now a central part.

3.5 The Dimensions of Platform Power

Let's break down some of the dimensions of platform power. Platforms hold considerable power, although it is not absolute (which we take up in the accountability section of this chapter). We focus here specifically on *politics* – again, expansively defined throughout this book in terms of matters of potential public concern.

In their important book *The Power of Platforms: Shaping Media and Society*, the media and communication scholars Rasmus Kleis Nielsen and Sarah Anne Ganter (2022) present an extensive discussion of platform power vis-à-vis publishers. We highlight and build upon a few of their central claims here.

Market Power

Perhaps one of the most obvious facts about the global economy is the increasing domination of advertising and information markets by large technology firms based primarily in the United States and China. The increasing concentration of market power means that companies such as Meta and Google have become central players in digital political advertising in the US and many countries around the world, attracting significant political ad revenues and being able to control data relevant to politics (Barrett 2021). Outside of companies such as Meta and Google, which count digital advertising among their primary sources of revenue, other platforms dominate other sectors. This includes cloud computing (Amazon and Microsoft), smartphones (Apple and Google), logistics and distribution (Amazon), and, increasingly, digital hardware and services (Meta).

The market power of platforms has downstream effects on politics. As digital advertising revenue migrates toward platforms, it moves away from journalism and other political media outlets. Meanwhile, platform control over digital advertising means they increasingly set the rules for political speech – and currently there are few forms of public accountability over their content and targeting rules.

For example, in the United States the decline in revenue for journalism (and especially newspapers) is an old phenomenon. Newspapers have been losing revenue to television and other media for decades. Regardless, this was amplified as non-profit platforms such as CraigsList captured classified advertising, and companies such as Meta and Google came to dominate markets for digital advertising. These market dynamics affect the revenue available to support things such as local journalism

(Hindman 2018), and shape the business strategies of the news media itself (Usher 2021). At the same time, platforms are also economic drivers of other industries in new ways, such as opening up local advertising markets – which in turn has lowered the cost of efficiently reaching local voters.

As platforms become the locus for political advertising, they in turn set the policies for paid political speech that candidates and causes must adhere to for access to their audiences (Barrett 2021; Kreiss & McGregor 2018, 2019). Meanwhile, state-backed or state-interested platform companies often have to abide by state rules over expression – increasingly a concern to American scholars as Chinese platforms including Weibo, WeChat, and TikTok have gained a dominant presence, rivaling (or exceeding) American giants such as Meta and Twitter.

Meanwhile, the dominance of a few platform companies in key software and hardware markets has enabled these companies to control access to audiences at various layers in the technology "stack" (Gillespie et al. 2020). The "stack" refers to the layers of technology – from hardware, operating systems, and services to web applications – which varying platforms exercise control over at different levels. Again, this market power has significant political implications. Amazon banned the right-wing Twitter-alternative Parler from its server infrastructure for a time after January 6, 2022, and Google initially denied the Donald Trump-backed alternative social media platform Truth Social access to its Android stores (the latter over a lack of content moderation policies). Regardless of the merits of any of these decisions, this means that a few commercial firms control access to significant portions of political audiences through their power over layers of the technology stack.

Distributional and Attention Power

Extending from this, companies such as Meta and Google in the United States, and Chinese-owned companies such as TikTok and WeChat, have increasing control over the distribution of information and public attention. Consider the ways in which many platforms are essentially privately maintained, public forums for much political news, media, debate, discussion, and contestation. It is impossible to imagine a political campaign today in many countries without accounting for the role of WhatsApp as a central vehicle for people to discuss politics; without Facebook being a key platform for campaigns to run targeted digital advertising to register voters and find supporters to volunteer and give money (Rossini et al. 2021); and without Twitter (especially in the United States) being the central vehicle for elected officials to issue press releases, respond to events (or incite them), and otherwise communicate with the press. Relatedly, political activists in countries around the world also use platforms such as Twitter in the attempt to influence the *American* press, especially when they want to get their messages in front of US elites.

Broadly, distributional power includes the ways in which platforms play increasingly important roles in controlling the flow of political communication in countries around the world. They do so in hybrid media environments where international and national television outlets, radio, and news websites continue to also play large roles shaping the distribution of political information and public and elite attention, to be sure. However, platforms are increasingly *the* central sites for the distribution of the content of these other media actors as well – in the process, giving them an outsized role in shaping public attention. And, as noted above, they do so through the policies, technical designs, and algorithms that reward certain types of content and select for certain types of engagement and not others – which in turn shapes the communicative incentives that many different political entities (including journalists) abide by.

Intermediary Power

Relatedly, platforms are intermediaries in a number of industries that they in turn indelibly shape. From public health to politics, commercial services to sports, entertainment to law and policymaking, platforms are now increasingly among the most important intermediaries that organize communication between various actors according to their own logics (Van Dijck et al. 2018). Indeed, platforms are a special kind of intermediary that not only serve as a go-between between content providers and audiences – they organize that content in deeply influential ways, including ordering it, incentivizing it, differentially making it accessible, determining what is acceptable and what is not, and ranking it (Gillespie 2017). In the process, these intermediaries structure interactions in particular ways.

Let's think about just a few of the ways platforms exercise intermediary power. By their very design, and depending on the platform, they structure *organizational* and *self-presentation* (by determining the categories for disclosure), *connections* (by the various ways they encourage ties to others or institutional bodies), *sociality* (by their differential capacity to support groups, anonymous versus public communication, the types of ties that are encouraged, etc.), *commercial transactions* (such as determining the possibilities for digital advertising and marketing, marketplace transactions, organizing interactions between buyers and sellers, etc.), and forms of *expression* itself (how many words or characters are permitted in posts, whether and how images render, the length of time available for videos or possibilities to livestream, etc.). In doing so, platforms serve as intermediaries that structure relationships across a host of different domains of political, social, economic, and religious life.

Content Power

Nearly all the major platforms have express content policies (and, as detailed above, when they control access to servers and stores, they also can force policies on other entities, including other platforms). These policies have outsized importance in politics, and have increasingly become a flashpoint around the world in debates over "free speech," especially notably with the rise of populist and authoritarian governments and politicians, anti-democratic movements, and mis- and disinformation.

It is worth remembering that content moderation policies are necessary for these commercial enterprises. Content policies are what enable platforms to run services that are free of pornography, for instance, or illegal activities such as the buying and selling of illicit drugs. Where platforms draw the line between what is permitted and what is not is often contested, however. While there is a large domain of content that is unquestionably and legitimately moderated by platforms (such as pornography and terrorist content), there are many, many debates around other significant categories of speech that these companies have sought to moderate in the face of internal, external, or commercial pressures. The more that political and social norms are unsettled and contested in societies, the more platform policies are the subject of political controversy – indeed, debates over platform content moderation efforts are often proxies for larger political struggles.

SPOTLIGHTED CASES

To provide a few examples of political controversies over content moderation, in the wake of the 2016 US presidential election there was increasing pressure on Facebook and Instagram, Google and YouTube, and Twitter to reduce hate speech, disinformation, and content that might dissuade people from voting – even though these things are very much allowed under the US's First Amendment (and there is often very little the US government can do to regulate this content). Many of these calls came in the wake of the high-profile revelations related to the Cambridge Analytica scandal – a company that obtained Facebook data on millions of Americans and Britons and engaged in targeted digital political advertising to sway them during the US presidential election and "Brexit," in contravention of the platform's policies – as well as Russian state-sponsored disinformation attempts during the cycle.

In response to public pressure in the US and European Union, over the past decade a number of platforms have developed an increasingly expansive (and often confusing) set of rules around permissible content, which are continual sites of challenge. These rules have proven difficult to enforce and justify. What exactly constitutes a false claim in politics, related to the processes and procedures of voting? Where is the line between raising legitimate questions about the fairness of a vote versus a strategic attempt to undermine electoral accountability? When is discussion about vaccinations for Covid-19 part of a good-faith debate as opposed to strategic attempts to undermine the public's faith in health systems? These are not easy questions, and platforms have routinely struggled with answering them. Even more, platforms are as conflicted as our *societies* increasingly are about the authority of, and trust we should place in, all sorts of knowledge-producing institutions, including journalism. And our societies are also conflicted about who we should trust to make judgment calls about speech – and, indeed, whether we should make them at all.

Some governments have sought to pass laws that promote freedom of expression in the wake of various crises – which remains a powerful democratic ideal. In the US, there have been no fewer than a dozen state and federal proposed bills requiring platforms to serve as neutral channels for speech since 2016, much in the way that phone companies are. In Brazil, populist President Jair Bolsonaro in 2021 implemented a rule requiring that social media platforms maintain their neutrality and support political freedom of expression. In many countries, platforms are often at the center of political struggles between some parties (including those with anti-democratic ends) that seek to elevate the freedom of expression beyond every other democratic value, and those that see the ways expression can be weaponized to undermine public discourse, democratic accountability, and democratic institutions (Franks 2020). Platforms, meanwhile, have their own values which shape what they are willing to support, countenance, and amplify. But they also have a set of commitments to their shareholders for maximizing revenue, as well as a set of near- and long-term market concerns, which means they rarely want to be the breeding ground for deception and disinformation and extremist political movements – which likely turns off many users, much like pornography does.

Economic Power

Many platforms also control an immense amount of capital that critics argue allows them to distort the market for goods and services and have outsized influence over labor markets. In the US and Europe, in particular, there are spirited debates over whether platforms concentrate too much economic power, distort prices and competition, and subvert markets in many sectors of the economy. As a result, there are ongoing struggles to regulate these platform companies amid debates over what the nature of the problem is, and what to do, in countries where platforms have taken on a significant role in economic and social life (Boczkowski & Mitchelstein 2021).

While we spend less time discussing the impact of platforms in domains outside of politics in this book, it is important to note the political aspects of things such as anti-trust law in the United States – where many prominent platforms are based. Various proposals, for instance, have argued that platforms distort various markets to such an extent that they need to be either broken up or prevented from making further acquisitions. Platforms, in turn, have argued that it is their very scale that enables them to effectively take action against things such as hate speech and disinformation, and the fragmentation of global public spheres and the comparatively fewer resources of smaller platforms would mean a proliferation of extremism across niche platforms. Potential regulatory efforts, in turn, have pointed to the ways in which many platforms have pursued growth at all costs, including when they lack resources and knowledge (such as language competency) to protect their users in new, or non-English-speaking, markets. At the same time, established platforms point to the emergence of new ones – such as the rapid global rise of TikTok – as evidence for the competitiveness of the markets they are in.

Technological Power

We have referred to "algorithms" before, but let's consider them in greater depth here. The term "algorithm" is used expansively in public discourse, including to deflect responsibility for human decisions, especially by platform companies looking to explain away some harmful aspect of their technology – such as statements that "the algorithm did it" (Lum & Chowdhury 2021). Etymologically, the word "algorithm" comes from the Greek word for number, "arithmos," and the Arabic word for calculation, "al-jabr" (from which "algebra" stems – see Striphas [2015]). Most definitions center on algorithms being a set of rules – a multiple-step process to produce specific outputs (Kitchin 2017) and a way of automated decision-making. Just like in a baking recipe, the automated decision-making behind the user interfaces of platforms consists of data (ingredients) and concise steps of execution (recipe instructions) processing the data.

SPOTLIGHTED CONTENT

Data are not neutral. After all, there are many things in the world that could be counted! How things are counted and why, what actions produce data and what do not, are all social – and often economic – decisions. Ultimately, data do not represent things that are actually in the world; they are "constructs" of things in the world. Moreover, data are uncertain, messy, imperfect, and social – so much so that, as Hong (2020) argues, datafication creates "data-driven fabrication" and, ultimately, "technologies of speculation," rather than objective truth.

Although they are often represented as purely technological, algorithms are human-made, and they run based on data that is both messy and constructed for particular organizational ends. In the context of platforms, algorithms are often commercial products. They are instrumental in that they are programmed to achieve certain goals, such as generating revenue according to business models; and they reflect the worldviews and experiences of their creators and the economic, political, and regulatory contexts they operate in. Algorithms can also have unintended consequences. As a growing number of researchers have documented, algorithms quite often produce discrimination and racist, sexist, and classist results – and, even worse, they scale, reinforcing and amplifying discrimination through biased automated decision-making (Eubanks 2018; Noble 2018; Sandvig et al. 2016).

How do the algorithms that platforms design and implement, and that in turn drive platforms, have power? In classical political theory, "power" refers to the opportunity to impose one's will on others, even against their resistance (Weber 1921/1968). Communication power, as Manuel Castells (2007) defines it, means that "the media are not the holders of power, but they constitute by and large the space where power is decided" (2007: 242). However, we see more expansive ways in which platforms wield power. Moisés Naím (2014), for instance, has elaborated on the classical definition: "Power is the ability to direct or prevent the current or future actions of other groups and individuals. Or, put differently, power is what we exercise over others that leads them to behave in ways they would not otherwise have behaved" (2014: 16). Naím distinguishes four power resources: persuasion, coercion, obligation, and rewards.

This is helpful for understanding algorithms and power. Here we can distinguish the power *of* algorithms, power *through* algorithms, and power *over* algorithms (Klinger 2023). With respect to the first, algorithmic systems can *persuade* (e.g. lure people into staying longer on platforms than they want to); they can *coerce* users (e.g. by giving users only defined options to communicate or behave, and foreclosing other options); they can *obligate* users to obey their rules out of "sunk-costs," or the time a user has already dedicated to a platform (e.g. users cannot migrate their network of followers from one platform to another, so that being de-platformed or leaving a platform is difficult); and they can *reward* users for compliant behavior (e.g. with more reach in return for personal data).

Programmers and designers, platform companies and advertising firms, even parties who create their own apps and harvest voter data, have power *through* algorithms. As detailed above, algorithms are social technologies and, as such, social biases get programmed into these technologies. The profession of programmers has long been riddled by a lack of gender, racial, ethnic, and class diversity. Although programming was originally a typical women's profession, today it is mostly white and Asian men who work in the tech industry in the US and Europe and design platforms, apps, dating portals, and messenger services. In Google's tech workforce at the time of this writing, for example, 36.9 percent of employees are white males, and 33.5 percent are Asian male workers. In contrast, only 0.9 percent of Google's tech employees are Black women, and 1.3 percent are Latinx/Hispanic women (Google 2021: 59).

There is also power *over* algorithms that only very few people can exercise. For instance, the Chief Executive Officer (CEO) of Meta, Mark Zuckerberg, can decide how much local journalism users find in their Facebook news feed, and can change this whenever he wishes – with massive effects on local news organizations. While Facebook is a complex company with a lot of considerations – such as commercial concerns – at the end of the day those who own or govern platforms have power over things such as algorithmic content moderation at massive scales, including the definitions of prohibited content. They also decide the performance goals of their algorithmic systems, how to weigh different types of popularity cues (such as likes, shares, comments), and whether and how the malevolent side-effects of their algorithms should be remedied, or not. And, taking this to an extreme, Elon Musk demonstrates (while we are writing this book) how one owner can disrupt, and capriciously make decisions that affect, millions of users on an entire platform.

Another prominent example is Facebook's changes in the run up to the 2020 election. That autumn, Facebook banned content from the international conspiracy movement QAnon. The platform also made the decision to tweak its news algorithms in the crucial period shortly before and after the 2020 US elections – to make the platform "nicer," to prioritize news from what the company considers authoritative sources as opposed to hyper-partisan sources, and to combat disinformation about the election. Soon after the election, however, and well before January 6, the platform generally rolled back a number of these policies (Joe Osborne, a Facebook spokesman, said this was "a temporary change we made to help limit the spread of inaccurate claims about the election" [Roose et al. 2020]). As the *New York Times* noted, "Other measures Facebook has developed to combat political misinformation and hate speech have been scaled back or vetoed by executives in the past, either because they hurt Facebook's usage numbers or because executives feared they would disproportionately harm right-wing publishers, several Facebook employees told The Times last month" (Roose 2020).

The rollback of these changes in turn likely created more opportunities for groups such as "Stop the Steal" to organize on the platform – of course, culminating in the attempted coup on January 6, 2021. Meanwhile, Twitter allowed Trump and other actors to spread lies about the vote in the aftermath of the election, stepped up enforcement after the violence at the US Capitol, and then stopped enforcing its "civic integrity" policies again in March 2021, according to public reporting (Dale 2022). Again, regardless of the merits of any of these policies, or their rollback, all of these examples illustrate the vast power platforms have over politics.

3.6 Summary

These events surrounding the 2020 US presidential election reveal the ways in which platforms such as Facebook are central to global politics. They are important forums for political debate and discussion, campaign attempts to mobilize and persuade their voters, and elected officials' communications with the electorate. At the same time, they are seedbeds for the attempts of elected leaders to undermine their accountability at the ballot box through false claims of electoral malfeasance, and of actors to spread public health misinformation. They provide key opportunities for elected officials to connect with voters, while also creating the means for those same leaders and their supporters to undermine democracy.

Through it all, their immense power is on display. In deplatforming the defeated former president, Facebook, Twitter, and Google took actions after January 6 that other media outlets were not willing to take – Trump coverage was not banned on CNN, for instance. Leaders across the globe – including former German Chancellor Angela Merkel – spoke out against the Trump ban, concerned about what concentrating vast power in a handful of companies meant for their own countries and legitimate political rule. Others sought to ensure platforms worked to their advantage. In September 2021, for example, then Brazilian President Bolsonaro signed a directive blocking social media companies from removing content and accounts. Turkey had earlier on introduced new legislation requiring platforms with over 1 million users to employ a local representative who would remove content if deemed necessary. A few months after officially banning Twitter, Nigeria's internet regulator also came up with proposals to regulate platform-based content in 2022.

While there may be more platforms, and different ones, in the future, their power is not likely to attenuate any time soon, given the central role they play in polities around the world. In the chapters that follow, we show that platforms are now central to how all the main actors in public discourse and democratic governance act to influence publics and public spheres, pursue policy and other ends, and secure and wield power. And, as we return to in Chapter 9, there are multiple mechanisms for platform governance – both self-governance through their policies and even independent oversight boards, and externally through public regulation.

Discussion Questions

- In most countries worldwide, Facebook is still the most important platform for political communication. However, newer and more popular platforms such as TikTok have emerged in the past years. Why is it that Facebook still remains a key player in political communication?
- Most commercial platforms are optimized for profit (e.g. through advertisements), not for facilitating meaningful public debate. If you were asked to design a platform that is beneficial for democracy and political discourse, what would it look like? What would be its key affordances?

Suggestions for Further Reading

Bucher, T. (2018) *If ... Then: Algorithmic Power and Politics*. New York: Oxford University Press.

Crawford, K. (2021) *The Atlas of AI: Power, Politics, and the Planetary Costs of Artificial Intelligence*. New Haven, CT: Yale University Press.

Gillespie, T., Boczkowski, P. J., & Foot, K. A. (eds.) (2014) *Media Technologies: Essays on Communication, Materiality, and Society*. Cambridge, MA: MIT Press.

Nielsen, R. K. & Ganter, S. A. (2022) *The Power of Platforms: Shaping Media and Society*. New York: Oxford University Press.

York, J. C. (2022) *Silicon Values: The Future of Free Speech under Surveillance Capitalism*. London: Verso Books.

4 Platforms, Public Spheres, and Public Opinion

Chapter 4 argues that political communication takes place in public spheres – networks or spaces where citizens and political actors come together, debate, discuss, form opinions, voice their grievances, find supporters for their causes, mobilize around issues, or fight about conflicting interests. Public spheres are often not harmonious spaces, but without them democracy cannot exist. This chapter presents various ideas about public spheres, and charts their digital transformations.

OBJECTIVES

By the end of this chapter, you should be able to:

- define public spheres
- understand publics, counterpublics, and affective publics
- explain how platforms shape public spheres
- describe what filter bubbles and echo chambers are, and discuss whether they really exist
- explain various meanings of "public opinion."

4.1 Introduction

Among the many changes that the Covid-19 pandemic brought about, it created an unexpected and mass-scale experiment. Perhaps for the first time in human history, public communication, and much of public life besides, were almost completely mediatized. In many countries, governments imposed lockdowns before vaccines were widely available. People around the world had to stay home completely for weeks or months, or were only allowed to leave their homes for essential shopping, doctors' appointments, or walking the dog. Even the number of contacts with people outside households were limited in many countries – for instance, to 2 people running errands, 6 people for a family gathering, or 30 people for a funeral. As a result, there were few opportunities for public life outside of media – citizens could not meet others in cafes, eavesdrop on conversations on public transportation, or chat with their neighbors in incidental encounters.

The "public sphere" is a concept scholars use to describe where the heart of political communication beats – and platforms play a central role in it. Despite its seemingly intuitive meaning, it is a very abstract concept. Scholars have conceptualized the public sphere as a forum, an arena, a system, and a network. There is not even agreement among scholars over whether there is one unified public sphere spanning all of society, or even the globe, or whether there are many and we should use the term in the plural, public *spheres*. The public sphere is not (just) a place, but it has spatial elements. It may not even be a "sphere," a metaphor that suggests a container of ideas, issues, and arguments, in a sprawling world of global communication networks. Indeed, it would be quite an understatement to say that the rise of platforms has challenged theories of the public sphere, as scholars have struggled to re-conceptualize the concept for at least a decade (Schäfer 2015), some even identifying a post-public sphere (Schlesinger 2020) or an anti-public sphere (Davis 2021).

While there is much debate over what, exactly, the public sphere is, it is undeniably useful as a tool to think with. Over the past 40 years, amid vast changes in media and technology, the concept of the public sphere has become one of the most prominent ways to understand the impact of media and technology on political communication.

The German philosopher Jürgen Habermas first developed the concept of the public sphere (*Öffentlichkeit*) in his famous 1962 book *The Structural Transformation of the Public Sphere* (translated into English in 1989) and he remains one of the most influential theorists of public communication. Habermas was the first to name and theorize the public sphere and its sociohistorical contexts as an independent source of authority over politics separate from private life.

Yet Habermas has only recently, at the age of 92, commented on how platforms impact democracy. Habermas argues that the printing press, invented in the 1430s, may have turned everyone into a potential reader. But it took many centuries after that before many countries achieved near-universal literacy (the 1800s and 1900s for most European democracies and the US). Similarly, platforms turn everyone into potential authors, but it will take some time until we have learned how to write in the service of "democratic" public discourse, grounded in the search for deliberative understanding. As Habermas argues (2021: 498): "A democratic system is damaged as a whole, if the infrastructure of the public sphere cannot direct the attention of citizens to the relevant issues that need to be decided, and can no longer guarantee the formation of competing public opinions, i.e., qualitatively filtered opinions."[1]

Habermas spent much of his career writing about what he believes is necessary for "democratic" communication. This includes the focusing of citizen attention, the identification of relevant and important issues, and the development of quality, competing opinions that can be debated. In the process, he also captures the deep tensions at the heart of political communication in the platform era. We celebrate how the Internet has granted many people new opportunities for democratic expression, even as we worry about the quality of that expression, the crowding out of substantive public debate, and the seemingly endless array of new crises that make sustained

[1] Author's translation, original quote: "Ein demokratisches System nimmt im ganzen Schaden, wenn die Infrastruktur der Öffentlichkeit die Aufmerksamkeit der Bürger nicht mehr auf die relevanten und entscheidungsbedürftigen Themen lenken und die Ausbildung konkurrierender öffentlicher, und das heißt: qualitativ gefilterter Meinungen, nicht mehr gewährleisten kann."

debate hard, if not impossible. Indeed, while Habermas originally focused on the harm commercialized media can do to democracy, the philosopher now argues that it is important for democratic societies to maintain professional legacy media and journalism (including commercial outlets) that enable the inclusion of many voices in public debate and the rational formation of public opinion.

In this chapter and book, we generally use the term "public spheres" in the plural form, acknowledging that there is not (and indeed there likely never has been) just the one overarching sphere for public discourse. Instead, we can understand public spheres as multiple, overlapping, and connected. Some are smaller, while others are larger. All public spheres are shaped by diverse communicative and technological dynamics and power, and span various populations, media, and platforms. Moreover, there have long been multiple public spheres because societies have long *excluded* some people from aspects of public life, including non-dominant racial, ethnic, and religious groups, and women.

4.2 Defining Public Spheres

How should we define the concept of "public spheres"? Broadly speaking, public spheres are located between civil society and political power. By "civil society," we mean the organized world of advocacy organizations, interest groups, trade unions, and other forms of formal political and social affiliation that represent groups and interests in public life. By "political power," we mean the formal bodies, entrusted by law, that organize aspects of human social, economic, political, and cultural life. They include entities such as executive agencies, state bureaucratic organizations, political organizations, and political institutions such as parties. These entities are created by legal and policymaking tools that grant them power, which they wield to organize and regulate human behavior.

In contrast, public spheres are generally loosely organized spaces for the formation of public opinion. To help us see how this works, let's start by differentiating public spheres from the state, the market, and the realm of private relations – even though public spheres are entangled with all of these things.

Public spheres are distinct from the state. Public spheres are forums where public opinion is formed, and where pluralist (i.e., many and different) and thus diverging interests are negotiated. Public spheres are conceptually separate from state institutions, such as parliaments, governments, or debates in constitutional courts. In contrast, public spheres are generally *self*-organized and not controlled or steered by formal institutions or power relations (ideally).

In classical political theory, the state consists of all power that its sovereign people transferred to it, such as the monopoly on the use of force. The state can tax people, enforce laws, incarcerate people, and in some countries execute death penalties. The state has an army; it can invade other countries. In one word, the state *is* power. In liberal democracies, this absolute power of the state and those who occupy its offices are (ideally) constrained by the rule of law. The rule of law creates accountability – everyone, even those representing or acting on behalf of the state, has to abide by the law, and the same rules apply to everyone, including state actors and state institutions.

The role of the state vis-à-vis public spheres is complicated. The state produces a lot of information that informs public life and debate (Friedland et al. 2006;

Schudson 1994), even as it also secures by law public spaces where citizens can assemble and speak (such as town squares, public media, and media licenses in the public interest). Moreover, many state institutions provide by law opportunities for public access to or comment on their workings (such as public comment periods for rulemaking). The rules that govern these things matter – even as the state facilitates spaces for public deliberation and the exchange of arguments, healthy public spheres still require independence from the state, and therefore there are often restrictions on what state entities can, and cannot, do (such as interfering in content.)

SPOTLIGHTED CONTENT

Changing technologies, especially infrastructural ones, have raised new and often pressing questions for the relationship between the state and public spheres. Who should control the data gathered through "smart city" technologies such as public Wi-Fi or facial recognition and closed-circuit television systems? There are many good reasons why the state should make these and other kinds of information and data accessible to citizens, including to even out information asymmetries between different groups of people. Citizens need to be able to challenge the state, its power, and authorities in the attempt to hold it accountable. Functioning public spheres are a prerequisite for democracy, and the tension is that they must be independent from the state, while also requiring state support in many cases.

Public spheres are distinct from the market. In classical liberal political philosophy, the "marketplace of ideas" is at the center of society. This goes back to the ancient Greek *agora*, the marketplace within the Greek city-states where the free, adult male citizens would meet and discuss matters of social concern. However, the metaphor of the "marketplace" does not mean that the public sphere is a commercial market where ideas are commodified and traded. The normative ideal is that free citizens exchange rational arguments, and the strongest argument wins a political conflict. This means the outcome is not determined by superior resources like power, money, or force.

It is important to make this distinction between the public sphere and the commercial marketplace because in everyday language we use many commercial metaphors like "buying someone's argument." The public sphere has *always* been connected to commercial places – the Greek marketplace, the bourgeois debating clubs in Viennese coffee houses, commercial newspapers, television journalism premised on advertising, and now the commercial digital platforms that sell target audiences to advertisers and commodify much of social life through data.

That said, the connection between public spheres and commercial contexts has always been a complicated one. Ideally, public spheres are open to *all* members of a society, which is not (always) the case in the proprietary structures of a market, or a platform. For example, a mall owner may exclude homeless people and certain types of speech in many countries; a coffee house can ban visitors who do not consume anything; a platform may geoblock or ageblock users – whereas truly public spaces or places or spheres are ideally unconditionally open to everyone. Platforms, just as malls or coffee houses, are proprietary environments that can and do exclude certain users and certain forms of speech – so much of the debate over platforms is exactly over what speech should and should not be allowed (i.e., the problem of content moderation), and who or what bodies should make these decisions.

At the same time, commercial spaces are often connected to the public sphere in a broader sense. While public spheres are conceptually distinct from commercial media processes, they are undoubtedly supported by them. This distinction means that, while platforms such as Facebook or news organizations such as the *New York Times*, *The Gleaner* of Jamaica, or the South African Broadcasting Corporation are important actors in public spheres, they do not encompass public spheres themselves.

This does not mean that public spheres are *practically* open to all. Scholars have long pointed out that non-commercial public spheres have long excluded women (Fraser 1990), non-dominant racial and ethnic groups (Squires 2002), and other groups in societies, including along the lines of religion, gender identity, sexual orientation, and class (e.g. Jackson et al. 2020). These exclusions reflect larger power differentials in society – especially the ability of the powerful to regulate access to public spheres, and especially their most important and influential forums. What is more, even without formal exclusion, there are often informal ways in which powerful interests and social and economic power shape access to many institutions and forums and the ability to speak to and be heard by publics more generally (Ananny & Finn 2020). In this context, sometimes commercial markets have been important drivers of expanding democratic inclusion (i.e., in the case of the LGBTQIA+ community).

Public spheres are distinct from the private. Already in the Greek city-states, the distinction between the public (*agora*) and the home (*oikos*) was very important. Back then, only matters of public concern were to be debated in the public forum, while matters of the family or the household had to remain private. That said, there was never a hard dichotomy of public versus private. Indeed, as we detailed in the opening chapter, an important aspect of political life is making matters of private life of public concern to address systemic problems. In our own time, think about domestic violence, gender and sexuality, economics, and class relations. These things at one time were strictly private, but activists made them the legitimate realm of public policy in the attempt to secure rights, pursue equality, or otherwise address what they saw as issues to be remedied through public policy.

More broadly, the private sphere, divided into the social and intimate spheres, is a prerequisite for the public sphere because it is often the source of topics, interests, attitudes, and identities that are the basis for politics.

Platforms have made public spheres more complicated. For one thing, they dissolve many boundaries between public and private or, at the very least, make our public and private selves more visible to more people. The difference between public and private is indeed a messy one, and often there are startling juxtapositions between public and intimately private matters on people's social media feeds. The "weak ties" facilitated by platforms, as well as information's potential to travel long distances during the platform era, have helped to create these juxtapositions. In his seminal work, Mark Granovetter (1973) showed that strong ties – the people closest to our hearts and minds – deliver mostly redundant information. In other words, those closest in our social circle tell us what we already know. On the other hand, weak ties – our loose acquaintances such as neighbors, high school friends, or friends of our friends – provide us with new information from socially more distant sources and communities.

It is precisely these weak ties that make up the major part of our networks on digital platforms. Indeed, a particular feature of platforms is that they bundle together many different types of social ties – such as friends from childhood, professional and work relationships, and communities of faith. This "context collapse" (Marwick & boyd 2011) has meant not only that we learn a lot of things about people that were often kept separate in the past (the private lives of our congregation members, for instance), but that information now increasingly flows across these networks in new ways.

SPOTLIGHTED CASES

Think about your own social media use. You might use TikTok to comment on Russia's invasion of Ukraine (a public matter) and then seamlessly post a video of your cat capriciously knocking things off of a table. Platforms also bundle many different types of relations and selves together. On Facebook, you might see the political ramblings of your uncle, juxtaposed with your sister's wedding announcement. While this mixture of public and private life was always a feature of public spheres (it is inconceivable to think that there was ever a purely public-oriented space of discourse), platforms make many aspects of ourselves and lives visible, and juxtapose them in new ways, all to people we have multiple and dispersed social, political, economic, and religious ties to.

Public Spheres

Against the backdrop of these considerations, we can understand public spheres as *self-organized forums, arenas, or networks in which public opinion formation takes place through discourse*. They are, *in principle*, open to the participation of all members of a society, who discover, deliberate about, or represent their interests, voice discontent, point to problems of public concern, exchange arguments, find supporters and allies for their causes, or mobilize on behalf of issues, people, or groups. In reality, however, they hardly ever are open to *everyone*. Illiterate citizens or members of non-dominant groups that face things such as discrimination and harassment encounter barriers to their participation. Historically, there have been legal and social forms of exclusion from public spheres in many countries around the world. Even more, public spheres (especially influential or powerful ones) often reward certain participatory styles – such as rationality, outrage, etc. – that perpetuate forms of social power (Krzyżanowski 2020; Rossini 2019).

Who participates, and how, matters because public spheres are central infrastructures in democracy. As Squires (2002) summed up, the public sphere consists "of physical or mediated spaces where people can gather and share information, debate opinions, and tease out their political interests and social needs with other participants." They are an "organizational principle of social and political order" (Andersen 2006: 219). An important function of public spheres is the public monitoring of society and state power. To the extent that political elites and formal sites of political power are oriented toward public opinion and discourse – if only to see how much they can get away with – it is a central form of contemporary democratic accountability.

Public spheres are also spaces where groups contest power – either to try to achieve it, or to hold on to it.

Only in and through public spheres do citizens create and get information about issues of common concern, hear various opinions and arguments, and give shape and voice to their own identities, preferences, and grievances (Moy 2020). It's where they learn about politics, policy, and the polity – how their society operates, what issues are currently at stake, and who fights over what, how, and why. Public spheres are where individual opinions, interests, and enthusiasm or outrage are aggregated into public opinion, common policy concerns, and even social movements. They are where ideas find supporters, stakeholders gather in groups, and movements gain momentum. And they are where people come to see themselves as members of social groups – different from, and at times opposed to, other social groups in the pursuit of political power.

There are a number of concepts related to public spheres. Similar to public spheres – but slightly different – is the concept of *publics*. As Warner (2002) has argued, there is *the public*, encompassing the totality of a society or community or nations, including everyone in it. This notion overlaps with the idea of a public sphere, but with less emphasis on spaces and more on *actors* and *addressing* them. There are also *publics* – which consist of concrete audiences, including "the kind of public that comes into being only in relation to texts and their circulation" (Warner 2002: 50). Publics in this sense emerge from groups or relations between strangers, including their interactions and communication. Publics are smaller than public spheres. One way to think about them is as building blocks. Publics might emerge around events or issues (Dewey 1927), such as transnational activist publics that are organized around certain issues and communicate across time and digital platforms and national borders, or be rooted in specific communities and comparatively more durable.

Where there are publics, we also find *counterpublics*. These are publics that are opposed to, in conflict with, or otherwise challenge the dominant public(s). In feminist scholar Nancy Fraser's famous criticism of Habermas's idealization of the liberal "bourgeois" (or middle to upper mercantilist-class) public sphere, she introduced the notion of "subaltern" counterpublics, in which historically non-dominant groups (women, people of color, LGBTQIA+ people, etc.) form alternative "parallel discourse arenas" (Fraser 1990: 67). As Warner (2002) and other scholars have pointed out, counterpublics are more than just alternative publics – they are consciously, even painfully, aware of their subordinate status and seek out their own venues to negotiate alternative identities and organize their own discourses that are not only separate from, but in contestation with, those of dominant publics.

Counterpublics can emerge around racial and ethnic identity, such as Black Twitter (Freelon et al. 2018; Graham & Smith 2016), or as sustained street protests against political dictatorships and corruption, as was the case with the Arab Spring (Al-Rawi 2014). They can be religious publics, such as Muslim bloggers in Germany (Eckert & Chadha 2013). Or they can emerge in comments sections on newspaper websites, weighing in on various issues in reaction to dominant discourse (Toepfl & Piwoni 2015). Researchers have recently expanded the concept of "counterpublics" to understand far-right and/or white supremacist discourses, in the process arguing that counterpublics are not necessarily pro-democratic or beneficial for democratic discourse (Kaiser & Rauchfleisch 2019; Tischauser & Musgrave 2020). The challenge with this approach is that it assumes that far-right or white supremacist discourses are actually *counter* to an underlying racial or social order – which is clearly not the case in many Western democracies.

In addition to her work on public spheres, publics, and counterpublics, Catherine Squires (2002) has theorized the diverse and varied ways in which people affiliate and gather with a range of different aims and goals in mind – all in the context of what they *can* do. Specifically analyzing multiple Black publics in the US, Squires notes that there are not just counterpublics, but also "enclaves" hidden from view that especially take root when people cannot openly engage in the public sphere (in the context of state or social repression; see also Van Duyn 2020). "Satellite" publics are separate from dominant and other publics by choice, to support identity and institution building, and engage with other publics at particular moments of strategic interest. In other words, "enclaved" publics have to keep their ideas and existence hidden from public view due to the threat of repression, whereas "satellites" willingly choose to eschew engagement with dominant publics. Scholars have built on this work, including showing how satellite cultures have helped to transform and transnationalize local issues and to transport them into European public spheres (Volkmer 2008).

4.3 Public Spheres in the Age of Platforms

The Internet and platforms have made public spheres and publics possible at new scales and across new timeframes and dimensions. Let's consider what has changed, for a moment. In the twentieth century, public spheres were always closely connected to media and communications technologies. Until the advent of the Internet, public spheres were dominated by mass media – again, in most countries, highly concentrated, powerful companies serving the same information unidirectionally to mass audiences. The Internet disrupted these media systems and changed both the information available in public spheres and how they emerge and form (Jarren et al. 2021). This disruption has occurred through the ways the Internet has afforded new, lower costs of communication at greater scales and new dynamics of public attention through new forms of communication flow. And the Internet has facilitated the rise of the platform companies that have emerged as dominant economic actors that structure the business and distribution models of mass media. Platforms also ushered in the algorithmic curation and filtering of communication, personalization of news feeds and search engines, and structuring of public attention at truly global scales.

As a result of all of these things, public communication became increasingly decentralized (although structured in new ways); political actors experimented with more participatory, dialogical forms of interacting in public spheres; and people around the world have an incredible wealth of information and communication at their fingertips. For example, mass media have diminished power to set the public agenda, or, as Chaffee and Metzger put it in an early 2001 statement: "The key problem for agenda-setting theory will change from what issues the media tell people to think about to what issues people tell the media they want to think about" (2001: 375). It turned out to be a bit more complicated than that. In any era, having money, holding a political position, or having social status meant being able to access mass media, and therefore the ability to speak to and be heard by publics. This remains true today, but the ability of the "people" to be heard has dramatically changed in significant ways, as a result of a number of media, political, and social forces.

For example, platforms support an incredible diversity of content and content providers, and have facilitated the emergence of smaller publics around a massively extended array of issues and topics, including at global scales. The Internet and platforms provide a means of communication and organization (Bennett & Segerberg 2013) that amplify the visibility and presence of various social and political movements, as well as shape new flows of communication and public attention. And the Internet facilitates new forms of commerce, consumption, and entertainment that shape politics as well, alongside new means of making private issues public. At the same time, platforms have given rise to more fragmented public spheres, as people have abundant choices of what to consume – including the choice to consume no political content at all (Bennett & Iyengar 2008; Dunaway & Graber 2022).

The Internet and platforms have ushered in all of these things in ways that are also structured and shaped by other forces. Consider again Figure 1 – economics (such as commercial models for internet delivery, access, and providing content), regulation (such as state rules around expression and liability), and social and political institutions (the Internet tends to get used in ways for which societies are already organized, although technology also works upon these institutions) all shape how media and platforms get taken up, and why. And this means that public spheres were never *just* the product of media and technology, but always the product of communication shaped and structured by many different forces that gave rise to them.

To take an example, platforms have, ironically, brought back much in the way of the centralization and concentration of information, in some respects. The Internet of 2023 is very different from the Internet of 2005, with the increasing concentration of ways of accessing content through platforms. In 2005, for instance, internet users might access the content they were interested in by going directly to the URLs of media outlets. In 2020, most internet users increasingly spent their time accessing content on TikTok, Facebook, WhatsApp, and other platforms that bundle together *many* different content providers, and serve them up through a mix of social and algorithmically curated mechanisms. At the same time, platforms have centralized social interactions online, even while facilitating the presence of a much wider array of information flows than we might encounter in daily life. For example, platforms combine *many* different forms of communication – direct communication between friends, communication from individuals to their social and professional networks, or even from individuals to thousands of followers or millions of platform users through the algorithmic processes TikTok is famous for.

In sum, the Internet and, especially, platforms provide much of the infrastructure for public spheres – the latter through their design and algorithms that shape who and what gets amplified, turned down, or filtered out, and how. Political actors in turn adjust their communication to the way in which media work (Esser & Strömbäck 2014; Mazzoleni 2008a; Strömbäck 2008). The concept of "media logic" captures the idea that media operate according to stable institutional and structural practices. In other words, there are certain rules of the game. And these rules of the game in the platform era are decisively different for traditional mass media and social or, more broadly, network media.

For example, a number of scholars have pointed to how the Internet and platforms have changed the logics through which political actors communicate. Poell and van Dijck (2013) differentiate between mass media logic and social media logic.

Social media logic, they argue, is "a particular set of strategies and mechanisms" (2013: 5) different from mass media logic in a few ways: social media are programmable and they are built around the principles of popularity, connectivity, and datafication, turning "into data many aspects of the world that have never been quantified before" (2013: 9). Klinger and Svensson (2015, 2016) argue that the Internet has changed how media producers create content (and who those producers are), how information is distributed and flows to and across audiences, and how people use media. In traditional mass media, information selection is exclusive and expensive, because it is journalists who do the job according to professional procedures and criteria. In an era of network media, everyone can become a producer of news, creating information according to personal tastes and preferences. Information in mass media occurs by broadcasting to known audiences, while with network media there is often no predetermined audience, but networks of (often, but not always) like-minded people. Finally, traditional mass media are used by often location-bound mass audiences (e.g. TV audiences in Italy or Indonesia), while network media are used by interest-bound networks of people who interact with one another.

These shifts, of course, have had a significant impact on how political actors adopt and adapt to network media, such as social media platforms. Both mass media logics and network media logics (ushered in with the Internet) overlap and intertwine; mass media logic is not becoming obsolete or marginal. For example, relevant information still mostly originates from journalistic content production, is distributed via established mass media, and is used by individuals with routine media habits. For political actors, this means that they must master the realms of both mass and social media.

To take one example, scholars have focused on the new importance of emotions in public life. While scholars have long noted that conceiving of public spheres as based on deliberation and rational, cool, fact-based exchanges is wrong, they have also pointed to the ways in which platforms heighten the role of emotions in public life (Lünenborg 2019; Papacharissi 2016). The intuitive, emotional, heated, and passionate aspects of public discourse have been heightened in the platform era, in part given the ways that psychological, social, and algorithmic processes select for this kind of expression and content (including for economic reasons). Scholars have increasingly noted how publics are organized around "affect" – or emotion and its intensity – in the platform era, for instance. "Affective publics" are "networked publics that are mobilized and connected, identified, and potentially disconnected through expressions of sentiment" (Papacharissi 2016: 312). The "intensity of emotion" (2016: 318) can disrupt dominant political storytelling and narratives. Affect is about gut feeling, dramatization, and perhaps even the creation of perceptions of alternative realities. While social movements and election campaigns have always been affective and included emotional appeals (e.g. Crigler 2007; Derks et al. 2008; Rußmann 2018), the increasing importance and immediacy of social media, user-generated content, mobilization through personal networks, and algorithmic curation further catalyze the role of emotions in political life. This affects political communication, such as during election campaigns, when attack messages yield more engagement and interactions than mere policy information postings (Boulianne & Larsson 2023).

One thing is clear – in the platform era, the role of emotion in public life has been intensified. And not only people, but also platforms, drive affective processes and, ultimately, shape the possibilities for and structures of publics. Facebook, for instance, attributed extra value to particularly emotional emojis, such as anger reactions, because posts that get more reaction emojis keep users more engaged, and engaged users are what Facebook's business model is built on. Journalists have learned that emotional content gets rewarded on platforms – leading to the increase of clickbait headlines and styles of journalism and political communication more broadly (Munger 2020). This reveals the power of platforms to *shape* journalism and political communication. While a cool, professional, and rational tone dominated the genre of what was considered "quality" journalism during the mass media era (certainly not cable news, talk radio, or the crime- and sex-driven tabloid press that often play important roles bringing people into the drama of public life), communication on platforms is driven more by affect and, as such, some political actors, journalists, and media outlets have adjusted their styles of communication.

While platforms have created new opportunities for participation in public spheres, including through affect, they have also given rise to new challenges. Disparities in digital access to platforms along the lines of gender, class, or education can make communicative participation hard. At the same time, mobile phones and other technologies have countered this in many countries (Dunaway & Searles 2022), including several African nations, where city dwellers are tapping into the new communications environment to improve their economic, social, and political conditions (Brinkman & de Bruijn 2018; Mutsvairo & Ragnedda 2018; Nothias 2020). Of increasing interest to scholars are the ways in which motivated actors – such as networks of right-wing white men – use things such as hate speech and harassment to foreclose the communicative participation of women and racial and ethnic minorities in various public spheres (Sobieraj 2020). For example, Harmer and Southern (2021: 2012) show how "digital microaggressions" on Twitter abuse female and minority-group members of parliament, and "serve as constant reminders of the marginalized status of female representatives, and women of color specifically, and should be conceptualized as forms of psychological and semiotic violence that reconstitute online political spaces as a hostile environment for women and may discourage women from seeking political office or compel women representatives to leave."

Platforms also now make instantaneous gatherings of strangers at a global scale newly possible, and increase the speed and volume of information (Vaidhyanathan 2018). That said, we have been increasingly forced to grapple with what is *positive* participation in public spheres. The growth of international conspiracy movements such as QAnon, for instance, is fueled by widespread participation but it is corrosive to democratic deliberation and political accountability (Marwick & Partin 2022), as is the rise of trolls (state-backed or otherwise) that undermine trust, authenticity, and democratic knowledge (e.g. Freelon et al. 2022). We turn now to consider the consequences of these changes in public spheres in the era of platforms.

4.4 The Consequences of Platforms for Public Spheres

After the initial years of the platform era saw a lot of democratic enthusiasm and techno-optimism in scholarly and public discourse, political communication has been haunted by the rise of disruptive phenomena such as disinformation, computational propaganda, hate campaigns, and platform manipulation, particularly in the years after 2016. We take stock here broadly of the democratic, and anti-democratic, effects of platforms on public spheres.

To start, as detailed above, public spheres are no longer as geographically or socially bound as they often were in the eighteenth or nineteenth centuries. Previously, public spheres were limited mostly by national or regional media systems. Today, however, platforms enable communication to operate at new scales, across multiple domains of life, and with greater decentralization. Platforms such as Facebook use algorithms to help their users find like-minded groups, whatever their interests are – connecting dog lovers, plane spotters, activists, or anti-Semites.

SPOTLIGHTED CONTENT

While we tend to think of media systems – and therefore public spheres – being regional and national during earlier centuries, there are very important exceptions. Empires and colonial systems were long premised on communication networks that tied together administrative sites for the purposes of coordination and control, including of military units and goods. This, in turn, supported information flows across vast scales. As one of the oldest institutions in the world, the Catholic Church has long had an established global communications network – one which often rode alongside colonialist and empire building projects. And economic trade has long been premised on regional and global communication networks, including the ships, trains, and telegrams that facilitated the flows of goods – and bodies – across the world. This means that media systems and public spheres have long had transnational and even global dimensions, even if we might think about our own era as uniquely interconnected!

As is clear, this is a two-sided coin. The same platforms that facilitate people getting involved in the political process or pursuing climate change activism, for instance, also support the creation of groups that promote extremism and hate. To take one example, an internal study at Facebook showed that the platform's algorithmic recommendation system actively drove users into far-right racist groups (Horwitz & Seetharaman 2020). While it can be quite beneficial for democracies when citizens easily find others to join a common cause, the same dynamic also makes it easy for people to rally around conspiracy theories or propaganda narratives. While these things have always been part and parcel of social life, changes in media and technology matter for how conspiracies and propaganda scale. Whereas the only conspiracy-theorist in town may have been lonely in the medieval city, she may have found some fellow travelers through newspaper ads in the era of mass media. But she might find a worldwide community reinforcing, creating, and supporting these beliefs in the age of platforms. Platforms have enabled even the most extreme fringe ideas to find supporters, friends, and followers, within countries or even worldwide – even as they have also fueled movements for climate, gender, and racial and ethnic justice.

SPOTLIGHTED CASES

Over the past decade, a steady stream of internal leaks from platform companies have caused a reevaluation of platforms' effects on democracies. For example, in an internal study, Twitter recently found that tweets from the political right and right-leaning news outlets are amplified by the platform's algorithms (Belli 2021) – but the company did not state why this was occurring. Meanwhile, the Facebook Papers leaked by whistleblower Frances Haugen in 2021 revealed, among other things, that the company's algorithms drive divisive content.

There are other concerns about platform effects on public spheres. Bennett and Pfetsch (2018) have argued that public spheres are becoming increasingly disconnected from traditional structures of media and journalism. As such, platforms are disruptive to important, information-producing institutions in the public sphere and lead to declines in trust and legitimacy in journalism. Pfetsch (2018) and Pfetsch et al. (2018) have developed the idea of "dissonant public spheres," arguing that we need to be clear-eyed about conflict being a central part of political life, and abandoning ideas that political actors seek consensus, deliberation, reasoned decision-making, or convergence (Pfetsch 2018: 60). The idea of dissonant public spheres captures the fact that there is often little agreement about important political topics among elected leaders, political organizations, and parties.

Even more troubling, scholars see dissonant public spheres as marked by a cacophony of voices and the "inability to communicate across difference" (Waisbord 2016: 2). In this view, political actors are not able, or not willing, to engage in rational discourse, seek understanding, exchange arguments, or even share a common perception of reality. Especially during campaigns, and in the course of public life more generally, political actors abstain from rational arguments: "They aspire neither to understand, nor deliberate or seek consensus" (Pfetsch 2018: 61).

A number of scholars have analyzed other dimensions of how platforms change public spheres. Bruce Bimber and Homero Gil de Zúñiga (2020) argue that social media have created "unedited public spheres" which provide contexts for obscure information sources, deceptive communication, and manipulated social signals. It is not all social media's fault; these researchers are careful to note that public spheres are not "truth machines" generally (2020: 708), just as platforms are not democracy machines. But these scholars argue that, through their affordances and algorithms, and the opportunities they provide to a wide range of actors to communicate at scale, platforms make it harder for publics to deliberate and separate truth from falsehood. What is needed, they argue, is more editing provided by institutional knowledge producers, such as professional journalists. These journalists would be enlisted in "operating a truth-biased filter on claims before they enter the broad public sphere, publicly identifying false claims that escape the filter, and providing signals about the provenance of truth claims such that interested parties can weigh evidence themselves" (2020: 710).

In this view, the more we communicate on platforms, the more important high-quality journalism becomes for a democratic society. This observation accords very well with the concept of "hybrid media systems" – the Internet, or platforms, have not replaced traditional media (or the need for them); they have diversified and decentralized the networks through which political communication takes shape and where public spheres emerge. But while platforms are very good at monetizing social relations, they are not particularly good at nurturing public spheres.

At the same time, the idea that the mere fact that journalists and other knowledge-producing institutions put good information into public spheres means that people will actually find it, and more importantly believe and trust it, is an increasingly dubious proposition. Indeed, much research has shown that people selectively expose themselves to information that accords with their pre-existing beliefs and are motivated to process information in ways that strengthen already held views. And, in a world where people have much more control over the political information they receive, this is a growing concern.

4.5 Filter Bubbles and Echo Chambers

It is worth mentioning here a very common concern about platforms and their impact on public spheres – namely, the emergence of so-called "filter bubbles" and "echo chambers." The idea behind these concepts is that both self-selected exposure (the media and content that users actively choose to inform themselves with) and algorithmic exposure on platforms (the content that platforms choose for their users' timelines, often based on monetized engagement) lead to bubbles of reinforcing like-mindedness (Möller et al 2018; Zuiderveen Borgesius et al. 2016). The argument itself is not new. Preferring like-minded information is rooted in human psychology and, for a long time in many places, media have been aligned with political views.

SPOTLIGHTED CASES

The idea of media aligning with political views for the purposes of effective representation is old. In Italy, the *lottizzazione* system distributed the public broadcasters of RAI (Radiotelevisione italiana) among the relevant political parties and thus introduced a purely partisan media system in 1975. Established much earlier, the *pillarization* in the Netherlands had separated society into groups based on religion and political beliefs – each with their own media, trade unions, schools, even sports clubs.

In digital environments, however, the concern is that media self-selection dovetails with algorithmic biases toward engagement to produce what scholars call "reinforcing spirals" (Slater 2007; Young & Bleakley 2020) of political information reception and belief. On platforms, users' own choices, as well as those of their networks, algorithms, and all sorts of political communicators, shape the political information that users see. Researchers fear that users may opt out of content they disagree with, and unfriend people with different opinions. And, as detailed earlier in this chapter, users also have opportunities to find other like-minded individuals on platforms, who are also sources of identity- and ideology-congruent political information and content

(Wojcieszak et al. 2022). Research has shown that Facebook users tend to follow incidental recommendations from close friends with similar political opinions, in essence creating self-reinforcing selective exposure (Kaiser et al. 2021). Meanwhile, algorithms tend to show users more content similar to what they have already engaged with, which selects against information they might disagree with or just not be very interested in.

As a result, so the argument goes, algorithms and users' own behavior lock users into digital environments that overwhelmingly confirm and reinforce their opinions. In this view, users have fewer opportunities to come across content they disagree with and that challenges them. The fear is that this leads users to radicalize without even noticing, and to become less and less able to communicate across political differences.

This would indeed be disruptive to public spheres – how could a society debate about public problems, find collective solutions, and understand the facts about the issues at stake if there is hardly any shared sense of reality?

Thankfully, the evidence for filter bubbles and echo chambers is mixed at best. Eli Pariser's famous book, *The Filter Bubble*, which did much to raise public and scholarly concerns about filter bubbles, was published in 2011. Since then, scholars have been trying to find empirical evidence for filter bubbles and related phenomena such as echo chambers, and have detailed a couple of mitigating factors that make them less of a concern than initially thought. First, it remains a truism that political information is a small minority of what people actually consume online, and generally most people around the world are not very interested in politics. To choose ideologically consonant information requires knowing what your own beliefs are and what is consistent about them, which only the most politically sophisticated and engaged can do with any regularity (Huttunen 2021; Parvin 2018; Wike & Castillo 2018; Willems 2012). While selective exposure has been increasing in the age of media choice (Arceneaux & Johnson 2013; Stroud 2011), scholars have consistently found that there is also a lot of incidental exposure to political information. People encounter news and political information – including across ideological differences – even when not actively searching for it, and even when not interested in news (Weeks & Lane 2020).

And, while most internet users avoid conflict and disagreement, some even enjoy and seek the fun of a hard debate (Svensson 2015). Meanwhile, scholarship has consistently demonstrated that internet use is associated with seeking out and being exposed to a wider array of media sources than in other information environments (Fletcher & Kleis Nielsen 2018). Moreover, hybrid media systems cut against homogeneous political information environments for many people. People are not confined to social media for news, for instance – they also watch TV, listen to radio and podcasts, and talk to their neighbors and colleagues.

To summarize the state of the literature on filter bubbles and echo chambers: it is complicated. In their meta-analysis of 55 empirical studies of echo chambers, Terren and Borge-Bravo (2021) found that methods matter. Studies based on digital trace data (i.e., based on users' own behaviors and exposure) tended to support the echo chambers hypothesis, while studies based on self-reported data (i.e., surveys) tended to reject it. Bruns (2019, 2021) argues that filter bubbles and echo chambers "constitute an unfounded moral panic that presents a convenient technological scapegoat (search and social platforms and their affordances and algorithms) for a much more critical problem: growing social and political polarization" (2021: 1).

Meanwhile, Dahlgren (2021) studied the underlying assumptions of the filter bubble argument and concluded that the concept contradicted previously well-established knowledge on selective exposure.

In a nutshell, while increasingly personalized information environments may lead to skewed, reinforcing information for some people, it does not mean that personalization impacts information levels or polarization on the level of society as a whole. That said, a number of scholars have rightly pointed to the fact that we should be concerned about dangerous phenomena even if they manifest among a small minority of platform users. Comparatively small numbers of politically extreme actors who are radicalized through spirals online, for instance, can still be capable of undermining democratic systems or causing political violence. (And a minority of global platform users can still be millions of people.) Even more, there are special concerns when politics spills over into other areas of social life, such as public health – which was revealed in the anti-vaccination and anti-masking political movements that likely cost thousands of lives. In short, while the vast majority of people have social networks that overlap across ideological divides and are not necessarily structured along political beliefs, others inhabit more ideologically cohesive social worlds. The question is: how many people need to inhabit closed social and political worlds for them to be dangerous for democracy?

In the end, technology alone does not determine society, and the claim that technology could lock people into inescapable bubbles wildly overestimates what technology can do. But technology is also undoubtedly part of society, and therefore reflects, and helps to constitute, our political and social lives.

4.6 Public Opinion

As this chapter has detailed, public spheres have been transformed by technologies and media in significant ways. This also means that public opinion – as the represented, collective expression of publics – is indelibly shaped by technologies and, especially in our own time, platforms. Platforms provide both a new communicative basis for the formation of public opinion and new means of representing it.

"Public opinion" refers to an approximation of what groups of people in a society think about issues, constructed through the efforts of researchers trying to measure or otherwise assess the attitudes, perceptions, feelings, and beliefs of people. While various ways of producing public opinion go back centuries, modern polling and public opinion research were born in the early twentieth century, and became standard research methods with Paul Lazarsfeld's studies at Columbia University, and George Gallup's accurate predictions of election results in the 1930s and 1940s in the US (Donsbach 2015).

While politicians and other political actors invoke public opinion and claim to represent it as a matter of course, the approach methodologically is generally premised on empirical procedures that assess attitudes and beliefs, both qualitatively among smaller samples (e.g. focus groups) and quantitatively among larger populations (e.g. through surveys, online polls, or population-based survey experiments [Mutz 2011]). Traditionally, scholars had to *ask* people about their attitudes – designing useful questionnaires and scales, attributing weight to questions, and carefully recruiting participants. For instance, to statistically generalize about society as a whole, researchers need representative samples (i.e., a selected group of random participants that resemble the age, gender, sociodemographic, and/or values patterns of the society). But sometimes the group to be surveyed is small or difficult to get to participate, for instance when studying radical groups or hidden populations such as illegal immigrants. In these cases, scholars would opt for snowball sampling, or recruiting participants with the help of previous participants. This way, one would waive the statistical generalizability of the results to obtain access.

The age of platforms has provided scholars with new methodological opportunities and tools to study public opinion. This is because people now actually write their thoughts down or perform them through things such as expressive posts on platforms such as TikTok. This means that people convey what they think (or what they wish other people believed they think) in social media posts, comments, and messages. Researchers then infer what people think by watching what they *do*, including clicking, sharing, downloading, and scrolling. Taken as a whole, people's behavior online creates a wealth of real-time "trace" data that can be used to infer public opinion.

The advantage of this is that researchers can study expressions of inferred opinions and beliefs without asking, and circumvent the many self-report downsides of surveys and polls. These downsides include the fact that people do not recall events accurately and there is no way to know whether they answer questions truthfully, as well as psychological problems such as social desirability effects (respondents give researchers the answers they think they want to hear) – all of which distort the results of surveys. Trace data from social media platforms apparently offer more direct access into what people believe through what they do, but they are also a complicated source of data. For one, the users (even more so, the most active users) of *any* platform are not representative of society as a whole. Twitter, for instance, is used by only a small minority of citizens in many countries. Moreover, as Jungherr et al. (2017) show, trace data from social media platforms often indicates attention rather than support. In other words, likes, shares, and comments show us what gets recognized, but not necessarily what people really like, love, or want. Following a party or politician on Twitter does not mean an intention to vote for them – perhaps it is just to keep an eye on a party one particularly dislikes (hate-following, e.g. Ouwerkerk & Johnson 2016).

4.7 Summary

While not easy, it is not impossible to change opinions and attitudes, and even the behavior, of people – and political communication is, in large part, about how political actors intervene in public spheres to try and achieve exactly that. In Chapter 6, we dive deeper into strategic communication, and in Chapter 7 we will explore how parties and candidates run campaigns, seeking to influence what people think, what they talk about, and whom they vote for. First, however, we turn to journalism as the most important source of information and influence on opinion formation in public spheres. Indeed, platforms have changed not only the role of journalism in public spheres, but also the very understanding journalists have of the public – with great consequence. Researchers have found that journalists not only look to social media to index public opinion, they represent social media back to political actors and audiences as *the* public (McGregor 2019). It is to the changing nature of journalism that we now turn.

Discussion Questions

- Elon Musk (and others) refer to Twitter as "the de facto public town square." What does this metaphor mean? What aspects of this metaphor fit, and what aspects do not? Can you think of a more fitting metaphor for Twitter?
- Although empirical studies have shown again and again that social media do not create filter bubbles and echo chambers – that they *do not* lock people into closed spheres of like-mindedness – the idea is very persistent and pervasive in public discourse. Why?

Suggestions for Further Reading

Bimber, B. & Gil de Zúñiga, H. (2020) "The unedited public sphere," *New Media & Society* 22(4): 700–15.

Bruns, A. (2019) *Are Filter Bubbles Real?* Cambridge: Polity.

Pfetsch, B. (2018) "Dissonant and disconnected public spheres as challenge for political communication research," *Javnost –The Public* 25(1–2): 59–65.

Wessler, H. (2019) *Habermas and the Media*. Cambridge: Polity.

5 Platforms and Journalism

Chapter 5 demonstrates that political communication has always been, and still is, closely tied to journalism, the institutionalized form of making and distributing news. The rise of platforms has challenged journalism and its practices and business models in many ways. The chapter shows how journalism and platforms are closely intertwined – much of the political content circulating on platforms originates from journalistic sources, and journalists use platforms as essential reporting sources and technologies.

OBJECTIVES

By the end of this chapter, you should be able to:

- define journalism
- identify business models for journalism in the platform age
- understand trends toward data journalism
- discuss emerging forms of journalism that take advantage of technological change.

5.1 Introduction

Journalism is a dangerous profession. If you get a chance, speak with Mexican journalists. They have harrowing stories to tell. From January to May 2022, 11 Mexican journalists were targeted and killed according to the Committee to Protect Journalists, a non-profit organization focused on press freedom. Correspondents for the UK-based global news outlet the *Guardian* called Mexico "the deadliest country for media professionals outside a warzone," according to Phillips and Espejel (2022), after Yesenia Mollinedo became one of the unlucky ones when unknown assailants pounced, killing her and a colleague, Sheila Johana García Olivera, on May 9, 2022. Mexican journalists have little political support. The nation's president, Andrés Manuel López Obrador, doesn't hide his disdain for journalists.

Sadly, Mexico is only one of the many countries across the world where working as a journalist can get you in trouble with political authorities, militia groups, or anyone opposed to press freedom and freedom of speech. To further demonstrate the perils of working as a journalist in many contemporary societies, two fellow female journalists, Chilean Francisca Sandoval and Al Jazeera's Shireen Abu Akleh, were killed during the same week as Mollinedo and García Olivera, both in the line of duty but in different circumstances.

Despite the dangers, journalism remains important, particularly in a platform era in which the process of news production is changing drastically in ways that present mounting challenges to longstanding news values, as Usher's (2014) ethnographic research at the *New York Times* over the course of several months concluded. In fact, we cannot do without it. This chapter will show why.

Many have proposed different definitions of journalism, some of which we will discuss in this chapter. Indeed, debates relating to journalism – what it *is*, what *sorts of claims* journalists make, what journalists *know*, and what journalism's *value* is to democracy – have grown up alongside the Internet and platforms, especially as the costs of producing media, finding audiences, and distributing news have fallen.

At its core, many researchers are adamant that journalism is about the pursuit of truth through the gathering, selection, and presentation of news (see Katz & Mays 2019; Kovach & Rosenstiel 2007). If you speak to many journalists, particularly in societies where journalism is highly valued, they will likely tell you that, among the reasons that drove them into the profession, are curiosity on the one hand, and the determination to seek and report truth in service of the public, on the other. Telling the truth often means holding public officials and other powerful people in society to account.

This is the ideal version of journalism. And it is one that often runs counter to the interests of the powerful. Not all countries are democratic, of course. Many do not respect citizens' fundamental rights of expression or their right to have a say in how they are governed. In backsliding or hybrid regimes, journalism is often a primary target among those looking to undermine knowledge- and accountability-producing institutions. Even in democratic countries, not all politicians are comfortable telling and dealing with the truth either, especially when it is inconvenient to them. As this chapter will reveal, journalism is considered a dangerous profession in many parts of the world for the simple reason that it is impossible to separate it from politics. Journalism is *inherently* political. Even journalists who claim to be the most objective and fair to all sides still make choices about what to cover, and, indeed, are engaged in work that fundamentally espouses the public's right to know. There is no more political claim than that.

Even with this common orientation among many journalists, there are many varieties of journalism *cultures*, defined as "a particular set of ideas and practices by which journalists legitimate their role in society and render their work meaningful" (Hanitzsch 2007: 369) – and especially in a world where platforms have changed what it means to be a publisher and who can speak to audiences. For decades, scholars in the field of journalism studies have conducted interviews, surveys, and observations to understand how journalists work in different settings and contexts, how their profession is organized, what ethical norms they follow, and how changes in media and technology impact the business and production models behind journalism. For example, the Worlds of Journalism Study is a major academic project that compares journalism cultures across 110 countries (during the 2013–23 wave), including editorial autonomy, journalistic roles, ethical orientations, and reporting practices.

One key finding is that journalistic practices, or what journalists *do*, shape relationships between media and political actors and how they communicate strategically.

For example, in cultures that emphasize the watchdog (or accountability) role of the press and have strong norms of objectivity, journalists keep distant relations with politicians (Norris 2014; Waisbord 2000). In different cultures, politicians, movements, or parties may be closely aligned with media organizations, and journalists embrace partisan, ideological, or identity orientations in their work (as Oates [2013] observes, including the Russian state-aligned media model, which limits the possibilities for a more open, democratic public sphere on the Internet). This means that there are varying political communication cultures across time and space – and, as this chapter shows, platforms indelibly shape them.

The purpose of this chapter is to help readers gain a deeper understanding of the relationship between journalism and politics in the platform era. We consider a number of scholarly concepts and theories that define and critique journalism and politics, and appraise journalism's role in political communication and politics, including the ubiquitous movements challenging or seeking to uphold social and political orders. We do so through a wide array of international examples that show why journalism's close relationship with politics is often adversarial, and consider how business models for journalism – especially fraught in the platform age – shape journalism's ability to be a knowledge-producing institution and hold power to account.

5.2 What Is Journalism?

There are many different views on what constitutes journalism (Ferrucci & Eldridge 2022; McNair 2003; Pavlik 2001; Zelizer 2005: 66). The journalism scholar Mark Deuze (2005: 458) takes one approach, focusing on the "values that journalism's ideology consists of" to define it. The "four Ps" definition of journalism adopted by Greste (2021) offers a different, more comprehensive perspective on how journalism should be conceptualized. The first "P" focuses on the person (i.e. the journalist), and includes factors such as sources of income, training, and employment status. The second "P" focuses on the product (i.e. what's being produced by the journalist), while the third "P" focuses on the journalist's purpose or mission. The last "P" is reserved for the process of gathering news.

This definition captures how, at the core, professionally trained journalists research, gather, prepare, and disseminate news and information with an audience in mind, to keep members of the public informed and educated about political, social, cultural, and economic developments within a given community, society, or region of the world. Amateur journalists can do similar things, even though in most cases they are not affiliated with news organizations and often pursue their trade independently from the market. Amateur journalists still engage in journalism regularly though, especially through the vast array of platforms and technologies that enable them to build and reach audiences with minimal capital.

Amateur journalists can also fall under the definition of "citizen journalism" (see Mpofu 2015; Nah & Chung 2020), which captures anyone who records, witnesses, or documents public events, especially at moments of great public import. Citizen journalism or participatory journalism (Mabweazara & Mare 2021) or the parallel market of information (Moyo 2009) has exploded during the platform era. Think about the Russian invasion of Ukraine in 2022. Citizen journalists reported from bomb shelters, and documented war crimes such as the use of cluster bombs against civilians and the devastating bombardment of civilian targets, including hospitals. Citizen journalists, enabled and empowered by digital technologies including platforms to produce and disseminate information, provide first-hand accounts about events, places, and situations where professional journalists lack access, or professional news does not meet the needs of affected communities (Miller 2019). Events often fashion people into citizen journalists. Think, for example, about the live documentation through mobile phones of police killings of Black people in the United States (Richardson 2020). Sometimes, citizen journalists are activists or have a distinct viewpoint rooted in a community. Others are in the right place at the right time and take full advantage of the advent of social media and other digital networks to report and distribute information and news.

While digital technology and platforms continue to revolutionize and disrupt journalism, including providing more opportunities for amateurs and citizens to fulfill this role, the purpose of the institution has more or less remained the same. Journalists have an obligation to tell the truth to some public (Balod & Hameleers 2021). However, *how* journalists tell the truth can vary significantly depending on outlets, ideology, and identity – which in turn are shaped by the political and media systems they are embedded in. Some journalists, and their outlets, believe their role is simply to produce facts about public life and present them to their audiences (and they often ignore the politics of why some things are considered 'facts' and 'public life' in the first place.) For others, working to convey the truth means making an argument and representing a community. For them, having a perspective about what facts are *important* and what facts *mean* are just as important as facts themselves.

For still others, journalism is about not only telling truth, but also acting on those truths, such as publicizing policy interventions to address what is wrong, or mobilizing public attention to spur governments to action. The degree to which journalists can tell the truth and how they tell it depends on who they work for, the political and media systems of the nations they live in or work from, and their own values, experiences, and status as journalists. For example, Tenenboim-Weinblatt (2014) conducted interviews with Israeli journalists to show how their reporting of social protests in the country during 2011 and 2012 was influenced by advertisers and editors.

To establish what is true and important, journalists analyze data in many forms, speak to sources, monitor what other media outlets are reporting, and select, frame, and disseminate to their network of audiences and readers what they think is important and newsworthy. Most journalists around the world see themselves engaged in a project to produce factual and authoritative reporting premised on carefully checking sources and data – all this in the institutionalized, professional manner of news production, guided by specific rules and norms. Of course, journalism is not perfect, and mistakes happen. But, at its core, journalism promises truthfulness – the intention to get it right, to carefully validate and verify information before publishing it, and to separate facts from opinions. However, a core question for journalism during this process is: *whose* truth? And what *constitutes* truth?

Let's take a look at elections to understand how complex reporting the truth can be. Election campaigns are heated in many countries. Many leaders or candidates on the ballot have questioned the fairness and legitimacy of democratic elections – sometimes without evidence (e.g. Donald Trump). Sometimes, though, questioning a vote can be legitimate. Vote-rigging claims were brought against President Denis

Sassou Nguesso of the Congo Republic after he won a presidential election in 2021 to extend his then 36-year rule. In both cases, journalists had important decisions to make. It is true that powerful political leaders said a vote was rigged (Trump) and that it was fair (Sassou Nguesso). Do journalists report the truth that both parties claim to have won an election? Do they independently report on the procedures of the election and judge its fairness? Do they juxtapose those who are on the ballot with non-partisan election administrators and treat them equally, or elevate one set of voices over the other? Some mix of all these things?

These are questions that journalists face every day, sometimes with dire consequences. For example, in many countries, particularly those that are home to long-serving political demagogues, such as Cameroon in West Africa, where President Paul Biya has been in power since 1975, journalists pursuing the truth are targeted by state-sponsored militias and security forces. Biya and his followers prefer their own version of truth. For many journalists in the country, though, it is obvious that, once a leader stays in power for such a long time as to be able to become one of the oldest presidents in the world, the truth cannot come from presidential palaces.

SPOTLIGHTED CASE

In March 2022, Russian President Vladimir Putin introduced a new media law, just after the invasion of Ukraine had started. The law threatens violators with 15 years' imprisonment for publishing alleged "false information" about the war in Ukraine. This includes claims journalists may make on platforms, such as the illegal use of the word "war," taking "censorship to new extremes," as the *New York Times* put it (Troianovski & Safronova 2022). As a consequence, many journalists left the country and independent news outlets closed.

Each year, Reporters Without Borders (see figure 2), a global press rights organization, releases its Press Freedom Index based on its assessment of press freedom across the world. According to the 2022 edition, the United States (ranked 42nd) and United Kingdom (24th) do not even feature in the top 20 of this internationally respected ranking, while the central American nation of Costa Rica features in the top 10. The bottom 6 countries, occupying 175–180, are China, Myanmar, Turkmenistan, Iran, the African nation of Eritrea, and North Korea. Other useful resources comparing media freedom and publishing annual reports include Freedom House's Press Freedom Index and the Internet Freedom Index.

There are many examples of the consequences that journalists face for reporting. Reporters Without Borders contends that 1,668 journalists have been killed worldwide between 2003 and 2022. For example, in November 2020, many international news agencies, including Voice of America (VOA), reported that approximately 1,000 journalists and protesters had been arrested in Belarus, just a few months after a disputed presidential election in which long-time leader Alexander Lukashenko claimed victory amid international outcry. As many as 60 journalists, 16 of them still languishing in state prisons at the time of this writing, were reported to complain of beatings at the hands of state agents (Plotnikova 2020). VOA reported that charges against

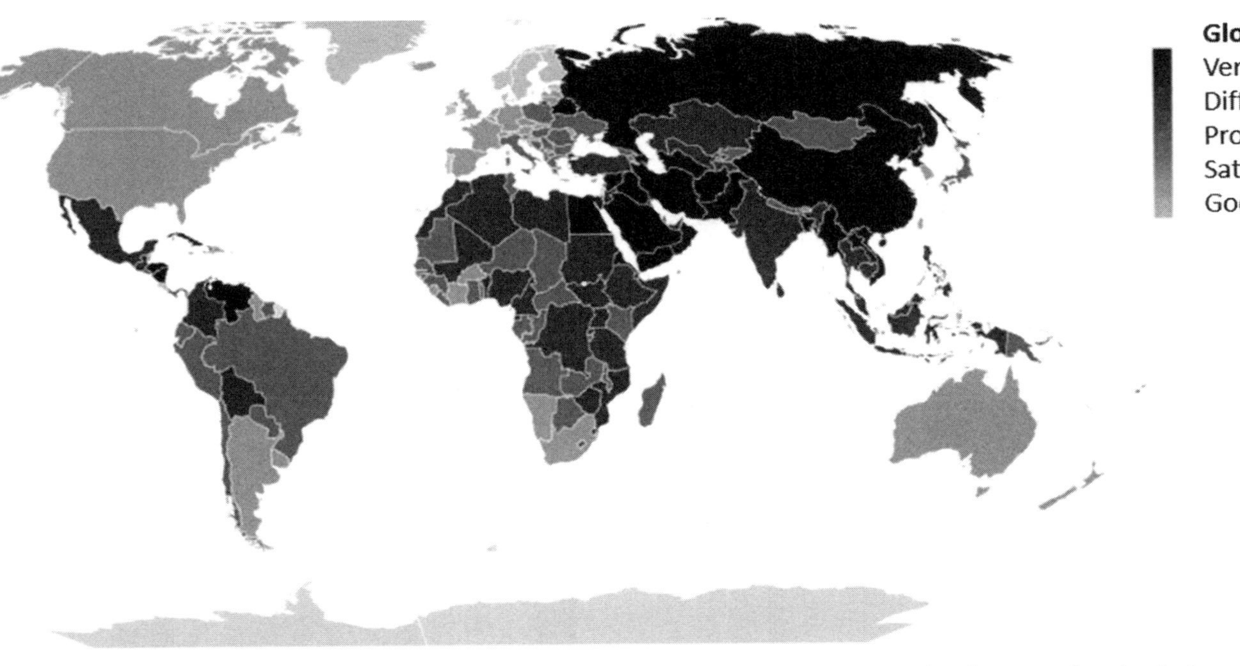

Figure 2 Reporters Without Borders 2022 Press Freedom Index: https://rsf.org/en/index

Good (global scores 85+), Satisfactory (85–70), Problematic (70–55), Difficult (55–40),Very Serious (40 and below). Map created by the authors

the journalists included "unlawful disobedience" or "taking part in an unsanctioned event" (Plotnikova 2020).

SPOTLIGHTED CASE

In power since 1994, Belarus's Alexander Lukashenko is considered Europe's last dictator, and he has a total disregard for dissent. Journalists working for reputed international media outlets including the British Broadcasting Corporation (BBC) and Associated Press (AP) have been detained in the past by the authoritarian, ice-hockey-loving president's state police. Lukashenko was back in the news in June 2021 after Belarusian authorities forced a Ryanair flight to divert in order to enable them to arrest an anti-government journalist – Roman Protasevich. One of the most totalitarian nations to live in, Belarus remains on US and European Union sanctions lists.

5.3 Journalism and Its Connections to Politics

In spite of the many dangers associated with the profession, and crises in public trust, many journalists continue to dedicate their lives to telling the stories of others, particularly of those who are unable to tell their own stories. This is an important journalistic function given that some of the things people are able to take for granted in some parts of the world are not always available in others. Indeed, core institutions of free societies (and journalists themselves) see journalists as protectors of a core human right of expression – which they uphold through their daily practices, including telling the stories of others.

SPOTLIGHTED CASES

The 2021 Nobel Peace Prize was awarded to journalists Maria Ressa and Dmitry Muratov, citizens of the Philippines and Russia respectively – two countries where journalists have often come under fire for doing their work. The Nobel Committee said the award was in recognition of "their efforts to safeguard freedom of expression, which is a precondition for democracy and lasting peace." This speaks volumes to journalism's important role in societies and commitments to its publics, particularly during an era when journalists face continued hostilities toward reporters' rights, including political and judicial harassment. That said, there can also be consequences for those who seek to repress journalism. Two-time Slovakian Prime Minister Robert Fico was forced to resign in 2018 after the politically motivated murder of investigative journalist Ján Kuciak and his fiancée, Martina Kušnírová.

Perhaps the power of the press vis-à-vis publics is most clearly demonstrated in the ways it continues to help to hold elected officials and governmental agents to account. Prominent politicians around the world have quit amid probes involving the disappearance of journalists, or after extensive news coverage of their affairs.

SPOTLIGHTED CASES

In Malta, Keith Schembri, the chief of staff to former prime minister Joseph Muscat, and tourism minister Konrad Mizzi were forced to resign in the wake of a probe into the car bomb assassination of investigative reporter Daphne Caruana Galizia in 2017. In Austria, extensive media coverage linking Chancellor Sebastian Kurz with bribery and embezzlement allegations forced him to quit in October 2021.

As this makes clear, on a very basic level, journalism and politics influence each other. Journalism is a precondition for democratic governing. Without reliable and trustworthy information about the political and social context, crises, political issues, and public problems, governmental and political actors, advocacy organizations, and citizens will find it harder to prioritize policy agendas, make decisions, and collaboratively solve problems. Indeed, without journalism, it is hard for a society to know itself in an immediate way. Journalism serves as one key social intermediary, aggregating the voices and grievances in a society and reflecting them back to that society in a way that makes politics possible. Citizens also need journalism to hold those in power accountable, to unveil scandals and corruption, or to draw attention to a lack of responsiveness to the people's needs – and compel action from those in authority.

Much research has focused on how journalists perform three essential functions in political life: gatekeeping, agenda setting, and framing. And while these functions and how they are carried out may have changed in the era of platforms (Entman & Usher 2018), they remain important and deserve our attention here.

Gatekeeping refers to the power of journalists to make important decisions shaping what publics know about the world, and what they do not know. The simple reason is that, every day, more things are happening than journalists can (and should) report about. Time is limited (and in earlier eras, space was too!), so they guard the "gates" to what a society gives its attention to, and determine what remains outside of public attention. In other words, gatekeeping "describes the powerful process through which events are covered by the mass media, explaining how and why certain information either passes through gates or is closed off from media attention" (Shoemaker & Vos 2009: 1).

Gatekeeping is a very useful process. Journalists reduce the amount of information pouring into public consciousness every day by selecting the most important things worthy and deserving of public attention, while (ideally) also keeping the junk, nonsense, and "bullshit" (Frankfurt 2009) out – or as Bimber and Gil de Zuñiga (2020) call it, they perform "epistemic editing." In the platform era, there are many more actors involved in gatekeeping – including trusted but non-institutional curators of news and information on social media (such as influencers, or opinion leaders with a specific domain of expertise). Meraz and Papacharissi (2016) call this "networked" gatekeeping. Australian scholar Axel Bruns (2005, updated in 2018) has also argued that, in the internet era, the secondary practice of *gatewatching* has emerged. This means that not only do (mainstream media) journalists select the information that is passed on to the public, other journalists, citizen journalists, bloggers, and social media users monitor the output of the prominent media outlets, taking up, criticizing, commenting on, extending, or sharing their coverage.

Agenda setting is about the choices and selections that journalists make, and how these affect public opinion. Agenda setting refers to the relationships between salient issues in the media (topics covered by and perceived as important by journalists) and salient issues in politics (topics in the public's mind or on the political agenda, i.e. perceived as important by the political elite). Coleman et al. (2008: 167) argue that "Agenda setting is the process of the mass media presenting certain issues frequently and prominently with the result that large segments of the public come to perceive those issues as more important than others. Simply put, the more coverage an issue receives, the more important it is to people."

Agenda setting is one of the essential concepts in journalism studies and political communication. Over the past decades, the theory has become more expansive, with researchers detailing "intermedia agenda setting" (transferring perceptions about the most salient issues from elite media to other media) and "second-level agenda setting" (where media do not just provide salience to issues, they define the salient attributes of those issues). Whereas *framing* offers media users a framework for interpreting a piece of news or information, second-level agenda setting highlights the specific characteristics of a piece of information. Also, agenda setting is about quantity – how often and how noticeably the media report about an issue, fashioning it onto the "agenda" of the public or political actors. Agenda setting impacts how media users think about politics and the world, including shaping perceptions of what issues are more important than others, and what problems politicians should more urgently deal with. The rise of platforms has afforded networked forms of agenda setting, for example when social media posts (such as trending Twitter topics) challenge authoritarian agenda setting by the state and state media (Fu & Chau 2014), or when issues circulate between Twitter and broadcast news (Su & Borah 2019).

Framing is among the most frequently used concepts in political communication research. Broadly, framing is not necessarily about *what* is being communicated (Adams & Kreiss 2021), but about *how* a story is told, how information is presented in a context for understanding it (Scheufele & Iyengar 2014; also see Scheufele 1999). One of the most influential scholars in framing research, Robert Entman (1993: 52), argues that to frame "is to select some aspects of a perceived reality and make them more salient in a communicating text, in such a way as to promote a particular problem definition, causal interpretation, moral evaluation and/or treatment recommendations for the item described." Frames: (1) define problems; (2) diagnose causes; (3) make moral judgements; and (4) suggest remedies. Entman also points to the power of framing, as frames "determine whether most people notice and how they understand and remember a problem, as well as how they evaluate and choose to act upon it" (Entman 1993: 54).

Think about a protest, for instance. Reporting about the protest could focus on the issues at stake (civil rights, or climate change) or it could present the protesters as troublemakers who cause traffic congestion and garbage in the streets. Indeed, research has shown that mass media tend to cover protests with hostile, negative framing (e.g. Gruber 2023), especially when protesters are members of non-dominant groups (Harlow et al. 2017, 2020). Or think about migration as a social issue. Journalists can write about migration as an opportunity for society (more diversity, bigger workforce) or as a threat to society (integration problems, pressure on welfare systems).

These examples all illustrate frames. More recently, scholars have shown that framing also happens on social media platforms across a much more diverse array of actors than in the mass media era. For example, prominent or popular users can become elevated to elite status within their network and shape reality perceptions through "networked" framing (Meraz & Papacharissi 2016), or frame "contestation" that challenges dominant frames (Knüpfer & Entman 2018; Knüpfer et al. 2022).

Journalists gatekeep, agenda-set, and frame political information, which are three key and interlocking ways they shape public opinion: (1) selecting the information that gets access to a mass audience (and the information that remains unnoticed) through gatekeeping; (2) then covering selected issues frequently, and thereby attributing salience and urgency to them through agenda setting; (3) and, finally, framing issues, which shapes how the public understands them.

The rise of platforms has reshaped this power of journalism. Journalists are still performing all these functions – they select information and make decisions about how often and with what frames they report about them – but now they are not alone anymore in doing so. They have lost the privilege of being the only – or even the central, in some cases – actors in a position that allows them to control access to mass audiences and diverse publics. Journalism can now be circumvented, and new gatekeepers and agenda setters such as popular "influencers" on social media have entered the stage – as have a wider range of "journalists," such as partisan and ideological actors. Teenagers streaming TikTok videos from their homes can have larger audiences than journalists, activists cover and report about their own protest events, and politicians use social media to directly converse with their voters and, quite importantly, also gain the attention and set the agendas and frames of journalists.

5.4 Journalism's Relationship with "Fake News"

As more actors have entered media ecosystems, in recent years researchers have documented and analyzed the growing rise of "fake news" ecosystems, "pseudo" information (Kim & Gil de Zúñiga 2020), and "pseudo journalism" (Egelhofer & Lecheler 2019). While the term "fake news" is capacious, it is worth addressing here. On one level, "fake news" refers to what researchers have identified as literally false information, and outlets that, despite the apparent markings of journalism, use sensationalized information, half-true or ambiguous claims, misinformation, or propaganda to mislead or deceive an audience, often for political or economic gain. At the same time, "fake news" is a term that has become weaponized in the hands of political elites looking to undermine journalistic accountability by casting legitimate news organizations and accurate reporting as "fake" (Polletta & Callahan 2019). Scholars are also increasingly concerned about hyper-partisan journalism (Heft et al. 2020; Rae 2021; Wischnewski et al. 2021). Writing in the US context, Mahone and Napoli (2020: n.p.) define it as "partisan media masquerading as state and local reporting and identify 400 partisan media outlets – often funded and operated by government officials, political candidates, PACs (political action committees), and political party operatives."

While scholars have pointed to many legitimate concerns with respect to the news media ecosystem, strategic political actors also use claims for "alternative facts" or notions about a "post-truth" era to sidestep being held accountable by making facts relative, negotiable, and subjective (Ladd & Podkul 2019; Waisbord 2018). While we discuss disinformation in greater detail in Chapter 10, here it is worth noting that journalists throughout the world have responded to growing challenges to knowledge-producing institutions and their profession through the fact-checking movement. Fact-checking takes a clear stance toward evaluating (not just reporting on) the claims of political leaders through independent verification and analysis (e.g. Walter et al. 2020). This is the embrace of factual and authoritative reporting explicitly designed to hold the powerful to account.

5.5 Journalists' Relationship to Their Publics

Knowledge about journalism and how the news is made is not only key to distinguishing high-quality news from "fake news," pseudo-journalism, and disinformation, it also plays an important role in how people select news sources. As Schulz et al. (2022: 18) found:

> Using online survey data from five Western countries, we find that higher news media knowledge – that is, knowledge about how the news is made – is positively associated with using social media as a source of news, but negatively associated with using it as the primary or only source of news. In other words, those who know more about how the news is made understand that social media can be a useful part of a wider news media repertoire, but also that it is sensible to combine it with other sources of information.

This is important, because journalists face a number of crises in their relationships with publics across the world. Even in countries where there are robust freedoms for the press, and protections for expression more generally, journalism faces other crises (see García-Avilés 2021; Nielsen 2016; Russial et al. 2015; Strömbäck et al. 2020; Williams 2017). This includes economic crises and a well-documented decline in public confidence and trust in journalists (Reuters Institute for the Study of Journalism 2022), especially amid heightened political attacks on journalists. Even still, scholars have also cautioned against universalizing these crises in journalism. Calling the debate about these crises "protracted and tedious," Mutsvairo et al. (2021) argue that obsession with globalizing crises in journalism fails to give credit to parts of the Global South where journalism is flourishing, including India and some parts of Africa and Latin America. Even when and where there are crises, they aren't always the same globally.

That said, declines in public confidence and trust in, and the politicization of, journalism in many countries are related in part to shifts in media and technology. Digitization has fundamentally changed how journalism operates in countries around the world, thanks largely to new mechanisms guiding the production of content online. User-generated content sits alongside citizen journalism, meaning that sources of information are harder to determine for publics. Technology has rapidly changed the ways in which journalism operates, for example in enabling new speed and efficiency, distribution mechanisms, and forms of public opinion, with potential consequences for public trust (see Braun 2013; McGregor 2019; Usher 2016). And, even as today's journalists require new skills to navigate terrains shaped by technologies, including social media platforms, journalism has faced new economic pressures and the nationalization of politics in countries such as the US, that run alongside shifts to digital advertising. Amid a loss of local and regional news in the US and parts of western Europe (but not in countries that better protect their journalism industries, especially through press subsidies), powerful national and global media outlets have taken their place, leading to a journalism of the elite and for the elite (Usher 2021).

Let's consider a few examples. The affordances of platforms impact the work of journalists in many ways that might result in shifts in professional values. A notorious example is "clickbait journalism" (Munger 2020). While catchy headlines in big letters have a long history in journalism – think of newspaper boys and girls and their cries of "extra, extra" to sell copies in the streets (DiGirolamo 2019; Linford 2022), or the exaggerated and sometimes entirely fabricated headlines in the yellow or tabloid press – digital media have helped change what a news audience is and how to get attention (Bosah 2018; Molina et al. 2021). In the era of print and broadcast journalism that dominated much of the twentieth century, publishers, reporters, and editors had a pretty precise idea of their standing audience size and composition. But when news competes for attention on platforms, and when business models move from standing subscriptions to ad-driven click-through rates, the headlines and teasers of stories become even more important than before (Hindman 2018).

Enter "clickbait," a communication strategy that presents information in a "curiosity-arousing way that entices readers to click on the referring article" (Lischka & Garz 2021). This approach to stories and headlines is widely used by *everyone*, from established media outlets, online news sites such as Buzzfeed, and tabloids to pseudo-journalistic or hyper-partisan sites. One reason publishers of all stripes have adopted this strategy is because it often works. Studies show that it is very common for users to share content on social media platforms without reading beyond the headline or teaser, including without even clicking on the content before sharing (Gabielkov et al. 2016). In 2020, Twitter even tried to mitigate this behavior by nudging users to read before sharing a link (Hern 2020).

For journalists, clickbait can be both beneficial in the short run for well-resourced outlets (such as increasing the number of clicks, thus enlarging audiences and raising income) and harmful (because it may pose a risk to credibility and reputation.) Indeed, studies have shown that tabloid-style coverage reduces public perceptions of journalistic credibility (Ladd 2012). Perhaps because of this, research shows that journalism outlets try to limit clickbait and balance its benefits and disadvantages. For example, Lischka and Garz's (2021) analysis of 37 German legacy news outlets and their articles posted on Twitter and Facebook showed that clickbait content was not frequent ("between 2% to 28% [of posts] on Facebook and 1% to 3% on Twitter"), with large variation among news outlets in terms of their production of clickbait. They also showed that a "moderate level of clickbait performs better than low or high levels." Thus clickbait journalism serves as an example of how some journalism outlets may "play" with the affordances of platforms and user behavior, adapting to hybrid information ecosystems and seeking to maximize attention and reach, while trying to preserve their credibility and reputation.

As detailed above, the availability of platforms has allowed a much wider range of voices to participate in the political matters that are important to them. This leaves many people, particularly those living in non-democratic societies or who were otherwise excluded from public spheres, feeling a sense of empowerment. Traditionally, journalists were the only ones sufficiently privileged to produce, write, and disseminate news. Non-democratic regimes knew that, once they silenced journalists, it was easier to stay in power. Meanwhile, for groups that did not gain access to the professional press, their issues and concerns often remained far from the political agenda.

Fast-forward to the twenty-first century and dynamics have changed considerably (Broersma 2022; Heinrich 2012). For one thing, journalism is no longer the primary informational actor working to hold political leaders accountable, and can work in tandem with digital activism. For example, Sudan's Omar Al Bashir castigated social media-organized protests and vowed they would not remove him from power. However, large-scale protests, helped in part by information-sharing among activists and journalists, played a large role in his military-led ousting in April 2019.

Journalism clearly still has a big role to play in the age of platforms, especially in amplifying some issues (Boydstun 2013) and voices and putting them in front of audiences such as elected officials, political candidates, other journalists, non-governmental organizations, bodies such as the United Nations, and foreign governments. Journalism remains an important source of the political credibility of candidates and the standing of those who are elected to serve. Astute politicians know how important it is to have a good relationship with journalists, because it can help to make or break their careers. News produced by journalists – including what they elevate and amplify from social media – is still critical in helping to focus public attention, signaling what is important, providing reliable daily sources of information, and representing the public to political leaders. Journalism helps shape the ideas we debate, and the realities and ends of political participation in many societies. News produced and shared by social media activists and publics and citizen journalists (Allan & Hintz 2019), then amplified by the professional legacy press, helps shape public opinion. It also influences what becomes the subject of governmental attention and the policymaking efforts of political parties.

5.6 Business Models for Journalism in the Platform Era

As detailed above, the profession of journalism in many countries around the world faces challenges as it battles falling revenues, in part the result of changing media technologies, consumer habits, and advertising models. Business models provide plans through which companies identify sources of revenue. Media outlets around the world have increasingly had to diversify their revenue streams in order to survive. Traditionally, the business model of journalism (for commercial, as opposed to public, outlets) rested on three streams of revenue: commercial advertisements, classified advertising, and subscriptions (for print). The advertising revenues of television journalism and newspapers had long been falling in many countries since the 1970s with the growth of cable media systems and increased media choice.

Classified advertising subsequently increasingly migrated online with the advent of the Internet, websites such as Craigslist, and specialized platforms like eBay, Airbnb, or Tinder. Companies such as Google and Meta capture large shares of audiences' time, attention, and dollars – with advertisers following suit. And subscriptions for many media outlets have been faltering, as citizens in many countries became used to free content on news sites, stopped seeking out news websites in favor of "news finds me" on social media platforms (Gil de Zúñiga et al. 2017), developed an overwhelming impression of information abundance (Bergström & Belfrage 2018), or otherwise struggled with financial hardship (although the extent these phenomena exist in countries is highly variable – see Reuters Institute for the Study of Journalism 2022). For example, of the 20 markets surveyed by the Reuters *Digital News Report 2022* (Reuters Institute for the Study of Journalism 2022: 19), an average of only 17 percent of citizens had paid money for online news, the highest share in Norway (41 percent), the lowest in the United Kingdom (9 percent).

Thus, changes in technology, business, and audiences disrupted the ways legacy media outlets had gained revenues for decades, forcing many to seek survival strategies (Marín-Sanchiz et al. 2021). In response, a number of outlets experimented with digital innovation (Pavlik 2022). Van der Beek et al. (2005) long predicted that paid content and paywalls would dominate the future of journalism, a reality we are now living to see. Some media outlets, such as Buzzfeed in the US, as detailed above, embraced clickbait headlines to build massive audiences (Lischka & Garz 2021). Others, such as the *New York Times*, embraced events and grew into vast, multimedia empires producing an array of email newsletters, podcasts, and specialized content like puzzles and cooking and athletic lifestyle brands – alongside its legacy newspaper. Others experimented with the form of journalism itself – such as US-based Axios's "smart brevity." At the same time, globally, writers turned to email newsletters to create individually monetized relationships with readers who subscribed. In some countries, governments doubled down on press subsidies to keep struggling outlets afloat (even as governmental support for media has been declining in many countries in Europe over the last few years) (Neff & Pickard 2021).

Other journalism outlets have begun to work more closely with the communities they serve. Glaser (2020) cites *Cable*, based in Bristol, UK, which has been transformed into a cooperative, allowing members to chip in with funding, earning themselves a say on major decisions associated with the publication. Some start-ups and newspapers and other outlets are embracing being non-profit entities, as an alternative business model. In many countries, non-profits have no obligation to pay tax, given their public mission. This includes the *Salt Lake Tribune* and *Chicago Reader* newspapers, which have become non-profit ventures (Glaser 2020). Rourke (2019) points to innovative techniques that reward readers for their loyalty, noting that "In India, Times Internet Limited rewards the reader with Timepoints for reading articles, watching videos, commenting and sharing posts, that can later be redeemed in attractive options such as travel, food, fashion and lifestyle." Community-based participatory initiatives using blockchain-based technology platforms is another way of working toward sustainability and survival for the media industry (see Voinea 2019). Some believe the blockchain, defined by Erkkilä (2018: 3) as "a technology that records transactions in a way that is distributed, immutable and openly available to anyone," has the potential to bring more transparency to journalism (Ivancsics 2019).

Donation-based journalism has increasingly become visible as well. Crowdfunding has become an additional (in most cases, not the only) stream of revenue.

The advantages are clear: many small donations support the creation of specific content, not a whole organization, and offer an easy way to amass revenue. This enables journalists to also assess how much public interest a potential story raises before working on and publishing it (Aitamurto 2019). Prominent examples of crowd-funded news outlets include deCorrespondent in the Netherlands (since 2013) and the Kyiv Independent (2022), Ukraine's English-language media outlet "created by journalists who were fired from the Kyiv Post for defending editorial independence" against its owner, who attempted to take over control of the newsroom. After only three months of existence, the Kyiv Independent became the key source for international readers about the Russian invasion in Ukraine in 2022. During that time, the Kyiv Independent raised 1.6 million pounds sterling on GoFundMe from 27,000 individual donations (as of August 1, 2022).

As advertising and subscription dollars get more competitive, public policymaking is often contested by monied interests. In a clash of media titans, recent measures to force Facebook to pay for media publisher content in Australia resulted in the American social networking giant blocking Australian users from sharing or viewing content on its platform (Isaac et al. 2021). Even though a deal to restore news on Facebook was reached, these policy actions and debates reveal underlying contests between media industry incumbents and platforms over news and information markets, and the ways in which attempts at public regulation ultimately involve making tough decisions to adjudicate the rival claims of different powerful actors. Now that Facebook has agreed to pay for content in Australia (Leaver 2021), many are keen to see whether other countries such as Canada, or those in the European Union, will develop similar legislation.

Journalism faces a difficult future, as Franklin (2011) predicted. For journalism outlets to receive philanthropic capital, government or community support, or revenue from paying customers, it is essential for journalism entities to maintain and enhance their credibility and reputation (Franklin & Carlson 2011). Trust is central to ensuring the sustainable future of journalism (Knudsen et al. 2021).

5.7 Data Journalism

As stated earlier, the loss of confidence in journalism is widespread and has diverse sources. One potential solution to this challenge has taken shape under the banner of "data journalism," which its adherents put forward both as an innovative way to keep citizens informed and as a new business strategy. The idea of data journalism is old. Ideas of the uptake of computers in reporting date from the 1970s, and with advances in computing, networked technologies, and processing power, there has been an explosion of interest in new forms of reporting (Meyer 2002).

In the digital age, journalism has taken on new quantitative dimensions. Scholars have described this variously as data journalism, computational journalism, and computer-assisted reporting (Coddington 2015). Definitions vary, but for the introductory purpose of this book, it suffices to say that "data journalism" is both a process and a product, which involves "gathering, cleaning, organizing, analyzing, visualizing, and publishing data to support the creation of acts of journalism" (Howard 2014: 4). In other words, data journalism involves finding and telling stories with and through data. Among examples of how data journalism provides new insights are the many dashboards on news portals that visualize complex issues, such as Covid-19 statistics or election campaigns on social media (Westlund & Hermida 2021) – not to mention the huge growth of audience analytics that shape which stories are reported on, how journalists frame them, and how they are presented to the public (Cushion et al. 2017; Nelson 2021; Nguyen & Lugo-Acando 2016).

Journalists have always used "data" in various forms, of course (Anderson 2018). Data includes both quantitative data, or numerical data on things such as public health statistics, and qualitative data, such as interviews. That said, increasingly journalists have turned to a new array of tools to produce quantitative data on social life and processes, such as platform apps and cloud computing for gathering and analyzing vast datasets. Data has also changed the role of technology and technicians in the practice and profession of journalism (see Weber & Kosterich 2018). Information technology experts are no longer aides and trouble-shooters, secondary positions to help journalists cope with technology. They are key players in the production of news. At its best, data journalism enables journalists to tell stories in new ways, mustering statistics and large-scale datasets to provide things such as graphic visualizations of the spread of Covid-19 in Asia and deaths from gun violence in the United States.

At the same time, we have to be cautious. The myth of "objective data" has been repeatedly debunked (e.g. Hong 2020). Data are not neutral collections of facts and figures, but constructs, results of operationalizations (translating messy concepts into quantifiable observations), and approximations. Data are uncertain, complicated, and representational in the sense that they are snapshots of the world, not the world itself. Data are always imperfect and must be put into relation with theories, analysis, and other data (Hong 2020). Even more, for data journalism to make high-quality contributions to public discourse, journalists need access to quality data and the resources and the skills to process it and understand and critique both data and results. Thus, data journalism is a very specialized field that is not available to all media outlets. For example, local newspapers only very rarely have the financial means or human capital to engage in data journalism.

SPOTLIGHTED CASE

One prominent example of data journalism is the international journalism collaboration around the Panama Papers, which the International Consortium of Investigative Journalists (ICIJ) described on its official website as a "giant leak of more than 11.5 million financial and legal records" which exposed "a system that enables crime, corruption and wrongdoing, hidden by secretive offshore companies" (ICIJ 2021a). ICIJ unveiled the Pandora Papers in October 2021, which exposed powerful politicians, celebrities, billionaires, and businessmen who held secretive offshore accounts (ICIJ 2021b). Using tools and techniques of computational analysis, journalists made sense of leaked data, identified the relevant stories in these massive data dumps, and told the world the stories hidden in the data. Indeed, data cannot speak for itself. Publishing the data itself does not hold the powerful accountable – journalists strive to understand, interpret, create narratives for, and visualize data in order to transform it into information and knowledge for news audiences.

5.8 Algorithmic Journalism

Like many fields in digital societies, journalism has become entangled with technology in many ways. While data journalism involves new forms of working with quantitative data and visualization techniques, algorithmic journalism refers to automation in content production and/or algorithmic optimization of content distribution. Algorithmic curation in search engines, news feeds, and on social media platforms has enabled people to better personalize the information they see (Zamith 2019).

There are four main areas of algorithmic journalism: automated content production, data mining, news dissemination, and content optimization (Kotenidis & Veglis 2021). Automated content production refers to the use of algorithms to actually *write* the news. Based on natural language generation (NLG), a form of artificial intelligence, an increasing number of media outlets use technologies to produce text for news that is rather simple and repetitive, such as weather or earthquake reports, stock-exchange news, or the coverage of sports events.

This approach to news is controversial. On the one hand, outsourcing routine tasks to automation is extremely fast and efficient. And it saves money – important, given that many newsrooms have faced painful budget cuts. It also frees journalists, pressed for time and resources, to focus on complex and substantial issues. On the down side, however, critics have voiced concerns about potential job loss for journalists, the risk of misinformation through incorrect data, and the potential watering down of journalism itself, moving it away from a craft toward an industrial assembly line of news (Latar 2018; Firat 2019). That said, journalists themselves see it as a supplement, not a replacement, for their work (Schapals & Porlezza 2020). These scholars found that journalists still see "journalism as a creative process; journalism as a uniquely individual craft; as well as the need to add background and context in order for recipients to contextualize information accordingly" (2020: 24).

The other aspects of algorithmic journalism are less controversial but still have important implications for the press and public life. Data mining, central to data journalism, refers to how the availability of data has made entirely new ways of reporting possible. Algorithms are now fundamental to the dissemination of news (Thurman et al. 2021) – this includes how journalism websites display content based not only on journalistic assessments of news value, but also on engagement, likes, and shares (to say nothing of the platform algorithms that shape how news is disseminated). Finally, content optimization refers to the ways that news organizations use algorithms to make design and display choices – including the choice of headlines and format of pages – that increase the probability people click, consume, and share content.

In *Automating the News*, Nick Diakopoulos argues that the future lies in the collaboration and co-evolution of technology, journalism, and society: "As the frontiers of what is possible to accomplish with automation, algorithms, and hybrid systems continue to expand, human journalists will still have a lot to add when it comes to complex communication, expert thinking, and ethical judgment" (2019: 40). After all, it is humans who create and maintain the algorithms and the work practices around them, even as evolving institutions and technologies change how journalism is practiced.

5.9 Summary

In this chapter, we have identified the theoretical and practical role of journalism in society, and detailed why journalism means different things in different societies. We discussed some of the roles and functions of journalism, as well as its relationship to democracy and the ethics of the profession. We also showed how journalism institutions take up new technologies, and are in turn transformed by them – with implications for the content journalists produce, the dissemination of news and media, and the creation and maintenance of publics.

Journalism takes root in many different societies and political systems – from democracies to one-party states. While we focused on the former here, it is worth noting that journalism is still practiced in countries that have great restrictions on the freedoms of the press and expression. Indeed, journalism in these countries often involves negotiations with state authorities, detailed restrictions on what can be reported and how, and normatively the privileging of state stability and social solidarity over accountability, free inquiry, and representing the public. As such, there are deeply contextual differences between global *journalisms* (such as in the United States versus postcolonial regions of the Global South).

Discussion Questions

- The rise of platforms, and the Internet more generally, have thoroughly disrupted the traditional business models for journalism. Why is it so complicated to find new business models to make journalism profitable in the age of platforms?
- Artificial intelligence and technologies for automated text generation are emerging at breathtaking speed (e.g. OpenAI's ChatGPT). How will they transform journalism?

Suggestions for Further Reading

Diakopoulos, N. (2019) *Automating the News*. Cambridge, MA: Harvard University Press.

Hanitzsch, T., Hanusch, F., Ramaprasad, J., & De Beer, A. S. (2019) *Worlds of Journalism: Journalistic Cultures around the Globe*. New York: Columbia University Press.

Scott, M., Wright, K., & Bunce, M. (2022) *Humanitarian Journalists Covering Crises from a Boundary Zone*. London: Routledge.

Usher, N. (2021) *News for the Rich, White, and Blue: How Place and Power Distort American Journalism*. New York: Columbia University Press.

Wahl-Jorgensen, K., Hintz, A., Dencik, L., & Bennett, L. (eds.) (2020) *Journalism, Citizenship and Surveillance Society*. London: Routledge.

6 Platforms and Strategic Political Communication

Chapter 6 introduces readers to strategic communication, which includes a wide array of things, including political marketing, advertising, public relations, lobbying, and public diplomacy. We discuss the history of these practices in Western democracies along with their theoretical and ethical underpinnings, and detail how platforms have changed strategic communication. In this chapter, we cover everything strategic that is not directly related to elections and movements. While election campaigns and movements are strategic communication, too, they each get their own chapter (Chapters 7 and 8, respectively).

OBJECTIVES

By the end of this chapter, you should be able to:

- give an overview of strategic political communication in the platform era
- have deep knowledge about strategic communication and changes in public opinion
- understand political marketing
- provide an assessment of public relations and public diplomacy
- explain concepts such as crisis communication
- discuss digital lobbying.

6.1 Introduction

Strategic political communication is as old as humanity itself. People have always sought to craft stories, make appeals, persuade and mobilize others, and otherwise forge forms of collectivity and solidarity to create and pursue some shared ends. Any attempt to legitimize a ruler or party or political system, persuade citizens about a political issue, convince advocacy organizations about a policy, or contest the meanings or understandings of actions or statements that concern public matters – or matters someone wants to make public – is strategic political communication.

By "strategic," we mean that there has to be intent behind the communication, whether it is to legitimate, persuade, convince, contest, or secure power in line with some pre-established political, social, or communicative goal. The idea of "strategy" requires whoever is doing the communicating – whether it is governments, campaigns, political leaders, non-governmental organizations, or citizens – to have something they want to achieve. This is different from processes like "deliberation," where the goal is to arrive at a shared set of ends in a mutual, or general, interest. Strategic communication might seek top convince people of shared ends and general interests, or it might be in the service of self-interest, personal ends, or achieving power over others. Strategic communication deserves its own chapter in this book because it goes *far* beyond election campaigns, which we focus on in Chapter 7.

This chapter concerns the broad spectrum of political actors – such as parties, regulatory agencies, social movements, elected leaders, and governments – who define goals and develop and pursue communicative strategies and tactics to achieve them. Advocacy groups, lobbyists, citizens, activists, local administrations, and even guerilla groups engage in strategic political communication. They vary in what they want to achieve, the means they employ to achieve their goals, how public their communication is, and even what they can legitimately do communicatively. Not all strategic communication takes place in the public eye, and communicators do not always seek to leverage the attention of the mainstream public to achieve their goals. Lobbyists, for instance, will often avoid public attention, especially if what they promote is unpopular or ill reputed. Lobbyists working for the tobacco or arms industries, for instance, often prefer direct connections with politicians rather than public campaigns in order to influence policymaking or avoid state regulation. Political groups may use public attention to build political pressure on decision-makers, presenting their goals as pressing issues for the common good (e.g. climate activists) or calling for immediate action around specific events that violate moral orders (e.g. protesters against police violence). Other groups might make more narrow appeals to identity groups to pursue or secure power (e.g. religious factions).

In other words, the nature of the goals and the type of actor shape what, how, when, and why actors engage in strategic communications – as do the broader sets of cultural meanings that provide structure and order to societies (see Adams & Kreiss 2021). In the twenty-first century in countries around the world, strategic political communication can take many, many forms. That said, strategic communication of many different stripes often takes shape through media. Indeed, the construction of monuments and the architecture of governmental buildings are media and forms of strategic political communication constructed to legitimate rule and enhance the power of office (J. D. Peters 2016; Sonnevend 2016). However, in this chapter, we focus on the changing nature of strategic communication in an era of digital media and technology platforms. This includes the ways in which public relations, political marketing, political advertising, and public diplomacy are taking on new casts as struggles to influence public opinion and journalism and even political debate are now increasingly conducted online.

6.2 Strategic Communication and Public Opinion in the Platform Era

Strategic communication is ultimately about persuasion. In the absence of coercion by force – and in lieu of other forms of political authority (such as religious authority) – democracies are generally premised on non-coercive forms of political consent. Securing political consent happens through contests to represent the public in a variety of elected offices; the need for legislators and regulators to (at least appear to) be responsive to public opinion; the expectation that government offices, the courts, and public officials have a degree of transparency and accountability for actions; and the hope that those governing will be responsive to public demands. And, in the platform era, this includes many new demands from the public for transparency from and accountability over a wide range of political, social, and commercial actors. Ultimately, these are ideals. In reality, in many democratic countries, elections are shaped by money and partisanship, leaders and legislatures are imperfectly sensitive to public policy preferences, and offices are unevenly transparent and accountable (e.g. Hacker & Pierson 2020). Different countries have taken varying approaches to dealing with these issues, including through creating agonistic (i.e. adversarial) monitory systems made up of many different actors (Keane 2018), but all democracies share a common orientation toward the need for much of everyday governance to be premised on consent, not force.

As such, strategic communication is central to democracy. In the course of governance, political actors need to *justify* their actions to the public, explain why they took the actions that they did, and defend them – and increasingly that means taking to social media. In democratic contests, such as elections, rivals have to make a case for why they are best positioned to represent the public and protect civic life, and why their opponent is not (Dayan & Katz 1992). And when political actors are accused of doing something wrong, or making a mistake, they have to defend themselves from institutions and actors seeking to hold them accountable (Alexander 2011). All of this is premised on strategic communication – the attempt to shape audiences' perceptions of public events and issues (Couldry et al. 2009; Scannell 1995).

The central battleground for strategic communication is public opinion, which is increasingly shaped, represented, and fought over on digital and social media platforms. At the heart of strategic communication, and professional practices such as public relations, is often a foundational concern with public opinion – representing it, strategically invoking it, or changing it (Strömbäck & Kiousis 2019). Public opinion can be a complicated and confusing concept (see our extended discussion in Chapter 4), but broadly we use it here to mean the representation of the attitudes or beliefs of some group of non-elite people.

A quick recap. Public opinion is about "the pictures in our heads," as Walter Lippman put it in his path-breaking book in 1922. Public opinion carries the internal paradox of being about both the individual opinions of citizens and their averaging to be a "public." Public opinion can be produced and represented for many ends: to predict election results, craft policies that are responsive to people's needs, estimate the (un)popularity of politicians and political decisions, reveal how citizens perceive other countries and their country's relations with them – in addition to many other things. The quality of these measurements depends on the empirical methods and how well they are applied. For instance, is a survey or an opinion poll representative of the population whose attitudes it seeks to measure? Does it create valid results – meaning can the questions asked actually indicate what they seek to measure?

Let us take a look at a few things. First, generally "public opinion" does not apply to institutions or elites. For that, we use phrases such as "elite opinion" (also the object of strategic communication – see Tedesco 2019) or focus specifically on what elites and institutions state or generally believe. At the same time, we are concerned with the *representation* of public opinion. As we argued above, *all* public opinion is represented in some way (e.g. Law 2009). Think of a survey about public attitudes toward climate change. The questions that researchers ask are what creates public opinion; the public's attitudes and beliefs did not manifest themselves independently from the survey. Even if some public got together and wrote a collective statement among its members, it would still be a representation of what that public believes because it selectively involves choices. In practice, many, many political actors create representations of public opinion (e.g. Herbst 1998) – journalists when they write on behalf of the public, lobbyists when they urge policymakers to pass a piece of legislation, political candidates when they make claims as to what publics want, and social movements when they chant "The people united will never be defeated."

To take this point further, because it is central to understanding strategic communication: public opinion is indelibly linked to the ways we have of representing it. Think, for instance, about how we know about what publics think, what their opinions are. Publics cannot tell us these things on their own. Opinions have to be represented in various ways. Historically, polling and surveys have been important ways of representing public opinion – those ranges of attention to issues, attitudes, beliefs, values, and priorities that some statistically represented publics hold (Igo 2007). There are many, many other ways of understanding public opinion though. Legislators often understand public opinion through the lens of what lobbyists and advocacy and interest groups bring to their attention. Journalists represent public opinion for elites and publics themselves through the production of their stories. Social media, in turn, have become key domains where actors create and represent public opinion (McGregor 2019). Platforms give rise to forms of public opinion through their affordances – the way that they create and organize certain forms of sociality and communication. They also represent public opinion in certain ways, such as through the analytics they provide to political practitioners (Kreiss & McGregor 2019). This is why platforms are central to strategic communication – and a central focus of parties, campaigns, candidates, and political leaders that are vying for power.

Strategic communication is the practice of influencing public opinion, but also of creating publics for strategic ends (Aronczyk 2013; Aronczyk & Powers 2010; Cronin 2018). Much of the work of strategic political communicators involves transforming formerly private individuals or associations into publics, and helping to create and define their interests. To take an example, environmentalists often appeal to consumers to make more sustainable lifestyle choices. When consumers do so, they are acting *politically* as a public in accord with a public issue (i.e. sustainability). Publics can also exist and endure over time – think of the ways in which organized religious groups argue for their values and interests, and advance a set of policy claims, sometimes over decades, as defined publics (Morehouse 2021). Often this persistence is premised on institutions, organizations, and media that support publics, provide them with resources and definition, and give shape to and represent their interests in consistent ways (Aronczyk & Espinoza 2021). Indeed, as we noted earlier, publics are often *made* through communication. This occurs whenever people are persuaded to recognize a shared interest with political implications and to come and work together to define goals and advance their aims, or when people are drawn to causes and engage in them socially and symbolically (Pacher 2018).

Strategic communication, then, is centrally concerned with the making, convening, mobilizing, persuading, maintenance, or manipulation of publics, and is intimately tied to the media systems it takes shape in. As a professional practice pursued by an identifiable and specialized group of people, it dates from the early 1900s in countries such as the United States, the result of growth in administrative and bureaucratic states and population growth, which made communication relating to politics and governance more complicated (Greenberg 2016). This was further facilitated by the growth of mass communication technologies throughout the course of the twentieth century in many Western democracies, and the increasing professionalization and institutionalization of journalism, as well as the marketing industry (Carlson et al. 2021). These developments meant that communication with publics took place across increasingly differentiated media with their own genres of communication, even as things such as the journalistic "beat system" (routine dimensions and areas of society that journalists cover, such as crime, business, the prime minister) meant reporting that standardized a number of events, occasions, and roles for political communicators.

While the core need to get messages to the public, or otherwise influence it in significant ways, is old, stragtegic communication took on increasingly specialized and mediated roles throughout the course of the twentieth century. For example, professional commercial advertising in the early twentieth century profoundly influenced the conduct of public affairs (Fowler et al. 2021a). In countries such as the US in the 1950s and 1960s, advertising was increasingly being based on psychological research, and with the widespread use of television a whole new world of potential advertising channels had emerged (Fowler et al. 2021a; Kaid & Johnston 2001). From the 1970s on, political advertisers and direct marketers developed an increasingly sophisticated suite of data-based tools to appeal to publics – such as direct mail, cable television advertising, and later the Internet and platforms (Baldwin-Philippi 2019).

There has long been debate and concern over the effects of these things. Initially, many policymakers, scholars, and experts believed that mass media heavily influenced what people thought. Take the myth about people fleeing in panic after the radio broadcast of Orson Welles's famous fictional news tale of alien invasion "War of the Worlds" in 1938. Or so the story goes – there is little evidence that anyone had panicked at all (Schwartz 2015). This myth resonated among journalists and publics deeply concerned with Nazi propaganda in the 1930s and 1940s. Many believed (then and now) that advertisements and other forms of strategic political communication are able to get directly into people's heads and manipulate their behavior – not so different than the "moral panics" about Cambridge Analytica after the Brexit referendum and the 2016 US election (see Jamieson 2020).

At the same time, research always painted a much more complicated picture than people as simple dupes of media messages (Neuman 2014). Research consistently shows how people are embedded in social networks that influence them, for instance, and engage in "motivated reasoning" to continue to believe in things that are already consistent with their identities, values, and beliefs (Vegetti & Mancosu 2020).

6.3 Strategic Communication in the Platform Era

If strategic communication is *old*, the contexts in which it takes place today are not. In fact, strategic communication has grown much more complicated in the past two decades. This is related to both technological and media change, as well as the social and professional practices of strategic communication that take shape on platforms. For much of the twentieth century in countries around the world, for instance, the media that strategic communication was practiced on were truly *mass*. This meant large-scale print publications (such as newspapers and magazines), radio, and television. What made them mass is that they reached large, generally geographically differentiated, publics. Of course, there have always been small-scale media, including petitions, fliers, pamphlets, newsletters, local broadcasters, and local-circulation or trade and industry group newspapers and magazines that created, sustained, or communicated between smaller-scale publics. And there have always been mass-circulation media that speak to ideologically distinct, partisan, and other identity group audiences, especially in countries with media systems that map onto the composition of groups in society. That said, mass, undifferentiated media became a central, if not dominant, feature of many countries over the course of the twentieth century, and the professional practice of specialized strategic communication reflected that.

With mass media, the construction of audiences was generally routinized (Davis 2002; Maloney & McGrath 2021). Professional journalists regularly produced news stories in standardized and consistent ways. Beat systems meant that, even if journalists did not know what the next day's news would be, they knew where to find it: at centers of government power such as legislatures, courts, executive offices, and police headquarters. Representatives of these agencies, as strategic communicators, subsidize news by providing information to journalists, while also seeking to represent their institutions in a strategically favorable light. Politicians developed press apparatuses – communications directors, press secretaries, etc. – to both communicate with their constituents and portray their actions in favorable ways. Organizations such as trade associations, advocacy organizations, and interest groups developed their own press operations and built regular ties with journalists in order to educate them on policy issues and have media coverage represent their preferred positions favorably.

These mass media systems did not disappear so much as newer media, and especially digital media, got layered onto them. This means media systems are "hybrid" and juxtapose newer and older technologies. This layering means a few things of relevance for strategic communication.

First, it means the increasing speed of information in political life. Many countries have moved from daily, 24-hour news cycles to "always on" news cycles that never really end, given continual, and fast, flows of information (Elmer et al. 2012). Second, it means the proliferation of publics and complex flows of political information. As we have documented throughout this book, while professional journalism remains important for organizing audiences and publics in public affairs, alongside this is the seemingly endless profusion of new groups and audiences sustained through communication, which give shape to social life (Bennett 2021; Entman & Usher 2018). This includes groups on Facebook organized around demographic or affiliational interests, network flows of political information built around social ties, curated flows and groups built around interest and identity, and "affective publics" shaped by emotional flows of communication (Papacharissi 2015).

Third, it has led to a profusion of professional and non-professional communicators. The Internet, and platforms especially, have dramatically lowered the cost and capital required to produce political information and speak to publics. This has had sweeping implications. This shift has allowed entirely new publishers to enter the market for political information – often with unclear journalistic or other editorial standards, hyper-partisan and interest group orientations, or organized around ideology and identity (Tandoc 2019). Meanwhile, it has opened political communication to a vast new array of people who were formerly effectively denied the opportunity to address publics, especially those far from the seats of power (Richardson 2019). Fourth, and related, with the dramatically lowered costs of communication has also come the rise of individuals and public collectives as key actors in political communication. This includes the ways in which newly communicatively empowered audiences have organized social movements, engaged in digital witnessing to hold power to account, and produced routine representations of politics (Chouliaraki 2015).

All of which has meant that public opinion – always a constructed phenomenon – has grown increasingly fragmented and diverse and represented in many different ways. All of these changes have meant a much more challenging strategic communications environment to navigate, but it has also created new opportunities to influence publics.

To start with, there are always *goals* for strategic communication campaigns. And these goals are often shaped by the even larger goals that a political organization has. To provide some examples, goals can entail many things, depending on the political actor (whether it is a non-governmental organization, a social movement, a political party, or anyone or anything else in between) and the context in which strategic communications take shape. For public health communicators, for instance, the public health goal might be to persuade people to get vaccinated during the Covid-19 pandemic, and the strategic communications goal might be to counter misinformation about the safety of vaccines or to develop pro-social messaging so people engage in protective health measures.

Political communicators might also have the goal of influencing smaller audiences that are influential in particular ways. Lobbyists who seek to influence legislation, for instance, might have the strategic communications goals of changing the minds of key legislators around their issues, or cultivating journalists to shape coverage in a way that pressures legislatures to vote a certain way, or collaborating with Instagram influencers or bloggers. Political strategic communicators often share the goal of introducing new ideas into policy or public debates – for example, about the very issues that we should be concerned about and what we should do about them (or not do). Or strategic communicators' goals can be to contest the dominant frames we have for talking about particular issues, such as whether climate change is a matter of public health or long-term economic stability, a humanitarian crisis or a natural one. The outcomes of framing contests often lead to particular definitions of the problem and influence the solutions posed to solve them (Knüpfer & Entman 2018).

SPOTLIGHTED CONTENT

Strategic communicators often have a goal of creating distinctions between groups, for their own gain. The goal here is to create *difference*. Political elites tell stories: stories about their nations' histories, the types of people who live within them and should live within them, the groups that they will represent, and the relationships between their citizens and the outside world.

As this shows, political elites work to strategically create and invoke political identities in order to pursue their objectives and goals. These "stories of peoplehood" (Smith 2003) are fundamental to politics, which is at its heart about the relationships between groups in societies – who has power (economic, cultural, social, political) and who *should* have power, and which ways of exercising authority and accountability in states are legitimate. The distinctions that political and social elites draw are fundamental to political communication and nations.

Think, for instance, about all the political conflicts over refugees and immigration that have wracked many Western democracies in the past 20 years (Benson 2013; Chavez 2001). Strategic communicators with different partisan and ideological perspectives have contrasting goals around communicating national identity: from a more restrictive, culturally homogeneous state, especially on the political right, to a more inclusive, expansive, and multicultural vision, especially on the political left. In the routine course of political events, strategic communicators fit their tactics into these larger narratives about what countries are and should be – with the goal of convincing publics of the rightness of their approach. These are, at heart, debates over who is granted citizenship, and who should be. For example, countries such as the United States, throughout its very short history as a multi-ethnic democracy, have been consumed with debates over difference and social and political power. Previously, the US had long secured, as a matter of law and of social norms, unequal power relations based on racial and ethnic categories of citizens. Meanwhile, European powers with their extensive colonial histories not only justified their global conquests through the lens of religious and racial and ethnic difference, they also created deep social-difference fissures in the countries they colonized, legacies that remain and structure power today.

The art and practice of making distinctions is not limited to political identities; there are many lines of difference central to the goals of strategic political communicators. They often seek to create symbolic lines of division between themselves and others across any number of dimensions – from interests, ideology, and geography to occupation, policy preferences, and values – to advance their goals and interests and those of the people they claim to represent. Parties create what are matters of public concern, for instance, and, as importantly, define the debates about why these things matter and what to do about them (Aldrich 2011). Parties in parliamentary documentaries stake out their issues and ideologies relationally to others, providing voters with choices at the ballot box based on these distinctions.

In other words, there are numerous goals that political communicators work toward and strategies for communicatively achieving them. In turn, political communicators have a number of different informational tools available, especially in the age of platforms. Broadly, we can think about political advertising (we discuss this in much greater detail in the next chapter and only touch on it here), political marketing, public relations, and, for governmental purposes, public diplomacy. These things have changed dramatically with media change, although at their heart they remain deeply indebted to their emergence during the course of the twentieth century in many Western democracies. They are also premised on *campaigns*, by which we mean sustained strategic political communications activity, often taking shape across multiple media and platforms, directed toward the goals and outcomes communicators seek to achieve. And, at their core, they often involve extensive research and data that inform goals, measure progress toward meeting them and the effectiveness of particular tactics, and enable strategic communicators to adjust tactics and goals in the middle of campaigns.

Let's consider a few domains of strategic communications in greater detail.

6.4 Political Marketing

As we have discussed throughout this book, platforms select for engagement. They seek to keep people using platforms in order to monetize their attention and time. This means that platforms incentivize the most engaging content that political organizations and groups promote on social media – which is often the most extreme, emotional, identity-based, or ideologically consistent. Central to understanding political marketing is recognizing that platforms are not neutral means of distributing political content, they *shape* that content in particular ways by creating incentives for political actors. And these incentives are often aligned with what is best for platforms economically.

These dynamics reveal how platforms are now central to "political marketing." By political marketing, we mean all attempts by political communicators to promote their policies or ideas, change public opinion, secure political office or political power, or shape public debate, policymaking, or governance more broadly. This is an expansive set of activities! They reflect the fact that, over the course of the twentieth century, strategic communications have grown much more central to governance and electioneering in many democracies, as theories, methods, and tools from commercial marketing have permeated political communication (Henneberg & Ormrod 2013; Lees-Marshment 2012). And, even more, they reflect the fact that there are many different political actors that are routinely engaged in strategic communications, from candidates and parties to advocacy organizations and interest groups. All of these entities engage in strategic communications, and platforms are newly central to just about everything that these groups do.

As with strategic communications more generally, political marketing proceeds from a set of goals that look different depending on the organization that is engaging in the political marketing campaign. These goals could span everything from persuading an electorate to vote for a particular candidate or endorse an issue in a referendum to changing public opinion on an issue about state spending or addressing climate change or public health measures. Political actors can use political marketing in the attempt to build support for a specific bill in a legislature, create accountability over a powerful institution such as the police or a regulatory agency, or change the minds of a small group of powerful legislators or party leaders on an important issue.

These different goals, in turn, give rise to different strategies or tactics. Marketing is a *holistic* approach to positioning some candidate, cause, organization, or party in relation to others in a field in a way that strategically furthers the organization's goals. This involves: (1) consideration of the organization's goals; (2) the field of allies and adversaries; (3) analysis of the state of play; and (4) the strengths and weaknesses of the organization symbolically and resource-wise. Political marketing involves a strategic approach to symbolically positioning the organization, in the attempt to convince some set of publics of things that further its progress toward its goals. And, to do so, strategic communicators use a rich set of tools from advertising to branding, from leveraging influencers to speeches by party leaders.

With their goals in mind, political communicators figure out whom they need and want to persuade, how best to reach and appeal to them, and what sorts of communication will likely be the most effective, and at which times. They also think expansively about how to create new publics, identities, or issues that help them advance their goals. Political marketing involves the development of a coherent set of narratives and messages, designed to achieve determined goals, delivered to some set of audiences, through an expansive set of communicative tactics.

Let's break this down. By "coherent set of narratives and messages," we mean that there is a *unified theme or set of themes* even if there are different types of communication or messages that convey them. There might not be any one theme to a campaign or cause (there might be a few, after all), but they are not infinite and should not be contradictory. This is important. Campaigns and causes *must* define themselves at some fundamental level, and this means making distinctions – this candidate is for *this* and against *that*; this cause means that *this* will happen and *that* will be prevented. Candidates and causes can entail a few different things, but in general these things should be coherent and they should be limited – research suggests that messages that have clearly identifiable core elements are the most successful at persuasion and garnering attention (Green 2021).

Of course, political life is more complicated than this. Politicians often avoid taking strong stances on issues, or are strategically ambiguous in their public pronouncements. They do so to give themselves maximum flexibility to respond to evolving situations, or to preserve the widest base of potential support. While this may work for a time, these are always decisions that come with the risk of being first defined by adversaries seeking to create their own distinctions. They might be criticized, if not for the policy positions themselves, then for being weak, noncommittal, indecisive, or pandering.

The choice of a theme or themes behind a candidacy or a cause reflects the *goal*. If the aim is to get a candidate elected, then that is the goal, and the choice of theme is shaped by a clear understanding of what needs to be accomplished (i.e. a majority of votes) and how best to accomplish it. For an election, this means accounting for such things as pre-existing public opinion, partisanship, political culture, and events in the world. For causes, this means an analysis of existing public sentiment, the field of adversaries and their interests and incentives, and targets and opportunities to persuade them.

By "delivered to some set of audiences," we mean a crucial part of the political marketing process. "Audiences" refers to campaigns and causes having a sense – however vague – of whom they need to reach and how best to reach them. One of the key shifts of the platform era is that we have many, many, many more vehicles for reaching publics than were ever imaginable before. Indeed, we have many new publics themselves – take, for example, communities built around interest and affinity, such as fan communities, or activism on platforms. Political marketers might make their fundamental appeals to journalists, seeking to influence coverage and raise public awareness of a candidate or issue. Or they might leverage journalism as a representation of public opinion as a way to pressure lawmakers to take action on some issue. They might reach out to fan communities directly through influencers, or make appeals for people to adopt the symbols of a candidate or cause as their own identity and spread it within their social networks (Penney 2017). They might stage high-profile actions in certain legislators' districts, take certain positions in ways that create allies or build coalitions, or work to shape public sentiment on social media as a means to influence the digital staffers of legislators.

All of this reveals the vast array of communication tactics now deployed in political life. From television appearances to staged events that influence journalists' coverage, from the performative use of Twitter to shape social media sentiment to the branding of causes in ways that convey partisan and social identities, from digital political advertising to TikTok posts – campaigns and causes think holistically about the communicative tools they have in the context of the goals they attempt to achieve. Political marketing, then, is the science and art of taking all of these things into account when determining what communications are most likely going to help political actors achieve their goals. These communicative tactics include messaging and framing, as well as the strategic presentation of campaigns and causes through branding – the process of creating cultural and social meanings around political symbols.

6.5 Public Relations and Public Diplomacy

Broadly, public relations (often falling under the broad label of "communications," or just "comms," for political practitioners) concerns the strategic work of creating and maintaining a positive public image for a political organization, campaign, cause, or candidate (Saffer et al. 2013). Often this is done through the creation and maintenance of relationships with key stakeholders – journalists, opinion leaders, influencers, various publics, etc. Communications professionals take into account the broad range of tools that they have at their disposal to achieve their goals. Some of these tools are very well established, such as press briefings, press conferences, and press releases that seek to set journalists' agendas and the frames they use to discuss politics. Public relations also includes the often extensive behind-the-scenes press work that goes into cultivating relationships with journalists and educating them about public issues or trying to influence patterns of coverage in a strategic way. And communications professionals also work to create public or other appearances for their campaigns or causes, including on television shows, coordinate speeches by key stakeholders, and plan rallies and events that seek to engage with members of the public and gain positive press attention.

In the platform era, there has been an increasing array of ways in which public relations professionals utilize new communicative capacities in the service of creating and fostering a positive public image for their candidates, campaigns, organizations, and causes. For example, press releases are now rarely just for journalists. The contemporary press release gets reworked across many different platforms (to fit with different genres of communication in accord with audience expectations) to appeal to wider publics, including networks of supporters who can engage with and share this content on social media.

Consider a politician who is running for office on a strong environmental platform and who wants to make a case for their candidacy in the aftermath of a natural disaster. Public relations professionals would issue press releases to journalists that detail the candidate's response to the disaster, attribute potential causes of the disaster, and propose potential solutions so it would not happen again or a district could be better prepared. Often, the details of these press releases would also be versioned on Facebook and Twitter and sent out through email. These campaign professionals would also proactively reach out to journalists to educate them on the issue. The politician might also hold an event and invite members of the press, elected officials, and the public to attend – this would happen through both emails directly to individual stakeholders, and promotions on platforms such as Facebook and Twitter. They might want to ask people to RSVP, in the process capturing emails that can then be added to build a list of media, supporters, etc. At the event, the politician speaks (itself a form of strategic communication) and that potentially shapes how the press understands the issue and coverage of it – in addition to the understandings people themselves have and post about on social media.

The politician's digital communications team then shares photos of the event on platforms such as Instagram and Facebook, quotes the politician's words on Twitter, and posts videos on YouTube (there are intricate gender dynamics at play in this – female politicians receive more "Likes" when they are visible in a picture, for instance [Brands et al. 2021]). The campaign hopes that supporters share this text and video within their own social networks, vastly expanding the reach of the communications, especially to those less attentive to politics, in the hopes they might be inadvertently exposed to political information (Scheffauer et al. 2021). Indeed, there is a shift in consumption habits, from a time when viewers had few options to turn away from mass media, ensuring *inadvertent audiences* (Prior 2007) for content, to the *viewer-choice era* (Lau et al. 2021) we are in today, marked by lots of choice in what, when, where, and how much viewers consume media.

Even this understates the possibilities for communication during the platform era and the many, many new possibilities public relations professionals have to cultivate relationships with stakeholders and burnish the public images of their campaigns and causes. While materials such as press releases and press packets have long been established as a genre, think about all the possibilities for platform communication – as well as how rapidly platforms themselves change. Posting on Facebook can include graphics and video or some combination of both, or videos can be streamed live (and archived) on YouTube. Campaigns can release a sequence of content across platforms that potentially reaches millions, including journalists. Tweets can be threaded to provide a more contextual view of events, and Instagram stories can provide more narrative stories. TikTok can reach millions with innovative content that animates political stories (Literat & Kligler-Vilenchik 2023). Meanwhile, the various forms of data provided by these platforms mean that the effectiveness of public relations strategies can be revealed in real time, such as sentiment analysis, shaping future messaging strategy through understandings of what worked and what did not.

Taking public relations to an international level, "public diplomacy" refers to state strategic communications to the populations of foreign countries or international audiences, which have as their intent to influence the attitudes of targets and put political pressure on foreign governments (Manor 2019). Public diplomacy can also be used for "nation-branding" to positively shape a country's image and reputation for audiences in other countries, including for economic reasons (Miño & Austin 2022). To pursue these goals, many countries broadcast television or radio shows in other nations, including in different languages – Russia Today is an infamous case in point, but also Germany's Deutsche Welle, Al Jazeera, the US's Voice of America, and the BBC's World Service, which reactivated two short-wave channels in Ukraine after the Russian invasion in 2022.

In the digital age, bots and state-affiliated troll farms (Howard et al. 2018) – most famously the Russian Internet Research Agency's attempt to influence elections or referendums around the world – have provided prominent cases of state-level attempts to influence public and electoral dynamics in other countries. These are simply the most extreme examples of what are often routine forms of engagement by many countries around the world that see strategic advantage in wielding informational dynamics to their advantage. The quarterly transparency reports by major platforms such as Facebook, Google, and Twitter, for instance, provide substantial evidence of state-backed networks attempting the malicious manipulation of foreign publics – and these reports are obviously limited to the cases detected and sanctioned by the platforms.

There are also more routine ways in which digitalization has influenced and transformed public diplomacy. Digitalization refers to "the way many domains of social life are restructured around digital communication and media infrastructures" (Brennen & Kreiss 2016). Diplomats, foreign ministers, and embassies have turned to social media for their external communications, and to some extent even for their internal communication. Ilan Manor (2019) gives the example of UN ambassadors using WhatsApp groups to coordinate their votes and resolutions, or nations using images for "selfie diplomacy." A key impact has also been that digital platforms opened the opportunity to speak to international audiences, and national ones, for a wider range of actors including NGOs, small activist groups, and even terrorist groups.

Thinking of extreme examples, we should take a look at strategic communication and public diplomacy in times of war, as both (or sometimes several) sides seek to frame war to their advantage. You may be familiar with the proverb that the first casualty is the truth when war breaks out. This reflects the level of strategic communication by parties in a conflict, and the fight over whose interpretations of events will prevail. Is the war legitimate? Is it a war, or just a special military operation? Who is to blame? Is it an act of aggression or self-defense? How many lies can be counted? Who is the victor; who lost the war?

In a digital environment, however, it is not only governments, professional media, and military actors who participate in the game of presenting, interpreting, and telling their version of events, but also civil society groups, individual stakeholders, networks of activists and partisans, and even celebrities.

SPOTLIGHTED CASE

Arnold Schwarzenegger posted a video addressed to the Russian people on Twitter on March 17, 2022, during the war in Ukraine. In the video, the Hollywood star and former governor of California first speaks about his connections with and his love for Russia, about his fond childhood memories of meeting a Russian weightlifter, and his own father's trauma as a soldier in World War II. He then tells his (presumed Russian) audience that they have been misinformed about the war and violence going on in Ukraine. He appeals to Russian soldiers to not get physically and mentally broken like his father by becoming guilty of war crimes, indirectly asking them to desert. It is a brilliant example of persuasive communication, employing psychological techniques to gain the trust of the audience and break their resilience against a message they might not want to hear. Interestingly, he also addresses Vladimir Putin directly – after all, @Schwarzenegger was one of only 22 accounts followed by the official Russian president's Twitter account, @KremlinRussia_E.

6.6 Crisis Communication

Crisis communication "can be defined as the strategic use of words and actions to manage information and meaning during the crisis process" (Coombs 2018). The idea of a "crisis process" refers to the fact that a crisis has several phases, each of which may require different approaches to strategic communication. Take, for instance, the crisis of a global pandemic, such as Covid-19. At its very core, it was a health crisis, forcing governments around the globe to take actions that affected the freedom of their citizens, such as imposing lockdowns or vaccine mandates. As the pandemic evolved and means of mitigation were developed, like tests and vaccines, the crisis communication of governments also changed. Because science delivered new knowledge frequently, the messages and measures needed to be adapted, and even sometimes reversed. This is very challenging for strategic communicators, because in such cases communications cannot be consistent, they need to reflect the current stage of an ever evolving situation and must take into account new insights into the crisis.

Among examples are the mask mandates that were differentially embraced in countries around the world. While most scientists believed at the beginning of the pandemic that masks would not help much, they became a key measure of limiting health risk in many countries later on, and governments the world over had to explain changes in policy to their citizens. In short: A crisis makes one of the most central requirements of strategic communication difficult: a consistent message. Crises "are fluid, and communicative demands can change as the crisis morphs" (Coombs 2018).

Even more, a massive crisis such as a pandemic does not remain a health crisis, but affects other parts of society as well. The Covid-19 pandemic soon led to economic crises in many countries, with steep increases in unemployment and precarious work; public education crises with home-schooling and closed schools; many social crises, such as increases in domestic violence, isolation, and depression among the most vulnerable groups in society; and certainly political crises, as governments struggled to find the right balance between public health and individual freedom. Each of these crises required their own communication strategies, adding to the complexity of governmental and stakeholder response.

Another aspect of crisis communication relates to organizational crises, when companies, NGOs, or government agencies face scandals and losses in reputation and trust. Crisis communicators have a number of different communicative strategies at their disposal to respond to reputational threats based on attributions of responsibility for crises. Depending on whether the organization is cast as the victim or the perpetrator, the effective response frames are well established, ranging from attacking accusers, finding scapegoats, and making excuses or justifications to accepting responsibility and offering changes and accountability (Coombs 2018). In the middle of an unfolding crisis, communicators have to be responsive to in-the-moment flows of information and the unfolding of public opinion on platforms such as Twitter, which they desperately try to stay on top of and even direct to shape public understanding and response to the crisis. This includes issuing tweets and statements with crisis responses while monitoring real-time public and stakeholder opinion and attempting to shape it. Depending on the crisis and culpability, organizations might use social media to self-disclose information, apologize, and seek to remedy the situation.

In other words, social media create new contexts for political crisis communications. In a meta-analysis of over 100 scholarly articles about effective social media crisis communication, Mats Eriksson (2018: 526) found five key tactics: "(1) exploiting social media's potential to create dialogue and to choose the right message, source and timing; (2) performing pre crisis work and developing an understanding of the social media logic; (3) using social media monitoring; (4) continuing to prioritize traditional media in crisis situations; and finally, (5) just using social media in strategic crisis communication." The latter can actually be a game-changer due to the speed of communication and the possibilities it opens to get a message out or respond to events, for instance during natural disasters, such as the devastating Italian earthquakes in 2016 (Splendiani & Capriello 2022).

SPOTLIGHTED CASE

Ukrainian President Volodymyr Zelensky took to Twitter to rally the support of Western democracies in the face of Russia's invasion of his country in February 2022. His message was simple: We are here, the government is staying, and working, and democracies have a responsibility to defend one of their own. He shared video messages on platforms and with new media, and appealed to foreign parliaments and governments via Twitter, successfully seeking support and to gain agency and symbolic power over the framing of the events.

6.7 Digital Lobbying

"Lobbying" refers to attempts to influence policymaking without being directly involved in the process (e.g. Hoffman 2015). As such, it takes place on an intermediary level – between stakeholder groups and those in political power. There are many forms of lobbying, but, as a professional occupation, lobbyists put forward the interests of the advocacy groups or industries who pay them to do so. They make their political networks and persuasive talents available to these groups, and represent their clients' interests or grievances to politicians in power.

Historically, the term "lobbying" reflects the intermingling of powerful people and members of parliament in hotel lobbies, antehalls of parliament buildings, or smoke-filled backrooms, where they cut deals and bargains away from the public eye. Indeed, lobbying is often considered a sinister, bad practice undermining the democratic process and policymaking for the common good. However, democracies thrive on pluralism – the coexistence of a plurality of particular interests that compete and conflict with one another in a marketplace of ideas. Thus, it is a fundamental right in democratic societies to petition decision-makers on behalf of the interest of one's group or community. Lobbyists also provide information, expertise, and connections around the issues and groups they represent, as a resource to politicians. In most democracies, lobbying is legally regulated, and usually lobbyist organizations or individual lobbyists register as such in parliaments. In fact, lobbying is quite pervasive in democracies. In the US, for example, the money spent on lobbying Congress and federal agencies has roughly doubled since 1998 ($3.7 billion US in 2022), while the number of active lobbyists remained about the same (Opensecrets 2022).

There are lobbyists on both (or many) sides of issues. Think of lobbyists who work for pro-life versus pro-choice groups, or those who represent public health organizations versus the producers of tobacco products and their employees. Traditionally, lobbying is a form of interpersonal communication, but it can be mediatized as well. Lobbying rarely seeks directly to mobilize large crowds, such as at rallies, demonstrations, or protests (although these things can be used in tandem with lobbying efforts to pressure targets). However, lobbyists can use platforms to get into close contact with their target audiences – politicians.

For example, with the advent of platforms, the costs of lobbying – defined expansively here in terms of direct appeals to policymakers – decreased, making it easier for small interest groups or communities to contact politicians directly. After all, not everyone can afford to pay a professional lobbyist, but platforms have made it much easier to approach politicians directly, not via a paid lobbyist, to get their attention.

One case to illustrate this is the "We are more than numbers" campaign of Norwegian mothers of chronically ill children in 2017, which Tine Ustad Figenschou and Kjersti Thorbjørnsrud (2020) analyzed in an interview-based study. Protesting against a proposal to reduce the welfare income of these families, a network of mothers posted "heart-wrenching public letters" on the Facebook pages of the country's prime minister and health and social ministers. A small ad hoc network of mothers engaged in personalized, emotional, and authentic storytelling, taking selfies at the bedsides of their children and providing first-hand accounts of their grievances. They targeted politicians directly by posting on their Facebook pages and tagging them in posts, but also strategically aimed for user engagement and, consequently, media coverage: "It sounds harsh, but sick children 'sell.' It is perhaps our strongest card because we can share our stories and others share theirs. This way we have managed to create massive engagement, likes and shares ... It evokes strong emotions because it is unfair and affects young, helpless, innocent children – who cannot stand up for themselves" (Ustad Figenschou & Thorbjørnsrud 2020: 174). The authors conclude that, while it was powerful, it also confronts the mothers with moral dilemmas such as invading the privacy of their children, and challenges them to negotiate their own roles as parents and as lay activists.

In their analysis of the logics of digital advocacy, Håkan Johannson and Gabriella Scaramuzzino (2019) argue that social media platforms opened up a new way of lobbying – not only seeking political influence, but building up political presence. Traditionally, lobbying meant negotiating directly with politicians. Now, digital media enable advocacy groups to establish themselves as political actors by demonstrating and amplifying their connections with politicians: "While a logic of influence presupposes a key message, a logic of presence is oriented towards promoting 'who you are' rather than 'what you stand for'" (2019: 1542).

6.8 Summary

In this chapter, we have seen how capacious strategic political communication can be in the time of platforms. In an era when press releases to journalists have become real-time tweets, strategic political communicators must be comparatively "always on," attuned to the dynamics of public opinion. They must be able and willing to respond to developments and issues on sites such as Twitter, and use many different strategies, tactics, media, and platforms to get their message out and shape journalistic coverage for strategic ends. And they must have the flexibility to realize their goals during complex unfolding events and in response to many different types of contestation. They do so with many new tools at their disposal, including paid platform communications to reach new audiences, and strategic platform influence campaigns to pressure powerful targets.

Discussion Questions

- What are the differences between strategic communication and political communication?
- Strategic communication is essentially about persuasion. How is persuasion on platforms different from persuasion through broadcasting?

Suggestions for Further Reading

Figenschou, T. U. & Fredheim, N. A. (2020) "Interest groups on social media: four forms of networked advocacy," *Journal of Public Affairs* 20(2): 1–8.

Holtzhausen, D. & Zerfass, A. (eds.) (2015) *The Routledge Handbook of Strategic Communication*. New York: Routledge.

Jamieson, K. H. (2017) *The Oxford Handbook of Political Communication*. Oxford University Press.

Lilleker, D., Coman, I. A., Gregor, M., & Novelli, E. (2021) *Political Communication and COVID-19: Governance and Rhetoric in Times of Crisis*. London: Routledge.

Strömbäck, J. & Kiousis, S. (eds.) (2019) *Political Public Relations: Concepts, Principles, and Applications*. New York: Routledge.

7 Platforms, Campaigns, and Campaigning

Chapter 7 focuses on how political actors in democracies contest and rally support during elections and referendums, including how they inform and mobilize supporters or de-mobilize supporters of their political opponents. Studies have repeatedly shown that political communication during these campaign periods is decisively different from "normal," non-electoral times. How political actors campaign depends very much on contextual factors, such as the dynamics of the political systems and media systems they take shape within. As we show, digital platforms have disrupted and transformed campaigning, moving us into an era of data-driven, personalized styles of campaigning.

OBJECTIVES

By the end of this chapter, you should be able to:

- provide an overview of platforms and elections
- explain the four ages of campaigning
- describe the relationship between elections and electoral systems
- discuss what role platforms play in elections
- understand campaign strategies, including gaining attention, interaction, persuasion, and mobilization
- understand trends in campaigning on platforms.

7.1 Introduction

In November 2020, a scandalous case of voter fraud rattled New Zealand. Election officials detected stuffed ballot-boxes – 1,500 presumably fraudulent ballots coming in from fake email addresses with the same IP address. Luckily, it was not an election for parliament or prime minister, but for the annual Bird of the Year contest. In New Zealand, this is a big thing – with campaigns and canvassing to mobilize the 55,000 voters who participate, and with politicians and celebrities endorsing their favorite bird candidates. In the end, the Kākāpō, a "fat flightless" and nocturnal parrot (Picheta 2020), won over the Little Spotted Kiwi to the surprise of many: "Outraged bird-lovers cried fowl on Twitter, calling it a 'total farce,' a 'stolen election,' as well as more colorful and unprintable terms," as the BBC reported (BBC 2021). There was a long history of controversy in this particular contest. In 2018, data scientists in charge of securing the election spotted and deleted 360 dubious votes, and in 2019 there was suspicion of Russian meddling – which eventually turned out to be legitimate votes from Russian bird lovers (that year, the Hoiho, a "beautiful but antisocial penguin," as the *Guardian* noted, won [Graham-McLay 2019]).

This perhaps humorous case illustrates a few important points. First, that campaigns and elections – in politics and elsewhere – must follow formal, institutionalized procedures to produce legitimate results that are generally accepted (including by defeated parties and their supporters), especially when things get messy. And, second, that campaigning is often affective and emotional (see Ridout & Searles 2011).

Democratic elections are among the most important institutions that humans have developed because they enable people to select their rulers and replace sitting ones in a non-violent way. Elections mean that power is only given to rulers for a defined, limited period of time, and that rulers can be held accountable for their actions at the ballot box. However, not all elections are *democratic* elections – free, fair, recurrent, and with transparent and legitimate results. And even fewer take place under conditions that secure the expressive rights of voters. For example, in many countries around the world, elections are recurrently held but serve only as a fig leaf to cover and legitimize authoritarian rule.

In this chapter, we focus on platforms and how they have shaped campaigns in democratic elections. We take up how political parties and candidates seek to gain the attention of, persuade, and mobilize voters – or dissuade and demobilize their competitor's supporters. Democratic regimes vary considerably when it comes to the stability and quality of their institutions, and there are many forms of quasi-democratic, hybrid, and non-democratic regimes. Democracies come into being, thrive, or suffer in conflict, and they can die. The very same is true for *the* key democratic institution: elections that mark the peaceful transfer of power. As the core mechanism of democracy, elections can be challenged, undermined, and manipulated. Research on democratic backsliding has shown that older forms of illegitimate power grabs, like coup d'états, have generally given way to legal attempts to undermine the peaceful transfer of power, such as the unaccountable expansion of executive power (see Erdogan in Turkey, or Orbán in Hungary) (Pirro & Stanley 2021), extra-legal harassment of the opposition, and the strategic manipulation of elections (Bermeo 2016).

Electoral accountability can be undermined through strategic claims that elections are not free and fair, or that the opposition is not legitimate or presents an existential threat to ways of life. Elites are *the* crucial actors in this. History has shown time and again that what political leaders and parties do is absolutely crucial for safeguarding, or undermining, electoral processes and the peaceful transfer of power. This is why so many democracies are under strain today. The stability of a democratic regime rests, in large part, on the belief of its leaders (Rosenblum 2010) and citizens (Bermeo 2016) that democracy is the best (or the least evil) political system. And they must have faith in playing the electoral game in the future – that they can lose today but still have the opportunity to win tomorrow and that the other side will honor this commitment. As such, parties and partisans must respect the outcome of elections even if their preferred party or candidate lost. If political adversaries become sworn enemies, elections are an Achilles heel for democratic legitimacy and a vulnerable target for demagogues. Once people lose their belief in the rightness of elections, or politicians seek to stoke that belief through cynical claims that seek to undermine perceptions of the safety and security of elections, democracy is in danger.

7.2 Four Ages of Campaigning

Just as video never killed the radio star, platforms are not replacing traditional campaign strategies or communication methods. Parties are still holding rallies, politicians meet-and-greet voters in public places, campaigners knock on people's doors, and parties print flags and T-shirts and give away buttons, lawn signs, and pens. And even though citizens increasingly get news and political information through platforms, mass media are still a key player in campaigns. But how can we account for these different tools and strategies in a more systematic way?

There are several approaches in political communication research to distinguish different "eras" of campaigning – each with their own predominant logic, organizational forms, tools, and strategies. It is important to understand that one era does not completely wipe away the preceding era. Instead, the tools, types of organizations, and strategies that dominate in one era often extend into new ones, although each era is shaped by its own predominant contexts and technologies. Building on Blumler and Kavanaugh's (1999) seminal work on three ages of political communication, we can differentiate four specific eras of *modern* campaigning (for the purposes of space, we focus only here on the twentieth and twenty-first centuries) (Blumler 2016; Kreiss 2016; Magin et al. 2017; Römmele & Gibson 2020; Semetko & Tworzecki 2017). These eras or ages describe what social scientists call "ideal types," not real types. Ideal types are abstractions that allow us to systematically reflect on the main characteristics of a period and what might be changing (or not) – even as, in reality, there is diversity in how parties and candidates mix and match elements from all eras in varying configurations.

Party-Centered Campaigning

This era describes electioneering and campaign tools and strategies based on the political communication that occurred through the strong party apparatuses that provided the organizational basis for much of electoral politics from the latter half of the nineteenth century to the 1950s in many countries of the democratic West – in addition to attendant media such as newspapers and radio. Campaigns generally were planned and coordinated by party leaders and the staffers of these organizations, as were the political messages they espoused. There was also a deeply social aspect of campaigning during this era, where the social identity of being involved in a particular party outweighed many other considerations, such as ideology. Parties also often delivered material rewards – such as jobs – to their partisans.

Mass Media-Centered Campaigning

When television became the dominant medium for entertainment and news in the 1950s and 1960s in many countries around the world, parties started to cater to the mass media in terms of its genres of coverage and the demands of audio/visual journalists.

This meant that parties started to plan their campaigns earlier in cycles, hired professional survey and advertisement experts to help to craft appeals and strategy, and developed their messages along the lines of media logics (such as sensationalism, sound bites, and appeals to the mass public [Rinke 2016]), rather than party logics (such as policy substance and directed communication to insiders and coalition partners as the target audience). This coincided with the growing use of statistical approaches to representing and understanding public opinion, through not only polling but also television ratings. For example, campaigns often sought to reach the mass public through broadcasting sound bites and having their candidates be on television as much as possible, such as debating live on TV.

The longer process of how parties adapted to the logic of mass media, generally called "mediatization," has been studied extensively in the field of political communication (Esser & Strömbäck 2014). This is a concept that Mazzoleni and Schulz (1999) and Strömbäck (2008), among others, have used to capture the transformative relationship between media and politics, particularly in a technologically driven era.

With the Internet and then platforms becoming a main source for news and political information, the next two eras are particularly interesting.

Target-Group-Centered Campaigning

With hundreds of cable and satellite television channels in the post-1970s era in many countries, the increasingly data-driven practice of sending direct mail to targeted groups of voters, as well as the emerging Internet with digital advertising, emails, digital newsletters, and websites, broadcasting messages to the mass public increasingly sat alongside what scholars called "narrowcasting" by the 1990s. No longer content to deliver one, general message for all (or many) citizens, political actors increasingly sought to tailor messages to predefined target groups (based on partisanship, consumer categories, race and ethnicity, religion, geography, social affiliation, etc.). Parties used multiple communication channels and marketing techniques to identify relevant target groups, rather than speaking to large comparatively undifferentiated publics. The larger shift during this time was the increasing importance of data and the technical systems to manage them, which Kreiss (2016) identified as a move toward "technology-intensive" campaigning: where everything campaigns did had an underlying technical, and often data, infrastructure. For example, in order to understand which groups to reach, how to reach them, and what to say, parties in the US developed large data infrastructures and the technical skills to manage and analyze them. This in turn was made more urgent by the increasing fragmentation of public attention across hundreds of media sites and outlets, which in turn meant it was harder to reach people and capture their attention.

Individual-Centered Campaigning

Extending this general trend toward the increasing importance of data in campaigning, the rise of technology and social media platforms – first in the United States and then far beyond its borders from 2008 and after – increasingly enabled parties and their candidates to send more personalized messages to voters by mining, compiling, and integrating data from public, party, and commercial databases and social media platforms, including on the online behavioral and communicative actions and social networks of voters, as well as online surveys and polls. In the US, campaigns increasingly moved to scoring individual citizens' probability of voting particular ways and espousing particular issue positions based on analysis of thousands (or even millions) of data points, and then crafted appeals to them across media (and even face to face at their doorsteps) based on these scores. Political ads were increasingly micro-targeted, not based on predetermined demographic or consumer categories, but based on these scores for groups of voters that shared particular characteristics, attitudes, or propensities. Meanwhile, parties experimented with tens of thousands of tailored messages, and evaluated and adjusted their strategies based on how these messages *performed* – such as tracking shares, likes, donations, comments, email sign-ups, etc., for each (Karpf 2016). A key aspect of individual-centered campaigning on platforms is that *future* messaging is shaped by the responses voters had to prior messages, such as engagements with ads.

We discuss political advertising in much greater detail below as a core campaign strategy in the platform era, but suffice it to say that we can see contemporary digital advertising as the coupling of marketing and data-driven logics, especially in countries with weak privacy regulation protecting citizens' data. Parties also increasingly hire data scientists, so that technology departments are not marginal members of teams, responsible for troubleshooting, but central units for strategizing and optimizing campaigns.

Römmele and Gibson (2020) further divide this fourth phase into two types of campaigning: a scientific type and a subversive type. Whereas the former involves using data science, algorithms, and machine learning as part of an integrated media strategy, the latter kind operates more on dark participation techniques, such as spreading disinformation, weaponizing social media against mass media to portray it as an enemy, and embracing disruptive foreign interference.

It is worth noting, as well, a shift toward explicitly social communication strategies for campaigns – basically, this is how campaigns account for the social embeddedness of individuals. Kreiss (2018) conceptualized this as a mix of data-driven practices combined with the comparatively older, social forms of political engagement common during the strong party era. Penney (2020) refers to the ways in which campaigns strategically look to disseminate messages through the cultivation of volunteers and supporters as forms of "citizen marketing" – and it is on full display in the ways that politically engaged people adopt the identities, symbols, and messaging strategies of parties and candidates on social media platforms. This, in turn, is also a central strategy of efforts at disseminating disinformation and propaganda, which can originate from campaigns and parties and flow through social networks, which we discuss in Chapter 10.

Taken as a whole, the Internet, and especially social media platforms, have substantially changed how campaigns are organized and run, and even who works on them, as parties and candidates have adapted to new technologies, high-choice information environments, and ever more complex political communication ecosystems. However, as our model described in Chapter 2 suggests, these technological effects are conditioned by the political and media systems that platforms are embedded in.

7.3 Platforms and Election Outcomes

Indeed, one thing is clear – elections are not won or lost on social media. It is a myth that former US President Barack Obama was successful in 2008 solely because he made brilliant use of emerging social media platforms, for instance by collecting small dollar donations – or that Donald Trump was elected because he successfully mobilized his supporters on Twitter. These things helped, of course. It is hard to imagine Barack Obama winning his primary against then-Senator Hillary Clinton if it was not for the campaign resources that he was able to garner online outside of formal party channels. That said, *many* factors were equally, if not more, important: television, Democratic Party coalitions, the partisan composition of the electorate during the general election, the economy, etc. Similarly, Donald Trump certainly helped to set the media's agenda through Twitter, which was especially consequential during the Republican primaries (Wells et al. 2020), but a lot of other factors mattered as well, including the fractured nature of the party he was competing in during the primaries and the fact that he was running against the incumbent party during the general election.

In short, the reality is that many factors influence election outcomes – especially structural factors such as the state of the economy and distribution of partisanship within the electorate. That said, campaigning matters, communicatively especially on the margins in shaping the contexts candidates run in and what voters think about when they vote. Campaigns "play the hands that they are dealt" and effective campaign strategies can generally seek to bend public discourse toward issues that are favorable to candidates and parties (e.g. Vavreck 2009), and the identities within the electorate they need to assemble a majority (Kreiss et al. 2020).

SPOTLIGHTED CASE

Barack Obama wielded platforms as a campaign tool in a larger political and social context that granted him opportunities. Obama leveraged the lowered cost of digital fundraising during the primaries to successfully challenge an unpopular party leader for the nomination (Hillary Clinton). During the general election, his campaign used platforms to amplify his message of hope, unity, and moving beyond the financial crisis, as well as to generate campaign resources and coordinate the massive amount of volunteers across the country willing to spend hundreds of hours knocking on doors for him.

Let's take an example. Trump was in the public eye long before the advent of social media (Baym 2019), although he skillfully exploited platforms to build a name for himself around the racist questioning of Obama's birthplace, and used Twitter adeptly to drive press coverage and amplify his messages (Su & Borah 2019). While there has been robust debate, there is only scant evidence that social media engagement directly translates into votes (Jungherr 2013). Even so, social media are impactful. With low barriers to entry and the potential to access large audiences, social media can help to equalize resources between challengers and incumbents, resource-rich and resource-poor candidates, and to level the playing field for smaller, newer parties. This is especially the case for parties that adapt to the affordances and incentives of social media platforms discussed above. At the same time, larger, well-established parties with significant resources can also benefit from digital media, especially given their ability to make large-scale investments in digital expertise and data (there is also evidence that platforms themselves subsidize these things for campaigns in many countries in exchange for advertising dollars [Kreiss & McGregor 2018]).

As revealed in our model, all of these dynamics take shape in particular political and media *contexts*, which is why it is impossible to definitively state the effects of platforms and social media on electoral outcomes! Indeed, research shows that all of these dynamics can take shape simultaneously, even when seemingly contradictory, depending on context (see Schradie 2019). For example, for many well-established parties, social media are extra, additional tools for campaigns – but they might be more constrained in using them, depending on the context, by institutional concerns that require careful coordination across many coalition members. Newcomers and underdogs can benefit from social media, such as the Five Star Movement in Italy, but not always or under all circumstances (political factors such as immigration, the economy, etc., provide differential opportunities to mobilize). Social media can sometimes shape internal party processes, such as nominations, enabling outsiders to gain power, with negative democratic effects (e.g. Trump). But this only happens in the right contexts, such as when parties are fractured – indeed, most research suggests that when institutional elites are aligned, outsiders rarely break through and win nomination contests, even if they get a lot of attention on social media.

In sum, while campaigns are about communication in the sense that candidates have to make appeals to voters to win their votes, many other structural and institutional factors matter for election outcomes as well. Platforms have not changed the fact that money is important for campaigning in many countries or that incumbency status helps electoral fortunes (such as in local elections: Lev-On & Steinfeld 2021). Platforms have not changed the fact that the hard work of going door to door to mobilize voters and making appeals to interest and advocacy groups and party advocates are still central aspects of political life. Even in the platform era, campaign periods are still different from non-electoral periods, marked by governance and policy concerns. The idea that politics would move to an era of permanent campaigning, in which parties and politicians would intensively communicate as if they were electioneering all the time, has been suggested repeatedly since 1982. This has not become a reality, even when social media platforms made it very easy to post a lot, all the time (Ceccobelli 2018; Larsson 2016; Vasko & Trilling 2019).

The sociologist Jennifer Schradie (2019) revealed just a few of the factors that shape how campaigns and advocacy groups take up digital and social media, including ideology, class, resources, organization, skills and practice, and political contexts. In doing so, Schradie moves us beyond narrowly digital-exclusive analyses of collective action focused on information costs, technological affordances, and digital sociality, and toward a much more nuanced analytical framework that accounts for forms of cultural, social, political, and economic capital that afford possibilities for digital action. Taking as her case US state-level politics on the left and right, Schradie shows how, despite the seemingly revolutionary promise of new digital technologies to bring about democratic ends, comparatively older forms of power remain. While a number of scholars have theorized phenomena such as "organizing without organizations" (e.g. Bennett & Segerberg 2013), these emerging forms seem timid in the face of entrenched power and other forms of capital.

Moreover, it goes without saying that there are many different kinds of elections, which also conditions the role of platforms in them. Again, these are features of political systems which shape how political actors use platforms and media. National presidential and parliamentary (or other legislative branch) elections are generally perceived to be the most important by both parties and citizens. Accordingly, parties make comparatively greater investments in these campaigns, and voter turnout is comparatively higher than in local or regional elections. Parties, candidates, and voters know that important issues and outsized political power is at stake in such elections. There are also local, regional, and, in the case of the European Union, transnational elections (Reif & Schmitt 1980). These elections are generally perceived as less important and yield lower voter turnout. Also, not all campaigns and votes are about who holds office. There are referendum campaigns such as the high-profile "Brexit" referendum about whether the UK should exit the European Union in 2016, but also on issues such as taxes or bans on facial coverings, as in Switzerland in 2021.

There are still, unfortunately, relatively few comparative studies of campaigning between countries, over time, or across platforms (Bossetta 2018; Haßler et al. 2021; Klinger et al. 2022a; Yarchi et al. 2021) and even fewer from the Global South (Jaidka et al. 2019). A majority of research in political communication focuses on campaigning in national elections (presidential or parliamentary elections). Comparative, cross-platform studies can analyze how the affordances of platforms impact citizen engagement, such as how the timing of posting and visual content can increase the attention of voters and whether responsive posts – such as when parties react to comments – yield more reactions or are shared and commented on more often (Koc-Michalska et al. 2021). Most studies focus on either Twitter or Facebook (and, thankfully, sometimes both – see Stromer-Galley et al. 2021). Researchers have focused on Twitter because data historically have been more readily available than with other platforms. They have analyzed Facebook because, as detailed above, it is the most popular platform or central to social life in many countries.

Even so, we have a number of key insights from an emerging body of research. In local elections, social media platforms generally play a smaller role than in national elections. That said, local politicians and administrators use social media more when these elections are more competitive, and in larger and wealthier municipalities (Silva et al. 2019). And studies mostly report that local media remain the most important channel of communication (Elvestad & Johannessen 2017) – that is, in regions where local media still exist (Darr et al. 2021). The continued importance of mass media even in the platform era is reflected in the fact that politicians use social media to attack journalists and run against the media (Rossini et al. 2021).

SPOTLIGHTED CASE

In European parliament (EP) elections, all 27 countries of the EU vote, generally on the same day(s) in basically the same institutional setting, to elect a parliament representing 450 million citizens. However, campaigns unfold differently across different media systems and political cultures. Even so, there are a number of commonalities. For example, in past elections (2009, 2014, and 2019), EP campaigns have remained mostly national campaigns, run by national parties on national issues. From a research perspective, the ability to compare campaigning on platforms across countries and over several election cycles is important, because it helps scholars to move beyond single-case studies (e.g. Twitter in Danish elections, or Facebook in Italian elections) and to generalize findings.

7.4 Campaigns and Advertising

Political advertising is a well-established way that candidates in democracies have of getting their messages in front of voters, or in front of other elites, journalists, and opinion leaders whom they seek to influence. In the US, political advertising dates back to when the first campaigns took shape to contest elections during roughly the mid-1800s (Schudson 1999). We focus on the US here because it has historically been the site of developments in political advertising, given its comparatively unregulated system of campaign finance and large size, which makes advertising essential to engaging audiences at scale. And numerous scholars have pointed to the ways in which American innovations often migrate to other political systems, albeit in the new political, media, and institutional contexts that transform them (McKelvey & Piebiak 2018; Negrine & Papathanassopoulos 1996).

By political advertising, we are speaking specifically of a "paid" or otherwise compensated relationship between an advertiser and some medium with access to voters' attention. Basically, advertisers pay to put their messages in front of voters, purchasing their attention. That is the ideal of advertisers – not all messages are noticed by the people advertisers try to reach, of course. Political advertising can also include things such as "in kind" donations of media space to reach audiences.

Political advertising in the United States and other Western democracies grew up alongside the development of commercial, mass-market models of news, especially newspapers, dating from the mid-1800s. As we noted in Chapter 5, when newspapers were generally appendages of political parties, candidates for office did not need to pay to get their messages out. Advertising, in turn, evolved as media did. Newspaper advertisements, for instance, were joined by radio and then television advertisements in the twentieth century. Often, political communicators purchased advertising in the attempt to gain access to large news audiences. Indeed, for much of the twentieth century in countries such as the US, advertising was a key mass-media tool that enabled campaigns and other interests to speak to relatively large, undifferentiated audiences.

As noted above, this focus on large-scale audiences in the United States began to shift in the 1970s through the 1990s with the rise of cable news, talk radio, and then the Internet – all of which offered up comparatively smaller, but potentially more influential (from a political perspective) and lucrative (from a donations standpoint) audiences. With cable news, talk radio, and the Internet serving up more social, ideological, and partisan communities of interest, candidates and causes could speak more narrowly to people most interested in public affairs and journalism. Even better from the standpoint of candidates (but maybe not democracy), with the growth of partisan media offline and online, campaigns could gain the attention of audiences who were already ideologically and politically engaged – and committed! Platforms amplified these trends with their unique coupling of content *and* data. In essence, political campaigns could discern which digital outlets and platforms their supporters or persuadable voters were on with data that were generated about audiences online. Parties and campaigns then merge these data with massive data sets on the electorate to create effective targeting and messaging strategies.

As we discussed above, during the era of platforms there was an explosion of data on members of the electorate – which is at the core of contemporary campaigning in the United States (and is less central, but still important, in other countries with comparatively stronger data protection and privacy laws) (Römmele & Gibson 2020; Kefford et al. 2022). Contemporary campaigns in many Western democracies have become a data- and analytics-intensive activity, whereby political professionals generate and process thousands or even millions of data points on members of the electorate to score them in the attempt to discern which voters to reach, how to reach them, and what to say to them to maximize their chances at electoral success.

That said, as our model specifies, there are significant variations in the uptake and practice of digital advertising depending on the political and regulatory context, even if in countries around the world it is increasingly a data-driven practice. As noted above, countries differ with respect to the data on the electorate that they allow parties and other entities to store and what they permit to be used in campaigning. The US is on the extreme end of the spectrum, with comparatively lax laws governing data privacy and regulating campaign practices – which generally fall under the legally protected category of political speech. In contrast, Germany has stronger laws governing the use of political data and campaign activities. For instance, campaigns are not allowed to combine individual-level data from one source with further information from other databases; data can only be collected if individuals explicitly agree; it is legally prohibited to store data for long periods; and parties must not store data on racial or ethnic origin or political, religious, or philosophical beliefs – restrictions that make micro-targeting or individual-level scoring impossible (Kruschinski & Haller 2017). And, even outside of national-level legal contexts, there are large differences in the use of data and political advertising between federal candidates in many countries – with their comparatively generous funding, large staffs, and large data operations at scale – and regional and local candidates who typically have fewer resources and are more reliant on parties (and, in the US, on commercial consultancies).

That said, there are some clear identifiable trends across many countries. First, the advertising money that is spent on digital media, as opposed to broadcast advertising, has grown exponentially over the past decade in many countries around the world (Fowler et al. 2021b). Second, the growth of digital media and platforms has meant new players shaping political advertising. Facebook (Meta) and Google dominate the market for commercial digital advertising in many countries, and therefore political digital advertising – which also means their policies have outsized effects on how political actors pay to get their speech in front of voters (Barrett 2021). The dominant platforms might be changing as well in an era when streaming services, from Amazon and Netflix to Apple, Disney, and Spotify, begin to take on outsized roles in television and radio markets.

Third, and related, even if political candidates do not bring their own data to the table, platforms can do it for them in many countries around the world – monetizing those voters who will be most likely to engage with advertising, and algorithmically promoting engagement and incentivizing advertising that increases it (Kreiss & McGregor 2018). Fourth, digital political advertising is one part of data-driven campaign strategies more generally, in the sense that campaigns use advertising to learn more about people, build their databases to be able to continually go back to people, and monitor the effectiveness of ads and specific messages – all of which informs other kinds of campaign communication (e.g., policy statements, speeches, rally locations, etc.).

To take a few examples, campaigns in many Western democracies use digital political advertising not only to put messages in front of voters, but to bring them into their databases, capturing email addresses as people click through to do everything from signing birthday cards and petitions to volunteering and donating. Indeed, in the platform era, there are many new opportunities for strategic political communicators to reach and mobilize voters for electoral gain. Political communicators often use digital advertising to identify potential supporters among groups in the electorate, whether they are based on ideology, partisanship, geographic region, demographics, or lifestyle or affinity group interests (made known to campaigns either through their own data or by the targeting affordances of platforms themselves).

SPOTLIGHTED CONTENT

When people click on links in digital ads, they reveal their interest in that campaign or cause. Campaigns can then reach these people again through what is known as "retargeting," which involves reaching out again (and again and again and again!) to people who behaviorally indicated this interest through clicking on a link. Or they can target across platforms – such as delivering digital ads to people who searched for particular things on Google.

In short, the same technologies that deliver an endless array of related digital advertising to you after you search for new sneakers or a jacket (and which also follows you around the Internet for months on Facebook, Instagram, and YouTube) get utilized in digital political advertising. And, just as campaigns use data to find supporters and those people they think are persuadable, make appeals to them, and then continually work to craft a relationship that results in money or volunteer hours or both, they use data to measure the effectiveness of their work. Campaigns and causes constantly run experiments (known as A/B tests) that seek to maximize the effectiveness of ads – utilizing analytics to produce the outcomes they desire (Karpf 2016).

Indeed, campaigns and causes will create many, many different versions of digital advertising, varying the color and shape of images, the font or content, the layout or design – everything that can be manipulated is! – to see what combination of elements perform the best. By "perform," we mean influence people to do whatever campaigns actually want people who see advertising to do: click on links, donate money, sign petitions, etc. The shift from mass media advertising – television, radio, newspapers, and magazines, for instance – has meant campaigns have increased ability to know how people are actually responding to political advertising, across a wide range of potential outcomes, from exposure to messages to behavioral outcomes.

Or even *perceptual* outcomes. While campaigns cannot necessarily know what is going on in people's heads, they can guess in the attempt to shape how people respond to messages. Commercial and political advertisers utilize a large set of tools at their disposal to try to discern the effects of advertising beyond the behavioral measures detailed above. For example, they run surveys of those who were exposed to ads to discern whether they noticed them, changed their opinion of something on the basis of them, or otherwise were psychologically responsive to an appeal. This happens through many of the same tools that platforms make available for digital advertising, and the results in turn shape future advertising decisions.

7.5 Campaign Platform Strategies: Attention and Interaction, Persuasion, and Mobilization and Demobilization

Attention and Interaction

In the early days of the Internet, candidates treated websites primarily as one-way, mass communication channels that delivered messages to voters. This began to change during the early and mid-2000s, as candidates gradually incorporated more interactive, and later social, elements into campaigns. In the first campaigns that were run on what we now would call "social media" platforms (a first generation of social tools, such as Meetup, Orkut, Friendster, and MySpace), both political actors and scholars saw their greatest potential in the interaction and dialogue that could take place between campaigns and their supporters, as well as between supporters themselves. Especially in the United States in the early 2000s, supporters and candidates began embracing the affordances of these technologies for volunteerism, fundraising, and supporter promotion of candidate messages – forms of interactivity that were often "structured" (Kreiss 2016) or "controlled" (Stromer-Galley 2019) toward the ends that campaigns and parties wanted to achieve.

There was nothing inevitable about this use of changing technologies by campaigns. As we detail in our model, political institutions, social dynamics that give rise to patterns of user behavior, and commercial contexts all shape the uptake of technologies in particular ways. In the United States case, for instance, there was no reason campaigns could not adopt more interactive and social elements of digital technologies in the mid- and late 1990s – instead, their model was a mass media one in which messages flowed one way to voters. In a similar fashion, US campaigns in the 1990s turned volunteers away in favor of advertising-centric approaches (see Nielsen 2012). There are many other examples. In Austria, it took until 2013 before all parties used social media as a campaign tool. When asked why, campaign managers cited a complex set of opportunities and concerns that reveal the social elements behind the uptake of new technologies. For example, they saw the potential for more interaction between parties, candidates, and citizens, but also expressed feeling pressured, fearing negative media coverage and ridicule if they did not use Twitter or Facebook or did not use them well, as well as being nervous about leaving the field open for fake party accounts or just generally missing the boat of modern campaigning, or failing at it (Klinger & Rußmann 2017).

Even more, *how* technologies are adopted is deeply shaped by institutional and social and cultural contexts. For example, electoral systems are deeply important – political actors largely see social media as being more powerful for candidates than parties, given the personalized genres of social media and expectations of audiences (Holtz-Bacha et al. 2014; McGregor 2018; Metz et al. 2020). Campaigners see social media as working best when the messages they craft fit their candidates' biographies and political styles, the varying audiences and affordances of platforms, the genres audiences expect, and the timing of the electoral cycle (Kreiss et al. 2018). They perceive authenticity to matter, as well – which is ultimately about convincing an audience that a performance is "real" and "true" to a self. Indeed, parties create what scholars call "authenticity illusions," staged events and strategically used authenticity markers in the self-presentation of their candidates in the attempt to convince audiences of their "realness" (Enli 2016).

This takes us back to interactivity. In general, despite the potential affordances of social media, empirical studies analyzing the campaign strategies of parties and candidates have repeatedly found much more broadcasting than interaction (Stromer-Galley 2000, 2019). Even today, parties and campaigns often use social media as another channel to unilaterally send out their messages to imagined audiences (Litt & Hargittai 2016), rather than engaging in bi- or multi-lateral exchanges with citizens (Filimonov et al. 2016; Kalsnes 2016). One important reason why is that parties and campaigns generally have a few clear goals – not only more votes on election days, but also usually volunteers and funds (depending on the country) to achieve that goal. As such, they adopt strategies they perceive as most efficiently meeting these goals. Another reason is capacity – interacting and engaging with potential supporters is deeply resource-intensive. This is why campaigns and parties have invested in more organizing models to build the capacity of volunteers to do this work themselves. In some countries, some campaigns that are more likened to movements (such as the Bernie Sanders presidential campaigns in the United States) use digital media to push organizing capacity down to volunteers. At the same time, campaigns are deeply time-delimited entities, which limits their long-term ability to build capacity and sustain political commitment – something that parties are better suited for (but long-term organizing lacks the energy and commitment by voters that is generated by campaigns). All of this limits the usefulness of interactivity when it comes to utilizing social media in the context of elections.

In the end, campaigns utilize many strategies and media concurrently to gain the attention of voters and spur the interaction that can make supporters more invested in campaigns and potentially turning into money and votes. On the basis of interviews with campaign managers in 12 European countries, Lilleker et al. (2015) found variation, but also a clear trend toward the embedding and integration of both new and older tools and platforms into campaign strategies. This underlines the fact that social media and microtargeted ads are by no means killing traditional campaign techniques, but they are adding to the strategic arsenal that practitioners use to contest elections.

Persuasion

Campaign communications are always forms of *strategic*, and attempts at *persuasive*, communication. Campaigns intentionally and purposefully attempt to change the attitudes, beliefs, and opinions of citizens – and even their identities and emotions – to convince them to vote for a party or candidate, give money, or volunteer (Barden & Petty 2012). Over the short term, this is hard. Political identities (especially partisanship), attitudes, and ideological beliefs are usually quite stable if the political system is (if not always coherent). This is because these things are formed through broader socialization processes and reflect our upbringing, social identities, social and economic environments, and ties to people close to us (Huddy & Bankert 2017; Jennings 2007). Research dating over 70 years has shown that interpersonal communication with family, friends, acquaintances, co-workers, and neighbors has a more important impact on political attitudes and behavior than mass media (Hopmann 2012). Research consistently shows that short-term campaign communications are most effective at manipulating the *salience* of issues and identities given these larger structural factors, even as, over longer time scales, identities and beliefs are conditioned by media and communication through socialization processes, including the media environments that over time shape what people believe about themselves and others; their understandings of themselves, their attachments, and different social groups; and their beliefs (Genner & Süss 2017). Changing people's opinion on issues is hard, but not impossible. For instance, when parties change their position on a major issue, they can be successful in switching their supporters' policy preferences, too (Slothuus & Bisgaard 2021).

It is in this context that social media have become such a potent tool for campaigners, and central to the persuasion efforts of campaigns. Social media integrate one-way mass media with social diffusion, attention, and persuasion processes. This is important because most people do not trust platforms (Reuters Institute for the Study of Journalism 2022) and they do not trust political advertisements. Yet on social media, political messages often appear in feeds from a network of family members, acquaintances, friends, and friends of friends. Thus, people encounter mediated, interpersonal political communication online, including shared mass media messages, often from far-flung networks of weak ties. This means that, increasingly, political messages are not (just) directly conveyed from a candidate or party, but passed socially through Facebook or WhatsApp groups, among people who might share personal or affinity ties. This matters. Research shows that interpersonal campaign communication can be effective, such as personal exchanges during canvassing (Johann et al. 2018), and that information conveyed on social media increases vote-choice certainty for young, inexperienced first-time voters (Ohme et al. 2018).

In this context, social media increasingly matter to campaigns for the varying identity and issue appeals they afford. Citizens have multiple, even conflicting, identities, ideologies, and interests, which parties vie not only to represent, but to give shape to. Candidates and parties work to make certain political identities and issues salient, and then seek to persuade voters to see themselves in these ways (see Jardina 2019) and to prioritize voting on the basis of them. This is complicated. Partisanship is not always in step with race, religiosity, and class, for instance. When it is time to vote, citizens have to choose what identity they prioritize in part based on what they see as the most politically salient, while politicians seek to persuade citizens to make that choice in particular ways (Baysu & Swyngedouw 2020; Weller & Junn 2018).

It works similarly with political issues. Voters might favor climate protection, universal healthcare, and low taxes. They might say "my body, my choice" when it comes to vaccines and, at the same time, prefer strong regulation on abortion. They might be progressive when it comes to social and cultural issues, but be die-hard conservatives on economic or tax matters. Most citizens might not even know their preferences with regard to complex issues such as foreign or telecommunications policy. Indeed, voters make irrational choices (Caplan 2011) and they are often not well informed or attentive to politics. In this context, politicians stake out positions, and seek to persuade voters both that *these particular issues* (i.e., what a candidate "runs" on) *are important* and that *their positions* (what a candidate proposes to do to solve a perceived problem) *are correct*.

Indeed, at this point, we know from nearly a century of research that people are often uninformed or misinformed (Lindgren et al. 2022), that they often have little intrinsic interest in politics, and it is only the most engaged who have coherent political identities or positions across a wide spectrum of issues (what researchers call "ideologies"). A politically realistic view sees politics in terms of the "heuristics" or shortcuts that people use to reason about politics, and especially political identity – from partisanship to any number of social cleavages. This has posed a challenge for scholars thinking about what "good citizenship" should entail. Already in 1999, journalism scholar Michael Schudson argued that, in the age of information abundance, the ideal should not be the informed citizen, but the "monitorial citizen" who knows just enough to pay attention during big crises. Schudson, in fact, noted that, historically, the idea of an "informed citizen" is a relatively recent ideal in the US and beyond, and that a politics of deference to social hierarchy, sociality, and rights are other models.

That people are not always informed about or attentive to politics, even in a platform age when we are awash in political information, is not all bad from a democratic perspective. People are busy caring for their families and working to make ends meet. They have different motivations and interest in following politics. They might be far more concerned with the workings of local state or welfare agencies, which affect their lives on a daily basis, than with the election of a distant president. They rely on heuristics such as partisanship to make choices when they are stretched thin or a ballot is simply overwhelming. And they might otherwise have knowledge of politics that affects their lives in ways seldom measured in national surveys – such as the ways in which unemployment agencies work. That said, we also know that people relying on social media for news in a passive, monitorial way – the "news finds me" phenomenon wherein people trust their networks to inform them when something relevant happens – has been shown to lead to lower political knowledge, less political interest, and thus, indirectly, to lower voter turnout over time (Gil de Zúñiga & Diehl 2019). And turnout is the clearest path toward political representation and favored policy outcomes. In other words, while being monitory might realistically capture citizens' attitudes toward political life, it is rarely a tool for building power.

In the end, elections in many countries are increasingly close races in which there is stability in partisan behavior, and small groups of swing or irregular voters decide who wins. In this world, only a small portion of the electorate needs to be actively persuaded – of how the incumbent did at managing the economy and crises, of who best represents people culturally and politically and economically and their interests, and of who is best poised to lead the nation into the future.

Mobilization and Demobilization

Another form of persuasion is mobilizing supporters. Especially in scenarios of strong partisanship, the persuasive task for campaigns is *mobilization* – rallying voters to your side through strategic appeals that strengthen identity, position outgroups, and defend or justify the actions of a party and reputation of its leaders. Mobilization has taken on increased importance in electioneering worldwide for a simple reason. It is much harder to convince undecided citizens that a party or candidate is the right choice for them than to activate and mobilize already convinced supporters to actually go to vote.

Candidates generally attempt mobilization through campaign appeals that activate, make salient, and double down on partisan identity, including through the use of aggressive metaphors (Kalmoe 2019), broadcast and targeted internet advertisements (Haenschen & Jennings 2019), wedge issues (Heinkelmann-Wild et al. 2020), and even sexism (Valentino et al. 2018). In the platform era, campaigns have also sought to mobilize supporters through the personal and social ties detailed above. Internal studies by Facebook in 2010 and 2012 claimed to show how strongly voters are influenced by their close friends on the platform. In a real-time experiment, Facebook measured the effect of a clickable "I voted" button in the US 2010 and 2012 elections and found that social norms, and social pressure, had a strong effect on mobilizing people to vote (Bond et al. 2012; Jones et al. 2017).

These experiments mirror findings from offline contexts, which show the outsized role that social pressure and social norms play in their potential to increase voter engagement. Facebook's experiments have been quite controversial. After all, they show Facebook's potential power to meddle in elections on massive scales, without transparency into their social experiments or accountability for their actions (Barrett & Kreiss 2019). Other studies have found similar results and underline that social media platforms hold the potential to increase voter turnout through social pressure (Haenschen 2016). What is important here is that these signals of social norms and social pressure are *not* getting people to do things they are not already inclined to do. In other words, these experiments are consistent with people's pre-existing political identities, interests, and inclinations, such as to vote itself.

Not only is mobilizing one's supporters through political communication a campaign strategy, so is the attempt to *demobilize* the supporters of one's political opponents. Germany's famed chancellor for 16 years, Angela Merkel, and her Christian Democratic Union have run very successful campaigns with this strategy. At its core, the idea is to avoid anything provocative, controversial, or polarizing that would mobilize opposition. They sought to make election campaigns as boring as possible, with the aim of demotivating the opponent's supporters from voting.

Another, more democratically problematic, strategy is to demobilize voters through negative campaigning. This has long been studied and debated in the academic literature, with experimental studies suggesting that negative ads can demobilize people (e.g., Iyengar & Simon 2000), while other research suggests the effects are mixed or even mobilizing for political opponents. Some scholars suggest that all forms of negative ads are anti-democratic because they drive a wedge between a party's politicians and supporters. Young Mie Kim et al. (2018) argued as much in her important study of Russian Internet Research Agency attempts to influence the 2016 US presidential election by serving negative ads to Democratic Party voters. Others point out that, under this definition, much of what campaigns routinely do, through either active campaigning or omission (see the example of Merkel above), would fit this definition.

Other scholars have focused on the work of candidates, or their supporters, to challenge the legitimacy of an election altogether. In a fascinating case study based on the 2018 municipal election in Jerusalem, Kligler-Vilenchik et al. (2021) show that the Jerusalem Twittersphere is segmented into a Hebrew part with a dominant mobilizing narrative, and a Palestinian segment portraying the municipal election as betrayal of the Palestinian cause, promoting electoral boycott, and establishing non-voting as a social norm: "Voting is thus *the opposite* of fulfilling one's democratic right; it is an act of betrayal of one's collective identity" (2021: 575).

Broadly, social media are the sites where mobilizing and demobilizing messages from candidates, parties, political actors, mass media, and interpersonal communication come together; are made visible and shared within networks; are curated, filtered, and amplified by algorithms; and transformed through social discourse.

7.6 Summary

This chapter focused on the core institution of democracy: competitive elections. Elections are the primary way in which citizens hold those who govern accountable. The peaceful transfer of power between parties who willingly lose to contest elections in the future is core to many of the freedoms that people enjoy in democracies.

Campaigns are required to contest elections. Campaigns are organized efforts that utilize a vast array of communicative tools – from candidate speeches and television talk-show appearances to emails and posts on social media platforms – to convince voters to elect their candidate, or not vote for the opposing side(s). Different electoral and media systems, as well as regulatory environments, shape how campaigns are organized and funded, the messages they craft, and the distinctions they draw in relation to opposition candidates and parties.

The relationship between social media – and platforms more generally – and campaigns is complex. Platforms are embedded in national systems that structure competitive elections, but they also provide technologies and incentives to those who contest public office. As a result, we have seen a number of important trends in campaigning that are amplified in the era of platforms, such as the use of data, personalization, identity appeals, and negativity. None of these things originated with platforms, but platforms foster and incentivize them in key ways.

In the end, platforms play a complex role vis-à-vis electoral institutions. It is undoubtedly true that platforms have provided candidates with a vast array of new tools to reach voters in increasingly personalized ways, which has spurred increases in political participation in many countries around the world. And platforms have facilitated movements (the subject of the next chapter) that can change perceptions of public issues and influence the choices of voters (Mutz 2022). At the same time, they have also created new opportunities for anti-democratic actors to capture party nomination contests and confuse and manipulate voters, which we turn to in Chapter 10.

Discussion Questions

- Platforms and their algorithms incentivize political parties to post aggressive messages, such as those negative in content and style, because these posts tend to yield more reactions, shares, and comments. What advice would you give to a party that wants to have more positive, policy-oriented communications with citizens while maneuvering social media?
- Parties and politicians are constantly experimenting with new and niche platforms. Think of a smaller platform that does not (yet) have mass political appeal (such as Mastodon) or one that campaigners have not widely adopted (like Pinterest or even Reddit) and devise a strategy for a campaign on this platform.

Suggestions for Further Reading

Bossetta, M. (2018) "The digital architectures of social media: comparing political campaigning on Facebook, Twitter, Instagram, and Snapchat in the 2016 US election," *Journalism & Mass Communication Quarterly* 95(2): 471–96.

Bruns, A., Angus, D., & Graham, T. (2021) "Twitter campaigning strategies in Australian federal elections 2013–2019," *Social Media + Society* 7(4): 1–15.

Ceccobelli, D. (2018) "Not every day is Election Day: a comparative analysis of eighteen election campaigns on Facebook," *Journal of Information Technology & Politics* 15(2): 122–41.

Haßler, J., Magin, M., Rußmann, U., & Fenoll, V. (eds.) (2021) *Campaigning on Facebook in the 2019 European Parliament Election: Informing, Interacting with, and Mobilising Voters*. Cham: Palgrave Macmillan.

Stromer-Galley, J. (2019) *Presidential Campaigning in the Internet Age*. New York: Oxford University Press.

8 Platforms and Movements

Chapter 8 covers movements. It seeks to deepen our understanding of how movements operate, and their potential power. It details types and theories of movements, the challenges they face, the tactics and methods they use, and their relations with media and governments – all against the backdrop of how they navigate and leverage digital information environments to achieve the visions they have for how the world should be.

OBJECTIVES

By the end of this chapter, you should be able to:

- provide an overview of social movements
- discuss theories that shape our understanding of social movements
- understand protest cultures in the digital age
- think about the future of social movements.

8.1 Introduction

When young Nigerians turned to Twitter to protest against police brutality in October 2020, it is likely that comparatively few people in other regions of the world had heard of the political controversies in Nigeria, the vast African country which is home to the continent's largest population. Twitter got much of the credit as demonstrations against the West African nation's abusive Special Anti-Robbery Squad (SARS) became visible across the globe under the #EndSARS banner. Messages of solidarity came from communities as far away as Washington DC, Mumbai, India, and Santiago, Chile, helping to sustain the popular social movement, which registered several successes, including the unexpected disbanding of the unpopular police unit.

Platforms have decisively changed the notion of what it means to be part of a movement, how movements emerge, gain force, and disappear, and the resources they have available and challenges they face. Platforms can help to rapidly globalize social struggles, connecting the world as activists shine hashtag spotlights on injustice. Platforms can empower youth and regions that often lack the mass media interest and global attention that can impose accountability on the powerful. And they can fashion global audiences into active participants in movements, or at the very least supporters and witnesses that help to sustain and animate them. This chapter details how contemporary movements increasingly have adapted to and take shape through the affordances, forms of shared symbols and sense-making, and opportunities for collective, connective, and affective action that platforms support. In short, in being central actors in media and political systems, platforms are indispensable to contemporary movements struggling for social change – or to prevent it.

Movements are everywhere. All you need is people. Once you have people, then you are likely to have movements of all kinds. Of course, movements existed long before we had, or knew someone who owned, a computer or a phone, or the platforms that are the subject of this book. That said, fueled by platforms, over the last two decades there has been an explosion in the visibility and power of movements, so much so that they seem to be transforming nearly every aspect of our political and social lives.

This chapter looks at the global wave of digital movements, which can encompass collectives of people working for change – or to prevent it – for any number of social, political, religious, economic, or environmental reasons. Movements all entail people who share a collective identity, beliefs, drive, and determination working to achieve or prevent change. It is a movement if the people involved in it have a shared identity and sense of purpose, although movements can take on many different organizational forms, as we detail in this chapter. And movements seem to be growing in importance. In an era dominated by a wide variety of increasingly visible challenges, ranging from racial injustice, sexism, climate change, and mental health to joblessness, immigration, and the Covid-19 pandemic, there cannot be a better time to talk about movements. Indeed, while many of these social problems have long existed, movements have helped us understand them as problems to be addressed through politics.

While movements all, more or less, strive for change – or to *prevent* change in the case of movements that protect existing orders – they use a wide variety of tactics and methods to achieve their goals. The idea of "social movements" is a broad category. While there are many different ends that movements can pursue (think about religious versus racial justice movements, for instance), researchers generally refer to "social" movements as those that seek to effect or prevent change in domains of life that are of shared concern (see Bennett 2005; Kavada 2018; Tuchman 1978). In short, social movements concern themselves with public matters (or matters that movements *want* to make a broad matter of public concern). There are many varieties of movements. Sometimes, social movements seek overtly political ends, in the sense that they are oriented to change the distribution of power in a society or polity, such as through campaign finance laws or tax rates. Or, sometimes, social movements have ends that are about the way people live, such as the environmental movement which, alongside policy change, seeks to transform the lifestyle choices that individuals make so they are more sustainable.

Movements can also seek or demand change – or frustrate it – through violent or non-violent means (Useem & Goldstone 2022). They can feature formal organizations (i.e., "social movement organizations" that act in institutionalized ways) or informal, non-centrally organized social actions (i.e., protests, marches). Or, most commonly, movements have both aspects – formal and informal, organized and unorganized elements. And movements can take root in democratic or authoritarian environments, although the latter often formally repress movements that pose a threat to the stability of regimes. In non-democratic societies where dissent often gets punished, movement groups silently deploy things such as "quiet encroachment" (Bayat 2013: 15) – the "silent, protracted, but pervasive advancement of the ordinary people on the propertied, powerful, or the public, in order to survive and improve their lives" (2013: 46). Regardless of the political system, however, social movements are ubiquitous – if not always visible. Every society has social movements. Some are more vocal; some prefer, or need, to be subtle.

As we will uncover in this chapter, movements have long played a key role in social transformations, and they have grown more visible in the platform era. Access to healthcare is not a right for everyone in many countries. People's voting rights have been taken away from them. There is increasing scrutiny of racial and gender injustice and child abuse. Organized or otherwise, peaceful or violent, social movements have fought for or against change. And social movements have to be dynamic to address the challenges facing various societies – and the forces that seek to limit their power. In a changing media and technological environment, where more people live out their daily lives online, existing and new social movements have developed new digital repertoires of collective action (Freelon 2014). As we emphasize in this chapter, during the platform era movements have flowered through new dynamics and processes and at new scales.

8.2 Defining Social Movements

While Lorenz von Stein's ([1848] 1964) book *History of the French Social Movement from 1789 to the Present* is often cited as the first study to use the term "social movement," movements themselves far pre-date the term. Indeed, we can think of a number of potent examples, including the American Revolution (Tilly 2004).

There are various definitions of social movements in scholarly literature. For example, Diani (1992: 1) defines social movements as "networks of informal interactions between a plurality of individuals, groups and/or organizations, engaged in political or cultural conflicts, on the basis of shared collective identities." This definition captures that social movements are "networks" made up of interlinked individuals and organizations. It details how their interactions are often informal, not formally organized (although they can be coordinated). It captures how conflict is at the core of movements – regardless of what these conflicts are over. And, finally, this definition captures the importance of collective identity to movements. Relatedly, other scholars have focused on how social movements form alliances and "develop structures of belief that critique the status quo, offer solutions to identified problems and justify political action to achieve change" (Gillan 2008: 247). This tells us that movements can knit themselves together – for example when environmental movement groups join forces with organized labor strategically to advance the goals of both groups.

Building from these and other scholars, we see social movements in the broadest sense as networks of actors organized around convergent identities and interests that pursue something that they believe is better than the status quo or what's currently on offer – or to prevent other movements from implementing their own version of social change. In our own era, democracies across the world are under strain (Repucci & Slipowitz 2021), which in many cases is both a product of movements and the cause of them. Movements sometimes destabilize democracy, either intentionally or unintentionally. Some nativist right-wing movements in Europe, for instance, seek to intentionally challenge democratic processes that lead to demographic change – such as legal immigration. Other movements strain societies by pushing for *more democratic* states. In this way, pro-democratic movements that seek equality under the law for *all* citizens, or equal democratic representation, can trigger movements that seek to prevent challenges to the existing social order. There is a destabilizing and anti-democratic white backlash to the Black Lives Matter movement in the United States, for instance, echoing the white dismantling of the democratic post-Civil War Reconstruction era over a century earlier (Hooker 2016).

Indeed, from Burkina Faso to Belarus, activists are demanding political change, some of them paying a heavy price for their public visibility. Recent challenges such as the Covid-19 pandemic have also given activists the opportunity to demand change in many regions of the world, including southeast Asia. For example, Corpuz (2021) argues that, using the pandemic for context and buoyed by events elsewhere such as the Black Lives Matter protests, citizens of Thailand, Indonesia, the Philippines, and other Asian nations are intensifying their online and offline efforts to fight state-sponsored limitations to civil and political rights. The pandemic has also provided activists in countries such as Switzerland with the opportunity to develop alternative ways to fight for their rights (Rauchfleisch et al. 2021). That said, in many societies, change is not easily achievable, which is why so many activists do not live to see the better world they spend their lives demanding. US political and social activist Martin Luther King Jr. is a notable example. Despite his widely recognized and remarkable role in shaping the success of the American Civil Rights Movement, King was assassinated on April 4, 1968, robbing him of an opportunity to enjoy the fruits of his long-standing, non-violent resistance against racial segregation.

Social movements have the potential to transform societies. They shape the political, social, and even economic direction of a country, for better or worse. They thrive through the commitment of their leaders and members, their networks of support – including institutions, journalists, and political entities – the national and local conditions and especially tolerance for dissent, their use of media to publicize their causes and win and mobilize supporters, and in some cases the transnational solidarity that comes through media.

SPOTLIGHTED CASE

The Rastafari movement is a good example of transnational solidarity. Even though its roots lie with socially disenfranchised Blacks living in Jamaica in the 1930s, the political and religious movement has since gained significant international visibility thanks to the musical works of the late Bob Marley and many other reggae icons who emerged from the Caribbean island of roughly 2.8 million people.

As noted above, social movements often contain social movement organizations (SMOs). Social movement organizations are formalized and centrally organized groups – such as advocacy or non-profit organizations – that are often issue- or cause-based. Examples include mainstream organizations such as Planned Parenthood (the abortion rights advocate and provider in the United States); radical political groups such as Somalia's Al Shebab, known for its audacious terrorist activities within and outside Somalia; and activist groups such as the Netherlands-based pro-environmental organization Greenpeace. SMOs also seek to promote or resist social change, be it environmental, political, economic, or cultural, and do so in conjunction with other movement actors. As formal organizations, they can often command resources (such as funding), volunteers, people, and media attention in routinized ways, and as such often take on coordinating or leadership roles in movements. They also can help to promote the wider movement by developing and maintaining ties to allies in the government, funding organizations, the media, and politics. SMOs often have significant power to "put into words what is wrong in society (a diagnosis), how this wrong should be ameliorated (a prognosis), and what people have to do to bring the needed changes about (motivation)" (d'Anjou & Van Male 1998). Because SMOs are often powerful organizations vis-à-vis other groups or informal networks of activists, sometimes tensions might arise over the future and direction of the movement. Large well-resourced organizations might protect their own position and status, or advocate more cautious and conservative courses of action than smaller groups with less to lose, more flexibility, or purer ideological commitments.

Indeed, as networks of many, and many different types of, groups, movements should not be seen as homogeneous entities. They are dynamic networks marked by change, conflict, and loose coordination – even as they pursue larger shared goals. As movements work to define their goals and identities, internal leaders compete to represent them. Movements can also work through institutional political channels, such as political parties, in the process transforming them into vehicles to pursue their aims. They can pursue their goals through disruptive actions or more diffuse forms of cultural change. Political leaders, in turn, often seek to ally with movements for mobilizational resources. And movements are not always *necessarily* political, although they might become political. For example, over the course of the second half of the twentieth century, white evangelical protestants who were part of a long-standing religious movement in the US went from being generally disengaged from formal politics and political institutions to advancing their concerns over communism, racial integration, and sex education through the vehicle of the US Republican Party (Butler 2021; Williams 2012).

Media are often central to movements and SMOs, as actors use them to circulate ideas and forge their identities, interests, values, and goals. Social movement actors also use media to coordinate their actions in pursuit of their goals in the public sphere and through political institutions in democracies. Media and social media have also been deeply important to many movements seeking to demonstrate their worthiness, unity, numbers, and commitment – which outsiders use to assess their legitimacy and power (Freelon et al. 2018; Tilly 1999; Tufekci 2014; Walgrave et al. 2022; Wouters & Walgrave 2017).

8.3 Theories that Shape Our Understanding of Social Movements

Looking at social movements through the lens of some major theories helps us to understand social movements and their changing dynamics and roles in societies.

Resource Mobilization Theory

In the 1960s and 1970s, social movements began to be a serious object of study as they became increasingly visible all around the world. Early on, scholars noted that resources play a key role in social movement processes. For example, to organize a successful protest, movements need to have adequate resources. As McCarthy and Zald (1977) argue, resource mobilization theory (RMT) showed that movements needed to be efficient at gaining and mobilizing resources if they hoped to be successful. Without sufficient money, time, human resources, and organizational skills, groups cannot successfully organize against the state or other powerful interests, which frequently have comparatively massive resources at their disposal, including even the police or intelligence services.

To gain resources, movements often rely on aligned groups, such as non-governmental organizations (NGOs), including foundations, that offer routinized ways to advance democratic change in certain countries. This, of course, also works for non-democratic or even anti-democratic groups who can attract funding and organizational support from aligned organizations, such as political parties (Ziblatt 2017). And, regardless of their ideology, movements rely as well on contributions from supporters, including those who volunteer their time and energy "in kind" to sustain a movement and its activities. Without sufficient funding, it is almost impossible to fight dictatorships – marginalized groups often do not gain voice unless their determination to push for change has adequate funding and organizational mechanisms supporting it. Indeed, organizations matter a great deal, because they help to routinize resources, including funding, communications, and allies.

SPOTLIGHTED CONTENT

A good example of a foundation is the Open Society Foundation (OSF), founded by American billionaire George Soros. OSF's mission is to provide funding avenues to civil society groups around the world, particularly those seeking to advance education, public health, independent media, and social justice. Given this work, Soros and OSF are often the subject of anti-Semitic conspiracy theories (Langer 2021). Other prominent American examples include the Ford and Rockefeller Foundations.

New Social Movement Theory

By the end of the 1960s, scholars were noting other dimensions of movements, beyond the importance of resources. European scholars, in particular, were pointing to the importance of transitions from industrial economies in many countries, and as such noting that movements were changing their orientation away from things such as class issues and toward culture and identity. These issues included various struggles for human rights, such as gay rights, in countries around the world. And while the workers' movement had for decades been a dominant orientation for movements, several issues such as gender, race, ethnicity, youth, sexuality, spirituality, countercultural values, environmentalism, and animal rights also came to the fore during this period (Buechler 2013). And yet, while many consider these cultural and identity issues, another way to think about many of these new movement orientations is through the lens of *democracy*. Identity-based movements are often oriented around achieving equality, equity, or justice for historically excluded, non-dominant groups. Think about the feminist movement, for instance, which seeks to achieve equal status for women both politically (such as rights and representation) and culturally (such as through empowering media and entertainment). Or movements for racial justice, which seek equal status as a matter of formal rights (as in ending police brutality) and social welfare (as in health-related disparities). And these new movement orientations sit alongside the explosion of new labor movement activity around the world, in the 1990s and again in the 2020s.

Deprivation Theory

Even with these new orientations for many movements, at the core there would be no social movements to talk about if some people living in a society or community did not perceive that they were deprived – whether this is a fact or a perception. As the examples above reveal, this can include class inequality, but also the deprivation of foundational rights of social and political equality or inclusion, more generally.

People seeking change take action because they have a set of grievances (perceived or real). In any given society, there are bound to be the less privileged and the privileged (Opp 1988). Absolute deprivation and relative deprivation differ in that the former focuses on the standing of the affected group separate and apart from that group's position in society, while the latter focuses on the group's unfavorable position or status vis-à-vis other groups in a given society (Sen & Avci 2016).

Not all deprivation leads to social movement activities, of course. There are many barriers to taking up collective action, even in societies that enshrine fundamental rights of expression and association.

SPOTLIGHTED CASE

Many Western societies have viewed Saudi Arabia's decision to deny women the right to drive as a human rights violation. The kingdom of Saudi Arabia, which, until its decision to grant women the right to drive in June 2018, was the only country in the world with such a law, argued the ban was in line with its strict brand of Islamic law, known as "Wahhabism." Obviously, such a law disadvantaged women drivers, but authorities in Saudi Arabia argued that this was a religious edict (despite being the only country in the world claiming as much). Once the right to drive was granted, the media focused on this path-breaking decision, but other issues, including the imprisonment of women's rights activists, did not get as much attention.

Political Process Theory

Scholars have argued that social movement dynamics, and especially success, are conditioned by political opportunities. In short, those in power, and arrangements of power (such as parties in government), matter. Under highly repressive governments, social movements face extreme conditions and barriers to success. Governments that are more tolerant toward a range of views, comparatively allow dissenting voices to flourish, leaving greater possibilities for social movements to thrive (Tilly 1978). That said, across all types of regimes (democracies included), dynamics among political elites matter for social movement organizing, collective action, and, ultimately, success (see Farthing 2019; Holdo 2020; Pettinicchio 2017). In countries where elites generally agree and are united in opposition to certain social movements, targeted actions against the state are likely to fail. Indeed, it is harder to even mobilize when people see few prospects for success. When elites are divided, however, movements have greater opportunities to win some to their side and advance their agendas. Relatedly, the environment external to states really matters. Foreign policy considerations deeply shape elite considerations of responses to social movements, for instance.

8.4 Movements in Platform Contexts

Everything about social movements, and our understanding of them, has drastically changed in contemporary societies. Digitalization shapes many of these changes. An increasingly digitalized society means that fewer resources are required for organizing collective action and getting a message out to the public – although *sustaining* collective action and *holding* public attention might be as, if not more, challenging (Tufekci 2017). Meanwhile, citizens and organizations have also had to devise new ways of organizing amid new possibilities, even as states have innovated in their informational operations to foreclose challenges.

Let's see these changes by first considering pre-digital-technology movement dynamics. Recall that a movement organizes people around a specific issue, ideology, identity, or set of grievances. Many people may share an interest in the outcome of, or be a stakeholder in, a conflict or a solution, having something in common that unites them for or against a cause. However, organizing people and turning them into a collective with an identity and getting them to engage in action is difficult. First of all, people need to be aware of not being alone in having a grievance or set of desired ends, of having something in common and being part of a group. Then they need to organize with others, and formulate and voice their discontent or their support for an issue – often in the face of repercussions. These repercussions can involve jail time and even death in repressive countries, or social ostracism in rights-granting democracies (Van Duyn 2021). And from there, it is still a long way to bringing people out on the streets. Even if it is safe to gather and protest, it still costs time, energy, and attention. People need incentives if they are going to get involved. After all, it is often less costly to just "free ride" on the backs of those willing to do the work (see Bimber 2017). In fact, classic theory on "collective action" (Olson 1965) identified early the problems that: (1) even though people share a common goal, they may not be able to act together and in a coordinated way; and (2) large mobilizations invite free-riders – people who perceive themselves sharing goals with a movement but fail to make contributions, while benefiting from the labor of others.

In this context, formal, collective-action organizations help to maintain, coordinate, control, routinize, and fund movements – organizations such as Greenpeace, Amnesty International, or World Wildlife Fund are examples of this development.

As detailed above, movements require a range of different resources to help them engage in collective action. This includes a core group that organizes events, sets and defines strategy, connects members or supporters, speaks to media and draws up campaigns, and of course raises money. Pamphlets must be printed, office space rented, computers and other information technology purchased, and telephone bills, Wi-Fi, and electricity paid for. In most democracies, demonstrations must be registered or coordinated with the state (such as through permits). For petitions, signatures must be collected. In short: movements cost a lot of money, time, and effort. This is why, traditionally, they tend to rely on organizations that can offer a headquarters, professional or paid staffers, and bank accounts.

Digital platforms, however, have changed these movement dynamics. As Lance Bennett and Alexandra Segerberg (2013) famously argued, based on their study of Occupy Wall Street – a protest action against gaping social and economic inequalities which began in New York and spread globally – and other movements, platforms have enabled new forms of *connective action*, in the form of self-organizing networks, and hybrid forms of collective and connective action, such as organizationally enabled networks.

SPOTLIGHTED CASE

The Fridays for Future movement mobilizes around the world for stronger action against the climate crisis. It all started with a 15-year-old Swedish schoolgirl, daughter of an opera singer and an actor – Greta Thunberg. She started to protest alone in front of the Swedish parliament, holding up a sign that said "school strike for climate." Soon more students joined her, and social media content about these protests helped transform Fridays for Future, as it was later called, into a global mass movement, with tens of thousands of mostly young people protesting not just online, but on the streets of their capitals and elsewhere. Thunberg spoke to the UN in 2018 and 2019, was named TIME magazine's Person of the Year, and has received several nominations for the Nobel Peace prize. The speed, scale, and global diffusion of Fridays for Future simply would not have been possible during the mass media era.

The Fridays for Future movement – famously founded by Greta Thunberg – grew, gained momentum, and even brought thousands of people around the world to the streets every week in large part through social media, and without any initial formal organizational backing. While, in the beginning, Thunberg's protests outside the Swedish parliament gained visibility due to prominent influencers on Instagram and other platforms, soon the movement itself became an online hit. It has all the characteristics of connective action: a decentralized structure predominantly supported through social media platforms, and a few spokespeople who serve as faces for mass media but remain in the background otherwise. And it shows us a key difference from movements in previous eras. It has spread not through centralized collective action messages (or frames) coordinated by formal, powerful organizations, but via personal expressions of concern and urgency shared over social media, which have echoed in millions of similar cries around the world. The same dynamics and patterns, of course, work on the other side of the political spectrum. Far-right, extremist movements have thrived on connective action. Indeed, these groups have been pioneers of using decentralized media to serve as a key form of organization while operating with limited public visibility (Belew 2018).

SPOTLIGHTED CASE

The far-right German movement PEGIDA (an abbreviation that translates to "Patriotic Europeans against the Islamification of the Occident") emerged in 2014 from a closed, then open, Facebook group of a small network of friends in the east German city of Dresden. They started weekly demonstrations disguised as "evening strolls" in December 2014, which soon grew to mass rallies of over 15,000 people, united in their protest against migration, and their disdain for government, democracy, and the state.

It is important to note here that connective action through platforms has not entirely replaced the need for comparatively older forms of collective action through formal organizations. Both forms coexist, interlace, and overlap. Movements in hybrid media systems can take on various stages of de/centralization – they can rely on social media platforms but still have an organizational core, offices, and several means of fundraising. In most cases, we see combinations of collective and connective action being especially powerful. This is because the advent of connective action and digital platforms has not solved the problem that only very few movements and NGOs like Amnesty International or Oxfam succeed in gaining and sustaining global public attention, especially over cycles of long, slow policymaking processes, which are often a target of movements. And the fragmentation of digital public spheres is making it even harder for smaller movements and NGOs to be seen and heard (Thrall et al. 2014).

8.5 Platforms and the Communication of Movements

As hinted at above, platforms have changed not only how movements organize, but also how they distribute their messages and mobilize support symbolically. There are at least three major differences between connective mobilization dynamics and more traditional collective action, specifically in the context of communication: the structural patterns of movement communication, the role of networked gatekeeping and superspreaders, and cross-platform dynamics.

Mobilization on social media platforms does not grow in concentric circles, from center to periphery, and it does not grow in a linear way. Lance Bennett and colleagues (2018) have shown that "peripheral networks" are key for mobilization, whereby messages that frame problems, create identities and grievances, and draw people into movements and mobilize them can come from anywhere, including places far from the center of organizational movement power. Networked mobilization often does not spill over from a core group to their closest supporters to their supporters' friends and so on. Instead, socially distant communities activate their networks and connect them to a group or cause. For instance, Bennett and colleagues found that celebrities like "movie stars, writers and politicians" and their fan networks played an important role in the Occupy movement and the (re-)framing of Occupy's central messages. While the Occupy Wall Street protest core was focused on issues around corruption and regulating banks, these peripheral actors (many influential in their own right in other domains) helped to turn public and journalistic attention to issues such as inequality in society.

The notion of peripheral networks is a very old one, similar to the idea of "weak ties" discussed in Chapter 4. To gain traction, an issue needs to move through peripheral networks, often socially far from the core group committed to it. This works not only with celebrity cheerleading (e.g. Instagram influencers promoting political movements or issues), but also with far-flung networks that connect institutional politics and extremist organizations. In a study tracing a far-right protest campaign against the United Nations Global Compacts for Migration (the first UN comprehensive global agreement on a common approach to international migration), Klinger et al. (2022) show that it was not networks around celebrities and politicians, but politically aligned yet differently situated groups that passed similar content between an extremist movement and a radical right party that could not endorse each other or communicate directly.

Another key element of networked mobilization is the role of hyperactive users, or "superspreaders." Online participation follows what scholars call a "long tail distribution" (Helles 2013). This means that only a small number of users comment and share a lot, while most users only "lurk" – they read and click, but only very rarely share or comment. That is the "long tail." As a result, the few most active users have a disproportionate impact on the distribution of messages on social media platforms. In the case of the far-right protest campaign against migration mentioned above, only 0.27 percent of Twitter users produced 21 percent of all interactions in the sample studied (Klinger et al. 2022b). Martini (2020) reports a similar pattern in her study of the German #metoo network on Twitter. Kennedy et al. (2022) found similar patterns in disinformation spread during the 2020 US presidential election. Papakyriakopoulos et al. (2019) made the more general point about how extremely skewed online participation is when finding that all users writing three or more comments on Facebook could already be considered "hyperactive" users, as 74 percent of Facebook users in their sample population made only one comment.

This pattern becomes even more pronounced by platform algorithms. When a platform like Facebook is built around the principle of "meaningful social interaction," such as rewarding posts that generate user engagement, these few hyperactive users in fact are gaming algorithms. The result is that a handful of influential, abusive, and aggressive users can often exert a massive influence over what other users see, and what they might not. As Hindman et al. (2022) put it, Facebook "has a superuser-supremacy" problem. On the flip side, a small number of superusers can also shape pro-democratic struggles.

For movements, this dynamic means at least two things. First, platforms make it very easy for a small number of users to become a loud minority, and to generate the impression of larger movements than may actually exist. It is very easy to amplify a small group and artificially inflate their size and importance. Second, if small movements strategically take advantage of these structural opportunities, they can grow fast and make an impact before (or even without) mobilizing large crowds. One example comes from some protests against Covid-19 regulations, masks, and vaccines in many countries. In Germany, for instance, a small minority of citizens, never more than 10 percent, managed to be loud enough to exert decisive pressure on the political agenda and political decision-makers, who subsequently shied away from vaccine mandates and canceled regulations long before the pandemic was actually over, at a time when infection rates were at an all-time high.

Finally, mobilization dynamics take place across platforms. Citizens may encounter information and messages from or about movements on WhatsApp or Telegram – in the form of YouTube videos. Movement content moves from legacy media portals and alternative media outlets via URL links through Twitter or Facebook, and across messenger services and crowd-edited archives such as Wikipedia. Unfortunately, there is still little research about these cross-platform dynamics (e.g. Theocharis et al. 2021) – including about the US right's strategic exploitation of these dynamics to spread messages and set the agendas of the professional press (see Marwick & Lewis 2021). Even so, it is hard to study because it is methodologically difficult to trace information flows and mobilizations in different data formats, and because most platforms share only limited data. As a result, researchers have so far focused mainly on Twitter, simply because, until April 2023, Twitter had made data more accessible for research than many other platforms.

8.6 State Activities against Social Movements

Institutional political leaders and states might be allied against movements. Even in modern democratic societies, clashes between governments and social movement groups are quite common. That's because social movements often make claims on state entities, which they in turn can resist (Dobson 2017). States have a diverse array of suppression methods at their disposal (Martin 1986). Legal mechanisms include surveillance, infiltration by police or investigative actions, the use of media such as press statements and interviews to discredit movements, and the targeting of leaders and groups with criminal charges or seizing their financial assets, as well as smear campaigns against their reputations. Extra-legal mechanisms include police intimidation tactics, violence including beatings and bombings, extra-judicial arrests of key people, or shootings targeting a social movement. And, of course, states can also invent many seemingly legal pretenses to legitimate these actions targeting social movements.

SPOTLIGHTED CASES

There are, sadly, many examples of state repression of social movements. Dutch police boarded a Greenpeace ship and arrested more than 20 activists who had staged a peaceful protest at a Shell oil refinery in the city of Rotterdam in October 2021. A month earlier, the Hong Kong Alliance in Support of Patriotic Democratic Movements of China, a local social movement group which holds annual events commemorating victims of the 1989 Tiananmen Square massacre, reported that police had arrested its leaders after they refused to release details relating to their funding sources. In the US, Black Lives Matter activists have been repeatedly targeted. High-profile members of a social group can also be threatened with job losses. For example, universities across the world have threatened or even dismissed staff for supporting or actively participating in the activities of a controversial movement.

States can also target the communications infrastructures that movements rely on (Howard 2020; Karpf 2019; Ndlovu-Gatsheni 2021; Segura & Waisbord 2016; Taberez 2018). This was a feature of state responses to the Arab Spring, to mixed success from the perspective of regimes. Tactics include throttling, surveilling, or shutting down the Internet entirely within national borders (Earl et al. 2022; Joshua & Edel 2021). According to Kapur (2022), Sri Lanka banned the use of Facebook, Twitter, YouTube, and WhatsApp in 2022 in anticipation of mass protests against the government, becoming the 11th Asian nation (30 in all as of April 2022) to ban social media as a measure of countering public protests since 2015. Digital surveillance has also become a common way for governments to intimidate activists. In 2017, the late Zimbabwean President Robert Mugabe became one of the first leaders in the world to appoint a minister for "Cyber Security, Threat Detection, and Mitigation." Critics voiced concern over this new ministry and what impact it would have on civil liberties, particularly freedom of speech, which was protected by the southern African nation's constitution.

Infiltration is another tactic used by governments to dispel threats from social movements. Counterintelligence mechanisms that stoke potential conflicts among movement leaders are designed to create factionalism and neutralize social movements. Authorities have been known to read dissidents' emails, hack their phones, or surveil them, seeking critical information about their activities. Undercover agents have been planted within social movements to collect information, and informers will sell information to intelligence services or spread gratuitous rumors for a price. These activities create unwanted divisions in an organization, weakening it. It is also common for leaders of movements opposed to governments to be discredited, by, for example, accusations of being a homosexual, rapist, or prostitute – attempts at character assassination to soil their image.

All of these intelligence activities can create paranoia among activists, effectively ensuring members lose focus or interest in a social movement – or they walk away because the costs are too high to bear. In fact, digital technology can make it even more difficult for activists to remain anonymous, because IP addresses, platforms with real-name policies, or tools like facial recognition surveillance can all compromise their personal data. Digital activism is neither ineffective, in the sense that it has no effects, nor risk free (Madison & Klang 2020).

8.7 Movements and Journalism

A large body of literature analyzes the relationship between journalism and movements. Scholars have noted, generally since the 1960s, that professional media and movements often have complicated relationships. Classic work on the Civil Rights Movement and the American anti-Vietnam War movement, for instance, showed how movements are reliant on mass media coverage to publicize their causes, gain supporters, and pressure lawmakers, and especially have leverage against states when there are foreign policy concerns (see Kennis 2021). And yet professional media also sensationalize movements, have their own agendas that might be far afield from a movement's own, choose framing that might undermine a movement, and elevate their own leaders of a movement, often based on charisma and media sophistication. Sociologist Sarah Sobieraj (2011) has shown how the press demand movements be "authentic" in not staging press conferences and events, yet also complain about their lack of professional media relations.

Indeed, in democratic regimes, professional practices and incentives often steer journalists to focus mostly or entirely on the most sensational aspects of events, such as violent acts, like throwing stones during demonstrations, chaos, or sheer spectacle – which may discredit movements. A study in Israel showed that professional values and organizational economic considerations led journalists to quickly fall in line with the dismissive editorial stance of their outlets despite initial sympathy for the 2011–12 social protests, which were opposed to rising costs of living (Tenenboim-Weinblatt 2014). For the United Kingdom, Gruber (2023) has shown, in a systematic analysis of 26 years of mainstream press coverage on protest, that the majority of reporting continues to be dismissive or hostile toward protests and social movements. Yet some scholars have argued that a growing proportion of news items also demonstrate legitimizing patterns more recently, providing more information about protesters' grievances and background on their issues. For the case of Brazil, Mourão and Chen (2020) have shown that journalist coverage of protest on Twitter followed the journalists' personal attitudes rather than professional values, reporting more favorably about left-leaning than about right-leaning protests.

And states can also use media to influence public opinion regarding the activities spearheaded by a particular social movement. Tactics include directly intimidating journalists to withhold coverage of or misrepresent pro-movement activities such as protest marches, or in some circumstances even paying journalists to create positive coverage of government activities (see Wallace 2020). As Moon's (2019) work in Rwanda shows, in authoritarian contexts, state actors can simply tell journalists what to do – who, in turn, often have to negotiate these directives with their professional values of autonomy. These dynamics might force journalists to underreport pro-movement activities in the face of reprisals.

8.8 Summary

Movements are ubiquitous in the platform era, and are shaping institutional politics as well as social orders. Scholars have identified key questions relating to the speed and scale and dynamics of movement mobilization, as well as the endurance of movements with respect to being able to resist state repression or implement movement goals through political means. Taken together, platforms have radically altered the contexts within which movements occur. In the next chapter, we turn to platform governance – which has deep implications for movements in structuring their organizational and discursive strategies.

Discussion Questions

- How can the logic of connective action and peripheral networks help us understand the spread of the QAnon movement?
- Freedom of speech versus freedom of reach: how could (and should?) platforms intervene when inauthentic mobilization happens, such as when superspreaders form loud minorities creating the false impression of grassroots movements?

Suggestions for Further Reading

Bennett, W. L. & Segerberg, A. (2013) *The Logic of Connective Action: Digital Media and the Personalization of Contentious Politics*. Cambridge University Press.

Brown, D. K. & Mourão, R. R. (2021) "Protest coverage matters: how media framing and visual communication affects support for Black civil rights protests," *Mass Communication and Society* 24(4): 576–96.

Harlow, S., Brown, D. K., Salaverría, R., & García-Perdomo, V. (2020) "Is the whole world watching? Building a typology of protest coverage on social media from around the world," *Journalism Studies* 21(11): 1590–1608.

Poell, T. & van Dijck, J. (2018) "Social media and new protest movements." In J. Burgess, A. Marwick, & T. Poell (eds.) *The SAGE Handbook of Social Media*. Los Angeles, CA: Sage, 546–61.

Treré, E. & Mattoni, A. (2016) 'Media ecologies and protest movements: main perspectives and key lessons', *Information, Communication & Society* 19(3): 290–306.

9 Platform Governance

Chapter 9 extends our model, arguing that platforms, and media in general, do not operate in a vacuum. To varying degrees, the legal, economic, and political contexts platforms operate in shape how they work, what their affordances are, how people use them, and their power in the world. Nation states and transnational organizations such as the European Union come up with legal and policy frameworks that govern media and platforms (or, as in the case of the United States, they largely fail to). Meanwhile, this chapter shows how platform companies introduce and constantly alter their own rules that internally govern how they are to be used, such as community standards and advertising content guidelines, and targeting affordances.

OBJECTIVES

By the end of this chapter, you should be able to:

- know the concept of platform governance
- understand the forms of and issues with media governance
- comprehend how platforms are governed globally
- discuss mechanisms for platform self-regulation
- understand Facebook's Oversight Board.

9.1 Introduction

In May 2014, a Spanish citizen (whose name shall remain unmentioned here, for reasons we are about to discuss) won a momentous verdict in the Court of Justice of the European Union (CJEU). In a nutshell, his problem was: if you want to find out about a person you don't know, you Google them – and what turns up in the search results can cause havoc in their lives. For this Spaniard, an old newspaper article showed up high in the search results, revealing that his house had been sold at a foreclosure auction in 1998 to repay a debt. Given that he earned his living as a financial consultant, he felt that this old and closed story was harmful for his professional career.

The Court ruled that, indeed, there was a "right to be forgotten" on the Internet, and that search engines are responsible for the content they show in their results, which must comply with EU privacy laws. On the first day of compliance,

Google received over 12,000 similar complaints and requests to remove private data from search results. The case had remarkable consequences for everyone. The Spanish citizen who started it all had won his case, his story was removed from Google search, and the original story about his debt could be forgotten – but it had by then received a lot of subsequent media coverage, ensuring its memorability. This is the so-called "Streisand effect" – the unintended consequence of increasing awareness for information one seeks to remove, named after American singer and actress Barbra Streisand, who tried to suppress a photo of her Malibu house from the California Coastal Records Project, thereby drawing massive attention to the photograph. For platforms, the case opened another gate for the role of governments and courts in shaping content regulation. And courts in many countries around the world began receiving similar complaints after the ruling.

The core of the debate is still controversial: while it may be understandable that people want to keep their "missteps" private, such as affairs, bankruptcy, and illegitimate children, and out of the public record if they affect their reputations and careers, what about the scandals of politicians (or would-be politicians), and those in power generally, in terms of their cases of corruption, sexual abuse, or war crimes? Isn't there also a right for the public to know – to archive for history, to hold people accountable, or to assess who should hold power? Justices and legislators are facing these tricky balancing acts to develop sensible rules and regulations that adjudicate between competing sets of interests and values. Platforms need to comply with different national laws and fulfill the competing demands of many different stakeholders (such as journalists and users), while often seeking to avoid government regulation and interference with their business models.

The idea of "platform governance" is expansive and covers cases such as these. It refers to different approaches to content moderation, such as platforms' own efforts at de-platforming, deleting messages, and flagging accounts, as well as platforms' own rules governing things such as hate speech and disinformation. It also covers the efforts by transnational bodies and states to set the rules platforms have to abide by or to hold them accountable for laws they developed in other domains (such as prohibitions against hate speech and terrorist content).

9.2 Governance as a Concept

Governance is an expansive concept that refers to a broad array of mechanisms to establish and maintain order. As we use it here, governance extends the scope of regulation and rule-making beyond state actors such as governments. In political science, for instance, global governance refers to all forms of regulation, including by entities beyond the nation state, such as international bodies, trade compacts, and treaties (e.g. Zürn 2018). Transnational organizations, such as the European parliament or European Commission, make decisions that affect and are binding on all 500 million inhabitants of the European Union. And these decisions often shape how corporations, including platforms, operate far beyond the borders of Europe. International treaties are often not legally binding, but they are a form of governance in the sense of creating orders that state actors abide by nevertheless.

The most obvious part of governance is the setting of rules. All organizations require recognizable governance. For example, governance provides structures through which organizations operate, including: defining things such as how members, management, and even citizens are held to account; the appropriate relationships and procedures for stakeholders to follow; and frameworks for monitoring relationships, rules, and the operation of other institutional processes. The systems and structures put in place create and administer policies and procedures and effectively define what governance entails. Governance creates rules or laws relating to issues such as conflicts of interest, equity, or inclusiveness. Almost all organizations have governance codes – such as shareholder documents, employee handbooks, and ethics codes – otherwise, they wouldn't be able to legally or functionally operate. And governance goes beyond the setting of rules – it also entails the enforcement of rules and the sanctioning of non-compliance. Indeed, what's the point of establishing rules, when you can't enforce them and punish disobedience? And governance is multidimensional – various governance systems intersect and overlap. These are important points, especially with regard to platform governance, as we will argue below in this chapter.

The idea of *media governance* specifically refers to the prescribed set of rules and regulations instituted to administer and influence the behavior of media within a particular context. Or, as Katzenbach (2013: 400) put it: "Under the umbrella term 'governance,' researchers have drawn their attention to the emergence, consolidation and transformation of various structures and processes that facilitate, constrain and coordinate the range of behavior of actors in a specific field." For our purposes, this is the field of media and platforms. Media governance sets the background conditions that media and platforms operate in, such as the incentives and limitations that influence how platforms emerge and function in the political system.

SPOTLIGHTED CASES

There are extreme cases of governance in many countries. Russia has long pressured American platform companies such as Facebook, Google, and Twitter to fall in line with limits on online freedom of expression, including through demands to take down content. States such as Belarus banned livestreams from protest events, and India has aggressively pursued Twitter and other platforms for harboring content in opposition to its ruling party. Indeed, in July 2022, Twitter sued the Indian government over its censorship laws that required companies to take down certain types of content and block accounts, passed under the pretext of preventing misinformation but broadly seen as an attempt at the politically motivated control of platform content (Singh & Conger 2022).

The attention that governments now pay to platforms and their role in political speech should be seen as the clearest signal yet as to their power to shape public discourse and politics – power that governments want to direct through media governance.

9.3 State Regulation and Self-Regulation

In general, when it comes to traditional legacy media, the more (and more complex) technologies are involved, the more the state engages in regulation. Newspapers, for instance, hardly face any state regulation when it comes to ownership in many countries. Television, on the other hand, was historically often shaped by state governance – especially given the historic scarcity of the broadcast spectrum (where only a certain number of channels were technically possible and permitted without interference) and its perceived power as a mass medium.

When there are only a few airwaves available for broadcasting, it takes governance to allocate who may use these frequencies, and for what purpose. From this logic, not only public service broadcasting emerged – ensuring that citizens get as much information as they need to make informed political choices across the limited radio spectrum – but also regulatory standards for those accessing the public airwaves, including commercial entities (such as outlets having to commit to using media in the public's interest).

In many countries, those seeking to operate a television station must apply for a broadcasting license. For example, while print media are entirely self-regulating in the United Kingdom, which means they operate independent of stipulated statutory rules, broadcast media outlets are subject to regulation through the Independent Television Commission (ITC) and the Radio Authority (RA), in observance of the Broadcasting Act of 1990 (Fielden 2016; Ruth 2019). In Mexico, community radios have fought for decades to be legally recognized and endowed with a regulatory framework defining how to obtain and keep broadcasting licenses. They have done so while operating in a legal gray zone – without a birth certificate (as "hijos naturales"), as Mexican journalist Julio DiBella (2005) put it. If there are no rules and no official registration, and broadly no transparent way to obtain a license, any community station operates at the arbitrary goodwill of those in power. Many community radio stations in other Latin American countries found or find themselves in a similar situation, facing a long fight for legal recognition and slow media reform processes. In Argentina, for example, it took 26 years to replace the authoritarian media law of its military junta (Harlow 2016; Klinger 2011; Lugo-Acando 2008). What these cases show is that non-regulation by the state can be an instrument for exercising power and repression, too.

In many media systems, governance also means self-regulation, or the rules that media organizations themselves set and enforce, sanctioning rule-breakers in cases of non-compliance. Most journalists around the world operate under codes of ethics that are established by professional journalism associations and press councils. It is normal for journalists in most countries to have ethical norms and principles that guide their conduct and professional activities (Hafez 2002; Hanitzsch et al. 2019; Limor & Himelboim 2006; Yang et al. 2016).

Media organizations also self-regulate around all sorts of other things, such as protecting minors, and in some countries have established authoritative bodies for complaints about false or unethical coverage. Often, self-regulation is designed to stave off the threat of state intervention and protect the autonomy of journalism and media organizations from the state. To take an example – in many countries, certain types of information (such as violence, pornography, etc.) are often seen as harmful

SPOTLIGHTED CASES

Ethics codes and self-regulation alone do not always work well. A good example is the infamous phone-hacking scandal in the United Kingdom. In 2011, journalists from the *News of the World*, one of the nation's oldest weeklies, were accused of hacking politicians' and celebrities' phones and other unethical conduct, including bribery in pursuit of stories. As a result of the scandal, after nearly 170 years of existence, the paper closed its doors. The scandal led to an investigation into the culture, practices, and ethics of the press, which resulted in the founding of the Independent Press Standards Organization (IPSO), an independent regulator of the press. Several newspapers, including *Financial Times* and the *Guardian*, however refused to be part of IPSO, preferring instead to establish their own complaints body (Greenslade 2014).

to children. Swedish law even prohibits the broadcasting of television commercials aimed at children under 12. The problem is that, in some contexts, protecting children may easily lead to the suppression of legitimate information, or censorship. Even more, many states have laws against things such as libel, or falsities that damage reputations, which political actors can wield to silence the press. Media actors therefore argue that it is important to have independent professional associations that provide guidelines or draw lines independent from the government, and according to professional judgments. Even so, a comparative study showed that journalists seek to avoid state intervention, but at the same time perceive the existing instruments of self-regulation as insufficient – due to a lack of incentives for organizations in media industries to accept or invest in media accountability (Fengler et al. 2015).

Other Key Players

Media governance involves more than state authorities and media organizations themselves. Civil society actors have a role to play in influencing public policy regarding platform or media regulation. As a reminder, "civil society" refers to the organizations and institutions that sit between the public and the government – such as non-governmental organizations, universities, and interest and trade groups. Civil society organizations can inform citizens about governance challenges, including actions they should consider taking when platforms regulate their speech. They can help steer a policy debate toward a direction considered to be in the interest of the public. With conspiracy theories, hate speech, and "fake news" designed to undermine democracy and other political institutions, it is important to have a vibrant and organized civil society.

Scientific discoveries and arguments led by scientists and social scientists also play a key role in driving the regulatory and governance agenda for media and platforms. Social scientists actively produce research-based work, which politicians and policymakers (ideally) use to inform and draft regulatory legislation. However, increasingly in many countries, researchers working at state-funded universities are not always free to openly criticize the government or to conduct public research that may irritate authorities.

SPOTLIGHTED CASES

In extreme cases, social scientists could get fired, jailed, or killed for their work. Faizullah Jalal, a respected political science and law professor at Kabul University, was arrested in January 2021 in Afghanistan for criticizing the Taliban leadership on social media, several international media outlets, including France24 and Al Jazeera English, reported. In the United States, in recent years, a number of states have worked to prevent researchers at public universities from activities such as testifying in court in contravention of state positions and teaching about racial inequality.

Other important players in media governance are digital dissidents or whistleblowers. The prevalence of digital technologies such as social media platforms has facilitated the distribution of dissident information – especially important in authoritarian countries – as well as whistleblowing in many governmental and corporate contexts. Whistleblowers such as former Facebook employee Frances Haugen have taken center stage in accusing big tech companies of alarming uses of personal data and weakening and damaging democratic processes across the world. In democracies, whistleblowers play an important role in holding power to account. They help "alert society to irregularities and practices that are unacceptable for democratic societies and harmful for citizens" (Høedt-Rasmussen & Voorhoof 2018: 3). In fact, Lewis and Vandekerckhove (2011) argue that transparency and accountability are important to healthy democracy, and thus unmasking wrongdoing should be tolerated. However, contemporary dissidents and whistleblowers – known for their formidable opposition to intelligence agencies, governments, and corporations – have also been harassed, hounded, or even jailed for disclosing information they believe is in the public interest, or for simply demanding change.

9.4 National and Transnational Media Governance

Other forms of media governance have regional, national, and transnational dimensions. Article 19 of the Universal Declaration of Human Rights adopted by the United Nations (UN) guarantees freedom of expression and information. In principle, that would be enough to provide the legal framework through which the right to free expression and information is guaranteed – but this declaration is not legally binding, like many international provisions. International organizations such as the UN often have the power to establish norms (how things should be or be done), but not the means to enforce them or sanction disobedience. It is also very challenging to make universally binding rules that are accepted across many nations. What works fine in the US may not in Europe, and regulatory solutions for problems in Europe may not travel well to Asian or African countries.

In fact, the regulatory differences between countries and regions open governance gray areas and economic opportunities. Media organizations and digital platforms benefit from such differences, for instance when choosing low-tax countries as their headquarters, or moving to countries with little regulation in crucial areas for their business. For example, a reason many global platforms such as Alphabet (Google) chose Ireland as their European headquarters is that the country offered them a safe haven from state and European regulation. This enabled firms such as Alphabet to economically prosper and grow without constraints, such as EU privacy laws, given that Ireland is soft on enforcing them (Murgia & Espinoza 2021). In addition, it is very difficult to get legal hold of companies that operate globally and that can easily withdraw from state regulation by just moving to another country. Messenger service Telegram, for instance, is notorious for escaping state-level regulations. Its founder, Russian tech billionaire Pavel Durov (who previously founded the Russian platform VKontakte and sold it to oligarch Alisher Usmanov in 2014) moved himself and Telegram to Dubai in 2017 after the Kremlin pressed him to hand over data. Conveniently, Dubai also has no personal income tax. Since then, Durov has acquired citizenship in various countries (Descalsota 2022), and claimed that Telegram will most likely not have any permanent location (Durov 2018). This, of course, makes it very hard to regulate the firm.

9.5 Governance Issues: Media Pluralism

Media governance has many dimensions, including creating frameworks for the availability of press, media, and broadcasting institutions in their plurality, which is often seen as the cornerstone of democracy (Brogi 2020). The normative ideal behind media pluralism is that having a wide range of different opinions in a democratic polity enables citizens to acquire a broad range of views and perspectives on the world they live in and ultimately make informed choices regarding the issues that affect them. Media pluralism can be understood based on the variety of media content (*internal pluralism*), and on the number of available channels and sources – and who owns them (*external pluralism*).

SPOTLIGHTED CASES

Media mogul Rupert Murdoch is a good example of a potential threat to international media plurality. Through his company News Corp, in the United Kingdom alone Murdoch owns many of the nation's leading national papers including the *Sun*, *The Times*, and *The Sunday Times*. He also owns the *Wall Street Journal* and the *New York Post* in the US, along with many newspapers in his native Australia including, at the national level, the *Australian*, the *Australian Associated Press*, News.com.au, and *Weekend Australian*, among several others. His media holdings also extend to TV channels, online-based content providers, magazines, and book publishers. In the US, he owns the Fox Corporation, including Fox News, a political media outlet aligned with the Republican Party.

The problem with media concentration from a democratic perspective is that, when more and more media are owned and operated by fewer companies, there is potentially less internal and external pluralism. And media owners can have tremendous political power should they decide to intervene in media coverage, as well as policy debates, to benefit their interests – Rupert Murdoch and the late Italian prime minister Silvio Berlusconi being just two particularly notorious examples. From an economic standpoint, however, media concentration makes perfect sense, as it enables companies to grow and benefit from synergy and scale effects. If you own a chain of cinemas, a movie production studio, and various TV channels, you control the whole chain of making movies, distributing them to audiences, promoting them, and offering actors cross-platform deals. Unfortunately, what works great in business is often not ideal for democracy, as it may narrow the voices and opinions visible in public debate. Alternatively, under the right ownership with public service-oriented values, profitable businesses can subsidize democratically important ones (as advocates for Amazon founder Jeff Bezos's tenure as the owner of the US's *Washington Post* argue). Regardless, in many cases media concentration did not just happen incidentally. It is the result of governance neglect (not regulating media markets) or even political intent (neglect of ownership regulation in return for favorable media coverage, such as in Mexico during the 70-year-long regime of the political party Partido Revolucionario Institucional).

The rise of the digital media, the Internet, and platforms was initially seen as an antidote to media concentration in the traditional media markets of newspapers, radio, and TV stations – broadly, a disruption of established media power. With digital broadcasting no longer being tied to the physical boundaries of radio waves or satellites, we increasingly live in high-choice media environments (van Aelst et al. 2017). And, for its utopian advocates, the Internet promised access and voice for everyone and an end to the age of information scarcity, physically limited airwaves (which provided a key rationale for media governance), and the power of entrenched cable and satellite broadcasters. With the Internet, many claimed that societies moved from the age of information scarcity to information abundance, and some may even say information overload.

That said, the problem of ownership and threats to pluralism has, however, not simply evaporated. Ownership of key properties on the global Internet today very much resembles highly concentrated traditional media markets, with a very small number of giant corporations controlling large digital platforms. While many of the largest, Western-oriented platforms are publicly traded companies, often one single individual has outsized control (e.g. Meta's Mark Zuckerberg, Tim Cook at Apple – and Elon Musk after he took Twitter private in October 2022). Moreover, from a pluralism perspective, van Aelst et al. (2017) also argue that information abundance does not necessarily result in more diverse information; media consumers might just get more of the same from fewer sources (the diversity paradox), and the demand for diverse information may not be as high as normative assumptions have suggested. That said, many other studies show that the use of platforms for news results in a far more diverse array of sources and content than from broadcast media, and the scale and scope of social networks as conduits for political news and information have resulted in a robust, diverse ecosystem for political content unprecedented in human history – often with accompanying problems of misinformation and disinformation, as we detail in the next chapter. At the same time, it is also clear that incumbent players, or those well established in other media, often carry their reach and clout online. As a study of Fox News revealed after the 2016 US presidential election (Benkler et al. 2018), the outlet reached far beyond those tuning into its cable broadcasts, amplifying its messages to millions of additional people online.

Internal and external media pluralism can be measured empirically and addressed in media regulation. Policymakers have a number of options. One is increasing the supply of quality and diverse information – such as through subsidies to public broadcasters (for example, the global BBC) or newspapers (as in Sweden's subsidies to local publishers). In many countries, regulatory authorities must green-light the mergers of large media companies, not only with regard to market competition rules, but also to protect pluralism. And media pluralism can be compared across time and countries. For instance, the Media Pluralism Monitor compares European countries and their media markets, focusing on the protection of pluralism, market plurality, political independence, and social inclusiveness of media (see Centre for Media Pluralism and Media Freedom 2022). Monitoring initiatives comparing the quality of democracy across the globe include indicators of media pluralism, for example the Sustainable Governance Indicators or Freedom House's Media Freedom Index. The assumption is that pluralism is essential for democratic health – although the growing problem of mis- and disinformation and propaganda detailed in the next chapter suggests that pluralism without consideration of actual content might have adverse effects, including empowering anti-democratic actors, state-backed efforts to meddle in other countries' affairs, extremist content, and claims that undermine knowledge-producing institutions.

9.6 The History of Platform Governance

Early enthusiastic claims about the Internet as a space were deeply libertarian, despite its roots in US Cold War military technology and academic research institutions (Turner 2006). The earliest global Internet had its roots in the US, although there were also other decentralized computer networks (the French Mintel System) and other political systems developed rivals more or less successfully (B. Peters 2016). The US Internet as a technology emerged at the intersection of Cold War military operations (its decentralized structure designed as a hedge against nuclear attack) and the ideology of Californian optimism and the communalist counterculture of early Silicon Valley (Svensson 2021; Turner 2010). Yet, by the 1990s, the Internet and "cyberspace" were rhetorically cast as absolutely free and unregulatable spaces. The massively popular and influential "A Manifesto for the Declaration of Independence of Cyberspace," penned in Davos by Grateful Dead lyricist John Perry Barlow, distilled this ethos of networked computing, contrasting a comparatively more open and accessible space of the mind – with a radical new freedom of expression, information abundance, and supposedly harmonious new forms of leveled social relations – with the top-down control of bodies and thought in the world of the flesh. This ethos also shaped many of the new platforms emerging in Silicon Valley during the early and mid-2000s, which adopted few explicit rules governing expression – an approach that soon proved unworkable, given pornography, threats, hate speech, and grift.

Even during its heady early days, however, the Internet still had forms of governance. US legal scholar Lawrence Lessig influentially noted that, even when other forms of regulation might be absent, "code is law." Lessig (2000) argued that the design and code of technologies worked to define what the Internet is, what it is not, and what users could do on sites and platforms. There were many other governance mechanisms as well, of course. In the US, Section 230 of the Communications Decency Act of 1996 was an important legislative act that shielded platforms from intermediary liability for what people posted on them, which was central to their growth (Citron & Wittes 2018). Beyond this, however, and despite the potential for many other forms of regulation, digital platforms faced few rules in many countries at the beginning of the twenty-first century. One reason is that they were quite successful in obfuscating the nature of their business, insisting that they were not "media" companies. In fact, the very term "platform" was helpful in avoiding regulation – it suggests an open, neutral, intermediary service, without any liability for content, and that falls outside of existing telecommunications and media regulations (Gillespie 2010).

That said, it is now clear that there are many different forms of governance brought to bear on the Internet generally, and platforms specifically. Contemporary scholarship thinks of the Internet in terms of a technology "stack" – with many layers that all introduce potential points for governance (Bratton 2016). Think about all the technologies and actors that are necessary to produce the Internet. You need undersea cables to connect across large geographic spaces, physical infrastructure (such as servers) to make webpages possible, hardware devices and software installed on them, domain hosting companies, internet service providers, international agencies such as ICANN (which assigns domain names), protocols and standards that govern how technologies communicate with one another and with users, in addition to all of the platforms and pages at the application layer of the Internet itself (DeNardis et al. 2020). There is governance at every level of the stack – from rules that govern the development of critical infrastructure to the policies of domain name providers. Indeed, sites hosting extremists worldwide such as 4Chan learned long ago how precarious access to the Internet can be, as the many intermediary companies that host sites, assign domain names, or facilitate payments have their own policies that platforms are subject to.

How should platforms be regulated and by whom? What should be regulated? And to what ends? Many societies, both in democratic and in non-democratic contexts, have recently moved to regulate social media. How this is being done is often completely different from country to country. Some countries have been accused of using social media regulation as a way of silencing dissenting voices. Turkey is a good example. Its social media legislation introduced in 2021 compels platforms with more than a million daily users to appoint a local representative whose task is to remove content should a court order it. It also forbids platforms from taking user data beyond the Turkish borders. Opponents of this law see the government's data localization attempts as an excuse to surveil citizens, especially those opposed to the ruling party. India and Uganda have introduced similar legislation. In 2022, Pakistan introduced its own version of a cybercrime law, which critics say is likely to be used against those opposed to the government. Cuba's social media law, introduced in 2021, explicitly punishes those who use platforms to criticize the government. Even Australia's proposed Social Media (Anti-Trolling) Bill, which is designed to force social media companies to release the identities of anonymous users whose posts may be deemed defamatory, has also come under heavy criticism, with opponents of the ruling party accusing the state of attempting to silence critics.

Germany and Austria are states that have adopted laws explicitly targeting hate and crime on social media platforms. For example, the German Network Enforcement Act of 2017 did not introduce any new regulation, but decreed that platforms with more than 2 million users in Germany must delete "obviously illegal content within 24 hours" – from hate speech to child porn to swastikas. Similar attempts in France hit a brick wall after the law was deemed unconstitutional. Another issue of state regulation is related to copyright issues for news publishers.

While many countries have tried before, in 2021 Australia successfully passed legislation that requires large tech platforms operating in the country to pay news publishers for news content that users share on the platforms. Amid political debates around the growing economic and political power of platforms, fair competition, and consumer protection that have been ongoing since 2017, the impetus behind this is that platforms make profits with content produced by journalists and media figures, while news media companies suffer. Indeed, as we detailed above, the business model of traditional media has come under pressure, as advertising revenue increasingly gets captured by platforms. More and more citizens get their news directly from social media instead of directly from media outlets or publishers. In Australia, that is 73 percent of internet users (Reuters Institute for the Study of Journalism 2021). This increases the incentives for companies to purchase ads on Google or Facebook rather than on news websites or radio broadcasts.

SPOTLIGHTED CASE

Before the Australian "News Media and Digital Platforms Mandatory Bargaining Code" was passed, it faced fierce opposition from Facebook and Google, despite wide political consensus on the matter in parliament. The companies not only threatened to leave Australia altogether with their services, but Facebook actually went ahead and deleted all content from the Facebook pages of Australian news outlets and prevented users around the world from sharing content from Australian news sites for approximately a week in February 2021 (Bailo et al. 2021b). The Facebook news ban used a broad definition of "news" as does the law – for example, the company banned the country's Bureau of Meteorology and public health institutions, even at a time of bushfires and a pandemic. Google inserted pop-ups on its search engine site to "warn" Australian citizens about the consequences of the new law. This move was heavily criticized by Australian politicians and finally Facebook returned to normal, stating that the company had reached a deal with the Australian government.

The Australian approach is innovative because it works on the principle of arbitration. It requires platforms and news companies to strike a deal, and if they fail, a public arbitrator will make a final decision for compensation with no room for middle ground (known as "pendulum arbitration"). The idea is that platforms will negotiate sincerely and pay larger sums through this mechanism of final arbitration. As a consequence, major platforms such as Google and Meta/Facebook have signed agreements with a range of publishers. Many countries have tried to implement legislation to make platforms pay content producers. In France, for instance, Google agreed to pay publishers in 2021. In May 2022, Google announced a deal with 300 publishers in the EU – with the amounts that will be paid undisclosed.

An important argument against the Australian approach was that these platform payments, in essence, were often going to large and profitable media companies – such as conservative Australian media mogul Rupert Murdoch's various holdings – and the government therefore was picking winners and losers in a media industry. On the other hand, as Bossio et al. (2022: 136) argue, it marks a turn in global platform governance, a "leading example of a global trajectory towards regulatory change, which sees governments move from a reactive regulation model to specific interventions around the governance of digital media spaces."

SPOTLIGHTED CASES

Major advancements in platform regulation have also come recently from the European Union, particularly with two game-changing initiatives: the Digital Markets Act (DMA) and the Digital Services Act (DSA), both of which have been in development since 2020 and passed in the EU parliament on July 6, 2022. The DSA considers platforms to be "intermediaries" and seeks to improve content moderation of illegal and harmful content, particularly on large platforms. While, in the US, platforms cannot be held accountable for hosting others' content (according to the above-mentioned Section 230), the DSA introduces a conditional liability exemption in Europe – if platforms know some content is illegal, they must remove it. It also forces platforms to be more transparent about algorithms and their effects on society, it includes bans on some forms of targeted advertisements, and it makes platforms assess and fix their "systemic risks." Meanwhile, in 2021, the European parliament approved a law compelling platforms to remove terrorist content in less than 60 minutes – otherwise, they risk heavy fines of up to 4 percent of their global revenue (Goujard 2022).

Looking forward, the emergence of Facebook whistleblower Frances Haugen, particularly her claims that Facebook makes profit from hate speech, has helped to spark calls for more regulation in countries around the world. Her claims that user safety was not Facebook's main concern as long as the company was making profit compelled many governments to introduce new regulatory frameworks targeting social media platforms.

9.7 Platform Self-Governance

In the absence of state regulation in many nations, but facing increasing public pressure, most platforms have developed and adopted extensive forms of self-governance since 2008. In the early days, there were few rules governing the content of posts or comments on Facebook and other platforms – either externally in the form of law and state regulation, or internally in the form of platform policies. Community (or other platform) rules generally emerged ad hoc and developed along with the growth of the platforms, especially the proliferation of controversies and subsequent challenges from users, as well as political pressure. In this sense, self-governance can be understood as a form of "reflexive coordination – focusing on those 'critical moments,' when routine activities become problematic and need to be revised" (Hoffmann et al. 2017).

Today, there is hardly any platform without some form of self-regulation, even if they claim to be open, free, and neutral. Self-regulation is not static, but constantly changing. The community rules of platforms, for instance, have changed many times and continue to do so rather frequently. In a study of shifts in platform policies, Barrett and Kreiss (2019) referred to this as "platform transience" and showed how it was often spurred by journalistic inquiries, changing commercial contexts, and user and political pressure. The Platform Governance Archive (https://pga.hiig.de) is a great resource in this regard, collecting key policy documents produced by Facebook, Instagram, Twitter, and YouTube and tracking their changes over time.

Self-regulation means that platforms set rules, enforce them, and sanction users according to their own policies. These are not without contestation, and their rules, decisions, and sanctions are at times extremely controversial and become high-profile cases. Facebook's and Twitter's decisions to ban former US President Donald Trump from their platforms after the attempted coup at the US Capitol on January 6, 2021 is a case in point (Trump was subsequently reinstated on both platforms). That was the final act in a long drama where Trump repeatedly violated, or walked right up to, an ever shifting line: numerous platform policies about election and census-related disinformation, hate speech, violent speech, and health misinformation. Indeed, platforms long let Trump get away with things they would not have permitted from other users on the theory that the public should have broad latitude to hear from its elected leaders. But, as we stated in Chapter 3, many of his supporters, and leaders around the world, did not agree with the decision to remove him from Facebook, Twitter, and other platforms. They instead thought this was an attempt to silence him, and them. That said, it is also clear that platforms only took this drastic step after a similarly drastic event: an attempted coup. It took *a lot* to get to the point where Trump was "deplatformed." Indeed, platforms often have little desire to be "arbiters of truth" when it comes to policing the expression of political actors (Kreiss & McGregor 2019).

These are all examples of the most prominent form of self-regulation: content moderation. Tens of thousands of workers, often outsourced to third-party firms, scan through millions of algorithmically flagged and user-reported posts, making decisions regarding whether a post, image, video, or some other content violated the platform's own community standards or rules. This is a tough, and in most cases also

SPOTLIGHTED CONTENT

One could write a book simply on platform policies relating to permissible speech. To provide just a snapshot of how complicated platform content moderation is in *one* domain, democratic processes, here are the findings of a report that tracked changes in platform policies from 2020 to 2022 (in advance of the midterm elections) in the United States. In an analysis of policy changes by Facebook and Instagram, Reddit, Snapchat, TikTok, Twitter, and YouTube, Kreiss and Brooks (2022) find:

- increased saliency of discussions in platform policy documents regarding social media's role in protecting elections and election integrity;
- reevaluations of previous thinking concerning "public interest" exceptions related to potentially false, harmful, or misleading posts;
- detailed outlines and approaches for handling challenges related to the upcoming 2022 US midterms by Meta, Twitter, and YouTube;
- updates to Meta political advertising and fact-checking policies;
- the continuation of Twitter's complete ban on political advertisements;
- YouTube's new election integrity policies in the wake of the 2020 election;
- few, but notable, changes to platforms' manipulated media policies, primarily concerning troll farms, impersonation, and spam.

a quite precarious and emotionally taxing, job, with long hours for low wages, as the documentary movie *The Cleaners* showed. Content moderation relies on automation – algorithms that probabilistically identify hate speech, toxicity, sexual or violent content, copyright infringements, and other problematic or illegal material. This approach helps platforms to accomplish at scale what human labor cannot (at the cost platforms are willing to pay).

While it may sound very practical to find technological solutions for these problems, practitioners as well as scholars are skeptical. Gorwa et al. (2020: 1) argue that:

> even "well optimized" moderation systems could exacerbate, rather than relieve, many existing problems with content policy as enacted by platforms for three main reasons: automated moderation threatens to (a) further increase opacity, making a famously non-transparent set of practices even more difficult to understand or audit, (b) further complicate outstanding issues of fairness and justice in large-scale sociotechnical systems and, (c) re-obscure the fundamentally political nature of speech decisions being executed at scale.

Moreover, these automated systems do not always not work well. During the Covid-19 pandemic, for instance, Facebook sent all human content moderators home, tasking only automated systems with content moderation. The result was less than optimal, with more content being flagged or removed, but much problematic content nevertheless remained on the platform (Scott & Kayali 2020).

Another problem contributing to the failure of content moderation is that so far it works most effectively (and often not even well) in English, not in other languages – while only about 5 percent of the world's population converses in English. The US has only a small percentage of the world's platform users; they are dominated by languages such as Chinese, Spanish, Hindi, and a long list of other languages. In cases where users communicate in a local Asian or African language, it simply means users are more likely to be on the receiving end of harmful content or hate speech that companies such as YouTube, Facebook, and Twitter may never even have an idea about. In Bangladesh, Facebook failed to recognize a hate campaign against the Rohingya Muslim minority, and even failed to detect calls to kill Rohingya in *paid* ads (Milko & Ortutay 2022). These are among the reasons the United Nations clearly pointed to Facebook's role in the ethnic cleansing that occurred (Beyrer & Kamarulzaman 2017). Moreover, harmful content shared, for instance, in a local African language could target a foreign national and the platform would likely never know about it.

Self-regulation is rarely transparent, mistakes abound, and there is often little users can do to hold platforms accountable for the decisions they make. Self-regulation often reinforces platforms' power because they predominantly regulate according to their own rules and do so in a non-transparent way that evades external monitoring, without any (or many) opportunities to appeal their decisions. The problem of non-transparency becomes most obvious (ironically) with regards to the transparency reports that large platforms such as Twitter, Google, and Facebook publish quarterly (after the German Network Enforcement Act made them do it). In these reports, these companies document how many "malicious manipulation" and fake accounts or networks they have detected and deleted. But there is no way to validate these reports from the outside. We are just expected to believe them.

The reality though is that, even as many want to see some form of regulation targeting social media platforms, there is no consensus on the right and effective way of doing it. Indeed, the political right in countries across the globe often sees the problem in terms of platform censorship of content, and makes arguments for regulation that would preserve free expression. One person's free expression, however, is another's hate speech, intimidation, and violence. Government leaders decry targeted political advertising – but fall silent when their campaigns and parties utilize the same tool to win elections. Many complain about emotional and identity appeals facilitated on platforms, and algorithms that promote content in divisive or polarizing ways, yet these are also key to the power of pro-democratic social movements such as the global Rhodes Must Fall.

Facebook has engaged in the most high-profile attempt to date to create a transparent and fair set of procedures to make content-related decisions. As such, it is worth examining the Facebook Oversight Board, and diving deeper into an innovative case of platform self-regulation and content moderation, and all the difficulties they entail.

9.8 The Facebook Oversight Board

The Facebook Oversight Board is the most ambitious attempt by a platform to date to address the fact that it is a de facto global speech arbiter and to develop a fair institution to wield that power. The legal scholar Kate Klonick (2019) details how Facebook launched its independent global Oversight Board in October 2020. The idea was to create a kind of global "supreme court" for speech that formalized a way of adjudicating global speech disputes on its platform. Broadly, the Facebook Oversight Board illustrates how the platform has become one of the most central forums for much political, cultural, social, and commercial speech across the globe today and, as such, among the most important decision-makers as to what types of speech are allowed.

SPOTLIGHTED CONTENT

Consider, for a minute, the very different categories of speech that Facebook has an important – if not *the* most important in some countries – say over:

- the posts of candidates for office and those of their political parties
- the pages of music producers seeking to build audiences for their creative work
- the posts and sharing of media between family members living apart
- the paid advertising of global companies such as Coca-Cola and Guinness.

Facebook has a say over an exceptionally broad and complicated array of speech on a global scale. Over the course of the nineteenth and twentieth centuries, governments and courts around the world developed a set of laws, policies, and legal interpretations that govern many types of speech – often in the context of the development of mass media. Various cases and lawmaking efforts have sought to balance rights, adjudicate between competing values (such as expressive freedom and protections from hateful and harmful speech), protect the expression of individuals and the well-being of society and minors (e.g. through laws that ban obscenity, punish defamation, or regulate when certain types of content can be displayed so minors do not encounter it), and govern things such as false advertising and deception to protect trust in commercial transactions. Governments around the world draw these lines in different places, reflecting their national histories, cultures, and politics.

For one *company* to have to govern all of these types of speech as a commercial platform, in accordance with multiple and disparate state laws in the countries it operates in around the world, is a monumental task. And Facebook routinely goes *beyond* various country-specific laws in regulating speech as a commercial platform (a basic right, notwithstanding applicable laws, to regulate its own platform in accordance with its own commercial and stakeholder interests that it generally enjoys in countries around the world.) Facebook often has more expansive rules governing its platform than many governments do, because it has a unique mix of stakeholders and orientations. As detailed above, it is a commercial business, meaning that it has an obligation to its shareholders and employees to return profits. As such, it often makes decisions in line with keeping its user base engaged on the platform (such as algorithmically promoting speech that is emotionally charged, but also policing content likely to turn many users off, such as pornography). It also has a set of *normative* expectations placed upon it by its users – those things that users simply expect the company to uphold. One of them is for Facebook to protect, in a broad sense, users' ability to say politically controversial things – just as, in free societies, constitutions prevent the government from censoring people except in extraordinary circumstances. And yet users also expect Facebook to protect them from harassment and hate speech that might cause them to not have a good experience on, or even leave, the platform. Another expectation is that Facebook allow users to access content of significant cultural importance – such as the famous photograph of a Vietnamese girl burned by American napalm during the Vietnam War, a focus of international controversy when Facebook banned it for a time because of child nudity.

The vast majority of the time, content posted on Facebook is not controversial. People write things to express their political views. Family members share photos of vacations. Old friends reconnect after decades apart. Star football strikers connect with their fans. Local businesses sell their wares. Individuals engage in transactions through Facebook's Marketplace. However, in the past decade, we have seen a number of high-profile, international controversies over many different categories of speech: mis- and disinformation, state-sponsored propaganda, the content and targeting of political ads, paid influencers working on behalf of candidates and corporations, breastfeeding promotion groups, discriminatory housing ads, hate speech, anti-democratic or violent organizing, terrorist videos, anti-vaccine groups, and international conspiracy movements such as QAnon. The list can go on and on. Facebook is not unique in facing these controversies – all major platforms have on one level or another been faced with these challenges. But it is the most prominent and visible platform that plays this quasi-public-sphere role – and despite TikTok's global rise, it does not play this role, yet.

Facebook has engaged in the most high-profile attempt to date to create a transparent and fair set of procedures to make content-related decisions. As such, it is worth examining the Facebook Oversight Board here. Some background first. Facebook is governed by its Community Standards, a loose and evolving set of rules that determine what users can say on the platform. In essence, it is the contract that users, and the company, agree to for using and providing the platform. It evolved from the origins of the company as a small start-up in Palo Alto, California, in the 2000s. Initially, speech rules were an afterthought as the fledgling company pursued explosive growth at all costs, and they developed in an ad hoc way on a case-by-case basis to solve pressing problems from the company's perspective. Its guiding ideal initially was free speech, which was reflected in both United States law and culture and the ethos of the tech industry at the time (Adams & Kreiss 2021).

That said, it also quickly became clear to the company that with growth came issues the early company was ill equipped to handle: users could harass one another, post revenge pornography, use racist and sexist language, or otherwise flood the site with imagery and content that diminished the experience for other users. It was as much a question of speech as of the company's growth and, well, the bottom line. The Facebook Community Standards initially grew up around solving problems in a pragmatic sense, addressing an issue and then trying to develop a rule or principle from it. Often, decisions were rooted in a goal of preventing harm. As this grew unwieldy, Facebook tried more explicitly to define an overarching set of principles to guide its content rules, which provided much of the shape the Community Standards have today.

The Community Standards outline broad principles, but the interpretation, application, and enforcement of them was left up to the discretion of the company – until the Oversight Board was granted review. Often, the company's interpretations of standards, the application of their decisions, and regulatory actions were not transparent or accountable to users or any other body. As such, the Facebook Oversight Board was created in an attempt, in part driven by external pressure, to become more democratic – providing greater consistency in, and transparency, accountability, and justification for, actions, and creating some mechanism to allow users to appeal the decisions the company was making.

The original idea for the Oversight Board was announced in November 2018, and it was formally launched in 2019. Broadly, the Board was tasked with interpreting Facebook's core values, which are "voice," balanced against "authenticity," "safety," "privacy," and "dignity," and its content moderation rules – the Community Standards – in the context of the decisions that the company makes. These Standards form the basis for what Facebook *looks for* as potential violations of content rules (and often through the algorithmic means detailed above), what users report as violations of the platform's rules, and the often opaque way that the company then reviews that content and takes action against it – a process that is based on that labor of the global army of often ill-paid and traumatized workers tasked with review discussed above.

The 11-member Board represents different regions around the world, and hears cases about content that is removed or kept up, although in practice this was originally limited to review over removed content. Users, and Facebook (in cases where the company itself wants guidance), can request a ruling. The Board selects its cases from user and company submissions, reviewing the decisions at issue, and ultimately makes a determination whether the decision was in line with Facebook's stated "policies and values" (Facebook 2023). Over time, the Board looks to establish precedent. However, the decisions of the Board are binding on Facebook in the context of that specific case, not on future cases of similar content. The Board can also make policy and process recommendations.

While the Oversight Board marks an unprecedented attempt at building due process and accountability into the content moderation decisions of the world's largest platform company, there have been vocal critics. Siva Vaidhyanathan (2021), for instance, has pointed out that, in restricting the Board's oversight only to *content* decisions (and initially only in the context of what gets taken down), the company did not address the important problem of the algorithmic decisions it makes – for instance, the choice to amplify certain content. Even so, there is nothing that would prevent the Board from expanding its jurisdiction in this way going forward or from making policy recommendations that relate to algorithmic functioning. And, in its first years, the Board issued a number of important rulings that overturned the company's decisions to take down content. Along the way, it consistently called Facebook to account for its lack of clarity and transparency, and flawed processes in its decision-making.

The most famous cases illustrate Facebook's global power to moderate political speech and how the company has sought to create some advisory and oversight mechanism given how high the stakes are. In the run up to the US 2020 presidential election, the company was faced with an increasingly hard set of challenges to its content moderation policies. These included the widespread phenomenon of Covid-19 mis- and disinformation, which were causing real-world harm in health behavior. During the US election itself, President Trump and members of the Republican Party repeatedly made false claims and allegations about the integrity and security of the election, as well as its processes and procedures. The company vacillated at first, declining to do much, but then rolled out new health and civic integrity policies, citing harm to public health and civic processes. At times – and inconsistently, but with increasing clarity as time went on – the company took action around protecting civic processes, such as limiting the ability of the president's disinformation to spread by restricting engagement on his posts. In the lead-up to November 2020, there were even more robust policy and enforcement actions, including bans on new political advertising pre- and post-election, takedowns of conspiracy movements such as QAnon, limits on the spread of a mainstream press story that the company determined to be disinformation, and, after the election, the removal of "Stop the Steal" groups on the platform. This culminated in the indefinite suspension of the president's Facebook and Instagram accounts in the wake of the attempted coup at the US Capitol on January 6, 2021 – a ban which the Oversight Board ultimately upheld, but sent back to Facebook for the company to clarify its policies and decision-making. In response, the company clarified that it was a two-year ban, set new policies for public figures during times of civil unrest, and outlined reinstatement conditions. Trump's Facebook and Instagram accounts were restored in February 2023.

9.9 Summary

To fully understand how political communication works, it is important to come to grips with the intricate governance processes covering media and platforms. Media, whether they are traditional or contemporary, play a prominent role in fundamentally shaping how we communicate politically. Different media systems exist. Some are authoritarian, while others are either free or partially free. Societies develop regulatory frameworks over time in accordance with their laws, values, principles, and the interests of many stakeholders that are involved in contested policymaking processes. Taken together, we can think of governance as being a key form of accountability that the state and the public have over what are often commercial interests, and as important means that media and platforms have for governing themselves – including through professional associations where they act collectively, and independent bodies that seek transparency and accountability.

Discussion Questions

- Draft core principles for new governmental regulation ensuring fair election advertisements on social media platforms.
- Content moderation is a key practice of platform self-regulation. However, content moderation cannot (yet) be fully automated. It rests on thousands of precariously employed moderators making millions of decisions (watch the documentary *The Cleaners*). Meanwhile, from a libertarian perspective one could argue that content moderation restricts freedom of expression. Do platforms really need content moderation? Why (or why not)?

Suggestions for Further Reading

Cowls, J., Darius, P., Santistevan, D., & Schramm, M. (2022) "Constitutional metaphors: Facebook's 'supreme court' and the legitimation of platform governance," *New Media & Society*: https://doi.org/10.1177/14614448221085559.

Gorwa, R. (2019) "What is platform governance?" *Information, Communication & Society* 22(6): 854–71.

Gorwa, R., Binns, R., & Katzenbach, C. (2020) "Algorithmic content moderation: technical and political challenges in the automation of platform governance," *Big Data & Society* 7(1): 1–15.

Napoli, P. M. (2019) *Social Media and the Public Interest: Media Regulation in the Disinformation Age*. New York: Columbia University Press.

Van Dijck, J., de Winkel, T., & Schäfer, M. T. (2021) "Deplatformization and the governance of the platform ecosystem," *New Media & Society*: https://doi.org/10.1177/14614448211045662.

10 Platforms, Misinformation, Disinformation, and Propaganda

Chapter 10 focuses on a set of current issues of central concern to contemporary democracies – namely, the relationship between information, polarization, mis/disinformation, propaganda, and public opinion. We define, theorize, and historicize these concepts, and discuss the types of information the public needs in democratic and other states. The chapter considers the role that fact-producing institutions play in political life, and asks what roles they should play. And we consider the responsibilities that platforms, journalism, and governments have for creating robust, democratic communication environments.

OBJECTIVES

By the end of this chapter, you should be able to:

- understand the relationship between platforms, information, and polarization
- explain concepts such as mis- and disinformation and propaganda
- consider how we can strengthen democratic information environments.

10.1 Introduction

"The Pope endorses Donald Trump for U.S. President!" screamed a Facebook post in the run-up to the US presidential election in 2016. In a world before Donald Trump was elected president of the United States, many dismissed this inconceivable bit of "fake news" as a joke. Who, after all, could seriously believe that the Argentine pope, widely seen as a reformer of the conservative Catholic Church, with his comparatively permissive views on homosexuality and embrace of welcoming refugees and being anti-poverty and anti-climate change, would publicly back the conservative, populist US presidential candidate who openly disparaged immigrants in racist terms?

In the years since, however, this particular piece of monetized "fake news" appears quite different: a harbinger of the deep threats to democracies around the world that would come into view in subsequent years. With the global rise of right-wing, populist, and authoritarian candidates and leaders – such as Viktor Orbán in Hungary and Jair Bolsonaro, who led Brazil until December 2022 – the spread of international conspiracy movements such as QAnon (Marwick & Partin 2022), anti-vaccine and health misinformation during the global Covid-19 pandemic (Gadarian et al. 2022), and the attempted coup at the US Capitol on January 6, 2021, many researchers, journalists, policymakers, and platforms themselves grew increasingly concerned about misinformation, disinformation, and propaganda on platforms as fundamental threats to democracy, including the potential role of these things in increasing polarization between various groups in society (Finkel et al. 2020).

In January 2018, in an interview with David Letterman, even former US President Barack Obama weighed in:

> If you are getting all your information off algorithms being sent through your phone and it's just reinforcing whatever biases you have, which is the pattern that develops, at a certain point, you just live in a bubble, and that's part of why our politics is so polarized right now. I think it's a solvable problem, but I think it's one we have to spend a lot of time thinking about.
>
> (Hamedy 2018)

While the research about the role of mis- and disinformation and propaganda in contemporary democratic crises across the world is deep, and deeply contested (for reviews, see Bennett & Livingston 2020; Jerit & Zhao 2020; Persily & Tucker 2020), virtually no one would doubt the increasing prevalence of information warfare on platforms being waged in, and between, countries around the world. This includes information warfare by states and groups vying for political power (Anderson 2021; Freelon & Wells 2020; Ong & Cabañes 2018). As a reminder, the idea of "democratic backsliding" refers to the general erosion of the institutions and norms of democracy (Levitsky & Ziblatt 2018), often in small ways that, taken together, undermine elections, the balance of powers, and the rule of law. Scholars broadly suggest that democratic backsliding or crises more generally occur because of polarization, declines in tolerance and faith in democracy among the public, growing views of the political opposition as illegitimate, the loss of press freedom or political and media coordination toward anti-democratic ends, elites eschewing norms that protect democratic processes and institutions, and, broadly, the erosion of mechanisms of accountability over political elites. Media and information, disinformation, and propaganda absolutely play roles in many of these processes, even if they might not be their primary drivers. That fact alone makes misinformation, disinformation, and propaganda a central problem for contemporary states. And, while none of these things originated with the Internet or social media, they afford potentially harmful communications at a scale unprecedented in global history.

10.2 Definitions and Delineations

First, we need some definitions of the important things discussed in this chapter. *Polarization* refers to the distance between groups on any one of a number of measures

(Iyengar et al. 2019). This can span the different political views groups hold, the social groups people perceive themselves identifying with, the moral values groups possess, and the feelings that groups have toward one another. Scholars roughly distinguish between *ideological polarization* (the distance between groups in terms of their policy preferences), *affective polarization* (the extent to which supporters of one group dislike the other group), and *social polarization* (the distance that social groups perceive themselves to be from one another) (Tucker et al. 2018).

Disinformation refers to false or misleading information that is produced with the intent to deceive, whereas *misinformation* is factually false, but lacks this intent (Freelon & Wells 2020). This means that disinformation is a subset of misinformation in being false information *plus* the intent to deceive (Vraga & Bode 2020). Disinformation, we shall soon see, is often a tool wielded in the pursuit of political power. *Malinformation* is a term that researchers use to capture information that combines truth and untruth, and/or strips context away from information, or is harmful and not necessarily false, all with the intent to deceive (Keller et al. 2020). *Propaganda* is related to all of these things, and generally refers to longer-term *campaigns* combining many different types of information which are designed to manipulate some target population (Reddi et al. 2021). It is important to understand that propaganda is more than just a piece of disinformation; it usually is used in contexts where the intent is to mislead, disrupt, or rally public support in a target population for strategic gain. Propaganda may even be "potentially factually correct information, but packaged in a way so as to disparage opposing viewpoints" (Tucker et al. 2018: 3).

As a shorthand, throughout this chapter we refer to "misinformation, disinformation, and propaganda" as MDP when we are discussing them together. Since 2016, there has been an explosion of research on all of these things, from the role of misinformation in shaping health outcomes and disinformation during the attempted coup of January 6, 2021 in the US, to the ways in which propaganda often works to racially polarize countries (Reddi et al. 2021). While it has new salience, MDP is an old concern. As the great American sociologist W. E. B. Du Bois (2014) wrote nearly a century ago, propaganda by historians helped to justify and legitimate continued racial inequalities in the US in the post-Civil War era. During World War II, the systematic development and dissemination of propaganda became a well-established tool of states challenging one another for the hearts and minds of people around the world (Tworek 2019). Nazi propaganda on radio in Germany legitimized the Shoah, the genocide of European Jews during World War II, and mobilized public support for the World War. Propaganda during the Cold War helped create the Manichean worldview of two opposing and irreconcilable systems (e.g. Rawnsley 2016), and was a key way the US and Russia worked to undermine governments in accordance with their strategic interests.

Other scholars have charted what is new in our era, especially the enormous reach and scale of mis- and disinformation on social media, including how platforms have enabled those with extreme views to find one another, make common cause, and take collective and connective action (Hart 2021). Others have analyzed the degree to which misinformation and disinformation leads people to have skewed understandings of everything from the efficacy of Covid-19 vaccines to the policy positions of political opponents or the integrity of elections (Kernell & Mullinix 2019; Tenove 2020). Still others take up the question of combating MDP – detailing necessary investments in fact-checking, quality journalism, local news, and civic literacy; tougher platform policies that root out harmful content; and government regulation to provide oversight for these commercial entities (e.g. Southwell et al. 2018).

10.3 The Dynamics of Platforms, Information, and Political Identity

Over the past ten years, scholars in many different countries have come to more fully appreciate the role of *identity* in politics (Sides et al. 2019). By "identity," we fundamentally mean difference – the understandings of the self and its relation to others premised on a set of distinctions that people make (Ellemers & Haslam 2012). Identities are the products of socialization and agency, the sense of ourselves we take on as we make our way in the world. Often, the most important social identities are those formed through socialization after birth. We are all born into families or relationships that tell us who we are as people – which people are the same as, similar to, or different from us (Eveland & Nathanson 2020). Individuals come to see themselves – through explicit teaching and being in the world – as a part of various social groups and, crucially, not a part of others. These most obviously include family and primary relationship units, but also geographic communities, and groups based on religion, class, sexuality and gender identity, race and ethnicity, class, etc.

It is clear that identities are a product of the stories we create for ourselves and those that are created for us and circulate in the world. People ascribe identities to other people and treat them on that basis. Think about all the ways groups relate visual markers for things such as race and class to people and treat them differently accordingly. And, sometimes, identities are structural in the sense that they are enshrined in law. Think, for instance, about countries with long histories of colonial occupation or racial discrimination that have formal legal definitions of various groups. Or think about identities that relate to citizenship status, or lack thereof. Sometimes, social identities are deeply rooted in history and culture in ways that provide the backdrop for that socialization process – people with shared multigenerational histories and stories of belonging and group status, for instance, such as religious communities. Sometimes, identities are received in the sense of things that are passed on within families without much thought, and sometimes they color everyday life and activities through explicit teaching – both of which can characterize partisanship and party member identities. Sometimes, identities are things that we come to recognize or embrace about ourselves, such as our sexuality and gender identities. And, sometimes, identities are more voluntaristic and expressive, such as sports fandom or musical taste groups.

Social scientists have long noted how identities provide a sense of belonging, place in the world, frame of reference, and set of stories that help make sense of life. What is important for our purposes are the ways that all sorts of identities can be made *political* through communication (Jardina 2019). An important part of what politicians and political leaders do is tell stories of identity – who is a part of groups and who is not, which groups are legitimate, which groups should lead, which groups have power and should have power, which groups compose a nation and which should, and what histories and struggles and triumphs groups of people share (Kreiss et al. 2020). In all countries, there are old and well-established "stories of peoplehood" (Smith 2003) that shape politics and political identity. These often relate to race and ethnicity, religion, and class, explicitly or implicitly, and they must be continually renewed and reinvested with political meaning so they stay salient as political identities. Media are central to identity as key sites for the creation and circulation of these stories of identification and belonging (Kreiss 2016; Peck 2019).

As for the power of identity, take, for instance, the idea of belonging to a specific "nation" – something that today is very close to the identity of many people, not only nationalists. People centrally identify as Americans, Italians, Germans, Panamanians, or New Zealanders. In nearly every country around the world, national belonging is a central identity (see Kohn & Calhoun 2017). However, the idea of nations is not very old, and most of the nations we know today did not exist before the nineteenth century. Until 1871, "Germany" was a patchwork of dozens of small dukedoms or kingdoms, and only exists in its current form since 1989. "Italy" only came into being in 1861 after a war of independence, and still many citizens identify as Tuscans or Venetians rather than Italians. Most African countries have borders that were artificially drawn by colonial powers in London or Paris, eventually leading to horrible wars between peoples who found themselves in "nations" that cut across their identities, territories, and allegiances. This means that a lot of cultural work had to go into solidifying the nation as an identity, suffused with perceptions of groups that are legitimately part of it. This work includes visual symbols (such as flags), myths (such as those of founding and battle), monuments and architecture (the design of state buildings and symbols asserted in public space), and stories told by political and social elites over time. Indeed, the most enduring stories are written in monuments and memorials, inscribed in stone and architecture, erected to ensure collective memory across generations (Edy 2006).

National identity is uniquely powerful, salient, and enduring. Other identities can be more hastily and temporally activated – such as when politicians make appeals to groups by adopting specific policy stances during the course of an election for electoral gain. Sometimes, identities are inherently political, although they can have strong lifestyle components as well – think about the environmental movement and green parties around the world. Sometimes, non-political identities can become political if groups perceive themselves to be under threat or work to advance their interests vis-à-vis other groups. At the same time, none of us is a member of just one group – we all carry multiple identities with us all the time (Hogg & Reid 2006): we are members of political parties, religious and geographic communities, have racial and ethnic identities, gender identities, etc. Social scientists refer to these as "cross-cutting" (Mason 2016) identities when they cross lines of social division.

Over the past few years, however, scholars have grown increasingly concerned with the ways partisanship in many countries becomes a mega-identity that subsumes many other social identities – a process that the political scientist Liliana Mason (2016) calls "sorting" in her studies of the US context. For example, in the paradigmatic case of the US, Democrats and Republicans are not just members of political parties, they are often members of increasingly cohesive, different social groups. Democrats are more multiracial and ethnic, tend to live more in urban areas, be more secular, and have lower class status on average. Republicans are generally white, populate more rural areas, are more religious, and tend to be wealthier.

None of these things applies to *all* Democrats or Republicans, of course – they are true on average. But one consistent finding is the increasing decline in cross-cutting identities as political parties become more homogeneously sorted, especially on racial and ethnic lines, which democracy scholars tell us raises the stakes of politics to be about not just winning an election, but preserving a way of life (Haggard & Kaufman 2021). The US is not alone, although these issues are exacerbated by a two-party, winner-take-all system. In many countries, for instance, social differences are increasingly being sorted into political causes and parties – and media are central to these processes (Walter 2022). As scholars have shown about the United Kingdom European Union membership referendum, and about tensions across Europe more broadly, racial, ethnic, and religious differences are increasingly the lines of political division (Caller & Gorodzeisky 2022; Sobolewska & Ford 2020).

Polarization occurs when groups, on any number of dimensions, come to perceive themselves as far apart, and view different groups more negatively (Wilson et al. 2020). As detailed above, ideological polarization refers to differences in political beliefs, for example regarding policies. Affective polarization refers to negative feelings about different groups (M. Wagner 2021; Wojcieszak & Garrett 2018). Social polarization (Goodman et al. 2022) refers to the perceived differences between groups of people. Moral polarization refers to different orientations groups have, in terms of values and beliefs about right and wrong (Tappin & McKay 2019). Sometimes, polarization is based on underlying structures, such as differences in race, ethnicity, and class in terms of wealth, access to political power, and health outcomes (Hooker 2009). Sometimes, polarization is more of a matter of perception or, more accurately, misperception, where we mischaracterize the other side (Garrett et al. 2019).

And, sometimes, polarization is the result of the *accurate* perception of the other side amid political and social conflict (Kreiss & McGregor 2022). Sometimes, polarization is rooted fundamentally in interest – the desire of groups to maintain, enhance, or achieve power. This brings up an important point because, whereas many researchers decry polarization itself, often they might be witnessing something far more disruptive to democracy – inequality. Indeed, challenges to inequality are often deeply polarizing because some groups are attempting to achieve equality while others are holding on to their power (Hooker 2009, 2016). The democratic threat here is not polarization, but the defense of inequality in the face of attempts at redress.

This brings us to an important insight. Much work on democracy and technology – or, more narrowly, polarization and technology – leads with looking at technological causes of our present democratic and social crises – with mixed results (Kubin & von Sikorski 2021; Tucker et al. 2018). In some ways, this makes sense. Media are often most visible to us, much more so than political or social structures. And because technology changes, people often assume that media and technology are driving other changes that we also perceive and see around us, such as growing acrimony in political debate or hardening lines of social division.

Indeed, while in the past decade there has been growing concern over things such as mis- and disinformation, which we turn to in greater detail below – especially the capacity of these things to skew the public's decision-making capacities during elections or understandings of public health – if identity is the real locus of politics, these things are less of a concern. For instance, in recent years, scholars have paid renewed attention to identity appeals in political communication – those attempts by political elites to craft salient political identities, appeal to these groups, claim to credibly represent them, mobilize them for electoral gain, and ultimately win power. In this world, it might be less important whether a citizen has limited knowledge of politics, or even holds correct views on policy or other matters; what matters is that they can perceive who will credibly represent their group interests.

Finally, we also have to be careful here about being overly concerned with polarization. Sometimes politics is not just about winning elections, but about achieving or protecting political equality, even as it can often be quite literally about preserving ways of life and social status. Polarization often stems from very real political conflicts between social groups over political, economic, cultural, and social power. And political elites and leaders in many different domains of social life often utilize communication and wield media to create lines of political and social difference in the course of pursuing political power for the interests they represent. Of course, they often do so while also affirming the institutional rules and broader civic commitments (such as honoring the results of elections) that lie underneath contests with political adversaries, but fundamentally politics is about creating, and mobilizing across, lines of difference. In the end, before we adopt any blanket concerns about polarization, we must evaluate the political and social status of various groups contesting power, and prioritize remedying inequality over social division.

10.4 Mis- and Disinformation and Propaganda (MDP)

Imagine a river. It is well established, always flowing, cutting deep grooves into the earth. When it rains, water flows from millions of smaller channels into the river, flowing downhill over mountains, hills, and grasslands and finding their way into the main channel.

Rivers provide an apt metaphor for misinformation, disinformation, and propaganda. As a reminder, misinformation generally refers to content that is false, but not propagated with the intent to deceive, while disinformation is deliberately crafted to deceive. Propaganda is a more expansive category of content that is intended to deceive or, more often, manipulate, and unfolds over time through *many* different messages and forms of communication. The content of propaganda *campaigns* might mix truth and falsehoods, half-truths, hyperbole, and other statements. But the content of propaganda is often not wholly made up; instead, it repurposes bits from established cultures and symbols, and often flows in deep, well-established currents alongside other ideas that are powerful.

There are a couple of different ways to think about misinformation, disinformation, and propaganda (MDP). Some questions include: Who or what groups are behind MDP, and what interests do they have? What are its dynamics, such as how does it spread, and why? And what are the consequences of mis- and disinformation and propaganda?

MDP as a Concern

MDP is not new. MDP has been a significant concern among researchers, governments, reformers, and civil society actors for a very, very long time, although we have not always used the same terms in public discourse. As Rachel Kuo and Alice Marwick (2021) point out in their historicization of MDP, we can think about campaigns in the US against immigrants and stories about "welfare queens" as examples of disinformation and propaganda – all during an earlier, mass-mediated era. Researchers and theorists have been writing about the roles of gossip, rumors, scandal, fabrications of political fact, campaigns to strategically undermine the standing of some political elites or public figures, among many other related things, in countries around the world since the 1800s, when a broader concern with the knowledge of the public first emerged (publics that were at the time deeply exclusionary on the lines of race, gender, and class).

Indeed, the relationship between information and public attitudes is a distinctly modern problem, dating roughly since the rise of public opinion as an independent force checking the king's sovereignty in the 1600s. Public debate about information and public opinion expanded considerably with the rise of popular sovereignty over the ensuing three centuries (although it took well into the twentieth century for the boundaries of the public to be extended to racial and ethnic minorities and women in many countries). Concern over the public's capacity to participate in politics was deeply rooted in democracies such as the United States, France, and the UK as debates over suffrage expanded – concerns that were often inflected with elite judgments and pretensions, and especially targeted at poorer groups and racial and ethnic minorities.

Today, researchers the world over have primarily focused on how MDP undermines the information and knowledge that citizens have, and, as such, see it as a significant threat to democracy. Because of MDP, individuals make less informed choices at the polls when choosing between candidates to represent them, or when they vote on specific issues through referendums. Secondarily, MDP distorts the shape of public opinion itself, either skewing it (in the case of misinformation) or distorting it strategically (in the case of disinformation and propaganda). The result is that politicians might have different incentives, or might respond differently, when faced with a skewed or misled public opinion that looks very different than if the public were ideally informed. Moreover, politicians might be able to avoid accountability at the ballot box or from other powerful institutions if public opinion is undermined (especially a concern with disinformation campaigns).

Another rather new aspect of MDP is what Yochai Benkler and colleagues (2018) have termed *network propaganda*. In part unique to the era of digital platforms, network propaganda does not emanate from one identifiable source – such as when a radio station or website is known as a propaganda channel, e.g. Russia Today. Instead, nearly identical propaganda messages come from multiple sources, or cross-reference and build onto one another, washed into citizen's social media feeds, chats, and search results from various directions (see Lukito 2020; Marwick 2018; Tripodi 2022). In this way, new networks of strategic, duplicitous actors on social media platforms can disguise propaganda as authentic, organic content from trusted contacts, even cloaking it as some sort of grassroots knowledge. The key lies in "discrete sources and narrative bits" (Benkler et al. 2016: 8) – propaganda messages are spread in various versions by multiple outlets, with the effect of "adding credibility and improving recall of the false, misleading or otherwise manipulative narrative in the target population" (2016: 8). Sometimes, these propaganda actors are domestic sources; at other times, they are foreign agents, and especially states, for example inauthentic networks from Iran meddling with US elections (K. Wagner 2021), Russian media such as Russia Today spreading anti-vaccine disinformation in Germany (Scott 2021), or religious groups in the US interfering with an abortion referendum in Ireland (O'Leary 2018).

Similar, but different, are the many new forms of *computational propaganda* that platforms afford and enable (Woolley & Howard 2017). The term "computational propaganda" is used to describe the phenomenon of intentionally spreading disinformation and attempting to manipulate public opinion through social media networks by making use of automation and digital tools such as social bots (Woolley & Howard 2018). Algorithms can deceive, and automated accounts (so-called "social bots") can multiply messages on a large scale. Numerous studies from various countries employing a broad methodological toolset have shown that social bots have been active in election campaigns in the past years (e.g. Bastos & Mercea 2019; Boichak et al. 2021; Ferrara 2017; Keller & Klinger 2018). And the effects of computational propaganda are rarely evenly distributed. Women and candidates from minority groups in particular face hate campaigns, harassment, and uncivil behavior on social media and comment sections of news portals, including from automated accounts, which may discourage these groups from participating in electoral contests and silence diverse voices (Beltran et al. 2021; Kenski et al. 2020; Krook & Sanín 2020; Rheault et al. 2019).

Computational propaganda may impact election campaigns in various ways – distorting the perceptions of the opinion climate (Matthes & Arendt 2016), silencing minority groups, or artificially amplifying fringe actors or opinions. Researchers applying agent-based modeling have even concluded that, in some settings, networks made up of 2–4 percent bots would be sufficient to turn the opinion climate and easily "sway public opinion – or the expression thereof.". This effect has also been found in real Twitter networks, which the company calls "malicious automation" in its quarterly transparency reports. Morales (2019) showed that, after Twitter had deleted more than 6,000 automated accounts that retweeted Venezuela's then-President Maduro in 2013, users' willingness to express criticism of the president, as well as support for the opposition, significantly increased. These bot accounts represented less than 0.5 percent of Maduro's followers, but the president's retweets dropped by 81 percent after their suspension.

The detection of bots is tedious and anything but an exact science – with limited data access to platforms, and tools and methods based on very different premises and definitions of "bots," scholars can only approximate how many bots there are (Martini et al. 2021; Schuchard & Crooks 2021). As a consequence, scholars have not yet found a way to prove (or disprove) the effects bots have (or don't have) on public discourse or election campaigns. Also, small numbers of superspreaders and superusers benefit from network effects and can have an overblown impact on online discourse and information flows – whether these accounts are automated, partially automated, or authentic. It is possible that hyperactive users or active, strategic groups coordinate their social media accounts, including automated ones, to have similar patterns in attempts to strategically manipulate public opinion.

Quandt (2018) argues that the idea of "dark participation" captures various forms of technology-enabled malign participation, which has surged with the rise of platforms. It includes various new actors (social bots, trolls, and inauthentic networks) and strategies (amplifying loud minorities, mass-reporting of accounts in order to take them down, and hijacking hashtags). Major platforms have sought to address some of these things, and report about their efforts to delete accounts and content in their transparency reports. For instance, in 2021, Twitter announced a new team to label social bots, with the aim of signaling malign automation while keeping "fun" bots on the platform (including introducing a "good bots label" [Twitter Safety 2021]). In a similar way, regulators around the world have started to recognize the disruptive potential of automated communication on platforms, and some have introduced an obligation for platforms to label social bots (e.g. in California and Germany). Even so, many smaller platforms struggle to develop countermeasures and, even when platforms take action, their measures often remain opaque, unverifiable, and irreplicable.

Bots and fake and spam accounts are not all there is. Photos or videos can be changed and faked with the intent to deceive. "Deep fakes" – seemingly realistic videos based on artificial intelligence that display somebody saying and doing things that are fake, through video and/or sound synthesis techniques – are still more a potential threat than a widespread reality, but provide a glimpse into what might soon be possible (Vaccari & Chadwick 2020). This is a technology that can put words into the mouth of literally anyone, creating false video and sound bites (in one instance, for example, of former US President Obama in one instance [Silverman 2018]). The manipulative danger posed by deep fakes has to do with two elements in particular: they potentially lend greater credibility to disinformation, and the technology is accessible even to laypeople.

All of these things, as well as MDP more broadly, potentially lead to a spiraling dynamic of less media and institutional trust. Deep fakes reinforce the epistemic crisis that has already gained momentum from the flood of disinformation during the Covid-19 pandemic. It is easier, when compared with the mass media era, to fashion alternative and conspiracy narratives and realities and make them plausible, as well as to delegitimize facts and scientifically sound knowledge. In relation to election campaigns, for instance, it can indeed have extremely disruptive effects if manipulated videos of politicians circulate. Diakopoulos and Johnson (2021) outline a few of them: deception and intimidation of viewers/listeners, reputation damages and harms to those misrepresented, and a broad undermining of trust in social institutions.

That said, the existing empirical evidence that MDP leads to less trust is not as straightforward (Valenzuela et al. 2022). Indeed, these concerns might be mitigated by the fact that much research suggests that there are other important considerations about public opinion we must account for. First, that the public – even at the best of times – is often ill informed, disinterested, not attentive, and ideologically incoherent when it comes to policy positions. Second, that a long, long line of research suggests that political elites are actually the ones who shape public attitudes, not the other way round. Third, that political elites may take their cues *less* from public opinion, and more from interest groups represented in their party coalitions.

That said, it is also clear that misinformation, disinformation, and propaganda have consequences, even if they might be rooted in deeper causes such as striving for political gain or financial profit.

SPOTLIGHTED CONTENT

As we have seen in countries from the United States to Brazil, mis- and disinformation about Covid-19 and the efficacy of vaccines have cost thousands of lives, prolonged the global pandemic, and resulted in more severe and deadly illness for millions around the world. In countries such as India and Ethiopia, misinformation, disinformation, and propaganda about minority racial and ethnic groups have resulted in systemic violence and attacks. While this symbolic violence often emerges from political interest, the types of toxic information circulated on platforms have exacerbated conflict and furthered the power of the individuals and groups behind it. This has opened an important debate globally over the harms that platforms potentially cause, and the approaches to internal and external regulation that might mitigate these harms.

10.5 How MDP Works

In 2018, a party in the opposition won a general election in Malaysia for the first time since independence in 1957. The previous party in power was made up of the political elite of ethnic and Islamic Malays, which held on to power in part through the creation and fostering of social difference and grievances along the lines of racial and religious conflict, which in turn provided the context for extremism and disinformation. In this context, MDP is both reflective of broader political struggles and structures of meaning, and a tool used by elites to manipulate and divide populations in the context of wider political and cultural conflict (Radue 2019). This raises a key point. While we often imagine MDP in terms of discrete bits of information that are false, deceptive, or misleading, information often only makes sense when fit within larger frameworks or structures of meaning. In other words, instead of focusing narrowly on the content of discrete pieces of information, think about the social and cultural structures that MDP is produced and embedded within. Often, MDP reveals worldviews that are required to make sense of it – and those worldviews come embedded with understandings of how the world *should* be, to which MDP appeals. At the root of all of these things is power – political, social, and economic, and the relative status of groups.

To provide a few examples: MDP often targets people with less power, or serves to enhance the power of those who already have it. In 2017, the Myanmar military took violent action against the country's Muslim minority: the Rohingya people. In the years leading up to it, Facebook was a site for the amplification of hate speech and violent incitement that helped lay the groundwork for ethnic cleansing. While hate speech – against the Rohingya, as against other minority groups, such as during the civil conflict in Ethiopia that also resulted in ethnic violence (Akinwotu 2021) – rarely originates on social media, platforms can become the key sites for the dissemination of well-established social and political discourses that marginalize people and justify violent actions.

The reality is that MDP is often a tool of political power wielded and deployed *against* those in marginalized positions with respect to race, ethnicity, gender, religion, or class. Sometimes, this means MDP directed at vulnerable people is designed to weaken their political position or keep them from doing things such as voting, or having a voice in public. Sometimes, MDP is directed toward a dominant group to amplify tensions with vulnerable groups. As such, MDP is not exclusively directed at vulnerable populations – if you think of international disinformation against vaccines, for instance, it moved seamlessly across class and racial and ethnic lines. However, the impacts of MDP on social groups are different. The consequences of being unvaccinated and having great healthcare, for instance, are often significantly less than if you are unvaccinated and have no healthcare access. At the same time, even something such as MDP directed against Covid-19 vaccines still accords with political interest (i.e., limiting the power of the state to regulate aspects of society, long a right-wing goal and the aim of numerous disinformation campaigns, including undermining the science around smoking and climate change).

Indeed, MDP often works to create doubt. Scholars have long pointed to the fact that ignorance is often not a *lack* of something: it is actively *produced*. Classic work in the sociology of science (Oreskes & Conway 2010), for instance, showed that, in cases from the safety of cigarette smoking to climate change, those seeking to undermine scientific consensus and policymakers' and the public's understanding of it sought to cultivate *doubt*. If we doubt the facts, for instance, there is less need to actually take actions to address public health or the melting of the icebergs. Relatedly, political scientists have shown how governments do not produce data and information on things they do not want to identify as public problems (Jones & Baumgartner 2005) – including gun violence in the US.

In other words, what MDP often does is create the conditions for people to doubt what is true, which in turn proves handy at staving off regulation (such as policy interventions) or content moderation by platforms. The most sophisticated purveyors of MDP will often not advance expressly false claims, but create doubt through the guise of asking an endless array of questions designed to undermine knowledge claims – from the efficacy of vaccines against Covid-19 to the reliability of an electoral vote count. Often, creating doubt works to undermine knowledge-producing institutions *and* the legitimacy of public action. More broadly, the cultivation of doubt can work to undermine *all* knowledge-producing institutions and a general sense of what is true among the public.

MDP often comes from the top. In summer 2021, in the face of disastrous losses from Covid-19, a state headed by India's ruling Bharatiya Janata Party began distributing herbal remedies for sick patients (Badrinathan 2021). Meanwhile, former Brazilian President Jair Bolsonaro emerged as the global leader of a "coronavirus-denial movement" (Ricard & Medeiros 2020). What these stories have in common is that MDP often originates from political elites, actors, and interests – and even when it does not, it is aided in its spread and credibility by the elites who embrace it. They are also likely the most persuasive actors. We have decades of political science research, for instance, that tells us that what elites say and do – on matters of policy and identity (as prototypes of what groups believe and consist of) – has particular influence on public opinions and attitudes. The upshot is that people – with limited time, effort, and interest – take their cues from elites as to what to believe and who to identify with – and that includes MDP.

SPOTLIGHTED CASE

In 2022, a group of Canadian truckers and activists calling themselves the "Freedom Convoy" shut down the city center in Ottawa, Canada, in protest against Covid-19 health measures, including mandated vaccinations. The protest quickly became a cause célèbre internationally, especially on the right in the United States, where Fox News and opinion shows such as Tucker Carlson's embraced and promoted it. However, not even the trucker's own labor union supported the protests, and over 90 percent of Canada's truckers were already vaccinated and not even affected by the new health measures. It turns out that the protest was fueled, in part, by a Bangladeshi marketing firm and right-wing political and media interests seeking to advance a narrative to undermine governmental authority.

MDP also flows across international boundaries and includes groups with very different motivations. The Canadian "Freedom Convoy" mentioned in the box was embraced not just by Fox News, but also apparently by a shadowy network of fraudulent Facebook groups that helped promote and fundraise for the protests (Reilly et al. 2022). Groups such as QAnon and international white supremacist groups were also involved in these protests. All of this reveals how MDP flows across international boundaries, and often involves people and groups with many disparate, but overlapping, interests: from the truckers engaging in protest, political entertainers looking to build audience share for ideological programs, marketers using social media, and conspiracy movements and political groups looking to recruit new members and advance right-wing projects.

Indeed, MDP is often reflective of political interests. As suggested above, even if misinformation does not originate with elites, organized interests will often harness it for their political ends. Take the example of vaccines. While there have long been anti-vaccine movements and sentiments, pre-Covid-19 they generally crossed the ideological spectrum in many countries around the world. During Covid-19, however, right-wing movements worldwide found that seizing on opposition to vaccines – and Covid-19 public health restrictions more generally, like the lockdowns and mask mandates which we saw in countries such as the United States, Canada, Germany, France, Sweden, Brazil, and India – could be framed in terms of religious purity and liberty and used for political gain on the right (Amin et al. 2017). Indeed, MDP often articulates a set of stories about the world that are mobilizational, and can infuse political institutions and movements with new life.

As such, MDP is often driven by concentrations of people with disparate aims and interests, and spreads through various means. As discussed above, studies suggest that, in the context of certain forms of misinformation, it is often a highly concentrated network phenomenon, where a small group of people are "superusers" responsible for the *vast* amount of the MDP that receives widespread circulation (Hindman et al. 2022). Studies have routinely found that a small number of people, sometimes working in concert and coordination, have been responsible for MDP across particular domains (e.g. González Bailón & Wang 2016; Klinger et al. 2022b; Papakyriakopoulos et al. 2019). This makes sense given what we know about the Internet – attention is not distributed evenly, but in ways that are highly stratified. Network effects mean those already with large followings (or those who port other forms of capital to the Internet) command significant attention. The influence of users is often the result of their ability to employ abusive, highly emotional, or controversial language that drives the engagement that platforms design for, given their commercial motivations. While elites and superusers are often responsible for originating MDP, it is frequently spread by those with a diverse set of attitudes and interests. People interact and engage with MDP to signal their social identities and political affiliations (Marwick & Hargittai 2019; Polletta & Callahan 2019); based on their trust in the source and understandings of recipients (Buchanan & Benson 2019); and for their own interests, including politics (Bennett & Livingston 2018) or even perceived altruism (Apuke & Omar 2021).

SPOTLIGHTED CONTENT

MDP is also a hybrid-media phenomenon. As the Canadian "Freedom Convoy" example cited above shows, MDP is often the product of the dynamics between movements and elites, playing out across many different media and platforms. While much public discourse and regulatory conversations the world over have narrowly focused on technology platforms such as Meta and Google Search, MDP does not respect arbitrary boundaries between media. The content of mass media such as newspapers and websites spills onto platforms, where people engage with and share it. The products of talk radio and podcasts in countries around the world make their way to WhatsApp and, with enough engagement, to national media outlets that command huge audiences.

Indeed, a tactic of media manipulators is often to seed and launder MDP across many media outlets horizontally and vertically – what scholars call "trading up the chain" (Krafft & Donovan 2020), moving content to more high-profile outlets where it can command much larger audiences. And what is articulated online often makes its way offline, as a study of the 2018 Zimbabwean national elections reveals (Chibuwe 2020).

MDP can also be weaponized by states and other political actors. It is, perhaps, the canonical example that MDP is a tool of states conducting information warfare. On the one hand, states such as Russia have used MDP in countries around the world to derive political advantage (Hellman & Wagnsson 2017). This is an old tactic, of course. Since World Wars I and II, and the long Cold War, states have long deployed propaganda and information tactics to shape public opinion in their favor. Meanwhile, as researchers have documented, given the outsized concern over MDP, it did not take long for claims of disinformation to become a potent political weapon. States have wielded claims of disinformation to support the political regulation of social media. Parties have sought to deploy the rhetoric of MDP against opponents. In this context, claims of concern over MDP themselves can be anti-democratic, limiting the political opposition and expression directed against the powerful.

Finally, a focus on MDP can serve to mask the political dynamics at play. There simply is no empirical evidence that the attempted coup on January 6, 2021 in the

United States took place because people were genuinely confused about the outcome of the election. Some people surely were. Many people surely were not. There is often a challenge in surveying people who have been exposed to MDP (it is not easy to find them, people are notoriously bad about recalling what they have seen and heard, and it is often difficult to be sure people are answering honestly versus in accordance with their self-interest). Moreover, we do not know why people answer surveys the way that they do. When Republicans in the United States say they believe that Trump won the election, are they saying this because they genuinely believe it? Or because they know it is what a Republican is supposed to say? Or because it fits with their political and social interests to believe as much? The reality is that empirical evidence is often murky about the consequences and effects of even the most visible cases of disinformation. In that light, we should not immediately look to MDP as a *cause* over and above other explanations, such as social identity, political and social interests, social status, and political power – which likely play a greater role in motivating events like those on January 6, 2021 (Feuer et al. 2022).

10.6 Public Knowledge, Information, and Democracy

Since the eighteenth century, many Western societies have tightly coupled an emphasis on the knowledge and fact basis of public reason and collective rationality with democracy, governance, and social cohesion. Central to this has been the idea that public opinion, democratic legitimacy, and democratic outcomes depend on a rational, and deliberating, public. Through the reasoned give and take of arguments, the public – and presumably its political leaders – will realize consensus, make good decisions, or, at the very least, make decisions that have democratic legitimacy. In accordance with this, over the past three centuries, many societies have developed various knowledge-producing institutions that serve governance and informed public opinion – in addition to informed *elite* opinion (i.e., those policymakers and regulatory offices that do the work of crafting legislation). Think about government survey offices, bureaus that produce economic statistics, and public health agencies, on one level. On another, universities that house, foster, and cultivate knowledge over long periods of time in accordance with the institutions of science and social science, premised on peer review systems to vet knowledge claims, serve a similar role. On still another is the international journalism that – while looking different in different countries and continually changing within countries – generally developed in many countries around the world as a structured, institutionalized way of: (1) producing current information about public and political life; (2) representing and mobilizing a range of political opinions in pluralistic societies; (3) holding elites accountable through communicative scrutiny and representations of public opinion; and (4) defining public standards of morality and ethics so violations of them became matters of public concern.

Over the past two decades, in many countries, trust in these institutions has been under considerable assault from a variety of pressures. The first is from political elites themselves, who in many locations have found political gain in attacking the press and other knowledge-producing institutions. They have done so variously to appeal to groups in the electorate, undermine their accountability both at the ballot box and in public opinion, pursue their agendas, and shape the contextual environment of public opinion and information to their long-term advantage. The second is the rapid expansion in many countries, over 40 years, of new and different types of communicative media, and especially the Internet. This has meant the explosion of ideological, interest, and (hyper)partisan media in many countries, from community and talk radio to partisan and identity-based publications that have found cheaper printing and distribution. Meanwhile, with the Internet and social media, it became possible for a much wider array of individuals to communicate at scale than in previous eras. This has fueled both an incredible array of political information and opinion, *and* new kinds of noxious, racist, and false information. It has also contributed to the addition into the public sphere of new voices that were closed off from addressing large audiences during the era of capital-intensive mass communications media – including racial and ethnic minority (Jackson 2022), trans- (Billard 2019), gender, and class groups (Jackson et al. 2020). Indeed, as a historical matter, public spheres in Western democracies have long been premised on colonial and racial projects that created the resource bases for European empires and exclusions of non-whites, women, and non-elite classes from addressing publics.

Indeed, and finally, we must note the global dynamics of inequality and citizenship that lie in the background of many political conflicts and make any simple story of "trust" deeply complicated and contested. While there have always been deeply stratified classes in many societies, since the advent of the "information age" – in which knowledge and technical systems increasingly structure many global economies – inequality has been on the rise. At the same time, the twentieth century witnessed many decolonization movements and postcolonial politics that featured struggles for political equality and civic incorporation – the basic granting of citizenship privileges and rights for formerly disenfranchised racial and ethnic minorities. In many countries, over the last century and a half, racial and ethnic minorities have challenged dominant groups over political and economic status.

Often, trust in knowledge-producing institutions plays out against these larger forces. Even though it is often valorized now, international journalism – as generations of scholars such as the Jamaican-born British academic Stuart Hall have demonstrated, for instance – often represents elite institutions, privileges existing systems, generally defends the status quo, and promotes established institutional orders – however unequal they might be. As noted above, W. E. B. Du Bois noted in the 1930s that academic knowledge itself was directed toward upholding unequal racial social orders. More contemporaneously, scholars of public health have long noted pervasive economic and racial and ethnic inequalities in the creation of health knowledge and outcomes, including deeply systematic ways that non-elites have been the subject of scientific knowledge that has devalued them (think about the global HIV/AIDS crisis, for instance, which was the focus of an international movement to challenge the structures of science that initially ignored and devalued the disease, and condemned its victims). Even when science is conscious of biases, interventions often follow economic and social disparities in structuring outcomes.

Against this backdrop, it is legitimate to ask how much trust individuals *should* have in knowledge-producing institutions. For platforms, the question of trust is multi-faceted – what sorts of information should platforms privilege, and why? What sorts of information should they reject in all its forms, and why? What institutions should they elevate and amplify? Why should people trust platforms to make these decisions over and above elected representatives or those who claim to serve public, not commercial, interests? Is the market mechanism of platforms sufficient to ensure their legitimacy and responsiveness to the public? Is the market mechanism of much journalism sufficient to secure its obligation to the public trust? In general, where should lines be drawn between expressive liberty and democratic harm – and should this be contingent on time, given that what we think we know is true at time A is rarely the same as at time B? And is there one line, or many potential lines, to be drawn in pluralistic public spheres?

The challenge, going forward, is to clearly identify how societies can balance the democratic potential of platforms with their harms. On the one hand, the democratic potential of social media is evident in the power and scale of global movements such as Black Lives Matter or Fridays for Future. On the other hand are the global flows of conspiracy movements such as QAnon and misinformation, fueled organically by millions of individuals around the world sharing their political opinions and (mis) understandings of facts, and often directed against those who lack social and economic power. We also need to account for what is disinformation and propaganda in the service of political interests – such as upholding unequal social orders, status, and power in democracies – versus what is solely an information problem. Indeed, of much bigger potential concern are the ways in which information gets wielded as a strategic political tool, one used to undermine accountability or otherwise expand political power. And, as detailed above, understanding how MDP accords with deep-rooted, well-worn grooves in culture – the things we are already organized to think and believe – makes it clear that our concerns are often only about the outwardly most evident and surface-level information.

10.7 What Should Be Our Response to MDP

So what do platforms, policymakers, civil society activists, and publics do about MDP? Individually, we all have an obligation to be cognizant and aware of the information we encounter and what we choose to place our trust in. A number of scholars have written about the problem of MDP through the lens of a public health crisis and the metaphor is a good one (Jamieson 2021). In a public health crisis, individuals are called upon to take actions that protect other individuals, especially the most vulnerable, even if it means sacrificing some of their own freedom. Think of Covid-19 masking, testing, social distancing, and getting vaccinated as measures not only to protect individuals, but as acknowledging people's responsibilities to others.

For individuals, vetting information and checking sources, taking a step back and refusing to engage with emotionally charged content if it undermines other people's dignity or equality, not sharing things that are problematic or racist, not sharing content before actually reading it beyond the clickbait headline and teaser, supporting family members and friends, trying to do outreach to those under the thrall of MDP, being an ally to those most vulnerable, and supporting trustworthy information producers are things that everyone can do. In addition, people can embrace a general ethical commitment to institutionally reliable, verifiable, or personally witnessed facts at the foundation of public debate – but also have the humility to acknowledge when we hit the limits of our understanding.

At the same time, just as the response to Covid-19 could not be wholly individual, nor can the response to our contemporary challenges with MDP. Individual actions only take us so far – think about the development of vaccines and their global distribution, the manufacture of masks, and the vast array of scientific research that was necessary to determine the causes, threats, and dangers of Covid-19. Wearing masks and getting vaccinated were individual responsibilities, but individuals could not produce vaccines alone, and neither can they combat MDP on their own. To do that, we need a strong collective response through our institutions. Below we discuss a few of the relevant considerations.

Where should platforms draw the line between legitimate expression and debate, and harmful mis- and disinformation? This has been a deeply fraught question in countries around the world, in part because societies themselves have drawn these lines in different ways. In essence, this is because there are different, often competing, principles at stake.

Platforms can and must do more. There are rival democratic values around freedom of expression and deliberation. Many countries want people to be free to express themselves as part of their democratic participation. At the same time, these societies also know that misinformation and disinformation harm the quality of information in the public sphere, and therefore the public's ability to reflect on political issues – even as hate speech and propaganda limit democratic inclusion. In some countries, such as the United States, the law protects the strong right of expression vis-à-vis the *government*, while letting private actors draw their own lines in some important respects (see Franks 2020). In other countries, especially those that have dealt with ethnic and racial violence such as Rwanda and Germany, the state has stronger restrictions against hate speech, given the capacity for social violence.

There are many different perspectives on expression that we are not going to resolve here. Broadly, global platforms have developed their own content rules governing things such as mis- and disinformation and hate speech, while also honoring the laws and regulations in the countries where they operate. These rules take shape for a variety of reasons. One is for commercial reasons: platform companies strive to grow and monetize their users, and as such need to create environments that people want to be a part of (most people, for instance, do not want to be exposed to racist content or medical disinformation). Another is for values: many US-based platform companies have their origins in particularly libertarian, "free speech" cultures. There are also social norms and values in the countries platforms operate in, to which they adapt their policies. And, of course, there are national laws governing types of speech and expression (such as defamation, child pornography, false advertising, deceptive business practices, discriminatory pricing, etc.) that platforms often have to adhere to (although in the United States, platforms are shielded from liability for the things their users post in many instances, under a law called Section 230 described above).

Platforms have many different approaches to speech regulation, so many that we cannot adequately cover them here, so we will discuss a company that has had *multiple* approaches toward expression, public health, and democracy – in a comparatively short amount of time. As already detailed in Chapter 9, Meta, the company behind Facebook, Instagram, and WhatsApp, has extensive Community Standards and an independent Facebook Oversight Board that provides review over content-related decisions. Much of Meta's policy approach was driven on a case-by-case basis – at least initially – which emerged in response to specific *problems*. These included grappling with what constituted acceptable nudity versus pornography. Think about breastfeeding, for instance, photos of which were initially banned on the platform until mothers around the world successfully challenged this policy on the grounds it was a natural act central to human biology and reproduction. Hate speech is banned by Meta as part of a commitment to creating an inclusive environment among users across its platforms, although its definition and prohibitions have continually evolved in response to new threats and changes in language – even as activists and journalists continually point out that the company does not do nearly enough to tackle the global scale of the problem, and especially lacks adequate language and country-specific expertise in developing nations. Indeed, an international United Nations report clearly implicated the company for its culpability in the ethnic cleansing of Rohingya Muslims, as detailed above, and in 2022 Facebook approved ads calling for ethnic cleansing during elections in Kenya (Cameron 2022).

In the end, there are no easy or clear answers. One of the authors of this book has argued that platforms can do a few things in the attempt to balance expression and democracy (Kreiss et al. 2021). The first is to create clear, democracy-worthy policies that account for national political contexts, including differences between dominant and marginalized groups. "Democracy-worthy" refers to policies that protect key democratic institutions such as elections, the peaceful transfer of power, and censuses, and strongly counter political and civil violence. Platforms can also hold political and social elites to higher standards, not lower ones, given the unique role elites potentially play in fomenting violence, declines in political tolerance, and delegitimizing elections. These policies must also be race/ethnicity conscious, informed by a clear understanding of power dynamics (in other words, speech that challenges dominant groups should not be treated the same as speech that targets subordinate ones). Platforms must develop clear procedures and enforcement mechanisms, including having adjudication processes for transparency and accountability over moderation decisions (this can also happen through third parties such as the Facebook Oversight Board). Finally, platforms should develop clear rules around data access for third-party accountability to ensure that policies, procedures, and enforcement are fair.

Among those important third parties are journalists. Global journalism plays a different role than platforms with respect to mis- and disinformation and propaganda. Rather than being in a position to take down content (or make decisions to leave it up), journalists have the opportunity to put public pressure on platforms, root out violations of policies, and bring issues to the attention of policymakers and regulatory agencies. As a part of public knowledge-producing institutions, journalists produce reliable content; hold platforms, politicians, and other political actors to account; and articulate the values and commitments of the democratic public. To take one example of these roles for journalists, in the past decade we have seen the international growth of the fact-checking movement – originating in the United States but now with global reach – which has taken a new, aggressive stance toward the truth in political claims. Think for a moment about how this represents a clear commitment for journalists. A contending professional journalism value is "balance," as is a commitment to representing many different sides of issues, regardless of whether they are grounded in fact or are consistent with democracy.

In reality, journalists often do a bit of all these things. Journalists, even those most committed to professional ideas such as "objectivity," have long drawn lines around what is allowed to have an airing in their outlets – such as choosing not to cover explicitly racist arguments or repeat hate speech in news coverage. Journalists often balance public interest in the speeches of elected representatives or those vying for public office with a concern over the danger of lies and falsehoods. The different orientations of journalists are also shaped by the many different varieties of media. Some countries, such as those in Scandinavia, are anchored by large public service broadcasters that provide a (relatively) shared set of information and stories about political life that people of all political persuasions orient toward. In other countries, there are more competitive partisan media systems that various political interests use to mobilize political constituencies to advance policy and other aims. Still others are oriented toward large, professional non-partisan commercial newspapers. In many countries, we also see a very important role for racial/ethnic media that have helped to organize along the lines of political identity and interests.

An unresolved tension with respect to the role of journalism and mis- and disinformation is the degree to which more organized media themselves can be the source of things that we find epistemologically dubious. This includes disinformation, lies, and hate speech from political leaders and elected officials that is often amplified through routine media coverage that would be defensible under many journalistic standards (Donovan & boyd 2021; Phillips & Milner 2021). Even worse, in much journalistic coverage of the non-factcheck variety, the truth status of these claims is often unquestioned, which means it might be legitimated in the minds of the public. And the process of establishing just what constitutes the "truth" is often far harder than many would allow. Meanwhile, as detailed above, much of the conflict in countries is often the result of fundamental underlying contests over power and status, contests that will not be resolved so easily by correcting mis- and disinformation – the latter of which, as detailed above, is often a tool. The reality is that, no matter how much countries would like to imagine that the tensions they experience are a result of media, the larger dynamics underlying mis- and disinformation are fundamental contests over power, status, citizenship, and the right to determine the future of countries. Journalism might tell these stories, but ultimately they are articulating ideas that provide frameworks for clashes in identity.

As such, given all of these considerations, as a prominent report has argued, rather than rely on after-the-fact takedowns of MDP, democratic societies should focus on building collective resilience to attempts at manipulation and produce more high-quality information for the public sphere (The Royal Society 2022). Global journalism and other knowledge-producing institutions have an important, indeed central, role to play in that.

10.8 Summary

Finally, there is so much we do not know about MDP. As we will return to in greater detail in Chapter 12, limiting politics to the ostensibly political – such as campaigns for office, formal elections and political organizations, and institutions such as parties – likely misses most of the sources of MDP in the world. Why? Because entertainment media, religious groups, social clubs – virtually any social gathering – are sources of political information and support political identities. While there has been some research into how these things "spill over" into politics, it is likely that we are still only at the very beginning of our understanding of the forces that shape the political world, including the narratives that shape what people believe are legitimate relations and values to hold.

Discussion Questions

- Clickbait practices help to spread MDP. How would you use clickbait to lure people into reading this chapter?
- What are potential dangers associated with "deep fakes" in the context of political communication? How could they be remedied or avoided?

Suggestions for Further Reading

Bennett, W. L. & Livingston, S. (eds.) (2020) *The Disinformation Age: Politics, Technology, and Disruptive Communication in the United States*. Cambridge University Press.

Freelon, D. & Wells, C. (2020) "Disinformation as political communication," *Political Communication* 37(2): 145–56.

Humprecht, E., Esser, F. & Van Aelst, P. (2020) "Resilience to online disinformation: a framework for cross-national comparative research," *The International Journal of Press/Politics* 25(3): 493–516.

Wasserman, H. (2020) "Fake news from Africa: panics, politics and paradigms," *Journalism* 21(1): 3–16.

Woolley, S. C. & Howard, P. N. (eds.) (2018) *Computational Propaganda: Political Parties, Politicians, and Political Manipulation on Social Media*. New York: Oxford University Press.

11 Platforms and Populism, Radicalism, and Extremism

Chapter 11 details how, in the past two decades, populist parties, politicians, and movements have been rather successful in elections and referendum campaigns. As in debates about polarization, digital platforms are often named as one potential reason for the recent surge of populism. The idea is that platforms provide an ideal environment for these things to take root, especially allowing populist political actors to mobilize and engage people away from gatekeepers in journalism and mass media. In this chapter we review the idea of populism, compare it with other related concepts such as radicalism and extremism – which share some common features but are distinct from each other – and address the role that platforms have in their promotion.

OBJECTIVES

By the end of this chapter, you should be able to:

- define populism
- imagine populism as communication
- question whether platforms are driving populism
- understand platform affordances and populism
- discuss concepts such as radicalism and extremism
- examine media and democratic backsliding.

11.1 Introduction

What do politicians as different as Brazil's former leader Jair Bolsonaro, Mexico's Andrés Manuel López Obrador, Alexandria Ocasio-Cortez and Marjorie Taylor Greene in the US, Hungary's Viktor Orbán, Israel's Benjamin Netanyahu, Turkey's (officially the Republic of Türkiye's) Recep Tayyip Erdoğan, or Ukraine's Volodymyr Zelensky have in common? You may have guessed it – all of them are listed as "populists" on Wikipedia ("List of populists" 2022). And while most of them are men, the smaller presence of women on this list along with Marine Le Pen in France, Alice Weidel in

Germany, or Pia Kjærsgaard in Denmark (Meret 2015), should not distract from the fact that women can be, or be accused of being, populists.

From this list alone, we can see that populism is a phenomenon on the left *and* the right that can be attributed to progressive and liberating, *and* illiberal and authoritarian, political actors. These leaders' diverse ideologies and policies mean that populism comes in many forms, facets, and degrees. Populism can stabilize countries after revolutions (e.g. in Mexico) or unconsolidate democracies in times of crisis (e.g. Bolivia), and it can hollow out the institutions of stable democracies (e.g. in the US). Populists tend to be rather talented and self-confident in political communication. The five-time president of Ecuador (1934–72), José María Velasco Ibarra, said, when learning that his campaign was out of money: "Give me a balcony and I will be president" (Knight 2012). And the label "populist" has itself become a tool of strategic communication, a derogatory term to attach onto a political opponent, to smear a campaign, or to delegitimize a government.

The term "populism" has been used to label and describe such a broad range of politicians, parties, and movements, that it has almost become an empty signifier – meaning too many things at once, and nothing at all. Some authors, for instance, refer to Donald Trump or Brazil's President Jair Bolsonaro as populists; others even declare them "wannabe fascists" (Finchelstein 2019). While fascism and populism share some typical elements, such as a Manichean ideology of friend/foe, they are distinct phenomena (e.g. fascism is often violent, populism is not.)

Given its complexity, it is important to learn what populism, and terms such as "radicalism" and "extremism" that are often used in conjunction with it, mean, and consider why and when these things can be a problem in polities – especially in an era of platforms. Indeed, today, populism is everywhere. It is evident in the news, in public discourses, on social media platforms, and in political communication research. At the same time, it is very hard to capture in a clear definition. Similar to famous problems in defining pornography, definitions of populism often come down to "I know it when I see it." What adds to the definitional problems is that, unlike nationalists, separatists, or even anarchists, few contemporary movements or political actors actually refer to themselves as "populists." Researchers even have trouble defining what the opposite of populism is: is it elitism (McGuigan 1992), pluralism (Hawkins & Rovira Kaltwasser 2017), or opposition to representative democracy (Hameleers et al. 2017)? No less contested is populism's relationship with democracy, since scholars see populism "both as a threat and a corrective to democracy" (Ernst et al. 2017: 1348).

These debates are not merely academic, ivory-tower skirmishes. Across Europe and other continents, political parties labeled as populists have been increasingly successful in elections, in part given the affordances of platforms. Over the past 30 years, the support for populist radical right-wing parties, in particular, rose to a level where it is greater than at any other point in time (Tartar 2017). In many democracies, populism is not only on the rise, it is also changing its face and direction. As one scholar described:

> The newly emerging type of populism is qualitatively different. First, this populism has gained ground in developed countries with consolidated democracies – rather than in the emerging markets. Second, the populists no

> longer pursue a traditional redistribution agenda. Instead, today's populists are positioning themselves as "nativists" protecting the "ordinary people" against the "cosmopolitan elites." There is a growing realization in political science ... that the conventional left–right dimension is no longer relevant. The radical left and right politicians now join forces to defend a parochial agenda against the mainstream center that represents markets and globalization.
>
> (Guriev 2018: 200)

Not only has the style and appearance of populism changed over the centuries, the emergence of digital and network media logic over the past decade has also transformed the communication environment in which populists mobilize support, and craft and disseminate their messages. Social media, in particular, shape opportunities for populists, enabling leaders and movements to directly communicate with their followers, thereby circumventing traditional gatekeepers, such as agenda-setting journalists and the so-called "legacy media" (Bucy et al. 2020).

In this chapter, we will differentiate populism from radicalism and extremism, and consider how populists benefit from platforms. First, let's turn to mapping the range of definitions of populism.

11.2 What Is Populism?

Populism has become a ubiquitous research topic. This is due in part to the rise of right-wing and left-wing populist leaders, parties, and movements in and beyond Western democracies; and also in part to populism being a mesmerizing, almost universal, phenomenon that is notoriously vague (Canovan 1999), promiscuous (Oliver & Rahn 2016), chameleonic (Taggart 2000), and an opaque zeitgeist (Mudde 2004) at the conceptual level, and one that poses an irresistible challenge to social scientists.

In the two decades since the publication of Cas Mudde's (2004) influential work referring to populism as a "thin" or "thin-centered" ideology, a near consensus emerged among scholars about its ideational character (Hawkins et al. 2012; Mazzoleni 2008b; Pauwels 2011). This approach broadly regards populism as *a set of ideas that focuses on pure and good people versus corrupt and bad elites, understood to be two homogeneous and antagonistic social entities.*

This antagonism takes shape alongside other ideational elements that give populism its meaning. They include a belief in the political supremacy of the will of the people, always defined exclusively (in terms of there being in- and out-groups), and invocations of a heartland as the symbolic and moral home of a people. The core of populism is the idea of a good and virtuous people: "virtue resides in the simple people, who are the overwhelming majority, and in their collective traditions" (Wiles 1969: 166). Populism seeks to create the illusion that the "people" are threatened from two directions: "elites" and out-groups. The former can be variously constructed depending on left- and right-wing varieties, including the wealthy, people who are highly educated, media professionals, or professors. Out-groups are often racial and ethnic minorities, or non-dominant groups such as migrants or religious minorities, that are seen as neither part of elites nor the true "people" (Müller 2017). Mudde (2004) calls this ideology "thin" because it builds on a limited conceptual core, unlike fully fledged ideologies such as socialism, Marxism, or liberalism. Populism often associates itself with other movements and ideologies, such as nationalism, instead of standing on its own feet.

Further, populism is *always* divisive and polarizing because it fundamentally casts some groups of people not only as not part of "the people," but as enemies of "the people." For right-wing populists, those enemies are often media and educational and cultural elites, as well as non-dominant racial, ethnic, and religious groups. For left-wing populists, elites are often those leaders of finance and business, while enemies are often groups that resist demographic and religious change or that side with entrenched interests.

Populism as an ideology has a supply side (political actors) and a demand side (segments of the electorate) (Rovira Kaltwasser 2018). Populists often have a vision of democracy in which there is a two-way relationship between leaders and the people, absent any institutional or media checks that would get in the way of this communion of leadership and people (Puhle 2019). Indeed, here we have another key element of populism: populists claim that one does not need political parties, civic associations, labor unions, or media anymore because they, the populists, and only they, directly embody, represent, and speak for "the people." Or, in the words of the late Venezuelan President Hugo Chavez: *El pueblo soy yo* – "I am the people."

While populism often receives its fair share of criticism from its collapse of complexity into simple, moral oppositions, as Canovan (1999: 3) noted: populism is "a shadow cast by democracy itself." Populism is the redemptive form of democracy that infuses public faith back into the pragmatic institutions that do the hard, grinding work of governing.

11.3 Who Is "a Populist"?

Populism can be studied from actor-centered and message-centered perspectives. In the first approach, researchers identify populist actors and then study their behavior and strategies, and compare them across time and countries. The problem with this approach is that often very different kinds of populists and populist parties or movements are grouped together. As a result, there is so far no definitive and conclusive list of "populist" parties in the world, although some attempts have been made (e.g. https://popu-list.org). The second approach focuses on typical populist elements in leader and party communication and tends to find populism of different degrees in almost all parties (e.g. Klinger et al. 2022a). It provides a more comprehensive account of prevalent populist communication, but it does not help much to identify populist actors.

The reality is that populism is anything but a new phenomenon. In the late nineteenth century, the People's Party was a populist party in the US. Like many populist parties and movements at that time, it was rooted in agrarian interests (e.g. the Russian Narodniki movement) and the social cleavage between urban and rural communities. Since then, populism has taken on the various forms delineated above, all centered around the core of a politics valuing the common people in opposition to established interests. Populism is fluid and apparent across the political spectrum, from the far right (e.g. Trumpism, Jair Bolsonaro in Brazil, Marine le Pen in France) to the far left (e.g. Evo Morales in Bolivia or Manuel López Obrador`s National Regeneration

Movement in Mexico). Populism often comes across as movements rather than organized political parties, because movements can often claim more closeness to the "people" and more distance from the "elites," such as in the Tea Party Movement in the US or the Five Star Movement in Italy.

Norris and Inglehart (2019) recently argued that the cultural cleavage between social liberals and social conservatives has fed into the increasing support for authoritarian populism in the US and in Europe, and provided a typology of European parties along a scale of cultural and economic values (Inglehart & Norris 2016). Within this framework, they single out presumed populist parties on the left and right of the political spectrum, among them several parties in government such as Switzerland's SVP (Swiss People's Party), but on the whole they are mostly fringe and opposition parties. However, their mapping of populist parties does not analyze the communication of, and direct messages sent out by, these parties.

11.4 Populism as Communication

De Vreese et al. (2018: 3) evoked the notion of "a new generation of populism researchers" – political scientists who recognize the "crucial importance" of communication for populism, and communication scholars who bring expertise on the logic of mass and networked media to this field. Understanding populism as communication enables researchers to bridge the current debates on whether or not populism is an ideology, a discourse, a mobilization strategy, an organizational type, or a political logic (Groshek & Koc-Michalska 2017; Moffit & Tormey 2014; Zulianello et al. 2018).

In the view of de Vreese et al. (2018), populism as a communication phenomenon includes typical elements of content and of style. According to this reading, populism is not about the attributes of an actor, but about what is communicatively done by an actor:

> the emphasis is on populist messages as independent "phenomenon as such" and no longer on a particular party family or type of politician. With populism "as content" we refer to the public communication of core components of populist ideology (such as people-centrism and anti-elitism) with a characteristic set of key messages or frames. With populism "as style," we refer to the fact that these messages expressing populist ideology are often associated with the use of a characteristic set of presentational style elements.
>
> (de Vreese et al. 2018: 3)

Focusing on populism as communication also helps researchers avoid another common problem of this research field – namely, that empirical studies measuring ideology, discourse, or organizational structures often find that "the usual suspects ... are not actually 'populist' at all" (Moffit & Tormey 2014: 381) while assumed non-populist actors may be populist. In other words, understanding populism as a communication phenomenon that is manifest and measurable in both the content and style of political messages often reveals a wider array of claims and actors than more narrow actor-centered approaches.

As indicated before, communicative populist appeals have three core elements – namely, appeals to the people, anti-elitism, and the exclusion of out-groups.

The People

Essentially, all populism appeals to "the people" (Canovan 1999) – not for the sake of the people as such, but in opposition to the communicatively constructed values and ideas of elites and certain minority groups who do not belong to the proper people. As an element of populism, "the people" is a rhetorical construct that is instrumental and can be exploited, and its meaning is not the same as the citizens or the population of a given territory. Instead, it is a socially and rhetorically constructed fiction that refers to some united and homogeneous group of ordinary people that are not the whole (as in the American phrase "the silent majority"). The people are often rhetorically constructed as united; guided by a practical common sense (as opposed to elite knowledge); endowed with the same interests, values, and opinions; and can be evoked in many collective forms such as the "nation," "peasants," "voters," or the "proletariat" (Rooduijn 2014).

In populist claims, the people are in a default state of crisis, threatened by others from outside their ranks (such as elites), which is why populism has been associated with a Manichaean perspective and a dualist worldview of us versus them. Thus, populism needs a culprit or an enemy that is always external to the people, in the form of anti-elitism or the exclusion of out-groups. Whereas anti-elitism represents a vertical antagonism toward the people, the exclusion of out-groups represents a horizontal antagonism (Jagers & Walgrave 2007). The construct of "the people" is anti-pluralist in the sense that there are no legitimate competing interests or values in a polity. The populist leader, party, or movement, meanwhile, is not just the representative of "the people," but the personification of "the people" – which is inherently undemocratic in the sense that the leader does not represent all the people that are governed under an elected office.

Anti-elitism

Whereas the people can include anyone who is not part of "the elite" (Hameleers et al. 2017), the notion of the elite is similarly flexible. In the rhetorical construction of populist claims, "the elite" refers to a homogeneous group with its identity based on antagonism directed at the people (Engesser et al. 2017). Elites are found in political, economic, and legal systems, in the media, and in supranational institutions (such as the United Nations, especially in the nationalist worldview). The core idea behind anti-elitism is the attribution of blame. When conjuring up a people in crisis, populists blame elites, since they are either unable or unwilling to represent the people's will and respect the people's sovereignty. Indeed, to a populist, problems *never* originate with "the people" – they are the victims of the elites which exploit them. Populism's opposition to complexity is connected to its anti-elitism. In the populist construction, "complexity is a self-serving racket perpetuated by professional politicians" (Canovan 1999: 6), suggesting that policy should be guided by the people's common sense that is actually pure, simple, and *right*. All that said, the degree of antagonism to elites varies by populist. While populism always presents itself as distinct from elites, rather than blaming or shaming elites, populists may comparatively place more emphasis on opposing other groups in society (Moffit & Tormey 2014).

Out-Groups

Some scholars contend that the exclusion of out-groups is not a key feature and element of populism as such, but only one of radical right-wing populism. However, de Vreese et al. (2018) argue that the exclusion of out-groups is found on both the right and the left side of the populist spectrum. The exclusion of "others" from the "true people" constitutes the horizontal dimension of populism. Elites are those in power and therefore the enemy from above; out-groups – groups that populists stigmatize as a threat or a burden to the people (Jagers & Walgrave 2007) – are the enemy from within society. Once more, the out-group is a construction of "a blameless in-group opposed to a culprit out-group" (Hameleers et al. 2017: 872). Rovira Kaltwasser (2018) differentiates between "exclusionary" and "inclusionary" populism. The former, rooted in notions of nativism and right-wing ideologies, opposes immigrants, ethnic and religious minorities, homosexuals, and welfare recipients. The latter form of inclusionary populism, a radical left-wing position, typically constructs a homogeneous group of victims out of those affected by alleged unjust socioeconomic policies and austerity measures.

SPOTLIGHTED CONTENT

Based on the contributions by Jagers and Walgrave (2007) and de Vreese et al. (2018), we can differentiate varying degrees of populism in the content of messages:

Full populism:	people + elite + out-group
Anti-elitist populism:	people + elite
Exclusionary populism:	people + out-group
Empty populism:	people

In sum, there are ways of understanding populism as a communication phenomenon that, to varying degrees, can be empirically identified in political messages. In this typology, the invocation of *the people* is at the core of populism. Full populism combines all three elements: of the people, plus construction of their enemies among elites and out-groups. Anti-elitism or the exclusion of out-groups alone does not constitute populism; both do so only in combination with the "people" element. Similarly, the invocation of the people without reference to any opposition to elites or out-groups can be seen as empty populism.

Regarding *content*, people, anti-elitism, and the exclusion of out-groups form three "pillars of populist discourse" (Bobba 2018). We must also take into account how populism manifests in the *style* of messages – that is, how actors present ideas and information. Populism is not about the attributes of a political actor, but about the actions of an actor. Populism is *performed*; it is what is said and how it is said (Bracciale & Martella 2017). Also, the performance of populism is not limited to the political right or left, since "politicians can slip in and out of the populist style" (Moffit & Tormey 2014: 393). Scholars have described the performative style of populism as direct and emotional (Canovan 1999), simple (avoiding complexity), and blunt. The populist transgresses the limits of presumed political correctness: "like a 'drunken guest' ... with 'bad manners' ..., the populist disrupts the normal dinner table, much to the discomfort, even alarm, of the usual patrons" (Oliver & Rahn 2016: 191). Populism is emotional, and populist rhetoric seeks to evoke emotions in audiences by purposefully breaching the taboos of mainstream politics and political culture (Krämer 2014), employing calculated provocations (Pauwels 2011), and taking on a narrative of underdogs (Mazzoleni 2008b), victimization, or other symbolic themes. These emotions emphasize fear and anger (Hameleers et al. 2017).

11.5 Are Platforms Driving Populism?

Recent empirical studies have begun to address how the proliferation of social media platforms provides opportunities for populists. Whereas previous research was limited to highly formalized genres such as public speeches and party platforms, social media enable scholars to monitor the use and effects of political communication in a more granular fashion, and in real time. Not surprisingly, populism has become a popular research topic of political communication scholars interested in the impact of social media platforms. Although the data are often proprietary and only partially accessible through software interfaces (application programming interfaces, or APIs), the availability thereof has nonetheless brought about an increase in quantitative empirical research designs on populist communication (Bobba 2018; Ernst et al. 2017; Hameleers & Schmuck 2017; Stier et al. 2017; Van Kessel & Castelein 2016; Zulianello et al. 2018). There is empirical evidence that purported populist parties have profited from social media (Bimber 1998; Bobba 2018). That said, there are limits to this. Studies show that populist parties often have a centralized structure and avoid internal dissent (Jacobs & Spierings 2019). A study on Twitter use by populist presidents in Latin America found that the prevalent communication mode remains top-down (Waisbord & Amado 2017). Surprisingly, in their social media practices, populist actors are not necessarily more apt to respond to and engage with the people (Spierings et al. 2019).

Few empirical studies have made comparisons of populist communication across countries, and even less so across time. Rooduijn (2014) set an example by using data obtained from newspaper articles, comparing five countries where, over two decades (1988–2008), populist parties (at the time) had varying success. A few studies, specifically involving social media, followed. For example, Ernst et al. (2017) analyzed 1,400 Twitter and Facebook postings from six countries, published by 88 politicians from 29 political parties. They found that parties at the fringes of the political spectrum and opposition parties were more prone to populist communication – a finding that should be tested in different situations (such as electoral and non-electoral periods). Engesser et al.'s (2017) comparative qualitative text analysis showed that "populism manifests itself in a fragmented form on social media" (2017: 1109), justifying the need for a differentiated and comparative look at party messages on Facebook or Twitter. Engesser et al. (2017) provided a useful operationalization, based on emotionalization and negativity (2017: 1282), to identify variations in populist content and style. Even though the thresholds they apply are debatable, Zulianello et al. (2018) compared the Facebook communication of 83 political leaders from six Western and Latin American countries, showing that populism as communication can be empirically identified and that it varies extensively across parties and actors.

SPOTLIGHTED CASES

Let's take more of an in-depth look into why populist communication might thrive on social media platforms. On one hand, populism benefits from collateral effects of platform business models. We have discussed before that Facebook, Twitter, Google's YouTube, and other sites are primarily advertising platforms. Of course, they are useful for a lot of things other than advertisements, but this is primarily how they monetize the vast amounts of data their users produce and attention they devote to these platforms. As a result, platforms are optimized to keep users for as long as possible on them and to increase their attention through user engagement. A sure way to keep users engaged is through affective communication, and particularly negative emotions, provoking anger, rage, and fear. This dynamic is not left to chance, but encouraged through platform algorithms. Facebook, for instance, diversified the old "Like" button with new buttons signifying emotional reactions (wow-astonishment, haha-humor and irony, sad, angry, love) in 2016. But Facebook did not treat those reactions equally. An "Angry" reaction was assigned five times the weight of an ordinary "Like."

This means that posts with angry reactions were deemed five times more valuable and that, consequently, the platform's algorithms would push more content like that: "Facebook CEO Mark Zuckerberg even encouraged users to use the angry face emoji to react to posts they didn't like, without the users knowing it would push more content they didn't like" (Lonas 2021).

Platform structures generally work very well for populist messages, which seek to make people angry at out-groups and elites, to promote or invent scandals, and to evoke perceptions of catastrophic governance failures that only the populist leader, party, or movement can save the "the people" from. One could argue that populist communication provides the perfect content for platforms – constant provocations, angry memes, and clickbait that keep users constantly engaged. At the same time, more broadly, platforms afford public communication outside and in circumvention of journalistic outlets. And it is popularity, and not news values or other professional journalistic criteria, that determines the relevance and reach of messages on social media. On social media, political leaders and parties remain in control of their messages. These political actors can tailor messages according to their target group's specificity, or use micro-targeting tools for political advertisements. Here are some other ways that the affordances of platforms suit the communication strategies of populists.

Constructions of the people

Populism claims to speak for "the people," and populists often emphasize the superiority of common sense over expert knowledge. To the populists, ordinary people, the proverbial women and men on the street, know what to do, whereas politicians and experts over-complicate matters to stay in power. As a result, populism is blunt, simple, never complicated. Social media are a perfect environment for such simple messages, as postings tend to be short, visual, and aim at immediate reaction. In 280 characters for a tweet or a quick-fire TikTok video, there is little space for long explanations, deliberations, musings, considerations, or arguments. The short format of social media posts also covers up the fact that populists often do not have and are not interested in any substantial argumentation. Koc-Michalska et al. (2021) found that the mean number of characters in a post in their sample of about 16,000 Facebook posts from 279 parties in the 2014 EP elections was 212 characters. Only 16 percent of posts consisted of only text, 45 percent contained photos.

Narratives of anti-elitism and anti-intermediation

A key narrative of populist messages is the vertical threat: the good "people" are in danger because of corrupt, evil, and/or incompetent "elites." Part of this narrative is the promise that the populist leader, party, or movement is different from these "elites," in that they are a direct embodiment of the people. Social media platforms provide a great resource to sustain this notion of a direct channel between the populist and the people. Donald Trump was by no means the only populist leader on Twitter, but his ascension to power is a great illustration of this narrative. His followers received tweets directly from him, with all the spelling mistakes and midnight tantrums signaling that it is not a PR team, but he himself, who is talking to his "people." Social media help to nurture the illusion of closeness, of a direct and unfiltered connection. Part of the narrative is that the populist does not need intermediation through journalism, opinion shows, parties, parliaments, and all the complex bells and whistles of the political and media system. The populist speaks directly to and for the people, and the people speak through him/her. Social media affordances cater to this illusion. This is particularly helpful when populists ascend to power and have to deal with the paradox of attacking the "elite" while themselves being the "elite."

Social media also enable populists both to circumvent mass media by creating their own channels and groups, and to attract the attention of journalists. As Jacobs et al. (2020: 615) have concluded, social media are "a new door into an old house," a new way to secure media coverage. An example of this is Donald Trump's quite successful strategic habit of tweeting whenever he had been garnering less attention from news media – with the aim of triggering more coverage (Wells et al. 2020). Again, social media help populists to navigate paradoxical situations of their own making – to attack mass media ("the lying media") while desiring mass media coverage, and to self-victimize ("we are silenced and canceled") while receiving large amounts of media coverage.

The "elites" that populism attacks are not only political elites and media, but also experts and scientists. Just like fascists, populists have an "elastic understanding of the truth" (Finchelstein 2020: 2). Their worldview is based on duality: there is only black and white, no gray, no nuances, no ambiguity or complexity. Populism has no appreciation for the intricacies of reality, the emergent nature of knowledge, or the limits of empirical evidence. Experts and scientists are only useful when they can be instrumentalized to support the positions of the populist. Populist messengers promise simple solutions for complex problems pertaining to "common sense" and the wisdom of ordinary citizens. As such, they tend to be diametrically at odds with science, facts, and the rather complicated processes of evidence-based, institutional politics.

Social media's affordances assist populists in distributing anti-science, anti-expert messages. High-information environments make it comparatively easy to bury truth under a flood of lies (or, as Steve Bannon concisely put it, "flooding the zone with shit"), making low-quality information widely available at no cost, while high-quality content remains gated behind the paywalls of journalism and academic publications. In the absence of "epistemic editing" by the public to sort truth from fiction (Bimber & Gil de Zúñiga 2020), populists need not fear being challenged on their claims, confronted with lying, or even sanctioned for it. On social media platforms, there are few with authority to edit, provide context, voice doubt, or disprove the false claims of populists. In addition, the layout of social media disguises the sources of information – populists and their supporters can easily distribute and amplify their messages in multiple similar versions to create the impression of a grassroots movement and widespread popular support. Of course, other, non-populist political actors can make the same use of social media's affordances. But platforms often serve the needs of populists because their only source of legitimacy is the illusion of speaking for "the people." Populists rarely have a substantial political agenda and policy proposals that actually work, so they mobilize on whatever issues evoke fear and anger. As an example, Germany's far-right populist (and in parts extremist) party AfD (Alternative für Deutschland) fervently campaigns on issues that enrage their base. If migration is not a hot issue, they simply turn toward climate policy (the elites will take our cars away) or health policy (Covid-19 is a hoax elites made up to take our freedom away).

Targeting and Ostracizing Out-Groups

The second horizontal threat for the good "people," so the populist narrative goes, comes from other groups in society who are, in the populist worldview, not part of the "people." A more fragmented public sphere and shifting demographics in many Western democracies provide more opportunities for such claims. Populist right-wing politicians often serve to stoke fear about changing demographics and presumed negative cultural, social, religious, and economic changes that will affect dominant groups. The emergence of many new right-wing media outlets (facilitated by the economic affordances of platforms), the increased communications capacity of far-right parties, and the easy spread and dissemination of anti-immigrant messages on platforms all contribute to the increased visibility of out-group threats. And, famously, Donald Trump's campaign used the targeted advertising affordances of platforms to stoke anti-immigrant fear, expressing themes that later resonated in mass shootings in the United States. In addition, many social media platforms are structured around social ties, and increasingly groups (TikTok breaks from this model in its personalized algorithmic structure). Many platforms are, at the same time, messenger services, news feeds, and tools to manage multiple groups users can join. While the evidence is lacking for filter bubbles and echo chambers on social media platforms on the whole, research has shown that people can radicalize in online groups, among like-minded others. In fact, an internal Facebook study revealed that "64% of all extremist group joins are due to our recommendation tools" (Hatmaker 2020).

The role of groups becomes quite obvious in the case of Telegram. Initially started as a messenger service, it is now a network of interconnected groups and channels. Users can easily search for groups and subscribe to them, and groups can be interlinked. These links create a rabbit-hole-like structure, because users can jump from one group or channel to another. The threshold is extremely low to encounter populist, radical, or extremist content, and in a rapidly escalating way. While, on WhatsApp, groups can have up to 200,000 subscribers, for Telegram there is no limit at the time of this writing. There are also fewer content moderation efforts by Telegram, a small company that has moved from Russia to Dubai, than by other major platforms. Telegram affords the mass distribution of voice messages, a popular feature that is used by conspiracy theorists and radical groups alike. Such a communication environment, structured around groups and subscriber channels, may help to reinforce and make plausible the populist narrative of duality, of friend versus foe, us versus them.

Beyond Telegram, social media offer low-threshold exposure and engagement – first there is a like, then a comment, and a user's timeline starts to fill with similar populist or radical postings. Because platform algorithms are based on previous behavior, each like, click, or comment matters for the subsequent delivery of content. A study using ideologically neutral bots has shown, for instance, that the first connections on Twitter have a strong impact on the news and information users are exposed to later on: neutral bots "with Right-wing initial friends are gradually embedded into dense and homogeneous networks where they are constantly exposed to Right-leaning content. They even start to spread Right-leaning content themselves" (Chen et al. 2021).

11.6 Radicalism and Extremism

"Populism" has become an umbrella term to describe a variety of parties and movements. Unfortunately, public discourse often confuses (or covers up) radicalism, and even extremism, with populism. In fact, populism has even been defined as "fascism adapted to democracy" (Finchelstein 2020). While this might hold some explanatory power in terms of far-right populism, it overlooks all the forms of populism on the political left. However, there are meaningful definitional lines between populism, radicalism, and extremism, as each is distinct from the other.

Cass Mudde (2007) has outlined the differences between them quite clearly. Both the radical right and the extreme (far) right are nationalist, xenophobe, and authoritarian, but the extreme right is also anti-democratic. The radical right is often uncompromising, its adherents want to drastically change society in line with a vision of a past, and it is sure of its ends – but in general the radical right pursues its agenda through democratic institutions such as elections, and engages in debates in the public sphere. In contrast, the extreme right is always against democracy; it seeks not to replace incumbents or change certain policies, but to either overthrow democracy as a political system or destabilize democracy by undermining and weakening its institutions. This is where fascism and the extreme right connect. Neither stops at diminishing the power of representative democracy – they want to end it. In contrast to populists and radical parties (on the right and left), extremists and fascists are violent in their rhetoric and behavior, and not only against people but also against nature (e.g. Bolsonaro's massive burning of the rainforest) or cultural artifacts (e.g. burning books or paintings).

But how can we distinguish populism, radicalism, and extremism beyond the right? What about radical progressive movements, such as radical environmentalists? As for radicalism, the key is challenging the status quo. Radicals want to change society; radicalism, in "advocating sweeping political change, represents a form of hostility against the status quo and its establishment" (Bötticher 2017: 75). They might not be willing to compromise, but are open to rational arguments and debate. They do not glorify violence or use all means to achieve their goals. On the left, radicals are often progressive, advocating for a golden future, while the radical right often seeks to re-establish a golden past. Left extremists, however, have anti-democratic, anti-elite, anti-establishment notions and dualist worldviews of friend versus foe, as well as the idea of a homogeneous people, with the aim of excluding everyone who does not belong to "the people" from society. Left extremists know no bounds to achieving this goal – there is absolutely no room for debate, no acceptance of diverse opinions or lifestyles, and they seek to "close the open marketplace of ideas" (Bötticher 2017: 75). As for their extremist right-wing counterparts, violence is seen as a legitimate means to gain and keep power and achieve left extremists' goals.

SPOTLIGHTED CONTENT

In sum, populism is quite common in democracies, and democracies can live with radicals – but not with anti-system, anti-democratic, uncompromising, and potentially violent extremists. Platforms offer various benefits for radicals and extremists, as they do for populists. Radicals and extremists can recruit and mobilize in unmoderated forums, and fly under the radar of the general public sphere and state authorities, not only in the Darknet, but also in interconnected Telegram groups and forums like 8kun. Extremists, located at the very fringes of society, use platforms to help them to gain visibility while circumventing mass media, and to connect with like-minded others and advertise acts of violence (e.g. broadcasting terror attacks as live videos, such as during the Christchurch massacre in New Zealand). In contrast to populists, extremists do not seek popular support, but mobilize among like-minded groups.

Social media provide a fertile ground for the spread of hate messages, conspiracy theories, and propaganda, particularly that which works against vulnerable groups, such as children, teenagers and young adults with still unstable political worldviews and incomplete political socialization, and racial, ethnic, and religious minorities. Schmuck et al. (2022) showed that large parts of youth encounter extremist content on social media platforms: "51% of all adolescents reported to be at least occasionally exposed to extremist content via social networking sites, 37% on video-sharing platforms ..., and 36% via instant messaging platforms" (2022: 9).

11.7 Summary

To conclude, populism, radicalism, and extremism share some features, but are not the same. This is important, not only for definitional reasons. Referring to extremists as populists downplays and trivializes the danger they pose for democracies. In the often heated debate around a so-called (and mostly fictional) "cancel culture" (Clark 2020), such as whether journalists or public discussions at universities should provide populists with a platform or not, the question should be whether we are dealing with populists, radicals, or extremists. One can have a rational dialogue with populists and radicals, and disagree with them, because they are open to arguments and not violent. There is no point to discussing politics with extremists, however, because they seek to overthrow democratic institutions and repress anyone who does not share their vision of society and the world. Moreover, the distinction between populism, radicalism, and extremism is important because all three of them can be used as strategic argumentative tools. Calling someone a "populist," "radical," or "extremist" delegitimizes their views, and can be used to silence them, or deny them voice. Thus, it is very useful to know what the concepts entail.

Discussion Questions

- Imagine you are asked to devise a communication strategy and action plan for (1) a populist, or (2) a radical, party or movement mobilizing around environmental issues. What would be this party's or movement's goals, how would they communicate (find a slogan or motto!), and what would they do to achieve their goals?
- Use ChatGPT (or another tool for automated text generation) to write a manifesto for a fictional populist movement and discuss the results.

Suggestions for Further Reading

Aalberg, T., Esser, F., Reinemann, C., Strömbäck, J., & Vreese, C. H. (eds.) (2017) *Populist Political Communication in Europe*. London: Routledge.

Hellmann, O. (2017) "Populism in East Asia." In C. Rovira Kaltwasser, P. Taggart, P. Ochoa Espejo, & P. Ostiguy (eds.) *The Oxford Handbook of Populism*. Oxford University Press, 161–78.

Mudde, C. & Rovira Kaltwasser, C. (2017) *Populism: A Very Short Introduction*. Oxford University Press.

Rovira Kaltwasser, C., Taggart, P., Ochoa Espejo, P., & Ostiguy, P. (eds.) (2017) *The Oxford Handbook of Populism*. Oxford University Press.

Siles, I., Guevara, E., Tristán-Jiménez, L., & Carazo, C. (2023) "Populism, religion, and social media in Central America," *The International Journal of Press/Politics* 28(1): 138–59.

12 Platforms, Politics, and Entertainment

Chapter 12 argues that political communication is not limited to the news or messages from candidates and parties, movements, or citizens. It is not always policy-oriented, concerned with national or world affairs, responding to pressing crises, or dead serious. In this chapter, we look beyond the typical content of political communication, such as journalism, news, and political messages. Instead, we explore politicians as celebrities, and celebrities who become politicians, and the role of music, streaming, film, and fashion in political communication. In short, we look at entertainment and other cultural forms as important sites of politics.

OBJECTIVES

By the end of this chapter, you should be able to:

- understand the relationship between politics and entertainment
- comprehend how politicians relate to celebrities
- discuss media monarchies and the Internet
- understand political influencers
- analyze music's role in political communication
- discuss movies, shows, and political communication
- evaluate how fashion relates to political communication.

12.1 Introduction

The research literature and public discourse about what "serious" politics is are dominated by elections, policymaking, and party communication. But political communication can be found in many places, narratives, and discourses far beyond political institutions and organizations. Remember the definition of political communication we provided in the opening of this volume. Political communication concerns all manner of things that relate to what we share and how we live with others. It also includes those things people *want* us to have a collective response to. As such, political communication is suffused throughout our everyday lives – it is in our sports and music, shows and TikTok feeds, and the places we gather to celebrate and worship.

Football players kneel during anthems before a game to protest police brutality and racism. Comedians and late-night talk shows engage in political satire and humorously criticize governments and politicians, as well as the rich and powerful. Politicians themselves appear in entertainment formats such as satirical TV shows (Zoonen et al. 2011), even as television shows portray governance (such as the US's *West Wing* and Denmark's *Borgen*), police and crime, and political authority, legitimacy, and succession (think *Game of Thrones*). Reality television and competition shows that incorporate audience participation (like voting) model and even enact new forms of citizenship (Ouellette & Hay 2007). And entertainment can make new political solidarities possible – think of the work of Eurovision bringing Europe together in a ritual of cultural citizenship (Vuletic 2018) or the central importance of television to the early Israeli state (Curran & Liebes 2002).

Meanwhile, thousands of memes circulate on social media platforms and in online groups, and sometimes they say so much more than many words could. Composed personal photos posted on social media convey volumes about how people wish to be seen and the ways that they perform their status for others, even as they reveal much about what is acceptable in cultures in terms of wealth, conspicuous consumption, and inequality. They also say a lot about how certain groups live – and, more importantly, *want* to live. Even before memes, comics and cartoons provoked debates and even triggered terror attacks (as in the case of *Charlie Hebdo* in 2015) or international conflict (as in the case of the 12 Mohammed caricatures published in Denmark in 2005; Bonde 2007). In authoritarian regimes, where press freedom and freedom of expression are repressed and censorship limits what can be said publicly, criticism and protest take place "between the lines" in theatre plays, jokes, or popular music (Scott 1985, 1990). Presidents publish their favorite songs on Spotify and other streaming services – carefully curated, of course. The clothes or jewelry political actors wear at certain events can be highly strategic and send powerful messages, just as do the celebrities and religious leaders they choose to bring onstage with them and the music they play at rallies.

In other words, political communication is not limited to formal politics, such as party platforms, speeches, or social media posts – it can be sung, it may rhyme, and it is often performed in symbolic, codified ways. Political communication happens far beyond what comes from official political actors, and includes all sorts of messages in everyday life, from the shows we watch on Netflix to the music that we stream. We often think about politics in narrow terms as the serious public business about matters such as war and peace, about gaining power and losing it, but politics gets worked out less visibly, more slowly, and more in the background of everyday life in the formats of music and entertainment as well, which shape important things such as political identity, interests, values, and power. This is what we cover here.

12.2 The History of Politainment and Infotainment

In 1985, American media theorist Neil Postman famously argued that we were "amusing ourselves to death," comparing media society to Aldous Huxley's dystopia in the novel *Brave New World*, published in 1932. Postman saw television news as an entertainment format, and commercial television in general as detrimental to reason, truth, and rational debate. Today, we can view this dour claim as a culmination of traditional media critique. For most of the twentieth century, scholars and intellectuals made a distinction between high culture (opera, theatre) and low culture (pop music, television, soap operas), serious news (national newspapers) and low-quality information (tabloids, talk shows, yellow press). Inherent in this distinction was the normative assumption that it required cognitive effort and education to acquire good information, while everything that is easy to watch or read also meant that it carried less valuable information.

This was both a classist and an elitist view that, at least in the United States, echoes various anti-immigrant reform movements in the late 1800s and early 1900s that valued "information-based citizenship" (Schudson 1998), whereby people dispassionately and rationally consider serious political matters, preferably in upper-class accents, as opposed to other ways of expressing and acting in politics. This narrative about serious politics and culture was not limited to information and political communication, it also extended to discourse about the arts. For instance, German philosopher and central figure of critical theory Theodor W. Adorno wrote several articles against jazz music and the cultural industries, which he saw as infested with commercialism, turning the arts into a mass culture of kitsch. Adorno was in turn heavily criticized for his theses, for example by historian Eric Hobsbawm who dismissed these writings as "some of the stupidest pages ever written about jazz" (Witkin 2000).

Thankfully, many correctives to these views also emerged in powerful ways. British cultural studies, with leading figures such as Stuart Hall and Raymond Williams, recaptured the importance of popular arts and entertainment for politics and power, showing how they were sites where ideologies were not only propagated, but also contested (see Morley & Robins 2001). Scholars such as Dick Hebdige (2012) showed how resistance subcultures could be built around style and cultural forms, with serious political consequences. American cultural studies advanced similar critiques and recaptured the importance of seemingly apolitical cultural forms for politics.

Black feminist activists and scholars, meanwhile, placed general forms of "consciousness-raising" (Combahee River Collective 1977) at the center of movement-building work, an important influence on subsequent movements that practiced lifestyles that marry culture, identity, and politics in the service of analysis and power (Collins 2002; Collins & Bilge 2020). Feminist scholars, meanwhile, advanced important ideas about the "personal is political," showing how the ways we order and live our lives in private and domestic spaces, and even the fantasies we share (such as romance novels), are deeply political and sites of power and contest (Van Zoonen 2006). Meanwhile, one of the most powerful, global political art forms – rap and hip hop – exploded any simplistic notion that politics was confined to the halls of parliaments and the pages of newspapers, that formal styles of address and debate are the sum total of political communication, and that there was easy distinction between supposedly "high" and "low" forms of politics and movements (Morgan 2021).

However, many (predominantly white and male) scholars, journalists, experts, and intellectuals carried on their view that the commercial cultural industry had a negative impact on the quality of the arts and public communication, on information and knowledge – a notion that outside of the US was often seasoned with anti-Americanism ("Disneyfication"), elitism, and classism. As Delli Carpini and Williams (2001) noted, the distinction between meritorious and less valuable contents resulted from an "elevation of that which was enjoyed by elites and a parallel devaluation of 'the popular.'" While this tendency has mitigated somewhat, you still see echoes of this today: in diatribes against social media demeaning our politics, concerns over youth forms of political engagement, and thinly veiled normative standards that encode upper-class forms of political discourse (Baym & Holbert 2019).

12.3 Politicians and Celebrities

One obvious way into analysis of the relationship of politics and entertainment is through one of its most visible lenses, the often permeable boundaries between politicians and celebrities.

Not all politicians are famous. In fact, the vast majority of them are not even well known. Most politicians work and campaign on local and regional levels – as mayors or local representatives in city councils, or they serve in regional or state parliaments. They inaugurate new malls and shops, visit kindergartens and factories, hold citizen consultation hours in their local offices, and give speeches at breeders' animal shows. Apart from their main representatives, most citizens may not be able to name their local politicians. Even on the national stage, only a few politicians appear on TV shows or have a large followership on social media, while most of their colleagues sit in committee meetings and on the back benches of parliaments (hence the derogatory term "back-benchers").

SPOTLIGHTED CONTENT

Some politicians become celebrities and icons of pop culture. In the US, the Kennedys and the Obamas are just two examples of politicians and their families that drew large crowds wherever they went and stirred tremendous public interest in their personal lives even after their terms ended (or after their deaths in the case of the Kennedys) – in who they hang out with, where they go on vacation, and what they wear, including among international audiences. Quite apart from their political roles, they became part of popular culture. Similarly, some activists ascend to the level of global icons through their work, resulting in their becoming public figures that are inspiring to millions – think Martin Luther King Jr., Nelson Mandela, Mother Theresa, Bishop Romero, and, more recently, Greta Thunberg, as just a few examples.

As politicians and activists ascend to national or international stages in popular culture, they no longer are just political leaders, they are cultural leaders shaping how people live and think, what they wear and how they talk (see Wells et al. 2021). In this, they have influence far beyond the political, over broader ways of life and thought. Often mass media are central to this story. Journalistic and other outsized media coverage of politicians' personal lives, work, and beliefs can portray these leaders in a charismatic way, effectively anointing them as celebrities.

Then, of course, there is the other way around: Celebrities who become politicians, or political leaders more generally. In a broad sense, there are many celebrity activists who have become political spokespeople for causes, for example American actors including Angelina Jolie, Leonardo DiCaprio, and Jane Fonda.

SPOTLIGHTED CASES

There are many examples of celebrities who have channeled their fame into political power, turning their fans and followers into a base for political mobilization. As one of the more infamous examples, Donald Trump should immediately come to mind. For Trump, decades spent in tabloid media in New York City and as a pop culture icon spring-boarded him to social media, which he in turn used as a platform to run for office (Baym 2019). But before him, Ronald Reagan and Arnold Schwarzenegger had transformed from actor and entertainer into a US president and governor of California, respectively. Ukraine's President Volodymyr Zelensky is another example. Before being elected president, he was an actor, starring in (and producing) a popular TV series in which he was a teacher who, after a rant about corrupt politicians filmed and uploaded to be a viral hit by his students, becomes the president of Ukraine. The name of the TV series (2015–19), *Servant of the People*, became registered as the name of the party for which Zelensky ran for president in reality, being elected in April 2019. Gul Panag is another example, a former Miss India and Bollywood actress, who has her own political foundation and rather successfully ran as a political candidate in the 2014 Indian elections.

Wood et al. (2016) further differentiate between superstar and everyday celebrity politicians. Superstar celebrity politicians rely more on broadcast media and have consciously staged marketing techniques and perform an exceptional role as strong, decisive leaders. Everyday political celebrities, on the other hand, rely more on digital platforms and (seemingly) spontaneous, ad hoc marketing techniques, performing authentic roles as flawed, regular folks.

Academic literature on celebrity politicians is torn between two normative approaches. On the one hand, scholars tend to see these celebrities-turned-politicians as a result of the "spectacularization" of politics, of the "dumbing down" of the culture, or a symptom of post-democracy – with pop culture and networks being more important than political hierarchies, identity politics, declining institutions, or party alignment (Street 2012). In this view, the rise of celebrity politicians is just another symptom of the hollowing out of democracy, a postmodern anything-goes attitude endangering the core norms and values of democracy and society. There is also the general phenomenon of celebrities who get involved in politics, for example by endorsing candidates, which can enhance politicians' credibility and trust, or be used to appeal to particular social groups in the electorate (Mishra & Mishra 2014; Pease & Brewer 2008).

On the other hand, a more optimistic view offers the interpretation that celebrity politicians mark a democratization process, as not only professional politicians with backing from the bureaucracy and party elites in smoke-filled back rooms can successfully run for office. Moreover, celebrity politicians may be able to engage and reach detached citizens with no or little intrinsic interest in politics, such as young voters and disappointed, disaffected citizens with low trust in traditional politicians. Not surprisingly, celebrity politicians are also linked to populism – they are usually charismatic leaders, selling themselves as being unique and different from professional politicians, candidates who do not "need" to be in politics, but do so out of the sheer necessity to save the nation (Bartoszewicz 2019; Nolan & Brookes 2015). While this might let would-be authoritarians come close to capturing political institutions such as parties or political power (e.g., Donald Trump), it might also elevate leaders who inspire broad popular support (e.g., Zelensky).

So, normatively, there are different perspectives on the issue. Either way, politicians who become celebrities or celebrities who become politicians wield media power over their more traditional counterparts. This should not be equated with political power, but it is not unimportant. Celebrities are often charismatic and already have or earn large follower bases on social media and elsewhere that they can leverage for resources. They have not only supporters, but also loyal fans who might not be turned off by policy failures or ethical scandals. They are accustomed to public appearances and professional image management, and used to being the object of the press – which in turn deploys celebrities to monetize their news products (see all the free media Trump received from journalists as a candidate). And they are often physically attractive and resourceful. On the other hand, they may not be acquainted with party bureaucracy and internal party conflicts, lack professional expertise in policymaking and running ministries or governments, and struggle to translate media capital into political capital to advance their priorities and agendas.

12.4 Media Monarchies and the Internet

Similar but different kinds of celebrity politicians are monarchs and royal families. They are superstars, their lifestyles and private affairs attract massive public attention (in most cases), and stories about them fill glossy celebrity magazines and can even cause global hypes and hysteria, as with the death of Diana, Princess of Wales, in 1997, or the "Megxit" of Prince Harry and his former actress wife Meghan in 2020. In many cases, royal families use this attention to re-direct focus on charitable causes and political issues such as landmines, climate change, or poverty (while sidestepping others, such as enduring legacies of colonialism).

Monarchs are not only celebrities, but also politicians. Depending on the political system, they are heads of state, some with the power to govern, others reduced to representative functions. Kings and queens, even in constitutional monarchies, can have far-reaching power, like the monarchs of Thailand or Morocco. Other monarchs have only ceremonial, symbolic functions, like Tennō, the emperor of Japan. But even these monarchs with only representative functions, such as the English royals, are key pillars for stabilizing democracy and its institutions.

SPOTLIGHTED CASES

Consider some examples of monarchy. In Spain, the dictator General Franco educated the young Prince Juan Carlos to become king of Spain after his death – who then steered Spain from dictatorship to democracy, playing a key role in Spain's transition to a constitutional monarchy in the 1970s. The late queen of the United Kingdom, Elizabeth II, always interpreted her role as politically neutral (despite, symbolically and otherwise, presiding over empire); she never openly expressed any political preferences and kept quiet even about major debates such as Brexit – yet she was famous for her subliminal political messages codified in attire, jewelry, and seemingly small accessories. When opening parliament in 2017, with Brexit on top of the session's agenda, for instance, for the first time she did not wear her formal gown and crown in the inauguration, but a blue dress and a floral hat that resembled the EU flag. When meeting Canada's Prime Minister Justin Trudeau in March 2022, shortly after the Russian invasion of Ukraine had begun, a massive floral bouquet of yellow and blue, Ukraine's national colors, was the dominant feature of the official photo's background. Monarchs are politicians – in obvious ways, when they hold political power, but also in more subtle ways when they do not and speak only through symbols.

However, monarchs are also quite different from other politicians. Their legitimacy does not rest on popular support or popularity; they do not win elections or depend on polling. Some of them are charismatic leaders; most of them are not. Their power rests on tradition, lineage, heritage, and, consequently, often on the belief of divine providence. Once acquired, power runs in a family, sometimes for centuries. Their political communication strategies are dynastic, focused not on the next electoral cycle, but on preserving the monarchy through generations (in this, monarchical institutions are similar to religious institutions such as the Catholic and Eastern Orthodox Church).

The communication strategies of monarchies were "mediatized" long before the term, or even modern political parties, existed. The UK's Queen Victoria was quite aware of the importance of her image and the impact the press had on public opinion, making her perhaps the "first media monarch" (Plunkett 2003). Also, the political communication of monarchies typically connects to entertainment and celebration: coronations and other festive events, parades, banquets, garden parties for accomplished citizens, pomp and circumstance, coverage in tabloids, and images on bits of material culture that are consumed by the public. This is no different in the digital age. At the time of this writing, the British royal family communicates on several websites, two official Instagram accounts (theroyalfamily, princeandprincessofwales) with a combined followership of approximately 27.5 million, on Facebook (TheRoyalFamily) with 6.5 million followers, a YouTube channel with 1.1 million subscribers, and on Twitter (@RoyalFamily, @KensingtonRoyal) with 8.4 million followers.

All the images and videos citizens encounter are strategic and symbolic expressions of dynastic monarchical claims that also affirm the existing political and social order. At the same time, they are also entertaining. When, for instance, Queen Elizabeth II posed in a photo together with her son, now King Charles III, her grandson Prince William, and her great-grandson Prince George, who is elevated by standing on a pile of books because he is only 3 years old, we see a cute, heart-warming family portrait. At the same time, the image carries a dynastic claim with the incumbent and three subsequent heirs spanning roughly 150 years of past and future rule of the House of Windsor. The image showcases that, after 70 years of Elizabethan rule, the three next kings are already in place to continue the line for generations. It is not circumstantial that the palace frequently releases photos of the royal heirs as formal portraits, or doing things like baking Christmas pudding together.

12.5 Political Influencers

With the rise of social media platforms and the increasing use of these platforms for political communication, a new type of micro-celebrity emerged: the so-called "influencer" (Khamis et al. 2017).

Influencers are people who are independent from established organizations (parties, companies, or NGOs) who have built up a large number of relations on social media (followers, channel subscribers) and generate a high frequency of interactions (likes, shares, comments) (e.g. Enke & Borchers 2019). This gives them and their content visibility, reach, and impact. They communicate strategically but attempt to do so authentically; most of them profit economically from their large fan base through sponsorships, advertisements, or micro-donations – but to be trusted by and hold on to an audience, they cannot be seen as crass commercial figures, but as honest brokers of trusted opinion. They are digital opinion leaders, with their leadership based in authenticity, and they appeal to their followers as real, casual, and knowledgeable peers (Riedl et al. 2021). This makes them very effective in promoting products, such as lipstick in make-up tutorials, but also potentially believable conveyors of "truths" and political opinion.

It remains a complicated question whether "influencers" really do influence (Vrontis et al. 2021), and where the threshold falls between a popular YouTuber or Instagrammer and an "influencer" in the sense we describe here. From the perspective of political communication, this is even harder to tell, because political influence cannot be measured by followers or ad revenue. Influencers diversify the spectrum of celebrities, because there are so many of them in countless fields of interest. Among citizens who use social media as a news source, for instance, influencers and celebrities dominate among the actors they pay attention to on YouTube, TikTok, Instagram, and Snapchat, the *Reuters Institute Digital News Report* (Reuters Institute for the Study of Journalism 2021) found. For instance, 36 percent pay attention to influencers and celebrities on TikTok, but only 14 percent to mainstream media and journalists, or 8 percent to politicians and activists (2021: 24). (That said, politics is likely still prominent on TikTok. A number of political studies of TikTok have found the platform to be a site for generating political conflict through memes [Zeng & Abidin 2021], and the platform has been a site for contested international relations [Mishra et al. 2022].)

Political campaigns and interests particularly target younger age groups through influencer marketing. It is not necessarily always the most prominent influencers, but "micro"-influencers with fewer than 10,000 followers who are recruited by parties and special interest groups to promote campaigns, often without their revealing they are being paid. As a researcher concluded: "This amounts to a new and growing form of 'inorganic' information operations – elite-dictated propaganda through trusted social media spokespersons. ... Such influencers, far from being 'volunteer digital door knockers,' are paid, highly organized surrogates of political campaigns failing to report this new mode of politicking" (Goodwin et al. 2020). Also, influencers are not only glamorous girls in luxurious settings showcasing brands, but also young and teenage boys mass-disseminating right-wing clickbait and memes (Cook 2020).

What makes this potentially effective is that platforms such as YouTube, Instagram, TikTok, or Snapchat are primarily used for entertainment (Reuters Institute for the Study of Journalism 2021) – which does not mean they are devoid of political content, but that they are places and spaces where the political and profane mingle. Political influencers on YouTube, TikTok, and Instagram can be found across the political spectrum. Many of them established their micro-celebrity for something else, but promote progressive causes – for example animal rights, environmental issues and action against the climate crisis, LGBTQIA+ and civil rights – as well. The far right has established many successful influencers who present anti-feminism, racism, and even anti-Semitism in a setting that seems to be all about lifestyle, food, music, fashion, and a good time.

Take as an example far-right influencer Brittany Pettibone, now married to the leader of the extremist Identitarian Movement, Martin Sellner, and posting also as Brittany Sellner. She posts videos about her motherhood and the "global tyranny" ("terrorizing children by making them wear masks" during the Covid-19 pandemic), about dating and "the war on feminine beauty." Pettibone emerged after 2016, in the wake of the Trump campaign and the QAnon #pizzagate conspiracy legend (Tangherlini et al. 2020), gaining traction on social media by posting increasingly radical tweets and videos. After 2017, her strategy shifted toward staged authenticity, posting behind-the-scenes and personal content from her life and family, including getting engaged and married to one of the most notorious leaders of the new right: "Pettibone mobilizes this aura of authenticity strategically to create a bond with her audience ... giving them the feeling that they really know Pettibone. The difference with non-political influencers is that networked intimacy and strategic authenticity are now being mobilized in support for metapolitical goals" (Maly 2020: 14).

Political influencers often successfully blend political and non-political topics, for example in the genre of feminist make-up tutorials (White 2018). Activists use the genre of make-up tutorials for their messages, a technique which has found its way into even more established formats. US Congresswoman Alexandria Ocasio-Cortez, for example, talked about her political views and issues on *Vogue* magazine's video channel while applying make-up, including addressing gender inequalities and racism while simultaneously talking about lipstick color and concealer. The video has over 3.6 million views (as of April 2022). Make-up tutorials are ubiquitous on YouTube, TikTok, and Instagram, and they come with an opportunity to talk about politics, being neither threatening nor boring.

Podcasts are another format from which influencers with large followings emerge. In 2020 and 2021, 31 percent of internet users accessed at least one podcast in the previous month, and they are most popular in Ireland, Spain, Sweden, Norway, and the US (Reuters Institute for the Study of Journalism 2021: 27). Especially during the Covid-19 pandemic, new podcasts have mushroomed – being locked-down at home, people had more time to both listen to and produce podcasts. On Spotify, comedian and actor Joe Rogan has become the most popular podcaster. In protesting against Rogan hosting controversial figures who spread disinformation about the Coronavirus, as well as his long history of racist remarks, singer Neil Young and other artists left the platform in January 2022. Spotify in turn argued that it removed over 20,000 episodes that had violated the platform's policies.

Podcasts are an important tool for becoming a political influencer, and for reaching a large audience with political messages, since platforms provide the necessary infrastructure to find networked audiences. Podcasts are also very popular among younger age groups, and people who extensively use podcasts for news often think podcasts help them to become more tolerant of other ideas, and to see themselves as part of a community (Bratcher 2022). Podcasts can create counterpublics for marginalized communities (Vrikki & Malik 2019), and they can impact election campaigns, as with the popular podcast Naneun Ggomsuda in the South Korean election of 2012 (Koo et al. 2015) or Rogan's embrace of US presidential candidate Andrew Yang in 2020 (Adams & Kreiss 2021). However, there is still only very little research on podcasts and streaming platforms, and their role in political communication.

12.6 Music and Political Communication

Music has always played a role in political communication. There is no mobilization or demonstration without protest songs, but also songs have been central to forging political identity, sustaining resistance, and conveying political hope for centuries. The French Revolution had its theme song, "La Marseillaise," which later became the French national anthem. Reggae is both a musical and a political movement, as we detailed in Chapter 8. Musical figures have spearheaded movements, such as the brilliant Fela Kuti's anti-authoritarian and anti-colonial activism in Nigeria (for which he paid a heavy price in arrest and persecution). It is impossible to imagine the anti-apartheid movement in South Africa, the Civil Rights Movement in the United States, or the resistance to Chilean dictator Augusto Pinochet without the songs that sustained resistance and hope in the face of repression. Or think about Christopher Street Day and Pride parades around the world, festivals commemorating the police violence against gay and lesbian people in the Greenwich Village neighborhood in New York in June 1969 and the ensuing protests that sparked the global gay liberation movement.

Politicians play music when they enter the stage or at their rallies. This is not always without conflict, as some artists do not want their music to be used for such events. In the case of Donald Trump, there is even a long list on Wikipedia naming all artists who have voiced opposition to using their music at his rallies, from Adele to The White Stripes ("Musicians who oppose Donald Trump's use of their music" 2022). There is also a very long history of politicians misunderstanding (or being indifferent to) the lyrics of the songs they claim, such as Bruce Springsteen's anti-Vietnam War masterpiece "Born in the USA" being embraced by conservative Republican Ronald Reagan. Some politicians, such as former US President Barack Obama, publish curated Spotify playlists for their fans and supporters. Music signals much about identity – both how politicians want to be portrayed, and whom they want to appeal to.

Music itself has also long been used for activism, such as the Live Aid concert in 1985, at that time the biggest rock concert ever, taking place simultaneously at

London's Wembley Stadium and the John F. Kennedy Stadium in Philadelphia, with a TV audience of 1.9 billion, roughly 40 percent of the world population. The line-up included the most famous global bands and singers, and its aim was to raise money and awareness to alleviate a ravaging famine in Ethiopia.

Music brings people and communities together, and identities (including social and political ones) are built around certain music styles and genres. Music sustains oppositional identities that have deep political implications – think of punk in the UK as a reaction to the monarchy, middle-class British life, and economic precarity, with bands such as the Sex Pistols and the Clash pursuing a defiant politics (Hebdige 2012). French-language hip hop among African immigrant communities in Paris offers voice against racism and poverty, and helps sustain political consciousness and protest. Music can also sustain conservative, revanchist politics – country music genres embraced by dominant groups, for instance, often make claims on the past and soil, with a nostalgia that fuels defensive politics. Belonging to a generation or a certain decade is often connected with music or specific songs. For instance, American journalist Chuck Klosterman (2022) has argued that the 1990s began on September 24, 1991, when Nirvana published their album *Nevermind*, with Grunge music effectively ending the 1980s – giving rise and voice to Generation X. Also in the United States, Black Lives Matter exists in a musical and political continuum with hip-hop groups, such as N.W.A. and Public Enemy in the 1980s and 1990s who critiqued police violence, and contemporaries like Kendrick Lamar whose anthem "Alright" was voiced by thousands in streets across US cities in the 2010s (Manabe 2019). Especially in world regions with little television and internet access, or low literacy rates, and in regions with strong traditions of oral history, radio broadcasts and music are key means of public communication – and therefore politics (e.g. Allen 2004).

Precisely because of its political import, there is also policing of music. In authoritarian regimes, music is often heavily censored – and even in democracies, public debates occur about music, such as how it could corrupt the youth, promote sex and drugs, stir conflicts, or provoke otherwise unwanted behavior. Authorities have tried to regulate music from ancient Greece to Italy in the nineteenth century, all the way to hip hop and punk. As John Street (2013) writes in his book about music and politics: "Throughout human history, music has been the source of fear and the object of repression. Every century on every continent has seen those in power – whether as church or as state – use their powers to silence certain sounds or performers" (2013: 9).

Aside from some notable exceptions, there is very little research on music in political communication – outside of cultural studies. Although streaming platforms use APIs through which data could be gathered, few scholars make use of them. Similarly, it is still rare that scholars use computational methods such as topic modeling or sentiment analysis on song lyrics, or publish on the politics of streaming (Passoth 2020).

12.7 Movies, Shows, and Political Communication

Scholars of mediation and mediatization have long argued that we know most of the world through media, or are influenced by media representations in the ways we perceive the world. This is particularly true of films and movies, especially when it comes to places and historical epochs that we cannot explore directly through personal experience. Visual communication is powerful, and many pictures in our mind are shaped by what we have seen in movie theatres, on television, or on streaming platforms such as Disney+, Hulu, or Netflix. In fact, a recent survey showed that US audiences often take fictional content for portrayals of real life. As many as 51 percent of respondents believed *The West Wing* to be a "very" or "somewhat" realistic portrayal of reality, 44 percent *The Crown*, 42 percent *House of Cards*, and 27 percent the streaming comedy *VEEP* (Ipsos 2022). And, indeed, the genre of movies and TV shows fictionally portraying political leaders and politics is very popular globally, as the international success of the Danish show *Borgen*, portraying fictional prime minister Birgitte Nyborg, demonstrates.

Visual platforms such as television, YouTube, or TikTok are predominantly used for entertainment, and much less for political information. But scholars have repeatedly shown that both can go hand in hand. For instance, in the late 1960s, scholars such as George Gerbner were already arguing that content on television, and in mass media more generally, over time "cultivated" a sense of a "mean world" more violent than it actually was, giving rise to fear and anxiety (for an appraisal, see Romer et al. 2014). So-called "soft news" programs, such as daily talk shows covering a wide range of topics, and satirical TV shows like *The Daily Show* or late-night shows in various countries have positive effects on political knowledge and political participation (Hoffmann & Young 2011; Kleinen-von Königslöw & Keel 2012; Reinemann et al. 2012). Groshek and Krongard (2016) showed that increased use of streaming television, for both political and apolitical content, can lead to higher online and offline political participation. Indeed, researchers have shown that apolitical content can provoke and sustain informal political talk, as with reality TV shows or soap operas that only obliquely touch on political themes (Graham & Hajru 2011). And it matters for political knowledge how much people talk about politics, even more than with whom they talk (Amsalem & Nir 2021)!

Popular movies and shows often revolve around political topics, and even fantasy shows can have political impact. Take, for instance, the uber-popular TV series *Game of Thrones* (2011–19), in which noble families fight for control over the fictitious lands of Westeros, while an ancient enemy returns after being dormant for millennia. In Spain, Pablo Iglesias, the leader of the left-populist PODEMOS party that evolved from the 15M indignados movement in 2014, has repeatedly used *Game of Thrones* for strategic party communication, mining the show for analogies and claims that connect with younger voters and activists. This includes comparing the newborn party to the character Daenerys Targaryan and gifting a DVD set to Spain's King Felipe ("you'll learn a lot"), as Virino and Rodriguez Ortega (2019) show in their illuminating analysis. The party leader has even edited a book on *Game of Thrones* (Iglesias 2015), with political science perspectives on the show, including how to gain and keep power, the plotting and scheming of political advisors, the ways of political violence, slavery, and how to end them, and building coalitions and breaking them up.

Finally, television and streaming, films and embedded videos on platforms are all part of the cultural materials that shape political identities, values, hopes, and aspirations. They represent (or critique) ways of life and legitimate and illegitimate political and social orders and forms of authority. They make arguments – often implicit – for how people should think about themselves and their relations to others and the world. So it is no surprise that shows also map onto political groupings, in terms both of who watches and enjoys them, and of who learns from them. In the end, like all pieces of culture, shows and films represent ourselves back to ourselves, even as they influence who we are and what we want to be in deeply political ways.

12.8 Fashion and Political Communication

Strategic communication in politics is not limited to oral, written, or even digitally mediated messages. In Chapter 1, we stated that, by "communication," this book means any form of symbolic expression, whether it entails spoken words, texts, visual symbols, digital videos, or, most likely, some combination of all the above. Similar to athletes, whose apparel carries the labels of their sponsors and advertising, the bodies, clothing, hair, and accessories of political actors and everyday people can be used as a canvas for symbolic expression.

The most obvious example perhaps is the clothing of kings and queens: jewel-laden crowns representing parts of their empires worn on the head; sashes and medals attached to their robes. They wear colorful fabrics so that they always stand out in a crowd and are visible for as many people as possible. National symbols commemorating battles, victories, and events that unite their subjects are coded into handkerchiefs, bags, or collars. Even dressing down, or wearing national street-fashion brands, works to convey being close to ordinary people. Being "normal" can be a statement (and an endorsement for the local fashion industry). Perhaps extreme, but fascinating, examples are figures such as Boris Johnson and, to some degree, Donald Trump. Both are wealthy men with access to bespoke and well-tailored suits, but they choose to wear ill-fitted suits and ties, eccentric hair styles, and, in the case of Trump, an infamous fake tan. In most cases (not Trump), politicians use dressing down to disguise their elite membership and wealth in the same way they tend to eat fast food and drink beer while on the campaign trail – creating "authenticity illusions" (Enli 2016) of being regular people with common tastes.

The clothing of political actors is often connected to gender debates. Candidates of all genders tend to use visual platforms such as Instagram to show a more personal, private, and human side of themselves – carefully curated, of course. Female candidates receive more likes when they are visible in pictures on Instagram (Brands et al. 2021). After all, women politicians find themselves under much more scrutiny when it comes to clothing and hairstyles than their male colleagues (Jansens 2019). For a long time, female politicians have copied a male power-suit style. Margaret Thatcher, the first British woman to serve as prime minister (1979–90) became known as the Iron Lady, not only because of her politics, but also for her power dressing and conservative style. Decades later, Prime Minister Theresa May became famous for her impressive collection of footwear, from leopard prints to shoes with lipstick kisses. Another option is to deflect attention by always wearing the same uniform style. Angela Merkel, for instance, has perfected this strategy, by wearing the exact same jacket in seemingly endlessly different colors over the course of her 16-year-long tenure as German chancellor. Whenever she side-stepped this path, e.g. in a low-cut dress in the Oslo opera-house, she caused quite a stir. Clothing is often culturally coded, and norms of appropriateness are always in flux. Think of discourses about cultural appropriation when white people wear dreadlocks or dresses with indigenous patterns. Also, gendered expectations apply. There are many pictures of male politicians posing in swimming shorts, visual statements of their fitness, masculinity, and virility, while women politicians are hardly ever seen in bathing suits or bikinis.

Politicians speak through fashion, for example when US Democratic Congresswomen wore all suffragette white for the 2020 State of the Union address to express solidarity with women and disenfranchised groups. In a similar vein, purple dominated the clothing of female actors in the Biden inauguration of 2021, a hint to bridging the bipartisan divide of Democrat blue and Republican red (Friedman & Steinhauer 2021).

SPOTLIGHTED CASE

Dressing casually is also a symbolic strategy in the politician's communication toolbox. During the first days of the Russian invasion in Ukraine in 2022, pictures emerged showing French President Emmanuel Macron in jeans and a hoodie and unshaven in his office at the Elysée Palace, instead of in his usual bespoke tailored suits. These pictures were by no means incidental snapshots, but a remarkably staged scene, taken by his official photographer in the final days of his presidential re-election campaign – attempting to portray a hard-working, never-tiring man. Debates ensued over whether he just looked incredibly sexy or was cosplaying Ukrainian President Zelensky (himself known for rugged military T-shirts during the Russian invasion of his country), because the hoodie carried an emblem of an elite parachute command in the French army.

There is also "brooch diplomacy," the art of speaking through jewels. The British Queen Elizabeth II was an infamous example, and hashtags such as #tiaraalert or #broochwarfare sprang up during state visits and other appearances, for example when she wore a brooch gifted to her by the Obamas during a Trump state visit in 2018. Another lover of brooches, former US Secretary of State Madeleine Albright explained her "pin diplomacy" in a CNN interview in 2015. When finding out the Russians had bugged the State Department, she wore a "very large" pin in the shape of a bug the next time she met with a Russian delegation, who, she claims, "knew exactly what I was saying" (CNN 2015).

Far beyond the political elite, clothing, hats, shoes, tattoos, etc., are signs and symbols of identities, including political ones. The ways in which people dress and present themselves are forms of communication about who they are, what groups they belong to, and the spaces that they navigate. As such, it is no surprise that dashikis, saris, western cowboy boots, and business attire convey political affiliations, ideology, and status – styles that are also reflected back to people, in turn, by the politicians and movement leaders who seek to lead them.

To sum up, the more visual content is posted on platforms, the bigger the role of visual symbols in political life. Words, oral, and written messages compete with silent symbolic statements in the attention economy. When the time for speeches and statements is limited, bold fashion statements can make headlines and drive user engagement, or stir outrage or viral dynamics online. Or they can more routinely signal social identity, political affiliation, and belief. At events and on magazine covers, in the spotlight with all eyes on them or routinely on Instagram, political actors can convey messages, encode ideologies, impact public opinion, without saying a word.

12.9 Summary

We hope it has become clear at this point that political communication is indeed expansive, and goes way beyond official party communication or government websites. It can be fun, entertaining, shocking, and surprising – we can find political communication in all sorts of unexpected places. Candidates campaign on dating portals such as Tinder and Grindr, politicians are expected to endure ridicule by comedians (such as during the traditional White House Correspondents' Dinner), and there is a whole host of political jokes (see, for instance, Samuel Schmidt's [2014] book on Mexican political jokes as social resistance), memes, gifs, cartoons, songs, and shows with political implications. And there is so much more that we have not covered here, such as the ways in which classical music and symphonic orchestras play an important role in public diplomacy and international relations (Gienow-Hecht 2015), and that there can be propaganda in ballet (Gonçalves 2019). Think about the role of politics in international sports events such as the Olympic Games or world championship games, with heads of states cheering their teams and visiting locker rooms as if on state visits and host countries using performance as opportunities for public diplomacy, or Formula One drivers donning T-shirts with peace messages in support of Ukraine during the Russian war there, or the debates after Fédération internationale de football association (FIFA) threatened to sanction soccer players who wore rainbow armbands in support for LGBTQIA+ rights during the World Cup in 2022 in Qatar. There are politics in online and video games, and deeply gendered and sexist stereotypes in games and gaming culture that are both political and shape ideas about roles for women. And, in due time, our attention might move from social media to the Metaverse or other forms of virtual reality, in which politics, power structures, contestation, and protests will take new, but very "real," forms.

Discussion Questions

- What are the potential gains and risks of working with social media influencers in political campaigns?
- What is the role of podcasts in political communication?

Suggestions for Further Reading

Jackson, S. (2021) "'A very basic view of feminism': feminist girls and meanings of (celebrity) feminism," *Feminist Media Studies* 21(7): 1072–90.

Murphy, P. D. (2021) "Speaking for the youth, speaking for the planet: Greta Thunberg and the representational politics of eco-celebrity," *Popular Communication* 19(3): 193–206.

Van Krieken, R. (2018) *Celebrity Society: The Struggle for Attention*. Abingdon: Routledge.

Williams, B. A. & Delli Carpini, M. X. (2020) "The eroding boundaries between news and entertainment and what they mean for democratic politics." In L. Wilkins & C. G. Christians (eds.) *The Routledge Handbook of Mass Media Ethics*. London: Routledge, 252–63.

Young, D. G. (2020) *Irony and Outrage: The Polarized Landscape of Rage, Fear, and Laughter in the United States*. New York: Oxford University Press.

13 Conclusion: Platforms and the Future of Political Communication

In the conclusion, we argue that this book developed a model to identify and critically consider what the authors believe to be the most relevant and pressing issues in political communication at a time of platforms. There are many challenges we face now, and many that lie ahead. We hope this volume provides a rising generation of political communication students, journalists, policymakers, and researchers with a framework and background context, as well as an overview of contemporary issues at the intersection of platforms and politics, to help inform their ideas, thinking, and work.

OBJECTIVES

By the end of this chapter, you should be able to:

- provide a summary of the book
- discuss what is covered, and not addressed, in this book
- identify future trajectories in political communication and research
- articulate the relationship between political communication and democracy.

13.1 Why This Book

Political communication is a field that has well-established research traditions that date in their current institutional form to the 1960s, with the establishment of the political communication divisions of the International Communication Association (ICA) and the American Political Science Association (APSA). During this comparatively short period of time for an academic field, many theories have been put forward to capture political communication processes (Blumler 2015), and a deep body of empirical research has shined a light on the workings of political communication around the world (Lilleker 2006). A number of scholars have proposed definitions of political communication to guide theoretical and empirical research. For example, Schuetz (2009: 758) defines *political communication* as communication between politicians, the media, and citizens with the aim of constructing "meaning about political practices." This idea includes how power is gained, exercised, and retained, along with how media messages enhance the power, credibility, and authority of political elites.

While this definition captures much academic research, our aim in this book was much broader. We sought in our model and definition of political communication to capture the ways in which the "political" spills out from many domains of social life, especially in the platform era, including our social identities, entertainment, movements, lifestyles, and health. Platforms are central to this. Our model centered platforms in this book because they provide the infrastructure for much modern-day political communication – and social life far beyond the political. And there is ongoing and significant public and scholarly debate about the consequences of sweeping changes in political communication, as the commercial models, content moderation, technological design, and algorithms of platforms interact with human psychology, individual preferences and identities, social and political structures, economics, and political institutions (Thorson et al. 2021).

As we have detailed, there is a dizzying array of findings (including contradictory ones) about platforms. Scholars find that social media could help reduce political misconceptions in the US (Garrett 2019), while studies in rural Pakistan revealed that exposure to social media leads to greater political awareness (Ahmad et al. 2019). Political knowledge and political participation could be gained through exposure to digital media (Dimitrova et al. 2014; Matthes et al. 2019). Meanwhile, scholars have also documented the rise of misinformation and disinformation corrupting the public sphere in countries around the world (Persily & Tucker 2020). Conditioning the effects of platforms on political life is how people use social media and other technologies in line with their pre-existing goals and identities (e.g., Knoll et al. 2020: 136), including political ones, dynamics that are captured in work on "uses and gratifications" (Katz et al. 1974) and theories of media and emotions (Lazarus 1991) and prototypes (Higgins 1996). These works take into consideration how people internally evaluate the benefits they gain from using certain media, how their previous experiences influence their media use, and how cognitive processing of media impacts opinion formation. In short, people and political systems are agents in media, not passive recipients of information, even as they are shaped by the choices and media environments they subsequently make (Webster 2014). And, while many point to the democratic challenges resulting from commercial and highly politicized digital ecosystems including misinformation, disinformation, propaganda, and polarization (Iyengar et al. 2019; Pennycook et al. 2021), there are also radical potentials for democracy that digital media afford – especially in terms of expanded public spheres that include many voices formerly excluded from participation (e.g., Gil de Zúñiga & Chen 2019; Jackson et al. 2020; McIlwain 2019).

While much of political communication research to date has been Western, and Western democracy-centric, throughout this book we sought to consider different regions around the world, including the Global South, while also examining political communication from the perspective of non-dominant groups to understand how they relate to and experience the changing terrains of globalized politics. This reflects the ongoing calls to diversify theory and research in political communication that have been loud and growing (Karam & Mutsvairo 2021; Lawrence & de Vreese 2020; Moyo 2020; Orgeret & Rønning 2020) – and the need to contextualize findings about things such as public opinion (Rojas & Valenzuela 2019). As our model details, and research has confirmed (Mutsvairo & Karam 2018; Shehata & Strömbäck 2011), political communication strategies are shaped by context, and structured by things such as race and gender (Abendschön & García-Albacete 2021; Ross 2017). As such, efforts to diversify and expand the field are essential, especially given global flows of communication and politics, unremitting changes to media and communication technologies, and the evolution of media and political systems (Klinger & Svensson 2016). For those countries that are not democratic, it is crucial to understand how the dissenting voices of journalists, civil society actors, or ordinary people persist even in contexts of state repression. For those that are, looking beyond the borders of democratic states offers a reminder of both the value and tenuousness of political rights and freedoms, a set of cases we can learn from, and a host of obligations to support efforts at justice, equality, and freedom.

We wrote this book with a specific aim in mind. Whether you are using this book as an undergraduate or postgraduate student, a scholar, politician, consultant, or citizen, we wanted to share some knowledge with you on the developments in political communication in an era of rapid technological change – and a framework for understanding them. While we discuss academic research in the field, we hope this book will also help to bridge the academic–professional divide (Nielsen 2018). The reality is that *all* sectors of the economy, aspects of our social and cultural lives, and institutions of our democracies are undergoing considerable change – and often strain – as platforms provide new economic incentives, empower new actors, and give rise to new opportunities for various social actors. We hope that this book provides a road map through some of these big issues in the context of politics – but, as we have also shown time and again, the line between what is economic, social, cultural, and political often moves. Indeed, it is often the work of politics to make things objects of public concern.

We write from the perspective of the first generation of political communication scholars that came up in a world where platforms were being widely used in politics. As such, we have been around for the entirety of work on political communication in the platform era, and watched (and participated in!) the transition from an earlier era of internet politics research. We have witnessed and researched radical changes in the capacities of political organizations, new possibilities for collective and even connective action, shifts in the economics and distribution of news and information, and changes in the organization of social and political life. This does not mean the internet and platforms brought about all of these changes on their own. Rather, as we have been at pains to emphasize throughout this book, our model is that technologies are introduced into political, social, economic, and technological environments where we are already organized to do things. People and institutions working in conjunction with technologies and media give rise to the political, and, as such, the very same platforms that support global movements for racial justice can also support would-be authoritarians.

We believe that bringing in examples and case studies from underrepresented nations from the southern hemisphere and in Asia helped illuminate these dynamics. If there has been any lesson for Americans and western Europeans to learn over the past decade, it is that their democracies are not unique, timelessly stable political systems that stand outside of history. Nor are they uncomplicated beacons of freedom and enlightenment. Not only do northern and Western democracies have a lot to learn from other countries that can shed light on their own crises and serve as models for their betterment, they have also played important, often unacknowledged, roles in destabilizing other governments – including democratic ones – through things such as Cold War interventions and deep legacies of colonialism.

At the same time, without looking globally at media and political communication, we risk falling back into the patterns of the past. Platforms are truly global, and the decisions they make in Silicon Valley and elsewhere have impacts around the globe – including their decisions *not* to invest in things such as content moderation language competency, a failure that has given rise to racial and ethnic violence and democratic destabilization. The research field of political communication is transnational – and the insights of our colleagues in countries around the world help us build generalizable knowledge about platforms and democracy. And if there is anything we know, from global economics to climate change, rarely is any one political issue a single national problem.

Taken together, this book has not only offered a new, platform-forward perspective on political communication, it has also sought to capture the advances in a field that continues to attract plenty of attention from students, academics, policymakers, journalists, and political actors.

13.2 What We Have Not Covered in This Book

This book serves as an introduction to political communication in the age of platforms. The topics and issues it presents are those the authors find essential in their own research and teaching. Of course, this is not a complete and fully comprehensive perspective – the book could have been three times as long (and actually was at a few points in the writing process!). The book inevitably had to make hard choices to leave some things out, or provide only cursory discussion of some others. For example, the book focuses more on platforms than on radio, long an important (and sometimes central) medium in many countries around the world. The field of political communication is broader, deeper, and much more diverse than any one book can map out.

So here are some things the book does not cover, or not as broadly or deeply as they would deserve. There is no chapter dedicated to theories or methods used in political communication. The book discusses theories and methods alongside relating key findings and ideas in the field, and in relation to topics and case studies, but does not separate these things out. The book is also deliberately expansive and does not honor boundaries between various fields (in ways, perhaps, other books would). This is because concepts and models used in political communication have frequently been borrowed from other, often neighboring disciplines, such as sociology, psychology, or information science. The book could have delved deeper into framing analysis, agenda-setting, gatekeeping, mediatization, and other theories, as many other books do. However, because there are a wealth of other venues detailing these concepts in great and accessible depth, this book focuses on platform analysis and research.

The field of political communication often focuses on empirical studies, and that often means quantitative research. Other books have presented statistical approaches, computational methods, topic modeling, automated content and framing analyses, and network analyses mapping large data sets from social media, and so on. This book generally does not discuss these things, except in a broad sense in relation to specific studies. To quickly provide an overview here, sometimes methods come from other fields, including computational science or digital linguistics, and involve off-the-shelf solutions and black-boxed tools. In principle, there is nothing wrong with this, but it also means that in some cases scholars have less control over the tools they use and their validity. At the same time, political communication scholars with training in the social sciences are increasingly confronted with the inflow of scholars from other fields, and their theoretical orientations and methods. Physicists and computer scientists, linguists and data scientists, have all taken an interest in political communication questions in recent years – for example studying the flow of political messages on social media in a similar way to how they study biological processes in complex systems. For instance, a team of computer scientists from Indiana University has programmed neutral social bots (the team calls them "drifters") circulating on Twitter to study the impact of first encounters on social media, and considers whether bias comes from platform features or user interactions (Chen et al. 2021). This is highly relevant research moving forward. Political communication has always been an inter- and transdisciplinary effort, and will certainly remain so – the question is whether it will remain a field dominated and largely shaped by the research questions of social scientists (Foucault Welles & González-Bailón 2020).

Additionally, there are also things that deserve more attention in the field of political communication in general, not just here in the book. These include visual communication, as in graffiti, memes, gifs, and videos. It is indeed astonishing how little research in political communication actually analyzes the visual content that social media provide; most studies are still based on text-only data from social media posts. One major reason for that, of course, is the limited data access platforms provide to scholars. It is painful to analyze thousands of Instagram posts if one has to capture screenshots to do it first. Other understudied areas include acoustics, including the role that podcasts play in political communication. And while scholars note that political communication can be embedded in entertainment formats, music, and fashion, such works are still too few and far between, and research on online and video games is almost entirely missing. We believe all of these things are particularly consequential for what is the most exciting area of political communication work at the moment: studies of identity.

Interpretation matters, as Anderson has argued, it is not enough to be "swimming in data points" (2021: 58), and scholars should put more effort into understanding the meaning of media texts, rather than just trying to measure their effects. Finally, we have emphasized throughout this book that perspectives on race and ethnicity, social status and social power, and colonialism and decolonization are often lacking in the field. We have sought to remedy that here – but as a field, we must do more on these fundamental drivers of political life in the future.

13.3 Future Trajectories

Political communication is going through a number of changes. By the time this book goes to press, undoubtedly there will be many things that have taken shape too late to be included here. We are likely to see continued democratic crises, even in established political systems. Right-wing populist and even authoritarian governments will likely come to power. There will be ongoing and intensifying debates about fundamental issues such as immigration, abortion, gun ownership, and safety in many countries, and climate change will continue to drive natural disasters, famines and food insecurity, global migration, political conflicts, and civil wars across the world.

To gain an in-depth understanding of political developments or problems across different political systems, it is important to institute comparative analysis (Blumler & Gurevitch 1975). Cross-national comparisons are a necessary instrument in understanding the existence of media, platform, technological, sociocultural, institutional, and other differences that variously shape political communication landscapes at the national level. There is an urgent need to extend such studies, especially to non-democratic regimes. Indeed, several recent transitions to democracy have happened, with authoritarian and military rulers ceding power to new leaders across the Global South – even as established democracies have slid into anocracies (mixed regimes) or authoritarian ones (Regan & Bell 2010). Understanding the role of political communication in countries experiencing crisis or transition is essential if researchers are to be able to accurately diagnose threats to democracy, take steps to consolidate free and fair elections, or promote liberalism in mixed regimes. In other words, we need comparative research across the whole scale of non-democratic, democratic, and mixed countries, be they under authoritarian or totalitarian rule, in transition, in the process of consolidating democracy, or backsliding into repression and illiberalism. This also means that the field needs not only cross-country comparisons, but also longitudinal ones across time.

Research will also continue seeking to analyze and document how interactive features and social media and other technology platforms shape political communication. Platforms will continue to have a big say in driving economic, social, and political developments in many societies, given their ability to amass data as a way of boosting their revenue models – even though they might not be the *same* platforms that are with us today. For instance, at the time of writing this book, only a few studies in political communication provided analyses of TikTok in campaigns, protests, movements, or politics more generally, even though there is vast agreement that the platform has rapidly become an important player globally (e.g. Bösch & Ricks 2021; Hautea et al. 2021; Literat & Kligler-Vilenchik 2023; Papakyriakopoulos et al. 2022; Vijay & Gekker 2021). This only further illustrates that, while studying platforms is nothing new in political communication, the field is evolving, along with digital technologies.

At the same time, societies will continue to need more research – and data access that affords it – on platforms' effects on political and social life, their reliance on data as a commercial strategy, and threats to personal privacy. It is also clear that platforms will continue, through their affordances, to play a large role in political mobilization, including global efforts to combat legacies of slavery and racism, flows of capital, and changing climates – and in movements in backlash to these. As platforms evolve and change, they will continue to shape opportunities and incentives for some political actors and movements, including ones that are a threat to democratic systems. Sadly, democratic backsliding will likely be with us for a while. Even so, while democratic performance has been in reverse gear in many countries, others have also made democratic gains. There needs to be further research in these areas.

Finally, moving the field forward also calls for more cross-platform research – as far as available data permit. In hybrid media systems, as we have argued many times throughout this book, information flows from newsportals via messenger apps through Twitter and other platforms, to take but one example. Studying discursive dynamics on only one platform – even the newest or most popular platform – often cuts off where ideas and voices come from, how they enter and exit public spheres. And, whereas the past ten years have seen a lot of market consolidation, with only a handful of platforms dominating markets globally, publics and audiences might be even more dispersed and fragmented in the future, as new platforms gain audiences and the Internet itself fragments according to different national and international governance systems.

13.4 Final Thoughts

We hope you have enjoyed reading this book as much as we enjoyed writing it. And we hope that you walked away from this text with a broader understanding of political communication in the platform era, and gained a framework for thinking through many of the changes that are shaping citizen expression, public debates, campaigns, journalism, elections, and movements in countries around the world. We also hope that you have an appreciation for what is distinctly new about political communication in the platform era, as well as the many continuities with the past – as power, political elites, and social hierarchies are very much still with us, even with dramatic changes in the means of communication and ways of contesting political issues. In sum, we aimed for this book to help you understand these changes, and especially the forces that shape platforms – from economics to governance – as well as the power platforms have, in turn, to shape commerce, politics, and powerful institutions.

Finally, most of all, we hope you have a newfound appreciation for the amazing possibilities for political expression and political action in the era of platforms – and the frightening threats to democracy those same platforms facilitate. The challenges of our world are vast – it will take all of us to reaffirm the importance of knowledge-producing institutions such as journalism, to reject cynicism and the demonization of our fellow citizens, to trust across lines of political difference and reject attempts to unfairly manipulate political processes, to hold platforms and other powerful interests accountable for their roles in democracy, and to truly embrace living in multiracial and multi-ethnic societies where everyone has the same political and civil rights. The road ahead will be hard – as this book has shown, authoritarian leaders and anti-democratic groups can use the very same platforms that promote expression and debate to undermine free and fair elections. However, in the end, we hope that you leave this book with a sense of the *possibility* for the democratic power of political communication in the platform era.

Revision: Chapter Objectives Revisited

1 Introduction: Political Communication in the Platform Era

- Detail the relationship between media, technology, and political communication.
- Provide working definitions of key terms used in this book.
- Understand how to use this book.
- Know the content that will be covered in this book.

2 Definitions and Variations of Political Communication

- Define political communication.
- Contextualize political communication from a global perspective.
- Understand the transition from the mass media era to the platform age.
- Explain the relationship between political systems, platforms, and political communication.
- Reflect on how political communication is mediated.

3 Platforms and Their Power

- Understand platforms and their roles in society.
- Analyze the dimensions of platform power.
- Understand technological power, including affordances and algorithms.

4 Platforms, Public Spheres, and Public Opinion

- Define public spheres.
- Understand publics, counterpublics, and affective publics.
- Explain how platforms shape public spheres.
- Describe what filter bubbles and echo chambers are, and discuss whether they really exist.
- Explain various meanings of "public opinion."

5 Platforms and Journalism

- Define journalism.
- Identify business models for journalism in the platform age.
- Understand trends toward data journalism.
- Discuss emerging forms of journalism that take advantage of technological change.

6 Platforms and Strategic Political Communication

- Give an overview of strategic political communication in the platform era.
- Have deep knowledge about strategic communication and changes in public opinion.
- Understand political marketing.
- Provide an assessment of public relations and public diplomacy.
- Explain concepts such as crisis communication.
- Discuss digital lobbying.

7 Platforms, Campaigns, and Campaigning
- Provide an overview of platforms and elections.
- Explain the four ages of campaigning.
- Describe the relationship between elections and electoral systems.
- Discuss what role platforms play in elections.
- Understand campaign strategies, including gaining attention, interaction, persuasion, and mobilization.
- Understand trends in campaigning on platforms.

8 Platforms and Movements
- Provide an overview of social movements.
- Discuss theories that shape our understanding of social movements.
- Understand protest cultures in the digital age.
- Think about the future of social movements.

9 Platform Governance
- Know the concept of platform governance.
- Understand the forms of and issues with media governance.
- Comprehend how platforms are governed globally.
- Discuss mechanisms for platform self-regulation.
- Understand Facebook's Oversight Board.

10 Platforms, Misinformation, Disinformation, and Propaganda
- Understand the relationship between platforms, information, and polarization.
- Explain concepts such as mis- and disinformation and propaganda.
- Consider how we can strengthen democratic information environments.

11 Platforms and Populism, Radicalism, and Extremism
- Define populism.
- Imagine populism as communication.
- Question whether platforms are driving populism.
- Understand platform affordances and populism.
- Discuss concepts such as radicalism and extremism.
- Examine media and democratic backsliding.

12 Platforms, Politics, and Entertainment
- Understand the relationship between politics and entertainment.
- Comprehend how politicians relate to celebrities.
- Discuss media monarchies and the Internet.
- Examine political influencers.
- Analyze music's role in political communication.
- Discuss movies, shows, and political communication.
- Evaluate how fashion relates to political communication.

13 Conclusion: Platforms and the Future of Political Communication
- Provide a summary of the book.
- Discuss what is covered, and not addressed, in this book.
- Identify future trajectories in political communication and research.
- Articulate the relationship between political communication and democracy.

References

Aalberg, T., Esser, F., Reinemann, C., Strömbäck, J., & Vreese, C. H. (eds.) (2017) *Populist Political Communication in Europe*. London: Routledge.

Abendschön, S. & García-Albacete, G. (2021) "It's a man's (online) world: personality traits and the gender gap in online political discussion," *Information, Communication & Society* 24(14): 2054–74.

Adams, K. & Kreiss, D. (2021) *Power in Ideas: A Case-Based Argument for Taking Ideas Seriously in Political Communication*. Cambridge University Press.

Ahmad, T., Alvi, A., & Ittefaq, M. (2019) "The use of social media on political participation among university students: an analysis of survey results from rural Pakistan," *Sage Open* 9(3): 1–9.

Aitamurto, T. (2019) "Crowdfunding for journalism." In T. P. Vos & F. Hanusch (eds.) *The International Encyclopedia of Journalism Studies*. Hoboken, NJ: Wiley-Blackwell, 1–4.

Akinwotu, E. (2021) "Facebook's role in Myanmar and Ethiopia under new scrutiny," *The Guardian*, October 7: www.theguardian.com/technology/2021/oct/07/facebooks-role-in-myanmar-and-ethiopia-under-new-scrutiny.

Al-Rawi, A. (2014). "The Arab Spring and online protests in Iraq," *International Journal of Communication* 8: 916–42.

Albert, J. & Spielkamp, M. (2022) "Digital Services Act: time for Europe to turn the tables on Big Tech," *Thompson Reuters Foundation News*, June 30: https://news.trust.org/item/20220630100725-mjbhd.

Aldrich, J. H. (2011) *Why Parties? A Second Look*. University of Chicago Press.

Alexander, J. C. (2011) *The Performance of Politics: Obama's Victory and the Democratic Struggle for Power*. Oxford University Press.

Allan, S. & Hintz, A. (2019) "Citizen journalism and participation." In K. Wahl-Jorgensen & T. Hanitzsch (eds.) *The Handbook of Journalism Studies*. New York: Taylor & Francis, 435–51.

Allen, L. (2004) "Music and politics in Africa," *Social Dynamics* 30(2): 1–19.

Amin, A. B., Bednarczyk, R. A., Ray, C. E., Melchiori, K. J., Graham, J., Huntsinger, J. R., & Omer, S. B. (2017) "Association of moral values with vaccine hesitancy," *Nature Human Behaviour* 1: 873–80.

Amsalem, E. & Nir, L. (2021) "Does interpersonal discussion increase political knowledge? A meta-analysis," *Communication Research* 48(5): 619–41.

Ananny, M. (2016) "Toward an ethics of algorithms: convening, observation, probability, and timeliness," *Science, Technology, & Human Values* 41(1): 93–117.

Ananny, M. & Finn, M. (2020) "Anticipatory news infrastructures: seeing journalism's expectations of future publics in its sociotechnical systems," *New Media and Society* 22(9): 1600–18.

Andersen, J. (2006) "The public sphere and discursive activities: information literacy as sociopolitical skills," *Journal of Documentation* 62(2): 213–28.

Anderson, B. (2006) *Imagined Communities: Reflections on the Origin and Spread of Nationalism*, 2nd edn. London: Verso.

Anderson, C. W. (2018) *Apostles of Certainty: Data Journalism and the Politics of Doubt*. Oxford University Press.

Anderson, C. W. (2021) "Fake news is not a virus: on platforms and their effects," *Communication Theory* 31(1): 42–61.

Aouragh, M. & Chakravartty, P. (2016) "Infrastructures of empire: towards a critical geopolitics of media and information studies," *Media, Culture & Society* 38(4): 559–75.

Apuke, O. D. & Omar, B. (2021) "Fake news and COVID-19: modelling the predictors of fake news sharing among social media users," *Telematics and Informatics* 56: 101475.

Arceneaux, K., and Johnson, M. (2013) *Changing Minds or Changing Channels? Partisan News in an Age of Choice*. University of Chicago Press.

Aronczyk, M. (2013) *Branding the Nation: The Global Business of National Identity*. Oxford University Press.

Aronczyk, M. & Espinoza, M. I. (2021) *A Strategic Nature: Public Relations and the Politics of American Environmentalism*. Oxford University Press.

Aronczyk, M. & Powers, D. (eds.) (2010) *Blowing Up the Brand: Critical Perspectives on Promotional Culture*. New York: Peter Lang.

Arora, P. (2019) *The Next Billion Users: Digital Life Beyond the West*. Cambridge, MA: Harvard University Press.

Badrinathan, S. (2021) "India is facing an epidemic of misinformation alongside Covid-19," *Washington Post*, June 07: www.washingtonpost.com/opinions/2021/06/07/india-misinformation-covid-19-pandemic.

Bail, C. (2022) *Breaking the Social Media Prism: How to Make Our Platforms Less Polarizing*. Princeton University Press.

Bailo, F., Meese, J., & Hurcombe, E. (2021a) "The institutional impacts of algorithmic distribution: Facebook and the Australian news media," *Social Media+ Society* 7(2): 20563051211024963.

Bailo, F., Meese, J., & Hurcombe, E., et al. (2021b) "Australia's big gamble: the news media bargaining code and the responses from Google and Facebook," *AoIR Selected Papers of Internet Research* 2021.

Baldwin-Philippi, J. (2019) "Data campaigning: between empirics and assumptions," *Internet Policy Review* 8(4): 1–18.

Balod, H. S. B. & Hameleers, M. (2021) "Fighting for truth? The role perceptions of Filipino journalists in an era of mis- and disinformation," *Journalism* 22(9): 2368–85.

Barden, J. & Petty, R. E. (2012) "Persuasion." In V. S. Ramachandran (ed.) *Encyclopedia of Human Behavior*, 2nd edn. London: Academic Press, 96–102.

Barrett, B. (2021) "Commercial companies in party networks: digital advertising firms in US elections from 2006–2016," *Political Communication* 39(2): 1–19.

Barrett, B. & Kreiss, D. (2019) "Platform transience: changes in Facebook's policies, procedures, and affordances in global electoral politics," *Internet Policy Review* 8(4): 1–22.

Bartoszewicz, M. G. (2019) "Celebrity populism: a look at Poland and the Czech Republic," *European Politics and Society* 20(4): 470–85.

Bastos, M. T. & Mercea, D. (2019) "The Brexit botnet and user generated hyperpartisan news," *Social Science Computer Review* 37(1): 38–54.

Bayat, A. (2013). "The Arab Spring and its surprises," *Development and Change* 44(3): 587–601.

Baym, G. (2019) "'Think of him as the president': tabloid Trump and the political imaginary, 1980–1999," *Journal of Communication* 69(4): 396–417.

Baym, G. & Holbert, R. L. (2019). "Beyond infotainment: political-entertainment media and electoral persuasion." In Elizabeth Suhay (ed.) *The Oxford Handbook of Electoral Persuasion*. Oxford University Press, 455–77.

Baysu, G. & Swyngedouw, M. (2020) "What determines voting behaviors of Muslim minorities in Europe: Muslim identity or left–right ideology?" *Political Psychology* 41(5): 837–60.

BBC (British Broadcasting Corporation) (2021) "New Zealand bat flies away with bird of the year award," *BBC*, November 1: www.bbc.com/news/world-asia-59115346.

Belew, K. (2018) *Bring the War Home: The White Power Movement and Paramilitary America*. Cambridge, MA: Harvard University Press.

Belli, L. (2021). "Examining algorithmic amplification of political content on Twitter": https://blog.twitter.com/en_us/topics/company/2021/rml-politicalcontent.

Beltran, J., Gallego, A., Huidobro, A., Romero, E., & Padro, L. (2021) "Male and female politicians on Twitter: a machine learning approach," *European Journal of Political Research* 60(1): 239–51.

Benjamin, R. (2019) *Race after Technology: Abolitionist Tools for the New Jim Code*. Cambridge: Polity.

Benkler, Y. (2006) *The Wealth of Networks*. New Haven, CT: Yale University Press.

Benkler, Y., Faris, R., & Roberts, H. (2018) *Network Propaganda: Manipulation, Disinformation, and Radicalization in American Politics*. Oxford University Press.

Bennett, W. L. (2005) "Social movements beyond borders: understanding two eras of transnational activism." In D. Della Porta & S. Tarrow (eds.) *Transnational Protest and Global Activism*. Lanham, MD: Rowman and Littlefield, 203–26.

Bennett, W. L. (2021) *Communicating the Future: Solutions for Environment, Economy, and Democracy*. Cambridge: Polity.

Bennett, W. L. & Iyengar, S. (2008) "A new era of minimal effects? The changing foundations of political communication," *Journal of Communication* 58(4): 707–31.

Bennett, W. L. & Livingston, S. (2018) "The disinformation order: disruptive communication and the decline of democratic institutions," *European Journal of Communication* 33(2): 122–39.

Bennett, W. L. & Livingston, S. (2021) *The Disinformation Age: Politics, Technology, and Disruptive Communication in the United States*. Cambridge University Press.

Bennett, W. L. & Pfetsch, B. (2018) "Rethinking political communication in a time of disrupted public spheres," *Journal of Communication* 68(2): 243–53.

Bennett, W. L. & Segerberg, A. (2013) *The Logic of Connective Action: Digital Media and the Personalization of Contentious Politics*. Cambridge University Press.

Bennett, W. L., Segerberg, A., & Yang, Y. (2018) "The strength of peripheral networks: negotiating attention and meaning in complex media ecologies," *Journal of Communication* 68(4): 659–84.

Benson, R. (2013) *Shaping Immigration News: A French–American Comparison*. Cambridge University Press.

Bergström, A. & Belfrage, M. J. (2018) "News in social media," *Digital Journalism* 6(5): 583–98.

Bermeo, N. (2016) "On democratic backsliding," *Journal of Democracy* 27(1): 5–19.

Beyrer, C. & Kamarulzaman, A. (2017) "Ethnic cleansing in Myanmar: the Rohingya crisis and human rights," *The Lancet* 390(10102): 1570–3.

Billard, T. J. (2019) "Setting the transgender agenda: intermedia agenda-setting in the digital news environment," *Politics, Groups, and Identities* 7(1): 165–76.

Bimber, B. (1998) "The internet and political transformation: populism, community, and accelerated pluralism," *Polity* 31(1): 133–60.

Bimber, B. (2017) "Three prompts for collective action in the context of digital media," *Political Communication* 34(1): 6–20.

Bimber, B. & Gil de Zúñiga, H. (2020) "The unedited public sphere," *New Media & Society* 22(4): 700–15.

Blair, A., Duguid, P., Goeing, A. S., & Grafton, A. (eds.) (2021) *Information: A Historical Companion*. Princeton University Press.

Blumler, J. (2015) "Core theories of political communication: foundational and freshly minted," *Communication Theory* 25(4): 426–38.

Blumler, J. G. (2016) "The fourth age of political communication," *Politiques de Communication* 6(1): 19–30.

Blumler, J. G. & Gurevitch, M. (1975) "Towards a comparative framework for political communication research." In S. H. Chaffee (ed.) *Political Communication: Strategies and Issues for Research*. Beverly Hills, CA: SAGE, 165–84.

Blumler, J. G. & Kavanaugh, D. (1999). "The third age of political communication: influences and features," *Political Communication* 16(3): 209–30.

Bobba, G. (2018) "Social media populism: features and 'likeability' of Lega Nord communication on Facebook," *European Political Science* 18: 11–23.

Boczkowski, P. J. & Mitchelstein, E. (2021) *The Digital Environment: How We Live, Learn, Work, and Play Now*. Cambridge, MA: MIT Press.

Bogaards, M. (2009) "How to classify hybrid regimes? Defective democracy and electoral authoritarianism," *Democratization* 16(2): 399–423.

Boichak, O., Hemsley, J., Jackson, S., Tromble, R., & Tanupabrungsun, S. (2021) "Not the bots you are looking for: patterns and effects of orchestrated interventions in the US and German elections," *International Journal of Communication* 15(2021): 814–39.

Bond, R. M., Fariss, C. J., Jones, J. J., Kramer, A. D., Marlow, C., Settle, J. E., & Fowler, J. H. (2012) "A 61-million-person experiment in social influence and political mobilization," *Nature* 489(7415): 295–8.

Bonde, B. N. (2007) "How 12 cartoons of the Prophet Mohammed were brought to trigger an international conflict," *Nordicom Review* 28(1): 33–48.

Bosah, G. A. (2018) "Digital media: changes in the news production and journalistic practices in Nigeria." Unpublished Ph.D. thesis, University of Leicester.

Bösch, M. & Ricks, B. (2021) "Broken promises: TikTok and the German election," Mozilla Foundation: https://assets.mofoprod.net/network/documents/TikTok_and_the_German_Election.pdf.

Bosch, T. (2017) "Twitter activism and youth in South Africa: the case of #RhodesMustFall," *Information, Communication & Society* 20(2): 221–32.

Bossetta, M. (2018) "The digital architectures of social media: comparing political campaigning on Facebook, Twitter, Instagram, and Snapchat in the 2016 US election," *Journalism & Mass Communication Quarterly* 95(2): 471–96.

Bossio, D., Flew, T., Meese, J., Leaver, T., & Barnet, B. (2022) "Australia's News Media Bargaining Code and the global turn towards platform regulation," *Policy & Internet* 14(1): 136–50.

Bötticher, A. (2017) "Towards academic consensus definitions of radicalism and extremism," *Perspectives on Terrorism* 11(4): 73–7.

Boulianne, S. (2015) "Social media use and participation: a meta-analysis of current research," *Information, Communication & Society* 18(5): 524–38.

Boulianne, S. (2020) "Twenty years of digital media effects on civic and political participation," *Communication Research* 47(7): 947–66.

Boulianne, S. & Larsson, A. O. (2023) "Engagement with candidate posts on Twitter, Instagram, and Facebook during the 2019 election," *New Media & Society* 25(10): 119–40.

Boydstun, A. E. (2013) *Making the News: Politics, the Media, and Agenda Setting*. University of Chicago Press.

Bracciale, R. & Martella, A. (2017) "Define the populist political communication style: the case of Italian political leaders on Twitter," *Information, Communication & Society* 20(9): 1310–29.

Brands, C., Kruikemeier, S., & Trilling, D. (2021) "Insta(nt)famous? Visual self-presentation and the use of masculine and feminine issues by female politicians on Instagram," *Information, Communication & Society* 24(14): 2016–36.

Bratcher, T. R. (2022) "Toward a deeper discussion: a survey analysis of podcasts and personalized politics," *Atlantic Journal of Communication* 30(2): 188–99.

Bratton, B. H. (2016) *The Stack: On Software and Sovereignty*. Cambridge, MA: MIT Press.

Braun, J. (2013) "Going over the top: online television distribution as sociotechnical system," *Communication, Culture & Critique* 6(3): 432–58.

Brennen, J. S. & Kreiss, D. (2016) "Digitalization." In K. B. Jensen & R. T. Craig (eds.) *The International Encyclopedia of Communication Theory and Philosophy*. Hoboken, NJ: Wiley-Blackwell, 1–11.

Brevini, B. & Swiatek, L. (2020) *Amazon: Understanding a Global Communication Giant*. New York: Routledge.

Brinkman, I. & de Bruijn, M. (2018) "Mobile phones in mobile margins: communication, mobility and social hierarchies in/from Africa." In B. Mutsvairo (ed.) *The Palgrave Handbook for Media and Communication Research in Africa*. Basingstoke: Palgrave Macmillan, 225–41.

Brock, A. (2020) *Distributed Blackness: African American Cybercultures*. New York University Press.

Broersma, M. (2022) "Walking the line: political journalism and social media publics." In J. Morrison, J. Birks, & M. Berry (eds.) *The Routledge Companion to Political Journalism*. London and New York: Routledge, 262–70.

Brogi, E. (2020) "The Media Pluralism Monitor: conceptualizing media pluralism for the online environment," *Profesional de la Información* 29(5): https://doi.org/10.3145/epi.2020.sep.29.

Brown, D. K. & Mourão, R. R. (2021) "Protest coverage matters: how media framing and visual communication affects support for Black civil rights protests," *Mass Communication and Society* 24(4): 576–96.

Bruns, A. (2005) *Gatewatching: Collaborative Online News Production*. New York: Peter Lang.

Bruns, A. (2018) *Gatewatching and News Curation: Journalism, Social Media, and the Public Sphere*. New York: Peter Lang.

Bruns, A. (2019) *Are Filter Bubbles Real?* Cambridge: Polity.

Bruns, A. (2021) "Echo chambers? Filter bubbles? The misleading metaphors that obscure the real problem." In M. Pérez-Escolar & J. M. Noguera-Vivo (eds.) *Hate Speech and Polarization in Participatory Society*. London: Routledge, 33–48.

Bruns, A., Angus, D., & Graham, T. (2021) "Twitter campaigning strategies in Australian federal elections 2013–2019," *Social Media + Society* 7(4): 1–15.

Buchanan, T. & Benson, V. (2019) "Spreading disinformation on Facebook: do trust in message source, risk propensity, or personality affect the organic reach of 'fake news'?" *Social Media + Society* 5(4): 1–9.

Bucher, T. (2018) *If ... Then: Algorithmic Power and Politics*. New York: Oxford University Press.

Bucher, T. (2021) *Facebook*. Cambridge: Polity.

Bucher, T. & Helmond, A. (2018) "The affordances of social media platforms." In J. Burgess, T. Poell, & A. Marwick (eds) *The SAGE Handbook of Social Media*. London and New York: SAGE.

Bucy, E. P., Foley, J. M., Lukito, J., Doroshenko, L., Shah, D. V., Pevehouse, J. C. & Wells, C. (2020) "Performing populism: Trump's transgressive debate style and the dynamics of Twitter response," *New Media & Society* 22(4): 634–58.

Buechler, S. M. (2013) "New social movements and new social movement theory." In D. A. Snow, D. Della Porta, B. Klandermans, & D. McAdam (eds.) *The Wiley-Blackwell Encyclopedia of Social and Political Movements*. Hoboken, NJ: John Wiley & Sons, 1–7.

Butler, A. (2021) *White Evangelical Racism: The Politics of Morality in America*. Chapel Hill: University of North Carolina Press.

Caller, S. & Gorodzeisky, A. (2022) "Racist views in contemporary European societies," *Ethnic and Racial Studies* 45(9): 1627–48.

Cameron, D. (2022) "Facebook approved pro-genocide ads in Kenya after claiming to foster 'safe and secure' elections," *Gizmodo*, July 29: https://gizmodo.com/facebook-kenya-pro-genocide-ads-hate-speech-suspension-1849348778.

Canovan, M. (1999) "Trust the people! Populism and the two faces of democracy," *Political Studies* 47(1): 2–16.

Caplan, B. (2011) *The Myth of the Rational Voter*. Princeton University Press.

Carlson, M., Robinson, S., & Lewis, S. C. (2021) *News after Trump: Journalism's Crisis of Relevance in a Changed Media Culture*. Oxford University Press.

Castells, M. (2007) "Communication, power and counter-power in the network society," *International Journal of Communication* 1: 238–66.

Ceccobelli, D. (2018) "Not every day is Election Day: a comparative analysis of eighteen election campaigns on Facebook," *Journal of Information Technology & Politics* 15(2): 122–41.

Center for Countering Digital Hate (2022) "TOXIC TWITTER: How Twitter generates millions in ad revenue by bringing back banned accounts": https://counterhate.com/research/toxic-twitter.

Centre for Media Pluralism and Media Freedom (2022) "Monitoring media pluralism in the digital era application of the Media Pluralism Monitor in the European Union, Albania, Montenegro, the Republic of North Macedonia, Serbia and Turkey in the year 2021": https://cadmus.eui.eu/handle/1814/74712.

Chadwick, A. (2017) *The Hybrid Media System: Politics and Power*. Oxford University Press.

Chaffee, S. H. & Metzger, M. J. (2001) "The end of mass communication?" *Mass Communication and Society* 4(4): 365–79.

Chakravartty, P. & Da Silva, D. F. (2012) "Accumulation, dispossession, and debt: the racial logic of global capitalism – an introduction," *American Quarterly* 64(3): 361–85.

Chavez, L. R. (2001) *Covering Immigration: Popular Images and the Politics of the Nation*. Berkeley: University of California Press.

Chen, W., Pacheco, D., Yang, K. C., & Menczer, F. (2021) "Neutral bots probe political bias on social media," *Nature Communications* 12(1): 1–10.

Chibuwe, A. (2020) "Social media and elections in Zimbabwe: Twitter war between pro-ZANU-PF and pro-MDC-A netizens," *Communicatio: South African Journal of Communication Theory and Research* 46(4): 7–30.

Chouliaraki, L. (2015) "Digital witnessing in conflict zones: the politics of remediation," *Information, Communication & Society* 18(11): 1362–77.

Citron, D. K. & Wittes, B. (2018) "The problem isn't just Backpage: revising Section 230 immunity," *Georgetown Law Technology Review* 2(2): 453–73.

Clark, M. D. (2020) "DRAG THEM: a brief etymology of so-called 'cancel culture'." *Communication and the Public* 5(3–4): 88–92.

Clarke, M. (2018) "Global South: what does it mean and why use the term?" *University of Victoria Global South Political Commentaries*, August 8: https://onlineacademiccommunity.uvic.ca/globalsouthpolitics/2018/08/08/global-south-what-does-it-mean-and-why-use-the-term.

Cline Center (2021) "It was an attempted auto-coup: the Cline Center's Coup d'État Project categorizes the January 6, 2021 assault on the US Capitol." Cline Center for Advanced Social Research: https://clinecenter.illinois.edu/coup-detat-project/statement_dec.15.2022.

CNN (2015) "The time America used this pin to rile the Russians," *Amanpour*, June 25: https://edition.cnn.com/videos/world/2015/06/25/intv-amanpour-madeleine-albright-russia-pin.cnn.

Coddington, M. (2015) "Clarifying journalism's quantitative turn: a typology for evaluating data journalism, computational journalism, and computer-assisted reporting," *Digital Journalism* 3(3): 331–48.

Coleman, R., McCombs, M., Shaw, D., & Weaver, D. (2008) "Agenda setting." In K. Wahl-Jorgensen & T. Hanitzsch (eds.) *The Handbook of Journalism Studies*. London: Routledge, 167–80.

Collier, D. & Levitsky, S. (1997) "Democracy with adjectives: conceptual innovation in comparative research," *World Politics* 49(3): 430–51.

Collins, P. H. (2002) *Black Feminist Thought: Knowledge, Consciousness, and the Politics of Empowerment*, 2nd edn. London: Routledge.

Collins, P. H. & Bilge, S. (2020) *Intersectionality*, 2nd edn. Cambridge: Polity.

Combahee River Collective (1977) *A Black Feminist Statement*. Boston, MA: Combahee River Collective.

Cook, J. (2020) "How conservative teens are meme-ing and monetizing the political divide," *The Huffington Post*, August 25: www.huffpost.com/entry/teen-instagram-influencer-maga-memes_n_5f43e20bc5b60c7ec4143b96.

Cook, T. E. (1998) *Governing with the News: The News Media as a Political Institution.* University of Chicago Press.

Coombs, W. T. (2018) "Crisis communication." In R. L. Heath & W. Johansen (eds.) *Encyclopedia of Strategic Communication.* Hoboken, NJ: John Wiley & Sons, 17–54.

Cooper, A. (2020) *Conveying Truth: Independent Media in Putin's Russia.* Boston, MA: Harvard University Shorenstein Center on Media, Politics, and Public Policy.

Coppedge, M., Gerring, J., Glynn, A., Knutsen, C. H., Lindberg, S. I., Pemstein, D., Seim, B., Skaaning, S. E., & Teorell, J. (eds.) (2020) *Varieties of Democracy: Measuring Two Centuries of Political Change.* Cambridge University Press.

Corpuz, J. C. (2021) "COVID-19 and the rise of social activism in Southeast Asia: a public health concern," *Journal of Public Health* 43(2): 344–65.

Couldry, N., Hepp, A., & Krotz, F. (eds.) (2009) *Media Events in a Global Age.* London: Routledge.

Cowls, J., Darius, P., Santistevan, D., & Schramm, M. (2022) "Constitutional metaphors: Facebook's 'supreme court' and the legitimation of platform governance," *New Media & Society*: http://doi.org/10.1177/14614448221085559.

Crawford, K. (2021) *The Atlas of AI: Power, Politics, and the Planetary Costs of Artificial Intelligence.* New Haven, CT: Yale University Press.

Crigler, A. N. (ed.) (2007) *The Affect Effect: Dynamics of Emotion in Political Thinking and Behavior.* University of Chicago Press.

Cronin, A. M. (2018) *Public Relations Capitalism: Promotional Culture, Publics and Commercial Democracy.* Cham: Palgrave Macmillan.

Crowley, D. & Heyer, P. (2015) *Communication in History: Technology, Culture, Society.* London: Routledge.

Curran, J. & Liebes, T. (2002) "The intellectual legacy of Elihu Katz." In T. Liebes & J. Curran (eds.) *Media, Ritual and Identity.* London: Routledge, 13–30.

Cushion, S., Lewis, J., & Callaghan, R. (2017) "Data journalism, impartiality and statistical claims: towards more independent scrutiny in news reporting," *Journalism Practice* 11(10): 1198–1215.

d'Anjou, L. & Van Male, J. (1998) "Between old and new: social movements and cultural change," *Mobilization: An International Journal* 3(2): 207–26.

Dahlgren, P. M. (2021) "A critical review of filter bubbles and a comparison with selective exposure," *Nordicom Review* 42(1): 15–33.

Dale, D. (2022) "Twitter says it has quit taking action against lies about the 2020 election," CNN, January 28: www.cnn.com/2022/01/28/politics/twitter-lies-2020-election/index.html.

Darr, J. P., Hitt, M. P., & Dunaway, J. L. (2021) *Home Style Opinion: How Local Newspapers Can Slow Polarization.* Cambridge University Press.

Davis, M. (2021) "The online anti-public sphere," *European Journal of Cultural Studies* 24(1): 143–59.

Dayan, D. & Katz, E. (1992) *Media Events: The Live Broadcasting of History.* Cambridge, MA: Harvard University Press.

De Vreese, C. H., Esser, F., Aalberg, T., Reinemann, C., & Stanyer, J. (2018) "Populism as an expression of political communication content and style: a new perspective," *The International Journal of Press/Politics* 23(4): 423–38.

Delli Carpini, M. X. & Williams, B. A. (2001) "Let us infotain you: politics in the new media age." InW. L. Bennett & R. L. Entman (eds.) *Mediated Politics: Communication in the Future of Democracy*. Cambridge University Press, 160–81.

DeNardis, L. (2009) *Protocol Politics: The Globalization of Internet Governance*. Cambridge, MA: MIT Press.

DeNardis, L. (2014) *The Global War for Internet Governance*. New Haven, CT: Yale University Press.

DeNardis, L., Cogburn, D., Levinson, N. S., & Musiani, F. (eds.) (2020) *Researching Internet Governance: Methods, Frameworks, Futures*. Cambridge, MA: MIT Press.

Derks, D., Bos, A. E. R., & von Grumbkow, J. (2008) "Emoticons in computer-mediated communication: social motives and social context," *Cyberpsychology and Behavior* 11: 99–101.

Descalsota, M. (2022) "Meet Pavel Durov, the tech billionaire who founded Telegram, fled from Moscow 15 years ago after defying the Kremlin, and has a penchant for posting half-naked selfies on Instagram," *Business Insider*, March 28: www.businessinsider.com/pavel-durov-telegram-billionaire-russia-instagram-wealth-founder-dubai-lifestyle-2022-3.

Deuze, M. (2005) "What is journalism? Professional identity and ideology of journalists reconsidered," *Journalism* 6(4): 442–64.

Dewey, J. (1927) *The Public and Its Problems*. New York: H. Holt & Company.

Diakopoulos, N. (2019) *Automating the News*. Cambridge, MA: Harvard University Press.

Diakopoulos, N. & Johnson, D. (2021) "Anticipating and addressing the ethical implications of deepfakes in the context of elections," *New Media & Society* 23(7): 2072–98.

Diamond, L. & Plattner, M. F. (2012) *Liberation Technology: Social Media and the Struggle for Democracy*. Baltimore: Johns Hopkins University Press.

Diani, M. (2021) "The concept of social movement," *The Sociological Review* 40(1): 1–25.

DiBella, J. (2005) "Un paso importante, un primer paso." In La Red de Radiodifusoras y Televisoras Educativas y Culturales de México, A.C. (ed.) *Democracia y medios públicos*. Mexico, D.F., 229–33.

DiGirolamo, V. (2019) *Crying the News: A History of America's Newsboys*. New York: Oxford University Press.

Dimitrova, D. V., Shehata, A., Strömbäck, J., & Nord, L. W. (2014) "The effects of digital media on political knowledge and participation in election campaigns: evidence from panel data," *Communication Research* 41(1): 95–118.

Dobson, C. (2017) *The Citizen Handbook*. Vancouver Citizens' Committee.

Donovan, J. & boyd, D. (2021) "Stop the presses? Moving from strategic silence to strategic amplification in a networked media ecosystem," *American Behavioral Scientist* 65(2): 333–50.

Donsbach, W. (ed.) (2015) *The Concise Encyclopedia of Communication*. Malden, MA: Wiley Blackwell Publishing Ltd.

Douek, E. (2020) "Governing online speech: from 'posts-as-trumps' to proportionality and probability," *Columbia Law Review* 121(1): 759–834.

Du Bois, W. E. B. (2014) *Black Reconstruction in America: Toward a History of the Part which Black Folk Played in the Attempt to Reconstruct Democracy in America, 1860–1880*. Oxford University Press.

Dunaway, J. & Graber, D. A. (2022) *Mass Media and American Politics*. Washington, DC: Congressional Quarterly Press.

Dunaway, J. & Searles, K. (2022) *News and Democratic Citizens in the Mobile Era*. New York: Oxford University Press.

Dunaway, J. & Soroka, S. (2021) "Smartphone-size screens constrain cognitive access to video news stories," *Information, Communication & Society* 24(1): 69–84.

Durov, P. (2018) [Twitter] January 17: https://twitter.com/durov/status/953449090930618368?s=20&t=ZdGMJksQ8xelO2xc52V7XA.

Earl, J., Maher, T. V., & Pan, J. (2022) "The digital repression of social movements, protest, and activism: a synthetic review," *Science Advances* 8(10): 1–15.

Eberl, J. M., Meltzer, C. E., Heidenreich, T., Herrero, B., Theorin, N., Lind, F., & Strömbäck, J. (2018) "The European media discourse on immigration and its effects: a literature review," *Annals of the International Communication Association* 42(3): 207–23.

Eckert, S. & Chadha, K. (2013) "Muslim bloggers in Germany: an emerging counterpublic," *Media, Culture & Society* 35(8): 926–42.

Edy, J. (2006) *Troubled Pasts: News and the Collective Memory of Social Unrest*. Philadelphia, PA: Temple University Press.

Egelhofer, J. N. & Lecheler, S. (2019) "Fake news as a two-dimensional phenomenon: a framework and research agenda," *Annals of the International Communication Association* 43(2): 97–116.

Eisenstein, E. L. (1980) *The Printing Press as an Agent of Change*. Cambridge University Press.

Ellemers, N. & Haslam, S. A. (2012) "Social identity theory." In P. van Lange, A. Kruglanski, & T. Higgins (eds.), *Handbook of Theories of Social Psychology*. London: Sage, 379–98.

Elmer, G., Langlois, G., & McKelvey, F. (2012) *The Permanent Campaign: New Media, New Politics*. New York: Peter Lang.

Elvestad, E. & Johannessen, M. R. (2017) "Facebook and local newspapers' effect on local politicians' popularity," *Northern Lights: Film & Media Studies Yearbook* 15(1): 33–50.

Engesser, S., Ernst, N., Esser, F., & Büchel, F. (2017) "Populism and social media: how politicians spread a fragmented ideology," *Information, Communication & Society* 20(8): 1109–26.

Engesser, S., Fawzi, N., & Olof Larsson, A. (2017) "Populist online communication: introduction to the special issue," *Information, Communication and Society* 20(9): 1279–92.

Enke, N. & Borchers, N. S. (2019) "Social media influencers in strategic communication: a conceptual framework for strategic social media influencer communication," *International Journal of Strategic Communication* 13(4): 261–77.

Enli, G. (2016) "'Trust me, I am authentic!': authenticity illusions in social media politics." In A. Bruns, G. Enli, E. Skogerbo, A. O. Larsson, & C. Christensen (eds.) *The Routledge Companion to Social Media and Politics*. New York: Routledge, 121–36.

Entman, R. M. (1993) "Framing: toward clarification of a fractured paradigm," *Journal of Communication* 43(4): 51–8.

Entman, R. M. & Usher, N. (2018) "Framing in a fractured democracy: impacts of digital technology on ideology, power and cascading network activation," *Journal of Communication* 68(2): 298–308.

Eriksson, M. (2018) "Lessons for crisis communication on social media: a systematic review of what research tells the practice," *International Journal of Strategic Communication* 12(5): 526–51.

Erkkilä, M. (2018) "What use is blockchain for journalism?" *POLIS: Journalism and Society*. London School of Economics.

Ernst, N., Engesser, S., Büchel, F., Blassnig, S., & Esser, F. (2017) "Extreme parties and populism: an analysis of Facebook and Twitter across six countries," *Information, Communication & Society* 20(9): 1347–64.

Esser, F. & Pfetsch, B. (2020) "Political communication." In D. Caramani (ed.) *Comparative Politics*. Oxford University Press, 336–58.

Esser, F. & Strömbäck, J. (eds.) (2014) *Mediatization of Politics: Understanding the Transformation of Western Democracies*. Basingstoke: Palgrave Macmillan.

Eubanks, V. (2018) *Automating Inequality: How High-Tech Tools Profile, Police, and Punish the Poor*. New York: St. Martin's Press.

Eveland Jr., W. P. & Nathanson, A. I. (2020) "Contexts for family talk about racism: historical, dyadic, and geographic," *Journal of Family Communication* 20(4): 267–84.

Facebook (2021) https://about.fb.com/news/2021/06/facebook-response-to-oversight-board-recommendations-trump.

Facebook (2023) https://transparency.fb.com/sr/oversight-board-charter-2023.

Farthing, L. (2019) "An opportunity squandered? Elites, social movements, and the government of Evo Morales," *Latin American Perspectives* 46(1): 212–29.

Fengler, S., Eberwein, T., Alsius, S., et al. (2015) "How effective is media self-regulation? Results from a comparative survey of European journalists," *European Journal of Communication* 30(3): 249–66.

Ferrara E. (2017) "Disinformation and Social Bot operations in the run up to the 2017 French presidential election," *First Monday*: https://doi.org/10.5210/fm.v22i8.8005.

Ferrucci, P. & Eldridge II, S. A. (eds.) (2022) *The Institutions Changing Journalism: Barbarians Inside the Gate*. London: Routledge.

Feuer, A., Haberman, M., & Broadwater, L. (2022) "Memos show roots of Trump's focus on Jan. 6 and alternate electors," *New York Times*, February 2: www.nytimes.com/2022/02/02/us/politics/trump-jan-6-memos.html.

Field, A., Kliger, D., Wintner, S., Pan, J., Jurafsky, D., & Tsvetkov, Y. (2018) "Framing and agenda-setting in Russian news: a computational analysis of intricate political strategies." In E. Riloff, D. Chiang, J. Hockenmaier, & J. Tsujii (eds.) *Proceedings of the 2018 Conference on Empirical Methods in Natural Language Processing*. Brussels: Association for Computational Linguistics, 3570–80.

Fielden, L. (2016) "UK press regulation: taking account of media convergence," *Convergence: The International Journal of Research into New Media Technologies* 22(5): 472–7.

Figenschou, T. U. & Fredheim, N. A. (2020) "Interest groups on social media: four forms of networked advocacy," *Journal of Public Affairs* 20(2): 1–8.

Figenschou, T. U. & Thorbjørnsrud, K. (2020) "'Hey there in the night': The strategies, dilemmas and costs of a personalized digital lobbying campaign." In H. Hornmoen, B. K. Fonn, N. Hyde-Clarke, & Y. B. Hågvar (eds.) *Media Health: The Personal in Public Stories*. Oslo: Scandinavian University Press, 165–85.

Filimonov, K., Rußmann, U., & Svensson, J. (2016) "Picturing the party: Instagram and party campaigning in the 2014 Swedish elections," *Social Media + Society* 2(3): 1–11.

Finchelstein, F. (2019). *From Fascism to Populism in History*. Oakland: University of California Press.

Finchelstein, F. (2020) *A Brief History of Fascist Lies*. Oakland: University of California Press.

Finkel, E. J., Bail, C. A., Cikara, M., Ditto, P. H., Iyengar, S., Klar, S., Mason, L., McGrath, M. C., Nyhan, B., Rand, D. G., & Skitka, L.J. (2020) "Political sectarianism in America," *Science* 370(6516): 533–6.

Firat, F. (2019) "Robot journalism." In T. P. Vos, F. Hanusch, D. Dimitrakopoulou, M. Geertsema-Sligh, & A. Sehl (eds.) *The International Encyclopedia of Journalism Studies*. Hoboken, NJ: John Wiley & Sons, 1–5.

Fletcher, R. & Kleis Nielsen, R. (2018) "Are people incidentally exposed to news on social media? A comparative analysis," *New Media and Society* 20(7): 2450–68.

Foucault Welles, B. F. & González-Bailón, S. (eds.) (2020) *The Oxford Handbook of Networked Communication*. Oxford University Press.

Fowler, E. F., Franz, M. M., Martin, G. J., Peskowitz, Z., & Ridout, T. N. (2021b) "Political advertising online and offline," *American Political Science Review* 115(1): 130–49.

Fowler, E. F., Franz, M. M., & Ridout, T. N. (2021a) *Political Advertising in the United States*. New York: Routledge.

Frankfurt, H. G. (2009) *On Bullshit*. Princeton University Press.

Franklin, B. (ed.) (2011) *The Future of Journalism*. London: Routledge.

Franklin, B. & Carlson, M. (eds.) (2011) *Journalists, Sources, and Credibility: New Perspectives*. London: Routledge.

Franks, M. A. (2020) "How the internet unmakes law," *Ohio State Technical Law Journal* 16(2020): 10.

Fraser, N. (1990) "Rethinking the public sphere: a contribution to the critique of actually existing democracy," *Social Text* 25/26: 56–80.

Freelon, D. (2014) "Online civic activism: where does it fit?" *Policy and Internet* 6(2): 192–8.

Freelon, D., Bossetta, M., Wells, C., Lukito, J., Xia, Y., & Adams, K. (2022) "Black trolls matter: racial and ideological asymmetries in social media disinformation," *Social Science Computer Review* 40(3): 560–78.

Freelon, D., McIlwain, C., & Clark, M. (2016) "Beyond the hashtags: #Ferguson, #Blacklivesmatter, and the online struggle for offline justice," Center for Media & Social Impact: http://cmsimpact.org/blmreport.

Freelon, D., McIlwain, C., & Clark, M. (2018) "Quantifying the power and consequences of social media protest," *New Media & Society* 20(3): 990–1011.

Freelon, D. & Wells, C. (2020) "Disinformation as political communication," *Political Communication* 37(2): 145–56.

Friedland, L. A., Hove, T., & Rojas, H. (2006) "The networked public sphere," *Javnost – The Public* 13(4): 5–26.

Friedman, V. & Steinhauer, J. (2021) "Purple was a popular color at the inauguration, and Bernie Sanders' mittens made a splash," *The New York Times*, January 20: www.nytimes.com/2021/01/20/us/politics/purple-inauguration.html.

Fu, K. W. & Chau, M. (2014) "Use of microblogs in grassroots movements in China: exploring the role of online networking in agenda setting," *Journal of Information Technology & Politics* 11(3): 309–28.

Fukuyama, F. (1989) "The end of history?" *The National Interest* 16: 3–18.

Gabielkov, M., Ramachandran, A., Chaintreau, A., & Legout, A. (2016) "Social clicks: what and who gets read on Twitter?" In S. Alouf (ed.) *Proceedings of the 2016 ACM SIGMETRICS International Conference on Measurement and Modeling of Computer Science*. New York: ACM, 179–92.

Gadarian, S. K., Goodman, S. W., & Pepinsky, T. B. (2022). *Pandemic Politics: The Deadly Toll of Partisanship in the Age of COVID*. Princeton University Press.

Gammelin, C., Fried, N., & Krach, W. (2021) "Das große Abschiedsinterview mit Angela Merkel," *Süddeutsche Zeitung*, October 22: https://projekte.sueddeutsche.de/artikel/politik/das-grosse-abschiedsinterview-mit-angela-merkel-e623201/?ieditorial=0.

García-Avilés, J. A. (2021) "Journalism as usual? Managing disruption in virtual newsrooms during the COVID-19 crisis," *Digital Journalism* 9(9): 1239–60.

Garland Mahler, A. (2018) *From the Tricontinental to the Global South: Race, Radicalism, and Transnational Solidarity*. Durham, NC: Duke University Press.

Garretson, J. J. (2018) *The Path to Gay Rights: How Activism and Coming Out Changed Public Opinion*. New York University Press.

Garrett, R. K. (2019) "Social media's contribution to political misperceptions in U.S. Presidential elections," *PLoS ONE* 14(3): 1–16.

Garrett, R. K., Long, J. A., & Jeong, M. S. (2019) "From partisan media to misperception: affective polarization as mediator," *Journal of Communication* 69(5): 490–512.

Genner, S. & Süss, D. (2017) "Socialization as media effect." In P. Rössler, C. A. Hoffner, & L. van Zoonen (eds.) *The International Encyclopedia of Media Effects*. Chichester: John Wiley & Sons, 1890–1904.

Gienow-Hecht, J. C. (ed.) (2015) *Music and International History in the Twentieth Century*. New York: Berghahn Books.

Gil de Zúñiga, H. & Chen, H. T. (2019) "Digital media and politics: effects of the great information and communication divides," *Journal of Broadcasting & Electronic Media* 63(3): 365–73.

Gil de Zúñiga, H. & Diehl, T. (2019) "News finds me perception and democracy: effects on political knowledge, political interest, and voting," *New Media & Society* 21(6): 1253–71.

Gil de Zúñiga, H., Weeks, B., & Ardèvol-Abreu, A. (2017). "Effects of the news-finds-me perception in communication: social media use implications for news seeking and learning about politics," *Journal of Computer-Mediated Communication* 22(3): 105–23.

Gillan, K. (2008) "Understanding meaning in movements: a hermeneutic approach to frames and ideologies," *Social Movement Studies* 7(3): 247–63.

Gillespie, T. (2010) "The politics of 'platforms'," *New Media & Society* 12(3): 347–64.

Gillespie, T. (2014) "The relevance of algorithms." In T. Gillespie, P. J. Boczkowski, & K. A. Foot (eds.) *Media Technologies: Essays on Communication, Materiality, and Society*. Cambridge, MA: MIT Press, 167–94.

Gillespie, T. (2017) "Platforms are not intermediaries," *Georgetown Law Technology Review* 2(2): 198–216.

Gillespie, T., Aufderheide, P., Carmi, E., Gerrard, Y., Gorwa, R., Matamoros-Fernández, A., & West, S. M. (2020) "Expanding the debate about content moderation: scholarly research agendas for the coming policy debates," *Internet Policy Review* 9(4): 1–30.

Gillespie, T., Boczkowski, P. J., & Foot, K. A. (eds.) (2014) *Media Technologies: Essays on Communication, Materiality, and Society*. Cambridge, MA: MIT Press.

Glaser, M. (2020) "Five business models for local news to watch in 2020," *Knight Foundation*, January 7: https://knightfoundation.org/articles/5-business-models-for-local-news-to-watch-in-2020.

Gonçalves, S. (2019) "Ballet, propaganda, and politics in the Cold War: the Bolshoi Ballet in London and the Sadler's Wells Ballet in Moscow, October–November 1956," *Cold War History* 19(2): 171–86.

González-Bailón, S. & Wang, N. (2016) "Networked discontent: the anatomy of protest campaigns in social media," *Social Networks* 44(1): 95–104.

Goodman, S., Tafi, V., & Coyle, A. (2022) "Alternative 'Lives Matter' formulations in online discussions about Black Lives Matter: use, support and resistance," *Discourse & Society* 34(3): 291–316.

Goodwin, A., Joseff, K., & Woolley, S. C. (2020) "Social media influencers and the 2020 US election: paying 'regular people' for digital campaign communication," Center for Media Engagement, The University of Texas at Austin, October 14: https://mediaengagement.org/research/social-media-influencers-and-the-2020-election.

Google (2021) "2021 Diversity Annual Report": https://static.googleusercontent.com/media/diversity.google/de//annual-report/static/pdfs/google_2021_diversity_annual_report.pdf?cachebust=2e13d07.

Gorwa, R. (2019) "What is platform governance?" *Information, Communication & Society* 22(6): 854–71.

Gorwa, R., Binns, R., & Katzenbach, C. (2020) "Algorithmic content moderation: technical and political challenges in the automation of platform governance," *Big Data & Society* 7(1): 1–15.

Goujard, C. (2022) "Online platforms now have an hour to remove terrorist content in the EU," *Politico*, June 7: www.politico.eu/article/online-platforms-to-take-down-terrorist-content-under-an-hour-in-the-eu.

Graham, R. & Smith, S. (2016) "The content of our #characters: Black Twitter as counterpublic," *Sociology of Race and Ethnicity* 2(4): 433–49.

Graham, T. & Hajru, A. (2011) "Reality TV as a trigger of everyday political talk in the net-based public sphere," *European Journal of Communication* 26(1): 18–32.

Graham-McLay, C. (2019) "New Zealand twitchy amid claims of Russian meddling in bird of the year contest," *The Guardian*, November 12: www.theguardian.com/world/2019/nov/12/new-zealand-twitchy-amid-claims-of-russian-meddling-in-bird-of-the-year-contest.

Granovetter, M. S. (1973) "The strength of weak ties," *American Journal of Sociology* 78(6): 1360–80.

Green, M. C. (2021) "Transportation into narrative worlds." In L. B. Frank & P. Falzone (eds.) *Entertainment-Education Behind the Scenes*. Cham: Palgrave Macmillan, 87–101.

Greenberg, D. (2016) *Republic of Spin: An Inside History of the American Presidency*. New York: W. W. Norton & Company.

Greenslade, R. (2014) "Financial Times rejects Ipso in favour of its own editorial complaints system," *The Guardian*, April 17: www.theguardian.com/media/greenslade/2014/apr/17/press-regulation-financialtimes.

Greste, P. (2021) *Define Journalism: Not Journalist*. Press Freedom Policy Papers. University of Queensland.

Groshek, J. & Koc-Michalska, K. (2017) "Helping populism win? Social media use, filter bubbles, and support for populist presidential candidates in the 2016 US election campaign," *Information, Communication & Society* 20(9): 1389–1407.

Groshek, J. & Krongard, S. (2016) "Netflix and engage? Implications for streaming television on political participation during the 2016 US presidential campaign," *Social Sciences* 5(4): 65.

Gruber, J. B. (2023) "Troublemakers in the streets? A framing analysis of newspaper coverage of protests in the UK 1992–2017," *The International Journal of Press/Politics* 28(2): 414–33: https:doi.org/10.1177/19401612221102058.

Guriev, S. (2018) "Economic drivers of populism," *AEA Papers and Proceedings* 108: 200–3.

Habermas, J. (1989) *The Structural Transformation of the Public Sphere: An Inquiry into a Category of Bourgeois Society*. Cambridge, MA: MIT Press.

Habermas, J. (2013) *Strukturwandel der Öffentlichkeit*. Frankfurt: Suhrkamp.

Habermas, J. (2021) "Überlegungen und Hypothesen zu einem erneuten Strukturwandel der politischen Öffentlichkeit." In M. Seeliger & S. Sevignani (eds.) *Ein neuer Strukturwandel der Öffentlichkeit? Sonderband Leviathan 37* (2021). Baden-Baden: Nomos, 470–500.

Hacker, J. S. & Pierson, P. (2020) *Let Them Eat Tweets: How the Right Rules in an Age of Extreme Inequality*. New York: Liveright Publishing.

Haenschen, K. (2016) "Social pressure on social media: using Facebook status updates to increase voter turnout," *Journal of Communication* 66(4): 542–63.

Haenschen, K. & Jennings, J. (2019) "Mobilizing millennial voters with targeted internet advertisements: a field experiment," *Political Communication* 36(3): 357–75.

Hafez, K. (2002) "Journalism ethics revisited: a comparison of ethics codes in Europe, North Africa, the Middle East, and Muslim Asia," *Political Communication* 19(2): 225–50.

Haggard, S. & Kaufman, R. (2021) *Backsliding: Democratic Regress in the Contemporary World*. Cambridge University Press.

Hajnal, Z. (2021) "Immigration & the origins of white backlash," *Daedalus* 150(2): 23–39.

Hallin, D. C. & Mancini, P. (eds.) (2011) *Comparing Media Systems beyond the Western World*. Cambridge University Press.

Hamedy, S. (2018). "Obama explains 'what the Russians exploited' in new interview with Letterman," CNN, January 18: https://edition.cnn.com/2018/01/12/politics/david-letterman-barack-obama-netflix-interview-russia/index.html.

Hameleers, M., Bos, L., & de Vreese, C. H. (2017) "'They did it': the effects of emotionalized blame attribution in populist communication," *Communication Research* 44(6): 870–900.

Hameleers, M. & Schmuck, D. (2017) "It's us against them: a comparative experiment on the effects of populist messages communicated via social media," *Information, Communication & Society* 20(9): 1425–44.

Hanitzsch, T. (2007) "Deconstructing journalism culture: toward a universal theory," *Communication Theory* 17(4): 367–85.

Hanitzsch, T., Hanusch, F., Ramaprasad, J., & De Beer, A. S. (eds.) (2019) *Worlds of Journalism: Journalistic Cultures around the Globe*. New York: Columbia University Press.

Harlow, S. (2016) "Social media and social movements: Facebook and an online Guatemalan justice movement that moved offline," *New Media & Society* 14(2): 225–43.

Harlow, S., Brown, D. K., Salaverría, R., & García-Perdomo, V. (2020) "Is the whole world watching? Building a typology of protest coverage on social media from around the world," *Journalism Studies* 21(11): 1590–1608.

Harlow, S., Salaverría, R., Kilgo, D. K., & García-Perdomo, V. (2017) "Protest paradigm in multimedia: social media sharing of coverage about the crime of Ayotzinapa, Mexico," *Journal of Communication* 67(3): 328–49.

Harmer, E. & Southern, R. (2021) "Digital microaggressions and everyday othering: an analysis of tweets sent to women members of Parliament in the UK," *Information, Communication & Society* 24(14): 1998–2015.

Hart, R. P. (ed.) (2021). *Fixing American Politics: Solutions for the Media Age*. London: Routledge.

Haßler, J., Magin, M., Rußmann, U., & Fenoll, V. (eds.) (2021) *Campaigning on Facebook in the 2019 European Parliament Election*. Cham: Palgrave Macmillan.

Hatmaker, T. (2020) "Facebook hits pause on algorithmic recommendations for political and social issue groups," *TechCrunch*, October 30: https://techcrunch.com/2020/10/30/facebook-group-recommendations-election.

Hautea, S., Parks, P., Takahashi, B., & Zeng, J. (2021) "Showing they care (or don't): affective publics and ambivalent climate activism on TikTok," *Social Media + Society* 7(2): 1–14.

Hawkins, K. A., Riding, S., & Mudde, C. (2012) "Measuring populist attitudes," *C&M Working Paper* 55.

Hawkins, K. A. & Rovira Kaltwasser, C. (2017) "What the (ideational) study of populism can teach us, and what it can't," *Swiss Political Science Review* 23(4): 526–42.

Hebdige, D. (2012) *Subculture: The Meaning of Style*. Hoboken, NJ: Taylor & Francis.

Heft, A., Mayerhöffer, E., Reinhardt, S., & Knüpfer, C. (2020) "Beyond Breitbart: comparing right-wing digital news infrastructures in six western democracies," *Policy & Internet* 12(1): 20–45.

Heinkelmann-Wild, T., Kriegmair, L., Rittberger, B., & Zangl, B. (2020) "Divided they fail: the politics of wedge issues and Brexit," *Journal of European Public Policy* 27(5): 723–41.

Heinrich, A. (2012) "Foreign reporting in the sphere of networked journalism," *Journalism Practice* 6(5–6): 766–75.

Helberger, N., Pierson, J., & Poell, T. (2018) "Governing online platforms: from contested to cooperative responsibility," *The Information Society* 34(1): 1–14.

Helles, R. (2013) "The big head and the long tail: an illustration of explanatory strategies for big data Internet studies," *First Monday* 18(10): https://firstmonday.org/article/view/4874/3753.

Hellman, M. & Wagnsson, C. (2017) "How can European states respond to Russian information warfare? An analytical framework," *European Security* 26(2): 153–70.

Hellmann, O. (2017) "Populism in East Asia." In C. R. Kaltwasser, P. A. Taggart, P. O. Espejo, & P. Ostiguy (eds.) *The Oxford Handbook of Populism*. Oxford University Press, 161–78.

Henneberg, S. C. & Ormrod, R. P. (2013) "The triadic interaction model of political marketing exchange," *Marketing Theory* 13(1): 87–103.

Herbst, S. (1998) *Reading Public Opinion: How Political Actors View the Democratic Process*. University of Chicago Press.

Hern, A. (2020) "Twitter aims to limit people sharing articles they have not read," *The Guardian*, June 11: www.theguardian.com/technology/2020/jun/11/twitter-aims-to-limit-people-sharing-articles-they-have-not-read.

Higgins, P. (1996) "The World Wide Web: an introduction," *Information Development* 12(3): https://doi.org/10.1177/026666699601200030.

Hindman, M. (2018) *The Internet Trap: How the Digital Economy Builds Monopolies and Undermines Democracy*. Princeton University Press.

Hindman, M., Lubin, N., & Davis, T. (2022) "Facebook has a superuser-supremacy problem," *The Atlantic*, February 10: www.theatlantic.com/technology/archive/2022/02/facebook-hate-speech-misinformation-superusers/621617.

Høedt-Rasmussen, I. & Voorhoof, D. (2018) "Whistleblowing for sustainable democracy," *Netherlands Quarterly of Human Rights* 36(1): 3–6.

Hoffmann, J. (2015) "Lobbying." In G. Mazzoleni, K. G. Barnhurst, K. I. Ikeda, R. C. Maia, & H. Wessler (eds.) *The International Encyclopedia of Political Communication*, 3 vols. Chichester: John Wiley & Sons, 660–4.

Hoffmann, J., Katzenbach, C., & Gollatz, K. (2017) "Between coordination and regulation: finding the governance in Internet governance," *New Media & Society* 19(9): 1406–23.

Hogg, M. A. & Reid, J. A. (2006) "Social identity, self-categorization, and the communication of group norms," *Communication Theory* 16: 7–30.

Holdo, M. (2020) "Power games: elites, movements, and strategic cooperation," *Political Studies Review* 18(2): 189–203.

Holtz-Bacha, C., Langer, A. I., & Merkle, S. (2014) "The personalization of politics in comparative perspective: campaign coverage in Germany and the United Kingdom," *European Journal of Communication* 29(2): 153–70.

Holtzhausen, D. & Zerfass, A. (eds.) (2015) *The Routledge Handbook of Strategic Communication*. New York: Routledge.

Hong, S. H. (2020) *Technologies of Speculation*. New York University Press.

Hooker, J. (2009) *Race and the Politics of Solidarity*. Oxford University Press.

Hooker, J. (2016) "Black Lives Matter and the paradoxes of U.S. Black politics: from democratic sacrifice to democratic repair," *Political Theory* 44(4): 448–69.

Hooker, J. (2017) *Theorizing Race in the Americas: Douglass, Sarmiento, Du Bois, and Vasconcelos*. Oxford University Press.

Hopmann, D. N. (2012) "The consequences of political disagreement in interpersonal communication: new insights from a comparative perspective," *European Journal of Political Research* 51(2): 265–87.

Horwitz, J. & Seetharaman, D. (2020) "Facebook executives shut down efforts to make the site less divisive," *The Wall Street Journal*, May 26: www.wsj.com/articles/facebook-knows-it-encourages-division-top-executives-nixed-solutions-11590507499.

Howard, A. B. (2014) "The art and science of data-driven journalism," Tow Center for Digital Journalism, Columbia University: https://academiccommons.columbia.edu/doi/10.7916/D8Q531V1.

Howard, P. N. (2010) *The Digital Origins of Dictatorship and Democracy: Information Technology and Political Islam*. Oxford University Press.

Howard, P. N. (2020) *Lie Machines: How to Save Democracy from Troll Armies, Deceitful Robots, Junk News Operations, and Political Operatives*. New Haven, CT: Yale University Press.

Howard, P. N. & Hussain, M. M. (2013) *Democracy's Fourth Wave? Digital Media and the Arab Spring*. Oxford University Press.

Howard, P. N., Woolley, S., & Calo, R. (2018) "Algorithms, bots, and political communication in the US 2016 election: the challenge of automated political communication for election law and administration," *Journal of Information Technology & Politics* 15(2): 81–93.

Huddy, L. & Bankert, A. (2017) "Political partisanship as a social identity." In W. R. Thompson (ed.) *Oxford Research Encyclopedia of Politics*. Oxford University Press, 1–31.

Humprecht, E., Esser, F., & Van Aelst, P. (2020) "Resilience to online disinformation: a framework for cross-national comparative research," *The International Journal of Press/Politics* 25(3): 493–516.

Hunter, E. (2018) "Newspapers as sources for African history." In T. Spear (ed.) *Oxford Research Encyclopedia of African History*. Oxford University Press, 1–34.

Huttunen, J. (2021) "Young rebels who do not want a revolution: the non-participatory preferences of Fridays for Future activists in Finland," *Frontiers in Political Sciences* 3(1): 1–11.

ICIJ (International Consortium of Investigative Journalists) (2021a) "The Panama Papers: exposing the rogue offshore finance industry": www.icij.org/investigations/panama-papers.

ICIJ (International Consortium of Investigative Journalists) (2021b) "Pandora Papers: an offshore data tsunami": www.icij.org/investigations/pandora-papers.

Iglesias, P. (2015) *Ganar o morir: lecciones políticas en Juego de Tronos*. Madrid: Ediciones Akal.

Igo, S. E. (2007) *The Averaged American: Surveys, Citizens, and the Making of a Mass Public*. Cambridge, MA: Harvard University Press.

Inglehart, R. F. & Norris, P. (2016) "Trump, Brexit, and the rise of populism: economic have-nots and cultural backlash," *Harvard Kennedy School Working Paper* No. RWP16-026. Cambridge, MA: Harvard Kennedy School.

Ipsos (2022) "Ipsos snap poll: TV shows and reality": www.ipsos.com/sites/default/files/ct/news/documents/2022-03/Ipsos%20TV%20Show-Reality%20Topline%20FINAL.pdf.

Isaac, M., Wakabayashi, D., Cave, D., & Lee, E. (2021) "Facebook blocks news in Australia, diverging with Google on proposed law," *New York Times*, February 17: www.nytimes.com/2021/02/17/technology/facebook-google-australia-news.html.

Ivancsics, B. (2019) "Blockchain in journalism," Tow Center for Digital Journalism, January 25: www.cjr.org/tow_center_reports/blockchain-in-journalism.php#journalism.

Iyengar, S., Lelkes, Y., Levendusky, M., Malhotra, N., & Westwood, S. J. (2019) "The origins and consequences of affective polarization in the United States," *Annual Review of Political Science* 22: 129–46.

Iyengar, S. & Simon, A. F. (2000) "New perspectives and evidence on political communication and campaign effects," *Annual Review of Psychology* 51(1): 149–69.

Jackson, J. M. (2022) "The militancy of (Black) memory: theorizing Black-led movements as disjunctures in the normativity of white ignorance," *South Atlantic Quarterly* 121(3): 477–89.

Jackson, S. (2021) "'A very basic view of feminism': feminist girls and meanings of (celebrity) feminism," *Feminist Media Studies* 21(7): 1072–90.

Jackson, S. J., Bailey, M., & Foucault Welles, B. (2020) *#HashtagActivism: Networks of Race and Gender Justice*. Cambridge, MA: MIT Press.

Jacobs, K., Sandberg, L., & Spierings, N. (2020) "Twitter and Facebook: populists' double-barreled gun?" *New Media & Society* 22(4): 611–33.

Jacobs, K. & Spierings, N. (2019) "A populist paradise? Examining populists' Twitter adoption and use," *Information, Communication & Society* 22(12): 1681–96.

Jagers, J. & Walgrave, S. (2007) "Populism as political communication style: an empirical study of political parties' discourse in Belgium," *European Journal of Political Research* 46(3): 319–45.

Jaidka, K., Ahmed, S., Skoric, M., & Hilbert, M. (2019) "Predicting elections from social media: a three-country, three-method comparative study," *Asian Journal of Communication* 29(3): 252–73.

Jamieson, K. H. (2017) *The Oxford Handbook of Political Communication*. Oxford University Press.

Jamieson, K. H. (2020) *Cyberwar: How Russian Hackers and Trolls Helped Elect a President: What We Don't, Can't, and Do Know*. New York: Oxford University Press.

Jamieson, K. H. (2021) "How conspiracists exploited COVID-19 science," *Nature Human Behaviour* 5(11): 1464–5.

Jansens, F. (2019) "Suit of power: fashion, politics, and hegemonic masculinity in Australia," *Australian Journal of Political Science* 54(2): 202–18.

Jardina, A. (2019) *White Identity Politics*. Cambridge University Press.

Jarren, O., Fischer, R., Seeliger, M., & Sevignani, S. (2021) "Die Plattformisierung von Öffentlichkeit und der Relevanzverlust des Journalismus als demokratische Herausforderung." In M. Seeliger & S. Sevignani (eds.) *Ein neuer Strukturwandel der Öffentlichkeit? Sonderband Leviathan* 37(2021). Baden-Baden: Nomos, 365.

Jennings, M. K. (2007) "Political socialization." In R. J. Dalton & H.-D. Klingemann (eds.) *The Oxford Handbook of Political Behavior*. Oxford University Press.

Jerit, J. & Zhao, Y. (2020) "Political misinformation," *Annual Review of Political Science* 23(1): 77–94.

Johann, D., Kleinen-von Königslöw, K., Kritzinger, S., & Thomas, K. (2018) "Intra-campaign changes in voting preferences: the impact of media and party communication," *Political Communication* 35(2): 261–86.

Johansson, H. & Scaramuzzino, G. (2019) "The logics of digital advocacy: between acts of political influence and presence," *New Media & Society* 21(7): 1528–45.

John, R. R. (2009) *Spreading the News: The American Postal System from Franklin to Morse*. Cambridge, MA: Harvard University Press.

Jones, B. D. & Baumgartner, F. R. (2005) *The Politics of Attention: How Government Prioritizes Problems*. University of Chicago Press.

Jones, J. J., Bond, R. M., Bakshy, E., Eckles, D., & Fowler, J. H. (2017) "Social influence and political mobilization: further evidence from a randomized experiment in the 2012 US presidential election," *PloS One* 12(4): 1–9.

Josua, M. & Edel, M. (2021) "The Arab uprisings and the return of repression," *Mediterranean Politics* 26(5): 586–611.

Jungherr, A. (2013) "Tweets and votes, a special relationship: the 2009 federal election in Germany." In I. Weber (ed.) *Proceedings of the 2nd Workshop on Politics, Elections and Data*. New York: ACM, 5–14.

Jungherr, A., Rivero, G., & Gayo-Avello, D. (2020) *Retooling Politics: How Digital Media Are Shaping Democracy*. Cambridge University Press.

Jungherr, A., Schoen, H., Posegga, O., & Jürgens, P. (2017) "Digital trace data in the study of public opinion: an indicator of attention toward politics rather than political support," *Social Science Computer Review* 35(3): 336–56.

Kaid, L. L. & Holtz-Bacha, C. (eds.) (2007) *Encyclopedia of Political Communication*. Los Angeles, CA: SAGE.

Kaid, L. L. & Johnston, A. (2001) *Videostyle in Presidential Campaigns: Style and Content of Televised Political Advertising*. Westport, CT: Praeger.

Kaiser, J., Keller, T. R., & Kleinen-von Königslöw, K. (2021) "Incidental news exposure on Facebook as a social experience: the influence of recommender and media cues on news selection," *Communication Research* 48(1): 77–99.

Kaiser, J. & Rauchfleisch, A. (2019) "Integrating concepts of counterpublics into generalised public sphere frameworks: contemporary transformations in radical forms," *Javnost – The Public* 26(3): 241–57.

Kalmoe, N. P. (2019) "Mobilizing voters with aggressive metaphors," *Political Science Research and Methods* 7(3): 411–29.

Kalsnes, B. (2016) "The social media paradox explained: comparing political parties' Facebook strategy versus practice," *Social Media + Society* 2(2): 1–11.

Kapur, M. (2022) "Sri Lanka is only the latest Asian country to ban social media," *Quartz*, April 5: https://qz.com/india/2150749/sri-lanka-is-among-30-asian-countries-to-have-banned-social-media.

Karam, B. & Mutsvairo, B. (eds.) (2021) *Decolonizing African Political Communication: Reframing Ontologies*. New York: Routledge.

Karpf, D. (2016) *Analytic Activism: Digital Listening and the New Political Strategy*. New York: Oxford University Press.

Karpf, D. (2019) "The campfire and the tent: what social movement studies and political communication can learn from each other," *Information, Communication & Society* 22(5): 747–53.

Katz, E., Blumler, J. G., & Gurevitch, M. (1974) "Utilization of mass communication by the individual." In J. G. Blumler & E. Katz (eds.) *The Uses of Mass Communications: Current Perspectives on Gratifications Research*. Beverly Hills, CA: SAGE, 19–32.

Katz, J. E. & Mays, K. K. (eds.) (2019) *Journalism and Truth in an Age of Social Media*. Oxford University Press.

Katzenbach, C. (2013) "Media governance and technology: from 'code is law' to governance constellations." In M. E. Price, S. G. Verhulst, & L. Morgan (eds.) *Routledge Handbook of Media Law*. London: Routledge, 399–418.

Kavada, A. (2018) "Connective or collective? The intersection between online crowds and social movements in contemporary activism." In G. Miekle (ed.) *The Routledge Companion to Media and Activism*. London: Routledge, 108–16.

Keane, J. (2009) *The Life and Death of Democracy*. London: Simon and Schuster.

Keane, J. (2018) *Power and Humility: The Future of Monitory Democracy*. Cambridge University Press.

Kefford, G., Dommett, K., Baldwin-Philippi, J., Bannerman, S., Dobber, T., Kruschinski, S., Kruikemeier, S., & Rzepecki, E. (2022). Data-driven campaigning and democratic disruption: evidence from six advanced democracies. *Party Politics* 29(3): 448–62.

Keller, F. B., Schoch, D., Stier, S., & Yang, J. (2020) "Political astroturfing on Twitter: how to coordinate a disinformation campaign," *Political Communication* 37(2): 256–80.

Keller, T. & Klinger, U. (2018) "Social bots in election campaigns: theoretical, empirical and methodological implications," *Political Communication* 36(1): 171–89.

Kennedy, I., Wack, M., Beers, A., Schafer, J. S., Garcia-Camargo, I., Spiro, E. S., & Starbird, K. (2022) "Repeat spreaders and election delegitimization: a comprehensive dataset of misinformation Tweets from the 2020 U.S. election," *Journal of Quantitative Description: Digital Media* 2: 1–49.

Kennis, A. (2021) *Digital-Age Resistance Journalism, Social Movements and the Media Dependence Model*. London: Routledge.

Kenski, K., Coe, K., & Rains, S. A. (2020) "Perceptions of uncivil discourse online: an examination of types and predictors," *Communication Research* 47(6): 795–814.

Kernell, G. & Mullinix, K. J. (2019) "Winners, losers, and perceptions of vote (mis) counting," *International Journal of Public Opinion Research* 31(1): 1–24.

Khamis, S., Ang, L., & Welling, R. (2017) "Self-branding,'micro-celebrity' and the rise of social media influencers," *Celebrity Studies* 8(2): 191–208.

Kilgo, D. & Mourão, R. R. (2019) "Media effects and marginalized ideas: relationships among media consumption and support for Black Lives Matter," *International Journal of Communication* 13: 4287–305.

Kim, J. M. & Gil de Zúñiga, H. (2020) "Pseudo-information, media, publics, and the failing marketplace of ideas: theory," *American Behavioral Scientist* 65(2): 163–79.

Kim, Y. M., Hsu, J., Neiman, D., Kou, C., Bankston, L., Kim, S. Y., & Raskutti, G. (2018) "The stealth media? Groups and targets behind divisive issue campaigns on Facebook," *Political Communication* 35(4): 515–41.

Kitchin, R. (2017) "Thinking critically about and researching algorithms," *Information, Communication & Society* 20(1): 14–29.

Kleinen-von Königslöw, K. & Keel, G. (2012) "Localizing *The Daily Show*: the *Heute Show* in Germany," *Popular Communication* 10(1–2): 66–79.

Kligler-Vilenchik, N., de Vries Kedem, M., Maier, D., & Stoltenberg, D. (2021) "Mobilization vs. demobilization discourses on social media," *Political Communication* 38(5): 561–80.

Kline, R. & Pinch, T. (1996) "Users as agents of technological change: the social construction of the automobile in the rural United States," *Technology and Culture* 37(4): 763–95.

Klinger, U. (2011) "Democratizing media policy: community radios in Mexico and Latin America," *Journal of Latin American Communication Research* 1(2): 1–20.

Klinger, U. (2023) "Algorithms, power and digital politics." In S. Coleman & L. Sorensen (eds.) *Handbook of Digital Politics*, 2nd edn. New York: Edward Elgar Publishing.

Klinger, U., Bennett, W. L., Knüpfer, C. B., Martini, F., & Zhang, X. (2022b) "From the fringes into mainstream politics: intermediary networks and movement–party coordination of a global anti-immigration campaign in Germany," *Information, Communication & Society*: 1–18.

Klinger, U., Koc-Michalska, K., & Rußmann, U. (2022a) "Are campaigns getting uglier, and who is to blame? Negativity, dramatization and populism on Facebook in the 2014 and 2019 EP election campaigns," *Political Communication*: https://doi.org/10.1080/10584609.2022.2133198.

Klinger, U. & Rußmann, U. (2017) "'Beer is more efficient than social media' – political parties and strategic communication in Austrian and Swiss national elections," *Journal of Information Technology & Politics* 14(4): 299–313.

Klinger, U. & Svensson, J. (2015) "The emergence of network media logic in political communication: a theoretical approach," *New Media & Society* 17(8): 1241–57.

Klinger, U. & Svensson, J. (2016) "Network media logic: some conceptual considerations." In A. Bruns, E. Gunn, E. Skogerbo, A. O. Larsson, & C. Christensen (eds.) *The Routledge Companion to Social Media and Politics*. New York: Routledge, 23–38.

Klonick, K. (2019) "The Facebook Oversight Board: creating an independent institution to adjudicate online free expression," *Yale Law Journal* 129(8): 2418–99.

Klosterman, C. (2022) *The Nineties*. New York: Penguin.

Knight, A. (2012) "Balcony politics," *The Guardian*, August 21: www.theguardian.com/world/2012/aug/21/balcony-politics-ecuador.

Knoll, J., Matthes, J., & Heiss, R. (2020) "The social media political participation model: a goal systems theory perspective," *Convergence: The International Journal of Research into New Media Technologies* 26(1): 135–56.

Knudsen, E., Dahlberg, S., Iversen, M. H., Johannesson. M. P., & Nygaard, S. (2021) "How the public understands news media trust: an open-ended approach," *Journalism* 23(11): 1–17.

Knüpfer, C. B. & Entman, R. M. (2018) "Framing conflicts in digital and transnational media environments," *Media, War & Conflict* 11(4): 476–88.

Knüpfer, C., Hoffmann, M., & Voskresenskii, V. (2022) "Hijacking MeToo: transnational dynamics and networked frame contestation on the far right in the case of the '120 decibels' campaign," *Information, Communication & Society* 25(7): 1010–28.

Koc-Michalska, K., Lilleker, D. G., Michalski, T., Gibson, R., & Zajac, J. M. (2021) "Facebook affordances and citizen engagement during elections: European political parties and their benefit from online strategies?" *Journal of Information Technology & Politics* 18(2): 180–93.

Kohn, H., & Calhoun, C. (2017) *The Idea of Nationalism: A Study in Its Origins and Background*. London: Routledge.

Koo, C., Chung, N., & Kim, D. J. (2015) "How do social media transform politics? The role of a podcast, 'Naneun Ggomsuda' in South Korea," *Information Development* 31(5): 421–34.

Kotenidis, E. & Veglis, A. (2021) "Algorithmic journalism – current applications and future perspectives," *Journalism and Media* 2: 244–57.

Kovach, B. & Rosenstiel, T. (2007) *Elements of Journalism: What Newspeople Should Know and the Public Should Expect*. New York: Three Rivers Press.

Krafft, P. M. & Donovan, J. (2020) "Disinformation by design: the use of evidence collages and platform filtering in a media manipulation campaign," *Political Communication* 37(2): 194–214.

Krämer, B. (2014) "Media populism: a conceptual clarification and some theses on its effects," *Communication Theory* 24(1): 42–60.

Kreiss, D. (2016) *Prototype Politics: Technology-Intensive Campaigning and the Data of Democracy*. New York: Oxford University Press.

Kreiss, D. (2020) "Media and social media platforms finally begin to embrace their roles as democratic gatekeepers." In D. Jackson, D. S. Coombs, F. Trevisan, D. Lilleker, & E. Thorsen (eds.) *US Election Analysis: Media, Voters and the Campaign*. Poole: Centre for Comparative Politics and Media Research, Bournemouth University.

Kreiss, D. & Barrett, B. (2020) "Democratic tradeoffs: platforms and political advertising," *Ohio State Technology Law Journal* 16(2): 493–519.

Kreiss, D., Barrett, B., & Reddi, M. (2021, December 13). "The need for race-conscious platform policies to protect civic life," Tech Policy Press: https://techpolicy.press/the-need-for-race-conscious-platform-policies-to-protect-civic-life.

Kreiss, D. & Brooks, E. (2022) "Looking to the midterms: the state of platform policies on U.S. political speech," Tech Policy Press: https://techpolicy.press/looking-to-the-midterms-the-state-of-platform-policies-on-u-s-political-speech.

Kreiss, D., Lawrence, R. G., & McGregor, S. C. (2018) "In their own words: political practitioner accounts of candidates, audiences, affordances, genres, and timing in strategic social media use," *Political Communication* 35(1): 8–31.

Kreiss, D., Lawrence, R. G., & McGregor, S. C. (2020) "Political identity ownership: symbolic contests to represent members of the public," *Social Media + Society* 6(2): 1–5.

Kreiss, D. & McGregor, S. C. (2018) "Technology firms shape political communication: the work of Microsoft, Facebook, Twitter, and Google with campaigns during the 2016 U.S. presidential cycle," *Political Communication* 35(2): 155–77.

Kreiss, D. & McGregor, S. C. (2019) "The 'arbiters of what our voters see': Facebook and Google's struggle with policy, process, and enforcement around political advertising," *Political Communication* 36(4): 499–522.

Kreiss, D., & McGregor, S. C. (2022) "A review and provocation: on polarization and platforms." *New Media & Society*: https://doi.org/10.1177/14614448231161880.

Kriesi, H. (2012) "Personalization of national election campaigns," *Party Politics* 18(6): 825–44.

Krook, M. L. & Sanín, J. R. (2020) "The cost of doing politics? Analyzing violence and harassment against female politicians," *Perspectives on Politics* 18(3): 740–55.

Kruschinski, S. & Haller, A. (2017) "Restrictions on data-driven political micro-targeting in Germany," *Internet Policy Review* 6(4): 1–23.

Krzyżanowski, M. (2020) "Normalization and the discursive construction of 'new' norms and 'new' normality: discourse in the paradoxes of populism and neoliberalism," *Social Semiotics* 30(4): 431–48.

Kubin, E. & von Sikorski, C. (2021) "The role of (social) media in political polarization: a systematic review," *Annals of the International Communication Association* 45(3): 188–206.

Kuo, R. & Marwick, A. (2021) "Critical disinformation studies: history, power, and politics," *Harvard Kennedy School Misinformation Review* 2(4): 1–11.

Ladd, J. M. (2012). *Why Americans Hate the Media and How It Matters*. Princeton University Press.

Ladd, J. M. & Podkul, A. R. (2019) "Sowing distrust of the news media as an electoral strategy." In Elizabeth Suhay (ed.) *The Oxford Handbook of Electoral Persuasion*. Oxford University Press, 1–49.

Lang, K. & Lang, G. E. (2009) "Mass society, mass culture, and mass communication: the meanings of mass," *International Journal of Communication* 3: 998–1024.

Langer, A. (2021) "The eternal George Soros: the rise of an antisemitic and Islamophobic conspiracy theory." In *Europe: Continent of Conspiracies*. London: Routledge, 163–84.

Larsson, A. O. (2016) "Online, all the time? A quantitative assessment of the permanent campaign on Facebook," *New Media & Society* 18(2): 274–92.

Latar, N. L. (2018) *Robot Journalism: Can Human Journalism Survive?* Hackensack, NJ: World Scientific.

Lau, R. R., Rogers, K., & Love, J. (2021) "Media effects in the viewer's choice era: testing revised agenda-setting and priming hypotheses," *Political Communication* 38(3): 199–221.

Law, J. (2009) "Seeing like a survey," *Cultural Sociology* 3(2): 239–56.

Lawrence, R. G. & de Vreese, C. (2020) "Transition essay," *Political Communication* 37(5): 591–2.

Lazarus, R. S. (1991) *Emotion and Adaptation*. New York: Oxford University Press.

Leaver, T. (2021) "Going dark: how Google and Facebook fought the Australian News Media and Digital Platforms Mandatory Bargaining Code," *M/C Journal* 24(2).

Lees-Marshment, J. (ed.) (2012) *Routledge Handbook of Political Marketing*. London: Routledge.

Lessig, L. (2000) "Code is law: on liberty in cyberspace," *Harvard Magazine* 1.

Lev-On, A. & Steinfeld, N. (2021) "Municipal campaigns on Facebook: what influences the scope of engagement and does it win votes?" In J. Lee, G. Viale Pereira, & S. Hwang (eds.) *Proceedings of the 22nd Annual International Conference on Digital Government Research*. New York: ACM, 104–12.

Levitsky, S. & Ziblatt, D. (2018) *How Democracies Die*. New York: Broadway Books.

Lewis, D. & Vandekerckhove, W. (2011) *Whistleblowing and Democratic Values*. Glasgow: International Whistleblowing Research Network.

Lilleker, D. G. (2006) *Key Concepts in Political Communication*. London: SAGE.

Lilleker, D. G., Coman, I. A., Gregor, M., & Novelli, E. (eds.) (2021) *Political Communication and COVID-19: Governance and Rhetoric in Times of Crisis*. London: Routledge.

Lilleker, D. G., Koc-Michalska, K., Negrine, R., Gibson, R., Vedel, T., & Strudel, S. (eds.) (2020) *Social Media Campaigning in Europe*. London: Routledge.

Lilleker, D. G., Tenscher, J., & Štětka, V. (2015) "Towards hypermedia campaigning? Perceptions of new media's importance for campaigning by party strategists in comparative perspective," *Information, Communication & Society* 18(7): 747–65.

Limor, Y. & Himelboim, I. (2006) "Journalism and moonlighting: an international comparison of 242 codes of ethics," *Journal of Mass Media Ethics* 21(4): 265–85.

Lindgren, E., Damstra, A., Strömbäck, J., Tsfati, Y., Vliegenthart, R., & Boomgaarden, H. (2022) "Uninformed or misinformed? A review of the conceptual–operational gap between (lack of) knowledge and (mis)perceptions." In J. Strömbäck, Å. Wikfors s, K. Glüer, T. Lindholm, & H. Oscarsson (eds.) *Knowledge Resistance in High-Choice Information Environments*. London: Routledge, 187–206.

Linford, A. L. (2022) "Extra: the history of America's girl newsies." Unpublished Ph.D. dissertation, University of North Carolina, Chapel Hill.

Lippmann, W. (1922) *Public Opinion*. New York: The Free Press.

Lischka, J. A. & Garz, M. (2021) "Clickbait news and algorithmic curation: a game theory framework of the relation between journalism, users, and platforms," *New Media & Society*: https://doi.org/10.1177/14614448211027174.

"List of populists" (2022) Wikipedia: https://en.wikipedia.org/wiki/List_of_populists.

Literat, I. & Kligler-Vilenchik, N. (2023) "TikTok as a key platform for youth political expression: reflecting on the opportunities and stakes involved," *Social Media+ Society* 9(1): https://doi.org/10.1177/20563051231157595.

Litt, E. & Hargittai, E. (2016) "The imagined audience on social network sites," *Social Media + Society* 2(1): 1–12.

Lonas, L. (2021) "Facebook formula gave anger five times weight of likes, documents show," *The Hill*, October 26: https://thehill.com/policy/technology/578548-facebook-formula-gave-anger-five-times-weight-of-likes-documents-show.

Lorenz-Spreen, P., Oswald, L., Lewandowsky, S., & Hertwig, R. (2023). "A systematic review of worldwide causal and correlational evidence on digital media and democracy," *Nature Human Behaviour* 7(1): 74–101.

Lu, Y. & Pan, J. (2021) "Capturing clicks: how the Chinese government uses clickbait to compete for visibility," *Political Communication* 38(1–2): 23–54.

Lugo-Ocando, J. (2008). "An introduction to the maquilas of power: media and political transition in Latin America." I J. Lugo-Ocando (ed.) *The Media in Latin America*. New York: McGraw-Hill, 1–12.

Luhmann, N. (2000) *The Reality of the Mass Media*. Stanford University Press.

Lukito, J. (2020) "Coordinating a multi-platform disinformation campaign: Internet Research Agency activity on three US social media platforms, 2015 to 2017," *Political Communication* 37(2): 238–55.

Lum, K. & Chowdhury, R. (2021) "What is an 'algorithm'? It depends whom you ask," *MIT Technology Review*, February 26: www.technologyreview.com/2021/02/26/1020007/what-is-an-algorithm.

Lünenborg, M. (2019) "Affective publics: understanding the dynamic formation of public articulations beyond the public sphere." In A. Fleig & C. von Scheve (eds.) *Public Spheres of Resonance: Constellations of Affect and Language*. London: Routledge, 29–48.

Lupien, P. (2013) "The media in Venezuela and Bolivia: attacking the 'bad left' from below," *Latin American Perspectives* 40(3): 226–46.

Mabweazara, H. and Mare, A. (2021) *Participatory Journalism in Africa: Digital News Engagement and User Agency in the South*. London: Routledge.

Madison, N. & Klang, M. (2020) "The case for digital activism: refuting the fallacies of slacktivism," *Journal of Digital Social Research* 2(2): 28–47.

Magin, M., Podschuweit, N., Haßler, J., & Rußmann, U. (2017) "Campaigning in the fourth age of political communication: a multi-method study on the use of Facebook by German and Austrian parties in the 2013 national election campaigns," *Information, Communication & Society* 20(11): 1698–1719.

Mahone, J. & Napoli, P. (2020) "Hundreds of hyperpartisan sites are masquerading as local news: this map shows if there's one near you," Nieman Lab, July 13: www.niemanlab.org/2020/07/hundreds-of-hyperpartisan-sites-are-masquerading-as-local-news-this-map-shows-if-theres-one-near-you.

Mailland, J. & Driscoll, K. (2017) *Minitel: Welcome to the Internet*. Cambridge, MA: MIT Press.

Malinen, S. (2021) "The owners of information: content curation practices of middle-level gatekeepers in political Facebook groups," *New Media & Society*: 1–18.

Maloney, K. & McGrath, C. (2021) "Rethinking public relations: persuasion, democracy and society," *Public Relations Education* 7(1): 220–6.

Maly, I. (2020) "Metapolitical new right influencers: the case of Brittany Pettibone," *Social Sciences* 9(7): 113.

Manabe, N. (2019) "We Gon'Be Alright? The ambiguities of Kendrick Lamar's protest anthem," *Music Theory Online* 25(1): 1–24.

Mano, W. (2010) *Africa: Media Systems*. London: Wiley.

Manor, I. (2019) *The Digitalization of Public Diplomacy*. New York: Palgrave Macmillan.

Margetts, H. (2018) "Rethinking democracy with social media," *The Political Quarterly* 90(1): 107–23.

Marín-Sanchiz, C. R., Carvajal, M., & González-Esteban, J. L. (2021) "Survival strategies in freelance journalism: an empowering toolkit to improve professionals' working conditions," *Journalism Practice* 11(1): 1–24.

Martin, B. (1986) "Suppression and social action." In B. Martin, C. M. A. Baker, C. Manwell, & C. Pugh (eds.) *Intellectual Suppression: Australian Case Histories, Analysis and Responses*. Sydney: Angus & Robertson, 257–63.

Martini, F. (2020) "Wer ist #MeToo? Eine netzwerkanalytische Untersuchung (anti-) feministischen Protests," *M&K, Themenheft Technik, Medien, Geschlecht Revisited* 68(3): 255–72: https://doi.org/10.5771/1615-634X-2020-3-255.

Martini, F., Samula, P., Keller, T. R., & Klinger, U. (2021) "Bot, or not? Comparing three methods for detecting social bots in five political discourses," *Big Data & Society* 8(2): 1–13.

Marwick, A. E. (2018) "Why do people share fake news? A sociotechnical model of media effects," *Georgetown Law Technology Review* 2(2): 474–512.

Marwick, A. E. & boyd, D. (2011) "I tweet honestly, I tweet passionately: Twitter users, context collapse, and the imagined audience," *New Media & Society* 13(1): 114–33.

Marwick, A. & Hargittai, E. (2019) "Nothing to hide, nothing to lose? Incentives and disincentives to sharing information with institutions online," *Information, Communication & Society* 22(12): 1697–1713.

Marwick, A. E. & Lewis, R. (2021) "Media manipulation and disinformation online," Data & Society Research Institute: https://datasociety.net/library/media-manipulation-and-disinfo-online.

Marwick, A. E. & Partin, W. C. (2022) "Constructing alternative facts: populist expertise and the QAnon conspiracy," *New Media & Society*: 1–21.

Mason, L. (2016) "A cross-cutting calm: how social sorting drives affective polarization," *Public Opinion Quarterly* 80(S1): 351–77.

Mattes, K. & Redlawsk, D. P. (2015) *The Positive Case for Negative Campaigning*. University of Chicago Press.

Matthes, J. & Arendt, F. (2016) "Spiral of silence." In K. B. Jensen & R. T. Craig (eds.) *The International Encyclopedia of Communication Theory and Philosophy*. Hoboken, NJ: Wiley-Blackwell, 1–8: https://doi.org/10.1002/9781118766804.wbiect147.

Matthes, J., Knoll, J., Valenzuela, S., Hopmann, D. N., & Von Sikorski, C. (2019) "A meta-analysis of the effects of cross-cutting exposure on political participation," *Political Communication* 36(4): 523–42.

Mazzoleni, G. (2008a) "Mediatization of politics." In W. Donsbach (ed.) *The International Encyclopedia of Communication*. Hoboken, NJ: John Wiley & Sons: https://doi.org/10.22059/JCSS.2020.7474.

Mazzoleni, G. (2008b) "Populism and the media." In D. Albertazzi & D. McDonnell (eds.) *Twenty-First Century Populism: The Spectre of Western European Democracy*. London: Palgrave Macmillan, 49–64.

Mazzoleni, G., Barnhurst, K. G., Ikeda, K. I., Maia, R. C., & Wessler, H. (eds.) (2015)

The International Encyclopedia of Political Communication, 3 vols. Chichester: John Wiley & Sons.

Mazzoleni, G. & Schulz, W. (1999) "'Mediatization' of politics: a challenge for democracy," *Political Communication* 16(3): 247–61.

McCarthy, J. D. & Zald, M. N. (1977) "Resource mobilization and social movements: a partial theory," *American Journal of Sociology* 82(6): 1212–41.

McGregor, S. C. (2018) "Personalization, social media, and voting: effects of candidate self-personalization on vote intention," *New Media & Society* 20(3): 1139–60.

McGregor, S. C. (2019) "Social media as public opinion: how journalists use social media to represent public opinion," *Journalism* 20(8): 1070–86.

McGuigan, J. (1992) *Cultural Populism*. London: Routledge.

McGuigan, L. (2019) "Automating the audience commodity: the unacknowledged ancestry of programmatic advertising," *New Media & Society* 21(11–12): 2366–85.

McIlwain, C. D. (2019) *Black Software: The Internet and Racial Justice, from the AfroNet to Black Lives Matter*. New York: Oxford University Press.

McKelvey, F. & Piebiak, J. (2018) "Porting the political campaign: the NationBuilder platform and the global flows of political technology," *New Media & Society* 20(3): 901–18.

McMillan Cottom, T. (2020) "Where platform capitalism and racial capitalism meet: the sociology of race and racism in the digital society," *Sociology of Race and Ethnicity* 6(4): 441–9.

McNair, B. (2003) *Sociology of Journalism*. London: Routledge.

McNair, B. (2017) *An Introduction to Political Communication*. London: Routledge.

McQueen, S. (2018) "From yellow journalism to tabloids to clickbait: the origins of fake news in the United States." In D. E. Agosto (ed.) *Information Literacy and Libraries in the Age of Fake News*. Santa Barbara, CA: Libraries Unlimited, 12–36.

Meese, J. & Hurcombe, E. (2020) "Facebook, news media and platform dependency: the institutional impacts of news distribution on social platforms," *New Media & Society* 23(8): 2367–84.

Meese, J. & Hurcombe, E. (2021) "Facebook, news media and platform dependency: the institutional impacts of news distribution on social platforms," *New Media & Society* 23(8): 2367–84.

Mendes, K., Ringrose, J., & Keller, J. (2019) *Digital Feminist Activism: Girls and Women Fight Back against Rape Culture*. Oxford University Press.

Meraz, S. & Papacharissi, Z. (2016) "Networked framing and gatekeeping." In T. Witschge, C. W. Anderson, D. Domingo, & A. Hermida (eds.) *The SAGE Handbook of Digital Journalism*. Los Angeles, CA: SAGE, 95–112.

Meret, S. (2015) "Charismatic female leadership and gender: Pia Kjærsgaard and the Danish People's Party," *Patterns of Prejudice* 49(1–2): 81–102.

Merkel, W. (2004) "Embedded and defective democracies," *Democratization* 11(5): 33–58.

Metz, M., Kruikemeier, S., & Lecheler, S. (2020) "Personalization of politics on Facebook: examining the content and effects of professional, emotional and private self-personalization," *Information, Communication & Society* 23(10): 1481–98.

Meyer, P. (2002). *Precision Journalism: A Reporter's Introduction to Social Science Methods*. Washington, DC: Rowman & Littlefield Publishers.

Miazhevich, G. (2018) "Nation branding in the post-broadcast era: the case of RT," *European Journal of Cultural Studies* 21(5): 575–93.

Milko, V. & Ortutay, B. (2022) "'Kill more': Facebook fails to detect hate against Rohingya," AP News, March 22: https://apnews.com/article/technology-business-bangladesh-myanmar-united-nations-f7d89e38c54f7bae464762fa23bd96b2.

Miller, S. (2019) "Citizen journalism." In J. Nussbaum (ed.) *Oxford Research Encyclopedia of Communication*. Oxford University Press.

Mills, C. W. (2017) *Black Rights / White Wrongs: The Critique of Racial Liberalism*. New York: Oxford University Press.

Miño, P. & Austin, L. (2022) "A cocreational approach to nation branding: the case of Chile," *Public Relations Inquiry* 11(2): 293–313.

Mishra, A. A. & Mishra, A. (2014) "National vs. local celebrity endorsement and politics," *International Journal of Politics, Culture, and Society* 27(4): 409–25.

Mishra, M., Yan, P., & Schroeder, R. (2022) "TikTok politics: tit for tat on the India–China cyberspace frontier," *International Journal of Communication* 16: 814–39.

Molina, M., Sunda, S. S., Le, T., & Lee, D. (2021) "'Fake news' is not simply false information: a concept explication and taxonomy of online content," *American Behavioral Scientist* 65(2): 180–212.

Möller, J., Trilling, D., Helberger, N., & van Es, B. (2018) "Do not blame it on the algorithm: an empirical assessment of multiple recommender systems and their impact on content diversity," *Information, Communication & Society* 21(7): 959–77.

Moon, R. (2019) "Beyond puppet journalism: the bridging work of transnational journalists in a local field," *Journalism Studies* 20(12): 1714–31.

Morales, J. S. (2019) "Perceived popularity and online political dissent: evidence from Twitter in Venezuela," *The International Journal of Press/Politics* 25(1): 5–27.

Morehouse, J. (2021) "Examining devotional campaigns and stakeholder-centric relationships in public relations materials: a case study," *Journal of Public Relations Research* 33(4): 209–30.

Morgan, M. (2021) "More than a mood or an attitude: discourse and verbal genres in African-American culture." In S. S. Mufwene, J. R. Rickford, G. Bailey, & J. Baugh, J. (eds.) *African-American English: Structure, History and Use*. London: Routledge, 277–312.

Morley, D. G. & Robins, K. (2001) *British Cultural Studies: Geography, Nationality, and Identity*. Oxford University Press.

Mouffe, C. (2002) "Which public sphere for a democratic society?" *Theoria* 99: 55–65.

Mourão, R. R. & Chen, W. (2020) "Covering protests on Twitter: the influences on journalists' social media portrayals of left- and right-leaning demonstrations in Brazil," *The International Journal of Press/Politics* 25(2): 260–80.

Moy, P. (2020) "The promise and perils of voice," *Journal of Communication* 70(1): 1–12.

Moyo, D. (2009) "Citizen journalism and the parallel market of information in Zimbabwe's 2008 election," *Journalism Studies* 10(4): 551–67.

Moyo, L. (2020) *The Decolonial Turn in Media Studies in Africa and the Global South*. Cham: Palgrave-McMillan.

Mpofu, S. (2015) "When the subaltern speaks: citizen journalism and genocide 'victims'' voices online," *African Journalism Studies* 36(4): 82–101.

Mudde, C. (2004) "The populist zeitgeist," *Government and Opposition* 39(4): 541–63.

Mudde, C. (2007) *Populist Radical Right Parties in Europe*. Cambridge University Press.

Mudde, C. & Kaltwasser, C. R. (2017) *Populism: A Very Short Introduction*. Oxford University Press.

Müller, J. W. (2017) *What Is Populism?* London: Penguin.

Munger, K. (2020) "All the news that's fit to click: the economics of clickbait media," *Political Communication* 37(3): 376–97.

Munger, K. & Phillips, J. (2022) "Right-wing YouTube: a supply and demand perspective," *The International Journal of Press/Politics* 27(1): 186–219.

Murgia, M. & Espinoza, J. (2021) "Ireland is 'worst bottleneck' for enforcing EU data privacy law – ICCL," *Irish Times*, September 13: www.irishtimes.com/business/technology/ireland-is-worst-bottleneck-for-enforcing-eu-data-privacy-law-iccl-1.4672480.

Murphy, P. D. (2021) "Speaking for the youth, speaking for the planet: Greta Thunberg and the representational politics of eco-celebrity," *Popular Communication* 19(3): 193–206.

"Musicians who oppose Donald Trump's use of their music" (2022) Wikipedia: https://en.wikipedia.org/wiki/Musicians_who_oppose_Donald_Trump%27s_use_of_their_music.

Mutsvairo, B. and Bebawi, S. (2022) "Journalism and the Global South: shaping journalistic practices and identity post 'Arab Spring,'" *Digital Journalism* 10(7): 1141–55.

Mutsvairo, B., Borges-Rey, E., Bebawi, S., Marquez Ramirez, M., Mellado, C., Mabweazara, H. M., Demeter, M., Glowacki, M., Badr, H., & Thussu, D. (2021) "Different but the same: how the Global South is challenging the hegemonic epistemologies and ontologies of Westernized/Western-centric journalism studies," *Journalism and Mass Communication Quarterly* 98(4): 996–1016.

Mutsvairo, B. & Karam, B. (eds.) (2018) *Perspectives on Political Communication in Africa*. London: Palgrave Macmillan.

Mutsvairo, B. & Ragnedda, M. (eds.) (2019) *Mapping the Digital Divide in Africa: A Mediated Analysis*. Amsterdam University Press.

Mutz, D. C. (2011) *Population-Based Survey Experiments*. Princeton University Press.

Mutz, D. C. (2022) "Effects of changes in perceived discrimination during BLM on the 2020 presidential election," *Science Advances* 8(9): eabj9140.

Nagy, P. & Neff, G. (2015) "Imagined affordance: reconstructing a keyword for communication theory," *Social Media + Society* 1(2): 1–9.

Nah, S. & Chung, D. S. (2020) *Understanding Citizen Journalism as Civic Participation*. London: Routledge.

Naím, M. (2014) *The End of Power: From Boardrooms to Battlefields and Churches to States, Why Being in Charge Isn't What It Used to Be*. New York: Basic Books.

Napoli, P. M. (2019) *Social Media and the Public Interest: Media Regulation in the Disinformation Age*. New York: Columbia University Press.

Ndlovu-Gatsheni, S. J. (2021) "Internationalisation of higher education for pluriversity: a decolonial reflection," *Journal of the British Academy* 9(s1): 77–98.

Neff, T. & Pickard, V. (2021) "Funding democracy: public media and democratic health in 33 countries," *The International Journal of Press/Politics*: 1–27.

Negrine, R. & Papathanassopoulos, S. (1996) "The 'Americanization' of political communication: a critique," *Harvard International Journal of Press/Politics* 1(2): 45–62.

Nelson, J. L. (2021) *Imagined Audiences: How Journalists Perceive and Pursue the Public*. New York: Oxford University Press.

Neuman W. L. (2014) *Power, State and Society: An Introduction to Political Sociology*. New York: McGraw-Hill.

Neuman, W. R. (2016) *The Digital Difference: Media Technology and the Theory of Communication Effects*. Cambridge, MA: Harvard University Press.

Neuman, W. R. & Guggenheim, L. (2011) "The evolution of media effects theory: a six-stage model of cumulative research," *Communication Theory* 21(2): 169–96.

Nguyen, A. & Lugo-Ocando, J. (2016) "The state of data and statistics in journalism and journalism education: issues and debates," *Journalism: Theory, Practice & Criticism* 17(1): 3–17.

Nielsen, R. K. (2012) *Ground Wars*. Princeton University Press.

Nielsen, R. K. (2016) "The many crises of Western journalism: a comparative analysis of economic crises, professional crises, and crises of confidence." In J. C. Alexander, E. Butler Breese, & M. Luengo (eds.) *The Crisis of Journalism Reconsidered: Democratic Culture, Professional Codes, Digital Future*. Cambridge University Press, 77–97.

Nielsen, R. K. (2018) "No one cares what we know: three responses to the irrelevance of political communication research," *Political Communication* 35(1): 145–9.

Nielsen, R. K. & Ganter, S. A. (2022) *The Power of Platforms: Shaping Media and Society*. New York: Oxford University Press.

Noble, S. U. (2018) *Algorithms of Oppression: How Search Engines Reinforce Racism*. New York University Press.

Nolan, D. & Brookes, S. (2015) "The problems of populism: celebrity politics and citizenship," *Communication Research and Practice* 1(4): 349–61.

Norris, P. (2014) "Watchdog journalism." In M. Bovens, R. Goodin, & T. Schillemans (eds.) *The Oxford Handbook of Public Accountability*. Oxford University Press: https://doi.org/10.1093/oxfordhb/9780199641253.013.0015.

Norris, P. & Inglehart, R. (2019) *Cultural Backlash: Trump, Brexit, and Authoritarian Populism*. Cambridge University Press.

Nothias, T. (2020) "Access granted: Facebook's free basics in Africa," *Media, Culture & Society* 42(3): 329–48.

Oates, S. (2013) *Revolution Stalled: The Political Limits of the Internet in the Post-Soviet Sphere*. Oxford University Press.

Ohme, J., de Vreese, C. H., & Albaek, E. (2018) "The uncertain first-time voter: effects of political media exposure on young citizens' formation of vote choice in a digital media environment," *New Media & Society* 20(9): 3243–65.

O'Leary, N. (2018) "Foreign groups invade Ireland's online abortion debate," *Politico*, May 17: www.politico.eu/article/foreign-groups-invade-ireland-online-abortion-referendum-debate-facebook-social-media.

Oliver, J. E. & Rahn, W. M. (2016) "Rise of the Trumpenvolk: populism in the 2016 election," *The ANNALS of the American Academy of Political and Social Science* 667(1): 189–206.

Olson, M. (1965) *The Logic of Collective Action: Public Goods and the Theory of Groups*. Cambridge, MA: Harvard University Press.

Oluwole, V. (2021) "Ethiopia is building its own social media platforms to rival Facebook, Twitter, WhatsApp," *Business Insider*, August 26: https://africa.businessinsider.com/local/markets/ethiopia-is-building-its-own-social-media-platforms-to-rival-facebook-twitter/v7dclfk.

Ong, J. C. & Cabañes, J. V. A. (2018) "Architects of networked disinformation: behind the scenes of troll accounts and fake news production in the Philippines," *Communication Department Faculty Publication Series* (University of Massachusetts Amherst).

Opensecrets (2022) Lobbying Data Summary Database: www.opensecrets.org/federal-lobbying.

Opp, K.-D. (1988) "Grievances and participation in social movements," *American Sociological Review* 53(6): 853–64.

Oreskes, N. & Conway, E. M. (2010) "Defeating the merchants of doubt," *Nature* 465: 686–7.

Orgeret, K. S. & Rønning, H. (2020) "Political communication in East Africa: an introduction," *Journal of African Media Studies* 12(3): 231–40.

Ouellette, L. & Hay, J. (2007) *Better Living through Reality TV: Television and Post-Welfare Citizenship*. Malden, MA: Blackwell.

Ouwerkerk, J. W. & Johnson, B. K. (2016) "Motives for online friending and following: the dark side of social network site connections," *Social Media + Society* 2(3): 1–13.

Pacher, A. (2018) "The ritual creation of political symbols: international exchanges in public diplomacy," *The British Journal of Politics and International Relations* 20(4): 880–97.

Pan, J. (2019) "How Chinese officials use the Internet to construct their public image," *Political Science Research and Methods* 7(2): 197–213.

Papacharissi, Z. (2015) *Affective Publics: Sentiment, Technology, and Politics*. Oxford University Press.

Papacharissi, Z. (2016) "Affective publics and structures of storytelling: sentiment, events and mediality," *Information, Communication & Society* 19(3): 307–24.

Papakyriakopoulos, O., Shahrezaye, M., Serrano, J. C. M., & Hegelich, S. (2019) "Distorting political communication: the effect of hyperactive users in online social networks." In IEEE INFOCOM 2019 – *IEEE Conference on Computer Communications Workshops*. Piscataway, NJ: IEEE, 157–64.

Papakyriakopoulos, O., Tessono, C., Narayanan, A., & Kshirsagar, M. (2022) "How algorithms shape the distribution of political advertising: case studies of Facebook, Google, and TikTok.". In V. Conitzer (ed.) *Proceedings of the 2022 AAAI/ACM Conference on AI, Ethics, and Society*. New York: ACM, 532–46.

Pariser, E. (2011) *The Filter Bubble: What the Internet Is Hiding from You*. London: Penguin.

Parvin, P. (2018) "Democracy without participation: a new politics for a disengaged era," *Res Publica* 24: 31–52.

Passoth, J.-H. (2020) "Music, recommender systems and the techno-politics of platforms, data, and algorithms." In S. Maasen, S. Dickel, & C. Schneider (eds.) *TechnoScienceSociety: Technological Reconfigurations of Science and Society*. Cham: Springer, 157–74.

Patalong, F. (2021) "Die Welt im Leserausch," *Spiegel Online*, March 16: www.spiegel.de/geschichte/wie-zeitungen-zum-massenmedium-wurden-die-welt-im-leserausch-a-466b1a31-3488-4e96-97c5-583d07b61789.

Pate, A. (2020) "Trends in democratization: a focus on instability in anocracies."

In J. J. Hewitt, J. Wilkenfeld, & T. R. Gurr (eds.) *Peace and Conflict 2008*. London: Routledge, 27–32.

Pauwels, T. (2011) "Measuring populism: a quantitative text analysis of party literature in Belgium," *Journal of Elections, Public Opinion and Parties* 21(1): 97–119.

Pavlik, J. V. (2001) *Journalism and New Media*. New York: Columbia University Press.

Pavlik, J. V. (2022) *Disruption and Digital Journalism: Assessing News Media Innovation in a Time of Dramatic Change*. London: Routledge.

Pease, A. & Brewer, P. R. (2008) "The Oprah factor: the effects of a celebrity endorsement in a presidential primary campaign," *The International Journal of Press/Politics* 13(4): 386–400.

Peck, R. (2019) *Fox populism: branding conservatism as working class*. Cambridge University Press.

Penney, J. (2017) *The Citizen Marketer: Promoting Political Opinion in the Social Media Age*. New York: Oxford University Press.

Penney, J. (2020) "'It's so hard not to be funny in this situation': memes and humor in U.S. youth online political expression," *Television & New Media* 21(8): 791–806.

Pennycook, G., Epstein, Z., Mosleh, M., Arechar, A. A., Eckles, D., & Rand, D. G. (2021) "Shifting attention to accuracy can reduce misinformation online," *Nature* 592: 590–5.

Persily, N., & Tucker, J. A. (eds.). (2020) *Social Media and Democracy: The State of the Field, Prospects for Reform*. Cambridge University Press.

Peters, B. (2016) *How Not to Network a Nation: The Uneasy History of the Soviet Internet*. Cambridge, MA: MIT Press.

Peters, J. D. (2016) *The Marvelous Clouds: Toward a Philosophy of Elemental Media*. University of Chicago Press.

Pettegree, A. (2014) *The Invention of News: How the World Came to Know about Itself*. New Haven, CT: Yale University Press.

Pettinicchio, D. (2017) "Elites, policy, and social movements." In B. Wejnert & P. Parigi (eds.) *On the Cross Road of Polity, Political Elites and Mobilization*. Bingley: Emerald, 155–90.

Pfetsch, B. (2018) "Dissonant and disconnected public spheres as challenge for political communication research," *Javnost – The Public* 25(1–2): 59–65.

Pfetsch, B., Löblich, M., & Eilders, C. (2018) "Dissonante Öffentlichkeiten als Perspektive kommunikationswissenschaftlicher Theoriebildung," *Publizistik* 63(4): 477–95.

Phillips, T. & Espejel, E. (2022) "Two slain in Mexico are the latest in unrelenting slaughter of journalists," *The Guardian*, May 9: www.theguardian.com/world/2022/may/09/mexico-journalists-killed-slaughter-amlo.

Phillips, W. & Milner, R. M. (2021) *You Are Here: A Field Guide for Navigating Polarized Speech, Conspiracy Theories, and Our Polluted Media Landscape*. Cambridge, MA: MIT Press.

Picheta, R. (2020) "Fat, flightless parrot named Bird of the Year after a campaign tainted by voter fraud," CNN: https://edition.cnn.com/2020/11/16/asia/kakapo-new-zealand-bird-vote-scli-intl-scn/index.html.

Pirro, A. L. P. & Stanley, B. (2021) "Forging, bending, and breaking: enacting the 'Illiberal Playbook' in Hungary and Poland," *Perspectives on Politics* 20(1): 86–101.

Plotnikova, A. (2020) "No guarantee of safety for media covering disputed Belarus election," VOA, November 11: www.voanews.com/a/press-freedom_no-guarantee-safety-media-covering-disputed-belarus-election/6198245.html.

Plunkett, J. (2003) *Queen Victoria: First Media Monarch*. Oxford University Press.

Poell, T. & van Dijck, J. (2013) "Understanding social media logic," *Media and Communication* 1(1): https://doi.org/10.17645/mac.v1i1.70.

Poell, T. & van Dijck, J. (2018) "Social media and new protest movements." In J. Burgess, A. Marwick, & T. Poell (eds.) *The SAGE Handbook of Social Media*. Los Angeles, CA: SAGE, 546–61.

Polletta, F. & Callahan, J. (2019) "Deep stories, nostalgia narratives, and fake news: storytelling in the Trump era." In J. L. Mast & J. C. Alexander (eds.) *Politics of Meaning / Meaning of Politics: Cultural Sociology of the 2016 U.S. Presidential Election*. Cham: Springer, 55–73.

Postman, N. (2006) *Amusing Ourselves to Death: Public Discourse in the Age of Show Business*. New York: Penguin.

Powers, M. (2018) *NGOs as Newsmakers: The Changing Landscape of International News*. New York: Columbia University Press.

Priolkar, A. K. (1958) *The Printing Press in India*. Mumbai: Marathi Grantha Sangrahalaya.

Prior, M. (2007) *Post-Broadcast Democracy: How Media Choice Increases Inequality in Political Involvement and Polarizes Elections*. Cambridge University Press.

Puhle, H.-J. (2019) "Populism and democracy in the 21st century," *SCRIPTS Working Paper* 2.

Quandt, T. (2018) "Dark participation," *Media and Communication* 6(4): 36–48.

Radue, M. (2019) "Harmful disinformation in Southeast Asia: 'Negative campaigning,' 'information operations' and 'racist propaganda' – three forms of manipulative political communication in Malaysia, Myanmar, and Thailand," *Journal of Contemporary Eastern Asia* 18(2): 68–89.

Rae, M. (2021) "Hyperpartisan news: rethinking the media for populist politics," *New Media & Society* 23(5): 1117–32.

Rauchfleisch, A., Siegen, D., & Vogler, D. (2021) "How COVID-19 displaced climate change: mediated climate change activism and issue attention in the Swiss media and online sphere," *Environmental Communication* 17(3): 313–21.

Rawnsley, G. D. (2016) *Cold-War Propaganda in the 1950s*. Cham: Springer.

Reddi, M., Kuo, R., & Kreiss, D. (2021) "Identity propaganda: racial narratives and disinformation," *New Media & Society*: https://doi.org/10.1177/14614448211029293.

Regan, P. M. & Bell, S. R. (2010) "Changing lanes or stuck in the middle: why are anocracies more prone to civil wars?" *Political Research Quarterly* 63(4): 747–59.

Reif, K. & Schmitt, H. (1980) "Nine second-order national elections – a conceptual framework for the analysis of European election results," *European Journal of Political Research* 8(1): 3–44.

Reilly, S., Stiles, M., Powers, B., van Wagtendonk, A., & Paladino, J. (2022) "The Canadian 'Freedom Convoy' is backed by a Bangladeshi marketing firm and right-wing fringe groups," *Grid*, February 11: www.grid.news/story/misinformation/2022/02/11/the-canadian-freedom-convoy-is-backed-by-a-bangladeshi-marketing-firm-and-right-wing-fringe-groups.

Reinemann, C., Stanyer, J., Scherr, S., & Legnante, G. (2012) "Hard and soft news: a review of concepts, operationalizations and key findings," *Journalism* 13(2): 221–39.

Repucci, S. & Slipowitz, A. (2021) *Freedom in the World 2021: Democracy under Siege*. Washington, DC: Freedom House: https://freedomhouse.org/report/freedom-world/2021/democracy-under-siege.

Retis, J. & Tsagarousianou, R. (eds.) (2019) *The Handbook of Diasporas, Media, and Culture*. Hoboken, NJ: John Wiley & Sons.

Reuters Institute for the Study of Journalism (2021) *Reuters Institute Digital News Report 2021*: https://reutersinstitute.politics.ox.ac.uk/sites/default/files/2021-06/Digital_News_Report_2021_FINAL.pdf.

Reuters Institute for the Study of Journalism (2022) *Reuters Institute Digital News Report 2022*: https://reutersinstitute.politics.ox.ac.uk/digital-news-report/2022/dnr-executive-summary.

Rheault, L., Rayment, E., & Musulan, A. (2019) "Politicians in the line of fire: incivility and the treatment of women on social media," *Research & Politics* 6(1): 1–7.

Ricard, J. & Medeiros, J. (2020) "Using misinformation as a political weapon: COVID-19 and Bolsonaro in Brazil," *Harvard Kennedy School Misinformation Review* 1(2): 1–8.

Richardson, A. V. (2019) "Dismantling respectability: the rise of new womanist communication models in the era of Black Lives Matter," *Journal of Communication* 69(2): 193–213.

Richardson, A. V. (2020) *Bearing Witness while Black: African Americans, Smartphones, and the New Protest #Journalism*. New York: Oxford University Press.

Ridout, T. N. & Searles, K. (2011) "It's my campaign I'll cry if I want to: how and when campaigns use emotional appeals," *Political Psychology* 32(3): 439–58.

Riedl, M., Schwemmer, C., Ziewiecki, S., & Ross, L. M. (2021) "The rise of political influencers: perspectives on a trend towards meaningful content," *Frontiers in Communication* 6: 1–7.

Rinke, E. M. (2016) "The impact of sound-bite journalism on public argument," *Journal of Communication* 66(4): 625–45.

Roberts Forde, K. & Bedingfield, S. (2021) *Journalism and Jim Crow: White Supremacy and the Black Struggle for a New America*. Champaign: University of Illinois Press.

Rojas, H. & Valenzuela, S. (2019) "A call to contextualize public opinion-based research in political communication," *Political Communication* 36(4): 652–9.

Romer, D., Jamieson, P., Bleakley, A., & Jamieson, K. H. (2014) "Cultivation theory: its history, current status, and future directions." In R. S. Fortner & P. M. Fackler (eds.) *The Handbook of Media and Mass Communication Theory*. Chichester: John Wiley & Sons, 115–36.

Römmele, A. & Gibson, R. (2020) "Scientific and subversive: the two faces of the fourth era of political campaigning," *New Media & Society* 22(4): 595–610.

Rooduijn, M. (2014) "The mesmerising message: the diffusion of populism in public debates in Western European media," *Political Studies* 62(4): 726–44.

Roose, K. (2020) "Facebook reverses postelection algorithm changes that boosted news from authoritative sources," *New York Times*, December 16: www.nytimes.com/2020/12/16/technology/facebook-reverses-postelection-algorithm-changes-that-boosted-news-from-authoritative-sources.html.

Roose, K., Isaac, M. & Frenkel, S. (2020) "Facebook struggles to balance civility and growth," *New York Times*, November 24: www.nytimes.com/2020/11/24/technology/facebook-election-misinformation.html.

Rosenblum, N. L. (2010) *On the Side of the Angels: An Appreciation of Parties and Partisanship*. Princeton University Press.

Ross, B., Pilz, L., Cabrera, B., Brachten, F., Neubaum, G., & Stieglitz, S. (2019) "Are social bots a real threat? An agent-based model of the spiral of silence to analyse the impact of manipulative actors in social networks," *European Journal of Information Systems* 28(4): 394–412.

Ross, K. (2017) *Gender, Politics, News: A Game of Three Sides*. Oxford: Wiley-Blackwell.

Rossini, P. (2019) "Toxic for whom? Examining the targets of uncivil and intolerant discourse in online political talk." In P. Moy & D. Matheson (eds.) *Voices: Exploring the Shifting Contours of Communication*. New York: Peter Lang, 221–42.

Rossini, P., Stromer-Galley, J., Baptista, E. A., & Veiga de Oliveira, V. (2021) "Dysfunctional information sharing on WhatsApp and Facebook: the role of political talk, cross-cutting exposure and social corrections," *New Media & Society* 23(8): 2430–51.

Rossini, P., Stromer-Galley, J., & Korsunska, A. (2021) "More than 'fake news'? The media as a malicious gatekeeper and a bully in the discourse of candidates in the 2020 US presidential election," *Journal of Language and Politics* 20(5): 676–95.

Rourke, M. (2019) "Emerging new business models for news media," Innovation Media Consulting Group, February 27: https://innovation.media/insights/emerging-new-business-models-for-news-media.

Rovira Kaltwasser, C. (2018) "Studying the (economic) consequences of populism," *AEA Papers and Proceedings* 108: 204–7.

Rovira Kaltwasser, C., Taggart, P. A., Espejo, P. O., & Ostiguy, P. (eds.) (2017) *The Oxford Handbook of Populism*. Oxford University Press.

Russial, J., Laufer, P., & Wasko, J. (2015) "Journalism in crisis?" *Javnost – The Public* 22(4): 299–312.

Rußmann, U. (2018) "Going negative on Facebook: negative user expressions and political parties' reactions in the 2013 Austrian national election campaign," *International Journal of Communication* 12(21): 2578–98.

Rußmann, U. (2021) "Quality of understanding in communication among and between political parties, mass media, and citizens: an empirical study of the 2013 Austrian national election," *Journal of Deliberative Democracy* 17(2): 102–16.

Ruth, E. (2019) *Media Regulation in the United Kingdom*. London: Article 19.

Saffer, A. J., Pilny, A., & Sommerfeldt, E. J. (2022) "What influences relationship formation in a global civil society network? An examination of valued multiplex relations," *Communication Research* 49(5): 703–32.

Saffer, A. J., Taylor, M., & Yang, A. (2013) "Political public relations in advocacy: building online influence and social capital," *Public Relations Journal* 7(4): 1–35.

Sandvig, C., Hamilton, K., Karahalios, K., & Langbort, C. (2016) "Automation, algorithms, and politics. When the algorithm itself is a racist: diagnosing ethical harm in the basic components of software," *International Journal of Communication* 10: 4972–90.

Scannell, P. (1995) "Media events," *Media, Culture & Society* 17(1): 151–7.

Schäfer, M. S. (2015) "Digital public sphere.". In G. Mazzoleni, K. G. Barnhurst, K. I. Ikeda, R. C. Maia, & H. Wessler (eds.) *The International Encyclopedia of Political Communication*, 3 vols. Chichester: John Wiley & Sons, 1–7.

Schapals, A. K. & Porlezza, C. (2020) "Assistance or resistance? Evaluating the intersection of automated journalism and journalistic role conceptions," *Media and Communication* 8(3): 16–26.

Schedler, A. (2001) "Measuring democratic consolidation," *Studies in Comparative International Development* 36(1): 66–92.

Scheffauer, R., Goyanes, M., & Gil de Zúniga, H. (2021) "Beyond social media news use algorithms: how political discussion and network heterogeneity clarify incidental news exposure," *Online Information Review* 45(3): 633–50.

Scheufele, D. A. (1999) "Framing as a theory of media effects," *Journal of Communication* 49(3): 103–22.

Scheufele, D. A. & Iyengar, S. (2014) "The state of framing research: a call for new directions." In K. Kenski & K. H. Jamieson (eds.) *The Oxford Handbook of Political Communication*. Oxford University Press, 619–32.

Schlesinger, P. (2020) "After the post-public sphere," *Media, Culture & Society* 42(7–8): 1545–63.

Schmidt, S. (2014) *Seriously Funny: Mexican Political Jokes as Social Resistance*. Tucson: University of Arizona Press.

Schmuck, D., Fawzi, N., Reinemann, C., & Riesmeyer, C. (2022) "Social media use and political cynicism among German youth: the role of information-orientation, exposure to extremist content, and online media literacy," *Journal of Children and Media* 16(3): 313–31.

Schradie, J. (2019) *The Revolution that Wasn't: How Digital Activism Favors Conservatives*. Cambridge, MA: Harvard University Press.

Schuchard, R. J. & Crooks, A. T. (2021) "Insights into elections: an ensemble bot detection coverage framework applied to the 2018 US midterm elections," *PLoS One* 16(1): 1–19.

Schudson, M. (1978) *Discovering the News: A Social History of American Newspapers*. New York: Basic Books.

Schudson, M. (1994) "The public sphere and its problems: bringing the state (back) in," *Notre Dame Journal of Law, Ethics & Public Policy* 8(2): 529–46.

Schudson, M. (1999) *The Good Citizen: A History of American Civic Life*. Cambridge, MA: Harvard University Press.

Schudson, M. (2002) "The news media as political institutions," *Annual Review of Political Science* 5(1): 249–69.

Schuetz, J. (2009) "Political communication theories." In S. W. Littlejohn & K. A. Foss (eds.) *Encyclopedia of Communication Theory*. Los Angeles, CA: SAGE, 758–61.

Schulz, A., Fletcher, R., & Nielsen, R. K. (2022) "The role of news media knowledge for how people use social media for news in five countries," *New Media & Society*: 1–22: https://doi.org/10.1080/17524032.2021.1990978.

Schwartz, A. B. (2015) *Broadcast Hysteria: Orson Welles's* War of the Worlds *and the Art of Fake News*. New York: Hill and Wang.

Scott, J. (1985) *Weapons of the Weak: Everyday Forms of Peasant Resistance*. New Haven, CT: Yale University Press.

Scott, J. (1990) *Domination and the Arts of Resistance: Hidden Transcripts*. New Haven, CT: Yale University Press.

Scott, M. (2021) "Russia sows distrust on social media ahead of German election," *Politico*, September 3: www.politico.eu/article/germany-russia-social-media-distrust-election-vladimir-putin.

Scott, M. & Kayali, L. (2020) "What happened when humans stopped managing social media content," *Politico*, October 21: www.politico.eu/article/facebook-content-moderation-automation.

Scott, M., Wright, K., & Bunce, M. (2022) *Humanitarian Journalists Covering Crises from a Boundary Zone*. London: Routledge.

Segura, M. S. & Waisbord, S. (2016) *Media Movements: Civil Society and Media Policy Reform in Latin America*. London: Zed Books.

Semetko, H. A. & Tworzecki, H. (2017) "Campaign strategies, media, and voters: the fourth era of political communication." In J. Fisher, E. Fieldhouse, M. N. Franklin, R. Gibson, M. Cantijoch, & C. Wlezien (eds.) *The Routledge Handbook of Elections, Voting Behavior and Public Opinion*. London: Routledge, 293–304.

Sen, A. & Avci, O. (2006) "Why social movements occur," *Bilgi Ekonomisi ve Yönetimi Dergisi* 11(1): 125–30.

Sen, A. & Avci, O. (2016) "Why social movements occur: theories of social movements," *Journal of Knowledge Economy and Knowledge Management* 11(1): 125–30.

Shehata, A. & Strömbäck, J. (2011) "A matter of context: a comparative study of media environments and news consumption gaps in Europe," *Political Communication* 28(1): 110–34.

Shoemaker, P. J. & Vos, T. (2009) *Gatekeeping Theory*. New York: Routledge.

Sides, J., Tesler, M., & Vavreck, L. (2019) *Identity Crisis: The 2016 Presidential Campaign and the Battle for the Meaning of America*. Princeton University Press.

Siles, I., Guevara, E., Tristán-Jiménez, L., & Carazo, C. (2023) "Populism, religion, and social media in Central America," *The International Journal of Press/Politics* 28(1): 138–59.

Silva, P., Tavares, A. F., Silva, T., & Lameiras, M. (2019) "The good, the bad and the ugly: three faces of social media usage by local governments," *Government Information Quarterly* 36(3): 469–79.

Silverman, C. (2018) "How to spot a deepfake like the Barack Obama – Jordan Peele video," *BuzzFeed*, April 17: www.buzzfeed.com/craigsilverman/obama-jordan-peele-deepfake-video-debunk-buzzfeed.

Singh, K. D. & Conger, K. (2022) "Twitter, challenging orders to remove content, sues India"s government," *New York Times*, July 5: www.nytimes.com/2022/07/05/business/twitter-india-lawsuit.html.

Sisodia, Y. S. & Chattopadhyay, P. (2022) *Political Communication in Contemporary India: Locating Democracy and Governance*. London: Routledge.

Slater, M. D. (2007) "Reinforcing spirals: the mutual influence of media selectivity and media effects and their impact on individual behavior and social identity," *Communication Theory* 17(3): 281–303.

Slothuus, R. & Bisgaard, M. (2021) "How political parties shape public opinion in the real world," *American Journal of Political Science* 65(4): 896–911.

Smith, R. M. (2003) *Stories of Peoplehood: The Politics and Morals of Political Membership*. Cambridge University Press.

Sobieraj, S. (2011) *Soundbitten: The Perils of Media-Centered Political Activism*. New York University Press.

Sobieraj, S. (2020) *Credible Threat: Attacks against Women Online and the Future of Democracy*. New York: Oxford University Press.

Sobolewska, M. & Ford, R. (2020) *Brexitland: Identity, Diversity and the Reshaping of British Politics*. Cambridge University Press.

Sonnevend, J. (2016) *Stories without Borders: The Berlin Wall and the Making of a Global Iconic Event*. New York: Oxford University Press.

Southwell, B. G., Thorson, E. A., & Sheble, L. (eds.) (2018) *Misinformation and Mass Audiences*. Austin: University of Texas Press.

Spierings, N., Jacobs, K., & Linders, N. (2019) "Keeping an eye on the people: who has access to MPs on Twitter?" *Social Science Computer Review* 37(2): 160–77.

Spivak, G. C. (2008) *Other Asias*. Malden, MA: Blackwell.

Splendiani, S. & Capriello, A. (2022) "Crisis communication, social media and natural disasters – the use of Twitter by local governments during the 2016 Italian earthquake," *Corporate Communications: An International Journal* 27(3): 509–26.

Squires, C. (2002) "Rethinking the Black public sphere: an alternative vocabulary for multiple public spheres," *Communication Theory* 12(4): 446–68.

Stier, S., Posch, L., Bleier, A., & Strohmaier, M. (2017) "When populists become popular: comparing Facebook use by the right-wing movement Pegida and German political parties," *Information, Communication & Society* 20(9): 1365–88.

Street, J. (2012) "Do celebrity politics and celebrity politicians matter?" *The British Journal of Politics and International Relations* 14(3): 346–56.

Street, J. (2013) *Music and Politics*. Cambridge: Polity.

Striphas, T. (2015) "Algorithmic culture," *European Journal of Cultural Studies* 18(4–5): 395–412.

Strömbäck, J. (2008) "Four phases of mediatization: an analysis of the mediatization of politics," *International Journal of Press/Politics* 13: 228–46.

Strömbäck, J. & Kiousis, S. (eds.) (2019) *Political Public Relations: Principles and Applications*. New York: Routledge.

Strömbäck, J., Tsfati, Y., Boomgaarden, H., Damstra, A., Lindgren, E., Vliegenthart, R., & Lindholm, T. (2020) "News media trust and its impact on media use: toward a framework for future research," *Annals of the International Communication Association* 44(2): 139–56.

Stromer-Galley, J. (2000) "On-line interaction and why candidates avoid it," *Journal of Communication* 50(4): 111–32.

Stromer-Galley, J. (2019) *Presidential Campaigning in the Internet Age*. New York: Oxford University Press.

Stromer-Galley, J., Rossini, P., Hemsley, J., Bolden, S. E., & McKernan, B. (2021) "Political messaging over time: a comparison of US presidential candidate Facebook posts and tweets in 2016 and 2020," *Social Media + Society* 7(4): 1–13.

Stroud, N. J. (2011) *Niche News: The Politics of News Choice*. New York: Oxford University Press.

Su, Y. & Borah, P. (2019) "Who is the agenda setter? Examining the intermedia agenda-setting effect between Twitter and newspapers," *Journal of Information Technology & Politics* 16(3): 236–49.

Svensson, J. (2015) "Participation as a pastime: political discussion in a queer community online," *Javnost – The Public* 22(3): 283–97.

Svensson, J. (2021) *Wizards of the Web: An Outsider's Journey into Tech Culture, Programming, and Mathemagics*. Gothenburg: Nordicom.

Taberez, A. N. (2018) *Political Communication and Mobilisation: The Hindi Media in India*. Cambridge University Press.

Taggart, P. (2000) *Populism*. Buckingham: Open University Press.

Tandoc Jr., E. C. (2019) "The facts of fake news: a research review," *Sociology Compass* 13: 1–9.

Tangherlini, T. R., Shahsavari, S., Shahbazi, B., Ebrahimzadeh, E., & Roychowdhury, V. (2020) "An automated pipeline for the discovery of conspiracy and conspiracy theory narrative frameworks: Bridgegate, Pizzagate and storytelling on the web," *PLoS One* 15(6): 1–39.

Tappin, B. M. & McKay, R. T. (2019) "Moral polarization and out-party hostility in the US political context," *Journal of Social and Political Psychology* 7(1): 213–45.

Tartar, A. (2017) "How the populist right is redrawing the map of Europe," Bloomberg, December 11: www.bloomberg.com/graphics/2017-europe-populist-right.

Tedesco, J. C. (2019) "Political public relations and agenda building.". In J. Strömbäck & S. Kiousis (eds.) *Political Public Relations: Principles and Applications*. New York: Routledge, 84–103.

Tenenboim-Weinblatt, K. (2014) "Producing protest news: an inquiry into journalists' narratives," *The International Journal of Press/Politics* 19(4): 410–29.

Tenove, C. (2020) "Protecting democracy from disinformation: normative threats and policy responses," *The International Journal of Press/Politics* 25(3): 517–37.

Terren, L. & Borge-Bravo, R. (2021) "Echo chambers on social media: a systematic review of the literature," *Review of Communication Research* 9: 99–118.

The Royal Society (2022) *The Online Information Environment: Understanding How the Internet Shapes People's Engagement with Scientific Information*. London: The Royal Society.

Theocharis, Y., Cardenal, A., Jin, S., Aalberg, T., Hopmann, D. N., Strömbäck, J., Castro, L., Esser, F., vanAelst, P., deVreese, C., Koc-Michalska, K., Matthes, J., Schemer, C., Sheafer, T., Splendore, S., Stanyer, J., Stępińska, A., & Štětka, V. (2021) "Does the platform matter? Social media and COVID-19 conspiracy theory beliefs in 17 countries," *New Media & Society*: https://doi.org/10.1177/14614448211045666.

Thorson, K., Cotter, K., Medeiros, M., & Pak, C. (2021) "Algorithmic inference, political interest, and exposure to news and politics on Facebook," *Information, Communication & Society* 24(2): 183–200.

Thrall, A. T., Stecula, D., & Sweet, D. (2014) "May we have your attention please? Human-rights NGOs and the problem of global communication," *The International Journal of Press/Politics* 19(2): 135–59.

Thurman, N., Lewis, S. C., & Kunert, J. (2021) *Algorithms, Automation, and News: New Directions in the Study of Computation and Journalism*. London: Routledge.

Tilly, C. (1978) *From Mobilization to Revolution*. Reading, MA: Addison-Wesley.

Tilly, C. (1999) "From interactions to outcomes in social movements." In M. Giugni, D. McAdam, & C. Tilly (eds.) *How Social Movements Matter*. Minneapolis: University of Minnesota Press, 253–70.

Tilly, C. (2004) *Social Movements, 1768–2004*. Boulder: Paradigm Publishers.

Tilly, C., Castañeda, E., & Wood, L. J. (2020) *Social Movements, 1768–2018*. Routledge.

Tilly, C. & Wood, L. J. (2020) *Social Movements, 1768–2008*. New York: Routledge.

Tischauser, J. & Musgrave, K. (2020) "Far-right media as imitated counterpublicity: a discourse analysis on racial meaning and identity on Vdare.com," *Howard Journal of Communications* 31(3): 282–96.

Tocotronic (2008) "Ich möchte Teil einer Jugendbewegung sein – International Version." In *10th Anniversary*. Hamburg: Rock-O-Tronic Records.

Toepfl, F. & Piwoni, E. (2015) "Public spheres in interaction: comment sections of news websites as counterpublic spaces," *Journal of Communication* 65(3): 465–88.

Treré, E. & Mattoni, A. (2016) "Media ecologies and protest movements: main perspectives and key lessons," *Information, Communication & Society* 19(3): 290–306.

Tripodi, F. (2021) "Ms. categorized: gender, notability, and inequality on Wikipedia," *New Media & Society*: 1–21: https://doi.org/10.1177/14614448211023.

Tripodi, F. B. (2022) *The Propagandists' Playbook: How Conservative Elites Manipulate Search and Threaten Democracy*. New Haven, CT: Yale University Press.

Troianovski, A. & Safronova, V. (2022) "Russia takes censorship to new extremes, stifling war coverage," *New York Times*, March 4: www.nytimes.com/2022/03/04/world/europe/russia-censorship-media-crackdown.html.

Tuchman, G. (1978) "The newspaper as a social movement's resource." In G. Tuchman, A. Kaplan & J. Benét (eds.) *Hearth and Home: Images of Women in the Mass Media*. New York: Oxford University Press, 186–215.

Tucker, J. A., Guess, A., Barberá, P., Vaccari, C., Siegel, A., Sanovich, S., Stukal, D., & Nyhan, B. (2018) "Social media, political polarization, and political disinformation: a review of the scientific literature," *SSRN Journal* 106(7): https://ssrn.com/abstract=3144139.

Tufekci, Z. (2014) "The medium and the movement: digital tools, social movement politics, and the end of the free rider problem," *Policy & Internet* 6(2): 202–8.

Tufekci, Z. (2017) *Twitter and Tear Gas: The Power and Fragility of Networked Protest*. New Haven, CT: Yale University Press.

Turner, F. (2006) "How digital media found utopian ideology: lessons from the first hackers' conference." In D. Silver & A. Massanari (eds.) *Critical Cyberculture Studies: Current Terrains, Future Directions*. New York University Press, 257–69.

Turner, F. (2010) *From Counterculture to Cyberculture: Stewart Brand, the Whole Earth Network, and the Rise of Digital Utopianism*. University of Chicago Press.

Twitter Safety (2021) [Twitter] October 30: https://twitter.com/twittersafety/status/1454214197647187975?s=11.

Tworek, H. J. (2019) *News from Germany: The Competition to Control World Communications, 1900–1945*. Cambridge, MA: Harvard University Press.

Useem, B. & Goldstone, J. A. (2022) "The paradox of victory: social movement fields, adverse outcomes, and social movement success," *Theory and Society* 51(1): 31–60.

Usher, N. (2014) *Making News at the New York Times*. Ann Arbor: University of Michigan Press.

Usher, N. (2016) *Interactive Journalism: Hackers, Data, and Code*. University of Illinois Press.

Usher, N. (2021) *News for the Rich, White, and Blue: How Place and Power Distort American Journalism*. New York: Columbia University Press.

Vaccari, C. & Chadwick, A. (2020) "Deepfakes and disinformation: exploring the impact of synthetic political video on deception, uncertainty, and trust in news," *Social Media + Society* 6(1): https://doi.org/10.1177/2056305120903408.

Vaidhyanathan, S. (2018) *Antisocial Media: How Facebook Disconnects Us and Undermines Democracy*. New York: Oxford University Press.

Vaidhyanathan, S. (2021) "Making sense of the Facebook menace: can the largest media platform in the world ever be made safe for democracy?" *New Republic* 252(1–2): 22–7.

Valentino, N. A., Wayne, C. & Oceno, M. (2018) "Mobilizing sexism: the interaction of emotion and gender attitudes in the 2016 US presidential election," *Public Opinion Quarterly* 82(S1): 799–821.

Valenzuela, S., Halpern, D., & Araneda, F. (2022) "A downward spiral? A panel study of misinformation and media trust in Chile," *The International Journal of Press/Politics* 27(2): 353–73.

Van Aelst, P., Strömbäck, J., Aalberg, T., et al. (2017) "Political communication in a high-choice media environment: a challenge for democracy?" *Annals of the International Communication Association* 41(1): 3–27.

Van der Beek, K., Swatman, P., & Krueger, C. (2005) "Creating value from digital content: e-business model evolution in online news and music." In *Proceedings of the 38th Hawaii International Conference on Systems Science*. Washington, DC: IEEE Computer Society, 1–10.

Van Dijck, J., Poell, T., & de Waal, M. (2018) *The Platform Society: Public Values in a Connective World*. New York: Oxford University Press.

Van Dijck, J., de Winkel, T., & Schäfer, M. T. (2021) "Deplatformization and the governance of the platform ecosystem," *New Media & Society*: https://doi.org/10.1177/14614448211045662.

Van Duyn, E. (2020) "Mainstream marginalization: secret political organizing through social media," *Social Media and Society* 6(4): 1–13.

Van Duyn, E. (2021) *Democracy Lives in Darkness: How and Why People Keep Their Politics a Secret*. New York: Oxford University Press.

Van Kessel, S. & Castelein, R. (2016) "Shifting the blame: populist politicians' use of Twitter as a tool of opposition," *Journal of Contemporary European Research* 12(2): 594–614.

Van Krieken, R. (2018) *Celebrity Society: The Struggle for Attention*. Abingdon: Routledge.

Van Zoonen, L. (2006) "The personal, the political and the popular: a woman's guide to celebrity politics," *European Journal of Cultural Studies* 9(3): 287–301.

Vasko, V. & Trilling, D. (2019) "A permanent campaign? Tweeting differences among members of Congress between campaign and routine periods," *Journal of Information Technology & Politics* 16(4): 342–59.

Vavreck, L. (2009) *The Message Matters: The Economy and Presidential Campaigns*. Princeton University Press.

Vegetti, F. & Mancosu, M. (2020) "The impact of political sophistication and motivated reasoning on misinformation," *Political Communication* 37(5): 678–95.

Vijay, D. & Gekker, A. (2021) "Playing politics: how Sabarimala played out on TikTok," *American Behavioral Scientist* 65(5): 712–34.

Virino, C. C. & Rodriguez Ortega, V. (2019) "Daenerys Targaryen will save Spain: Game of Thrones, politics, and the public sphere," *Television & New Media* 20(5): 423–42.

Voinea, C. F. (2019) "Political culture research: dilemmas and trends," *Quality & Quantity* 54: 361–82.

Volkmer, I. (2008) "Satellite cultures in Europe: between national spheres and a globalized space," *Global Media and Communication* 4(3): 231–44.

Voltmer, K. (2013) *The Media in Transitional Democracies*. Cambridge: Polity.

Von Stein, L. (1964/1848) *History of the French Social Movement from 1789 to the Present*. New York: Bedminster Press.

Vraga, E. K. & Bode, L. (2020) "Defining misinformation and understanding its bounded nature: using expertise and evidence for describing misinformation," *Political Communication* 37(1): 136–44.

Vrikki, P. & Malik, S. (2019) "Voicing lived-experience and anti-racism: podcasting as a space at the margins for subaltern counterpublics," *Popular Communication* 17(4): 273–87.

Vrontis, D., Makrides, A., Christofi, M., & Thrassou, A. (2021) "Social media influencer marketing: a systematic review, integrative framework and future research agenda," *International Journal of Consumer Studies* 45(4): 617–44.

Vuletic, D. (2018) *Postwar Europe and the Eurovision Song Contest*. London: Bloomsbury.

Wagner, K. (2021) "Facebook says most 'inauthentic' networks start in Russia, Iran," Bloomberg, May 26: www.bloomberg.com/news/articles/2021-05-26/facebook-says-most-inauthentic-networks-start-in-russia-iran.

Wagner, M. (2021) "Affective polarization in multiparty systems," *Electoral Studies* 69: 1–39.

Wahl-Jorgensen, K., Hintz, A., Dencik, L., & Bennett, L. (eds.) (2020) *Journalism, Citizenship and Surveillance Society*. London: Routledge.

Waisbord, S. (2000) *Watchdog Journalism in South America: News, Accountability, and Democracy*. New York: Columbia University Press.

Waisbord, S. (2016) "Disconnections: media sociology and communication across differences." Paper presented at the annual conference of the International Communication Association, Fukuoka, Japan.

Waisbord, S. (2018) "Truth is what happens to news: on journalism, fake news, and post-truth," *Journalism Studies* 19(13): 1866–78.

Waisbord, S. & Amado, A. (2017) "Populist communication by digital means: presidential Twitter in Latin America," *Information, Communication & Society* 20(9): 1330–46.

Walgrave, S., Wouters, R., & Ketelaars, P. (2022) "Mobilizing usual versus unusual protesters: information channel openness and persuasion tie strength in 71 demonstrations in nine countries," *The Sociological Quarterly: Journal of the Midwest Sociological Society* 63(1): 48–73.

Walker, C., Kalathil, S., & Ludwig, J. (2020) "The cutting edge of sharp power," *Journal of Democracy* 31(1): 124–37.

Wallace, P. (2020) *India's 2019 Elections: The Hindutva Wave and Indian Nationalism*. New Delhi: SAGE.

Walter, B. F. (2022) *How Civil Wars Start: And How to Stop Them*. New York: Crown Publishing Group.

Walter, N., Cohen, J., Holbert, L. R., & Morag, Y. (2020) "Fact-checking: a meta-analysis of what works and for whom," *Political Communication* 37(3): 350–75.

Warner, M. (2002) "Publics and counterpublics," *Public Culture* 14(1): 49–90.

Wasserman, H. (2020) "Fake news from Africa: panics, politics and paradigms," *Journalism* 21(1): 3–16.

Weber, M. (1921/1968) *Economy and Society: An Outline of Interpretive Sociology*. New York: Bedminster Press.

Weber, M. S. & Kosterich, A. (2018) "Coding the news," *Digital Journalism* 6(3): 310–29.

Webster, J. G. (2014) *The marketplace of attention: How audiences take shape in a digital age.* Mit Press.

Weeks, B. E. & Lane, D. S. (2020) "The ecology of incidental exposure to news in digital media environments," *Journalism* 21(8): 1119–35.

Weller, N. & Junn, J. (2018) "Racial identity and voting: conceptualizing white identity in spatial terms," *Perspectives on Politics* 16(2): 436–48.

Wells, C., Cramer, K. J., Wagner, M. W., Alvarez, G., Friedland, L. A., Shah, D. V., Bode, L., Edgerly, S., Gabay, I. & Franklin, C. (2017) "When we stop talking politics: the maintenance and closing of conversation in contentious times," *Journal of Communication* 67(1): 131–57.

Wells, C., Friedland, L. A., Hughes, C., Shah, D. V., Suk, J., & Wagner, M. W. (2021) "News media use, talk networks, and anti-elitism across geographic location: evidence from Wisconsin," *The International Journal of Press/Politics* 26(2): 438–63.

Wells, C., Shah, D., Lukito, J., Pelled, A., Pevehouse, J. C., & Yang, J. (2020) "Trump, Twitter, and news media responsiveness: a media systems approach," *New Media & Society* 22(4): 659–82.

Wessler, H. (2019) *Habermas and the Media*. Hoboken, NJ: John Wiley & Sons.

Westlund, O. & Hermida, A. (2021) *Data Journalism and Misinformation: Handbook on Media Misinformation and Populism*. London: Routledge.

White, M. (2018) "Beauty as an 'act of political warfare': feminist makeup tutorials and masquerades on YouTube," *Women's Studies Quarterly* 46(1/2): 139–56.

Wike, R. & Castillo, A. (2018) "Many around the world are disengaged from politics," Pew Research, October 17: www.pewresearch.org/global/2018/10/17/international-political-engagement.

Wiles, P. (1969) "A syndrome, not a doctrine: some elementary theses on populism." In G. Ionescu & E. Gellner (eds.) *Populism: Its Meaning and National Characteristics*. London: Weidenfeld, 166–79.

Willems, W. (2012) "Interrogating public sphere and popular culture as theoretical concepts on their value in African studies," *Africa Development* 37(1): 11–26.

Williams, A. T. (2017) "Measuring the journalism crisis: developing new approaches that help the public connect to the issue," *International Journal of Communication* 11: 4731–43.

Williams, B. A. & Della Carpini, M. X. (2020) "The eroding boundaries between news and entertainment and what they mean for democratic politics." In L. Wilkins & C. G. Christians (eds.) *The Routledge Handbook of Mass Media Ethics*. London: Routledge, 252–63.

Williams, D. K. (2012) *God's Own Party: The Making of the Christian Right*. Oxford University Press.

Wilson, A. E., Parker, V. A., & Feinberg, M. (2020) "Polarization in the contemporary political and media landscape," *Current Opinion in Behavioral Sciences* 34: 223–8.

Wischnewski, M., Bruns, A., & Keller, T. (2021) "Shareworthiness and motivated reasoning in hyper-partisan news sharing behavior on Twitter," *Digital Journalism* 9(5): 549–70.

Witkin, R. W. (2000) "Why did Adorno 'hate' jazz?" *Sociological Theory* 18(1): 145–70.

Wojcieszak, M., Casas, A., Yu, X., Nagler, J., & Tucker, J. A. (2022) "Most users do not follow political elites on Twitter: those who do show overwhelming preferences for ideological congruity," *Science Advances* 8(39): eabn9418.

Wojcieszak, M. & Garrett, R. K. (2018) "Social identity, selective exposure, and affective polarization: how priming national identity shapes attitudes toward immigrants via news selection," *Human Communication Research* 44(3): 247–73.

Wolfsfeld, G., Sheafer, T., & Althaus, S. (2022) *Building Theory in Political Communication: The Politics–Media–Politics Approach*. New York: Oxford University Press.

Wood, M. Corbett, J., & Flinders, M. (2016) "Just like us: everyday celebrity politicians and the pursuit of popularity in an age of anti-politics," *The British Journal of Politics and International Relations* 18(3): 581–98.

Woolley, S. C. & Howard, P. (2017) *Computational Propaganda Worldwide: Executive Summary*. Oxford: Project on Computational Propaganda.

Woolley, S. C. & Howard, P. N. (eds.) (2018) *Computational Propaganda: Political Parties, Politicians, and Political Manipulation on Social Media*. New York: Oxford University Press.

Wouters, R. & Walgrave, S. (2017) "Demonstrating power: how protest persuades political representatives," *American Sociological Review* 82(2): 361–83.

Yang, A., Taylor, M., & Saffer, A. J. (2016) "Ethical convergence, divergence or communitas? An examination of public relations and journalism codes of ethics," *Public Relations Review* 42(1): 146–60.

Yarchi, M., Baden, C., & Kligler-Vilenchik, N. (2021) "Political polarization on the digital sphere: a cross-platform, over-time analysis of interactional, positional, and affective polarization on social media," *Political Communication* 38(1–2): 98–139.

York, J. C. (2022) *Silicon Values: The Future of Free Speech under Surveillance Capitalism*. London: Verso Books.

Young, D. G. (2020) *Irony and Outrage: The Polarized Landscape of Rage, Fear, and Laughter in the United States*. New York: Oxford University Press.

Young, D. G. & Bleakley, A. (2020) "Ideological health spirals: an integrated political and health communication approach to COVID interventions," *International Journal of Communication* 14: 3508–24.

Zamith, R. (2019) "Algorithms and journalism." In J. Nussbaum (ed.) *Oxford Research Encyclopedia of Communication*. Oxford University Press, 1–21.

Zelizer, B. (2005) "The culture of journalism." In J. Curran & M. Gurevitch (eds.) *Mass Media and Society*, 4th edn. New York: Hodder Arnold, 198–214.

Zeng, J. & Abidin, C. (2021) "'# OkBoomer, time to meet the Zoomers': studying the memefication of intergenerational politics on TikTok," *Information, Communication & Society* 24(16): 2459–81.

Ziblatt, D. (2017) *Conservative Political Parties and the Birth of Modern Democracy in Europe*. Cambridge University Press.

Zoonen, L. V., Coleman, S., & Kuik, A. (2011) "The elephant trap: politicians performing in television comedy." In K. Brants & K. Voltmer (eds.) *Political Communication in Postmodern Democracy: Challenging the Primacy of Politics*. London: Palgrave Macmillan, 146–63.

Zuboff, S. (2019) *The Age of Surveillance Capitalism: The Fight for a Human Future at the New Frontier of Power*. New York: Public Affairs.

Zuiderveen Borgesius, F., Trilling, D., Möller, J., Bodó, B., De Vreese, C. H., & Helberger, N. (2016) "Should we worry about filter bubbles?" *Internet Policy Review: Journal on Internet Regulation* 5(1): 1–16.

Zulianello, M., Albertini, A., & Ceccobelli, D. (2018) "A populist zeitgeist? The communication strategies of Western and Latin American political leaders on Facebook," *The International Journal of Press/Politics* 23(4): 439–57.

Zürn, M. (2018) *A Theory of Global Governance: Authority, Legitimacy, and Contestation.* Oxford University Press.

Index

Italics refer to tables.